THE KINGS & QUEENS OF
ENGLAND

THE KINGS & QUEENS OF
ENGLAND

EDITED BY

W.M. ORMROD

TEMPUS

First published 2001

PUBLISHED IN THE UNITED KINGDOM BY:
Tempus Publishing Ltd
The Mill, Brimscombe Port
Stroud, Gloucestershire GL5 2QG
Tel: 01453 883300
www.tempus-publishing.com

PUBLISHED IN THE UNITED STATES OF AMERICA BY:
Tempus Publishing Inc.
2 Cumberland Street
Charleston, SC 29401
Tel: 1-888-313-2665
www.arcadiapublishing.com

Tempus books are available in France and Germany from the following addresses:

Tempus Publishing Group
21 Avenue de la République
37300 Joué-lès-Tours
FRANCE

Tempus Publishing Group
Gustav-Adolf-Straße 3
99084 Erfurt
GERMANY

British Library Cataloguing in Publication Data.
A catalogue record for this book is available from the British Library.

ISBN 0 7524 1988 9

Typesetting and origination by Tempus Publishing.
PRINTED AND BOUND IN GREAT BRITAIN.

Front Cover, left to right: Edward III; Henry VIII; Alfred; Charles I.
Back cover: Charles II; Jane Seymour.

CONTENTS

THE CONTRIBUTORS

THE EDITOR

W.M. Ormrod is Professor of History at the University of York. He has written extensively on medieval Britain: his other books include the major modern study of Edward III, *The Reign of Edward III* (also published by Tempus), along with *Political Life in Medieval England, 1300-1450*, (with Anthony Musson) *The Evolution of English Justice: Law, Politics and Society in the Fourteenth Century*, and (with Phillip Lindley) *The Black Death in England*.

THE CONTRIBUTORS

David Bates is Edwards Professor of Medieval History at the University of Glasgow. He has written extensively on medieval Britain and France, and his books include the major modern study of William I, *William the Conqueror* (also published by Tempus), *Domesday Book* (with Elizabeth Hallam), and *Regesta Regum Anglo-Normannorum: The Acta of William I (1066-1087)*.

Jeremy Black is Professor of History at the University of Exeter and specializes in the history of the early modern period and the eighteenth century, though his writing also spans many periods and themes in British and European history. He is the author of numerous books, including *A History of the British Isles, The Penguin Dictionary of Eighteenth Century History*, and *Maps and History*.

S.D. Church is Senior Lecturer in History at the University of East Anglia and works on English and continental history of the high Middle Ages, with special emphasis on the Angevin period and the reign of King John. His publications include *The Household Knights of King John* and *King John: New Interpretations*.

John Morrill is Professor of British and Irish History at the University of Cambridge, and Vice Master of Selwyn College; he is also Vice President of the British Academy. He is an expert on the history of British Isles during the early modern period, and his recent publications include *The Oxford Illustrated History of Tudor and Stuart Britain* and *Revolt in the Provinces: The English People and the Tragedies of War, 1634-48*.

A.J. Pollard is Professor of History at the University of Teesside and a highly regarded and prolific historian of medieval England, specializing in the fifteenth century. His books include *The Worlds of Richard III* (also published by Tempus), *The Wars of the Roses*, and *Richard III and the Princes in the Tower*.

A.W. Purdue is Senior Lecturer and Staff Tutor in History at the Open University. His publications, written jointly with J.M. Golby, include *The Civilisation of the Crowd: Popular Culture in England 1750-1900*, *The Making of the Modern Christmas*, and *The Monarchy and the British People, 1760 to Present* (also published by Tempus).

Richard Rex is Lecturer in Church History in the University of Cambridge and Fellow and Tutor of Queens' College. He has researched and written extensively on Tudor England and is the author of *The Tudor Dynasty* (forthcoming from Tempus), *Henry VIII and the English Reformation*, and *The Lollards*.

Alex Woolf is Lecturer in Celtic and Early Scottish History and Culture at the University of Edinburgh and is an expert in early medieval history. He contributes regularly to scholarly publications and is author of the forthcoming *From Pictland to Alba: Scotland in the Viking Age* and *The Kingdom of the Picts* (forthcoming from Tempus).

Thanks to Paul N. Dobson for compiling the genealogies and index.

INTRODUCTION

The history of the English and British monarchy spans fifteen hundred years and encompasses many of the principal events in the wider story of Britain's past. The history of monarchy is certainly an account of the emergence of political unification: the rulers of England acquired lordship of Ireland in the twelfth century and appropriated the sovereignty of Wales in the thirteenth; and when the previously independent ruling house of Scotland – the Stuarts – assumed the English throne in 1603, they set in motion the process that would lead to the formal union of Great Britain. One of the greatest challenges to the monarchy in this long process has always been to create a sense of identity with its acquired territories. The problem was evident within England itself when successive 'foreign' dynasties – Scandinavian, Norman, Angevin, Stuart and Hanoverian – acquired the throne. But such monarchs usually found it possible, at least within a generation or two, to acquire sufficient cultural identity with their English subjects to be thought of as credible and potentially worthy rulers. Not so the position in Ireland, Wales or Scotland, where there was enduring suspicion of rulers who chose London as their capital and the English Home Counties as their main place of residence. These tensions partly accounted for the cessation of the Republic of Ireland in the early twentieth century and help to explain the continuing hostility towards Westminster-based government evident in modern Wales and Scotland.

Under these circumstances, the most remarkable thing about the British monarchy must surely be its ability to survive. Whereas other European monarchies were overthrown or reduced to the position of mere token heads of state, the British kings and (more especially) queens of the nineteenth and twentieth centuries went from strength to strength, reviving the mystique of their office, offering charismatic leadership, and providing (at least until very recently) a model of family life respected and emulated by large numbers of their subjects. For some generations, the stability of the throne has been managed and achieved through a judicious mixture of tradition and modernization. Each new ruler continues to be crowned and anointed: the office they hold is represented (as it was in the Middles Ages) as divinely sanctioned, and involves (as it has done since the Reformation) specific responsibilities to the established religion of the Church of England. But modern rulers have also embraced new technologies of communication, to the extent that they now, in effect, hold court through the medium of television. The balance between the ceremonious and the populist approaches is an issue on which the royal family itself, and many of its subjects, remain divided, and it is uncertain what new brand of monarchy might yet be experienced in the twenty-first century. What remains virtually undisputed is the extraordinary capacity of that monarchy, in every sense, to endure.

GENEALOGIES

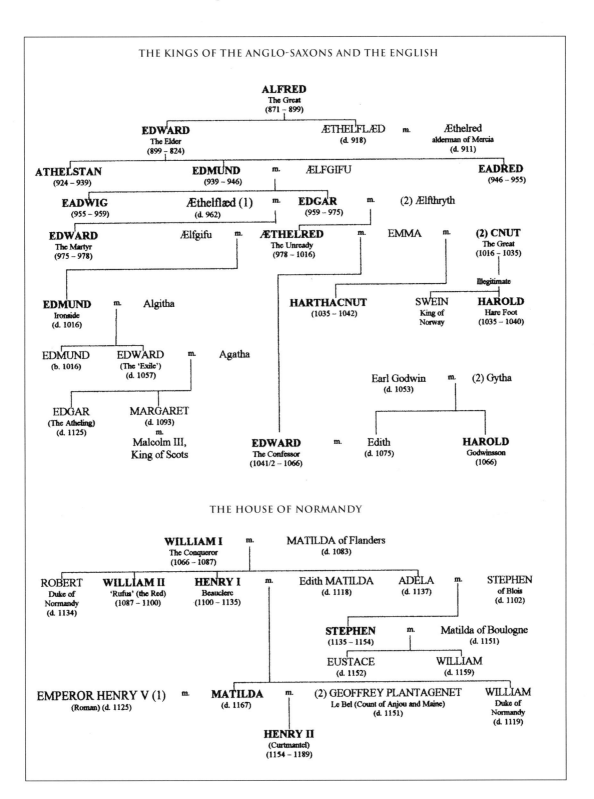

THE KINGS OF THE ANGLO-SAXONS AND THE ENGLISH

ALFRED
The Great
(871 – 899)

EDWARD
The Elder
(899 – 824)

ÆTHELFLÆD
(d. 918)
m.
Æthelred
alderman of Mercia
(d. 911)

ATHELSTAN
(924 – 939)

EDMUND
(939 – 946)
m. **ÆLFGIFU**

EADRED
(946 – 955)

EADWIG
(955 – 959)

Æthelflæd (1)
(d. 962)
m. **EDGAR**
(959 – 975)
m. (2) Ælfthryth

EDWARD
The Martyr
(975 – 978)

Ælfgifu m. **ÆTHELRED**
The Unready
(978 – 1016)
m. **EMMA** m.
(2) CNUT
The Great
(1016 – 1035)

Illegitimate

EDMUND
Ironside
(d. 1016)
m. Algitha

HARTHACNUT
(1035 – 1042)

SWEIN
King of
Norway

HAROLD
Hare Foot
(1035 – 1040)

EDMUND
(b. 1016)

EDWARD
(The 'Exile')
(d. 1057)
m. Agatha

Earl Godwin
(d. 1053)
m. (2) Gytha

EDGAR
(The Atheling)
(d. 1125)

MARGARET
(d. 1093)
m.
Malcolm III,
King of Scots

EDWARD
The Confessor
(1041/2 – 1066)
m.
Edith
(d. 1075)

HAROLD
Godwinsson
(1066)

THE HOUSE OF NORMANDY

WILLIAM I
The Conqueror
(1066 – 1087)
m. MATILDA of Flanders
(d. 1083)

ROBERT
Duke of
Normandy
(d. 1134)

WILLIAM II
'Rufus' (the Red)
(1087 – 1100)

HENRY I
Beauclerc
(1100 – 1135)
m.
Edith MATILDA
(d. 1118)

ADELA
(d. 1137)
m.
STEPHEN
of Blois
(d. 1102)

STEPHEN
(1135 – 1154)
m. Matilda of Boulogne
(d. 1151)

EUSTACE
(d. 1152)

WILLIAM
(d. 1159)

EMPEROR HENRY V (1)
(Roman) (d. 1125)
m. **MATILDA**
(d. 1167)
m. (2) GEOFFREY PLANTAGENET
Le Bel (Count of Anjou and Maine)
(d. 1151)

WILLIAM
Duke of
Normandy
(d. 1119)

HENRY II
(Curtmantel)
(1154 – 1189)

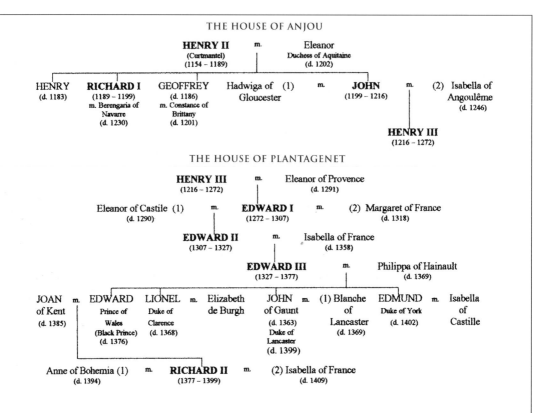

THE HOUSE OF ANJOU

HENRY II m. Eleanor
(Curtmantel) Duchess of Aquitaine
(1154 – 1189) (d. 1202)

HENRY | **RICHARD I** | GEOFFREY | Hadwiga of (1) | m. | **JOHN** | m. | (2) Isabella of
(d. 1183) | (1189 – 1199) | (d. 1186) | Gloucester | | (1199 – 1216) | | Angoulême
| m. Berengaria of | m. Constance of | | | | | (d. 1246)
| Navarre | Brittany
| (d. 1230) | (d. 1201)

HENRY III
(1216 – 1272)

THE HOUSE OF PLANTAGENET

HENRY III m. Eleanor of Provence
(1216 – 1272) (d. 1291)

Eleanor of Castile (1) m. **EDWARD I** m. (2) Margaret of France
(d. 1290) (1272 – 1307) (d. 1318)

EDWARD II m. Isabella of France
(1307 – 1327) (d. 1358)

EDWARD III m. Philippa of Hainault
(1327 – 1377) (d. 1369)

JOAN m. EDWARD | LIONEL m. Elizabeth | JOHN m. (1) Blanche | EDMUND m. Isabella
of Kent | Prince of | Duke of | de Burgh | of Gaunt | of | Duke of York | of
(d. 1385) | Wales | Clarence | | (d. 1363) | Lancaster | (d. 1402) | Castile
| (Black Prince) | (d. 1368) | | Duke of | (d. 1369)
| (d. 1376) | | | Lancaster
| | | | (d. 1399)

Anne of Bohemia (1) m. **RICHARD II** m. (2) Isabella of France
(d. 1394) (1377 – 1399) (d. 1409)

THE HOUSES OF LANCASTER AND YORK

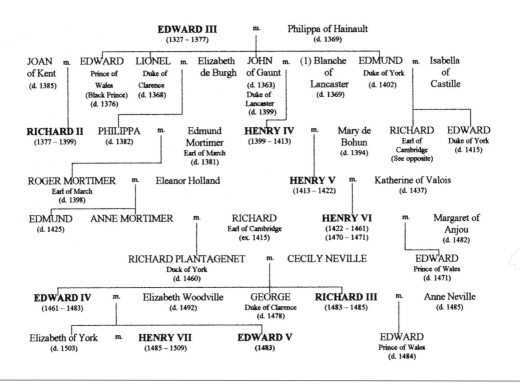

EDWARD III m. Philippa of Hainault
(1327 – 1377) (d. 1369)

JOAN m. EDWARD | LIONEL m. Elizabeth | JOHN m. (1) Blanche | EDMUND m. Isabella
of Kent | Prince of | Duke of | de Burgh | of Gaunt | of | Duke of York | of
(d. 1385) | Wales | Clarence | | (d. 1363) | Lancaster | (d. 1402) | Castile
| (Black Prince) | (d. 1368) | | Duke of | (d. 1369)
| (d. 1376) | | | Lancaster
| | | | (d. 1399)

RICHARD II | PHILIPPA | m. | Edmund | **HENRY IV** | m. | Mary de | RICHARD | EDWARD
(1377 – 1399) | (d. 1382) | | Mortimer | (1399 – 1413) | | Bohun | Earl of | Duke of York
| | | Earl of March | | | (d. 1394) | Cambridge | (d. 1415)
| | | (d. 1381) | | | | (See opposite)

ROGER MORTIMER m. Eleanor Holland   **HENRY V** m. Katherine of Valois
Earl of March   (1413 – 1422)   (d. 1437)
(d. 1398)

EDMUND | ANNE MORTIMER | m. | RICHARD | **HENRY VI** | m. | Margaret of
(d. 1425) | | | Earl of Cambridge | (1422 – 1461) | | Anjou
| | | (ex. 1415) | (1470 – 1471) | | (d. 1482)

RICHARD PLANTAGENET m. CECILY NEVILLE   EDWARD
Duke of York   Prince of Wales
(d. 1460)   (d. 1471)

EDWARD IV | m. | Elizabeth Woodville | GEORGE | **RICHARD III** | m. | Anne Neville
(1461 – 1483) | | (d. 1492) | Duke of Clarence | (1483 – 1485) | | (d. 1485)
| | | (d. 1478)

Elizabeth of York | m. | **HENRY VII** | **EDWARD V** | EDWARD
(d. 1503) | | (1485 – 1509) | (1483) | Prince of Wales
| | | | (d. 1484)

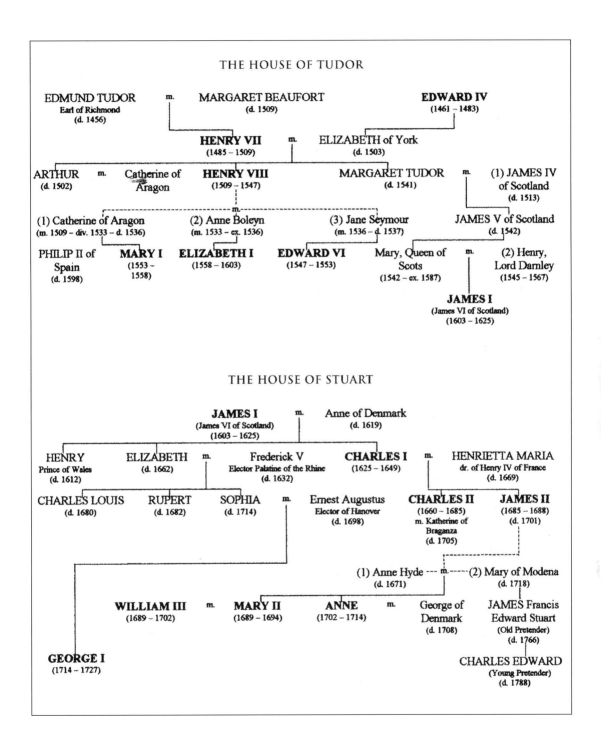

THE HOUSE OF TUDOR

EDMUND TUDOR
Earl of Richmond
(d. 1456)

m.

MARGARET BEAUFORT
(d. 1509)

EDWARD IV
(1461 – 1483)

HENRY VII
(1485 – 1509)

m.

ELIZABETH of York
(d. 1503)

ARTHUR
(d. 1502)

m.

Catherine of
Aragon

HENRY VIII
(1509 – 1547)

MARGARET TUDOR
(d. 1541)

m.

(1) JAMES IV
of Scotland
(d. 1513)

(1) Catherine of Aragon
(m. 1509 – div. 1533 – d. 1536)

(2) Anne Boleyn
(m. 1533 – ex. 1536)

(3) Jane Seymour
(m. 1536 – d. 1537)

JAMES V of Scotland
(d. 1542)

PHILIP II of
Spain
(d. 1598)

MARY I
(1553 – 1558)

ELIZABETH I
(1558 – 1603)

EDWARD VI
(1547 – 1553)

Mary, Queen of
Scots
(1542 – ex. 1587)

m.

(2) Henry,
Lord Darnley
(1545 – 1567)

JAMES I
(James VI of Scotland)
(1603 – 1625)

THE HOUSE OF STUART

JAMES I
(James VI of Scotland)
(1603 – 1625)

m.

Anne of Denmark
(d. 1619)

HENRY
Prince of Wales
(d. 1612)

ELIZABETH
(d. 1662)

m.

Frederick V
Elector Palatine of the Rhine
(d. 1632)

CHARLES I
(1625 – 1649)

m.

HENRIETTA MARIA
dr. of Henry IV of France
(d. 1669)

CHARLES LOUIS
(d. 1680)

RUPERT
(d. 1682)

SOPHIA
(d. 1714)

m.

Ernest Augustus
Elector of Hanover
(d. 1698)

CHARLES II
(1660 – 1685)
m. Katherine of
Braganza
(d. 1705)

JAMES II
(1685 – 1688)
(d. 1701)

(1) Anne Hyde
(d. 1671)

m.

(2) Mary of Modena
(d. 1718)

WILLIAM III
(1689 – 1702)

m.

MARY II
(1689 – 1694)

ANNE
(1702 – 1714)

m.

George of
Denmark
(d. 1708)

JAMES Francis
Edward Stuart
(Old Pretender)
(d. 1766)

GEORGE I
(1714 – 1727)

CHARLES EDWARD
(Young Pretender)
(d. 1788)

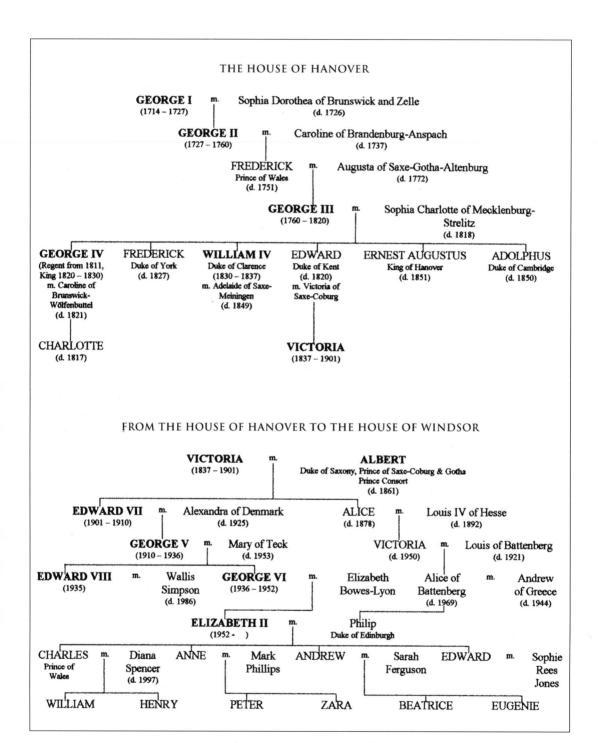

THE HOUSE OF HANOVER

GEORGE I   m.   Sophia Dorothea of Brunswick and Zelle
(1714 – 1727)   (d. 1726)

GEORGE II   m.   Caroline of Brandenburg-Anspach
(1727 – 1760)   (d. 1737)

FREDERICK   m.   Augusta of Saxe-Gotha-Altenburg
Prince of Wales   (d. 1772)
(d. 1751)

GEORGE III   m.   Sophia Charlotte of Mecklenburg-
(1760 – 1820)   Strelitz
       (d. 1818)

GEORGE IV	FREDERICK	**WILLIAM IV**	EDWARD	ERNEST AUGUSTUS	ADOLPHUS
(Regent from 1811, King 1820 – 1830) m. Caroline of Brunswick-Wölfenbuttel (d. 1821)	Duke of York (d. 1827)	Duke of Clarence (1830 – 1837) m. Adelaide of Saxe-Meiningen (d. 1849)	Duke of Kent (d. 1820) m. Victoria of Saxe-Coburg	King of Hanover (d. 1851)	Duke of Cambridge (d. 1850)

CHARLOTTE
(d. 1817)

VICTORIA
(1837 – 1901)

FROM THE HOUSE OF HANOVER TO THE HOUSE OF WINDSOR

VICTORIA   m.   **ALBERT**
(1837 – 1901)   Duke of Saxony, Prince of Saxe-Coburg & Gotha
       Prince Consort
       (d. 1861)

EDWARD VII   m.   Alexandra of Denmark   ALICE   m.   Louis IV of Hesse
(1901 – 1910)   (d. 1925)   (d. 1878)   (d. 1892)

GEORGE V   m.   Mary of Teck   VICTORIA   m.   Louis of Battenberg
(1910 – 1936)   (d. 1953)   (d. 1950)   (d. 1921)

EDWARD VIII	m.	Wallis Simpson (d. 1986)	**GEORGE VI** (1936 – 1952)	m.	Elizabeth Bowes-Lyon	Alice of Battenberg (d. 1969)	m.	Andrew of Greece (d. 1944)
(1935)								

ELIZABETH II   m.   Philip
(1952 -)   Duke of Edinburgh

CHARLES	m.	Diana Spencer (d. 1997)	ANNE	m.	Mark Phillips	ANDREW	m.	Sarah Ferguson	EDWARD	m.	Sophie Rees Jones
Prince of Wales											

WILLIAM	HENRY		PETER	ZARA		BEATRICE	EUGENIE

1

THE KINGS OF THE ENGLISH FROM EARLIEST TIMES TO 1066

ALEX WOOLF

In the fifth to seventh centuries AD, substantial parts of Britain were invaded and settled by a series of tribesmen from northern mainland Europe collectively referred to as the Anglo-Saxons. By the end of the seventh century, these tribes had spread out to encompass most of present-day England and much of southern Scotland. By the end of the seventh century, twelve principal Anglo-Saxon kingdoms had emerged: those of the Bernicians, the Deirans, the Lindesfarona, the East Angles, the Middle Angles, the Mercians, the Hwicce, the Magonsaete, the Gewisse, the South Saxons, the Cantware and the East Saxons. Of these, three were to become especially dominant: the Bernicians in the North, the Mercians in the Midlands and the Gewisse in the South. The spread of Christianity amongst these Germanic-speaking peoples around 600 greatly enhanced the office of king and helped to promote a sense of common cultural and political identity. The Bernician monk Bede, writing *c*.730, listed seven rulers in the period up to 671 who held *imperium* (overlordship) over all the 'South Angles' (by which he meant all the Germanic peoples south of the Humber, the boundary between the Deirans and the Lindesfarona). In the ninth century, the West Saxon text known as the *Anglo-Saxon Chronicle* added another more recent king to this list and gave these *imperium*-holders the title of *Bretwalda* or *Brytenwalda* (meaning either 'wide-ruler' or 'Britain-ruler'). Under King Alfred and his successors in the tenth century, the kings of the West Saxons asserted the right to rule most of what is now England, and were an influential and sometimes dominating force over the rulers of native British peoples in parts of Wales, Scotland and Ireland.

THE KINGS OF THE CANTWARE ('KENT')

The history of the Anglo-Saxon kingdoms traditionally begins with the history of Kent. The reasons for this are twofold. First, Bede, followed by the *Anglo-Saxon Chronicle*, claimed that the first leader of the Germanic invaders of Britain was the same man who appears at the head of the list of Kentish kings, Hengest. Secondly, Kent was the first kingdom to receive

Christianity, and thus had the oldest archive of historical documents. If we look at the pedigree stretching back from the first Christian king, Æthelbert, who died in 616, however, it is clear that Hengest cannot have lived much earlier than *c*.500, whereas we can be certain that the coming of the Anglo-Saxons took place at least half a century before that. Two solutions present themselves: either Hengest was not really the ancestor of the Kentish kings, or he was not really the leader of the first invasion. It is hard to choose between these two options. Archaeology, however, does suggest that there was a second Germanic influx in Kent, of a distinct southern Scandinavian tribe called the Jutes, around 500, so it is possible that Hengest was the first Jutish leader in Kent but not the first German in Britain. The dates accorded him in the ninth-century *Anglo-Saxon Chronicle* cannot be trusted.

With Æthelbert, the third of the *imperium*-holders listed by Bede, we are on much firmer ground. He seems to have married a Christian princess, Bertha, from Francia (the region across the Channel in what is now the Low Countries and France) at a time when his father, Eormanric, was still king in Kent. By the mid-590s, however, he himself was king and he wrote to the pope, Gregory the Great, asking that missionaries be sent to convert his people. Gregory's responses survive and it is clear that he believed Æthelbert was *rex Anglorum* – 'King of the English' – evidence that even at this early date the term *Angli* had the double meaning of 'Angle' and 'Anglo-Saxon'. Gregory sent the monk Augustine to Kent, having him made a bishop on the way, to convert Æthelbert and his people. Rather curiously it is clear that Bertha, who was already a Christian, had brought with her on her marriage a Frankish bishop, Liudhard. Possibly Æthelbert was wary of Frankish political intentions towards his kingdom and may have felt that getting missionaries from Rome rather than the Frankish kingdoms was one way of preventing a fifth column from entering the country.

After Æthelbert's death his son Eadbald succeeded to the kingdom. Eadbald (616-40) had not grasped the full implications of being a Christian. He married his father's widow (marriage to stepmothers seems to have been quite common, as it prevented disputes over inheritance) and engaged in other activities that were regarded as pagan by the missionaries. Bishop Laurence, now the leader of the mission, managed to bring Eadbald around by convincing him that he himself had been assaulted and beaten by St Peter as a punishment for not keeping the king on the straight and narrow. Anxious for the welfare of his father's friend, King Eadbald set aside his stepmother and returned to the fold of the Church. Eadbald further promoted the cause of the Church by giving his sister Æthelburh in marriage to the Deiran King Eadwine in 625. This helped to spread Christianity into the northern part of England. All subsequent Kentish kings were descended from Eadbald.

Kent seems to have been divided into two provinces at this time: that of the Cantware proper, with its bishop at Canterbury, and, west of the Medway, another province with a bishop at Rochester. Archaeologically, West Kent had more in common with East Saxon territories just across the Thames than it did with the Jutish East Kent. The west sometimes had its own kings as well. At times these were junior members of the Jutish dynasty, but some of them had names like Swæfheard and Sigered, which look suspiciously East Saxon. It is perhaps best to think of the land between the Medway and the Thames as debatable, sometimes looking north and sometimes east.

Of the later kings, the most notable are Hlothere (673-85) and Wihtred (690-725) who both produced law codes, expanding on a practice begun by Æthelbert. The three Kentish codes attached to the names of these kings are the earliest English law. After Wihtred, the importance of the Kentish kings declined. They lost out to the growing power both of the Mercians and of the church at Canterbury, which now housed an archbishop claiming ecclesiastical jurisdiction throughout Britain. The second half of the eighth century saw direct Mercian intervention, including the imposition of Midland princes into the kingship (Cuthred, 798-807, and Baldred, 823-5). In 825 the kingdom was 'liberated' by the West Saxons, who subsequently bestowed it on their heirs apparent. After 860 it became fully absorbed into their kingdom.

THE KINGS OF THE EAST ANGLES

The kingdom of the East Angles was probably more powerful than the surviving sources would suggest. This is the region of England that was most severely affected by the Viking invasions of the later ninth century, and no native documentation has survived. It contains the richest pagan burial yet recovered from Anglo-Saxon England: the famous ship-burial at Sutton Hoo. This has been claimed as the burial, or at least cenotaph (no body was found), of King Rædwald (d. *c*.625), the grandson of Wuffa, from whom the royal dynasty was named the Wuffingas. Rædwald is said to have converted to Christianity at the court of Æthelbert of Kent, but to have been persuaded by his wife not to renounce paganism altogether. This, it is argued, explains the presence of Christian paraphernalia in the Sutton Hoo tomb, despite its generally pagan character. Rædwald clearly put a lot of store by his wife's advice, for some years later he received messengers from Æthelfrith of Bernicia offering him great rewards if he would murder or hand over Eadwine, an exiled Deiran prince who was a warrior of his household. When she heard of this, the queen told Rædwald that to do such a thing would dishonour him before all men, so he changed his mind and instead went to war with Æthelfrith. In a battle on the River Idle in Nottinghamshire, he slew the Bernician king and was subsequently able to place Eadwine on the Deiran throne. It is probably this great victory that made him one of Bede's *imperium*-holders.

Rædwald's son and successor Eorpwald converted to Christianity properly but was slain by his pagan subjects in *c*.627, and the kingdom remained pagan for a further three years. In *c*.631 Rædwald's stepson Sigibert returned from exile in the Frankish kingdom, converted, and began to promote Christianity. Within a few years he retired to a monastery but returned to the world when an invasion by the Mercian King Penda took place. He was killed in battle (*c*.637) and was succeeded by Rædwald's nephew Anna. Anna lasted until about 654, when he too was killed by Penda, who seems to have been supporting a bid for power by Anna's brother, Æthelhere. Æthelhere died the following year, alongside Penda, in battle with the Bernicians at Winwæd.

Of the deeds of later kings we know little. King Ealdwulf (663-713) seems to have been a great patron of the Church even though he could remember that pagan temples remained standing in his own childhood. As in Kent, conflict with the Mercians dominated the later history of the East Angles. One king, Æthelbert (779-94), was invited to the court of the Mercian King Offa and summarily executed. His body was taken to Hereford (near where the execution had taken place) and his grave became the site of a cult. The ninth-century kings are known mostly from their coins and some of them may have been Mercian, or even West Saxon, intruders. In 869 King Edmund, a young warrior, was slain by the Vikings. He too became venerated as a saint and his tomb lay in the monastery of Bedricesworth, now known as Bury St Edmunds. After him there were two shadowy kings, an unknown Æthelred and Edmund's son-in-law Oswald. After that, we know of two Danish kings, Guthrum (880-90) who made peace with Alfred the Great, and Eohric (890-902) who was killed at the Battle of the Holme. It was another fifteen years before the East Anglian territory was absorbed into the new English kingdom; but who its kings were in the intervening period is not known.

Left to right, top to bottom   2. Coin of Cuthred, King of the Cantware (798-807).
3. Coin of Baldred, King of the Cantware (823-5).
4. Coin of Offa, King of the Mercians (757-96).
5. Offa's wife, Cynethryth, the only Anglo-Saxon queen to have coins issued in her name.
6. Coin of Peada, King of the Middle Angles (d. 656).
7. Coin of Ecgfrith, King of Northumbria (d. 685).
8. Coin of King Eadbert, King of Northumbria (737-58).
9. Coin of Edmund, King of the East Angles (d. 869).
10. Coin of Guthrum, Danish King in East Anglia (880-90).

THE KINGS OF THE DEIRANS

The province of the Deirans roughly equated with the later county of Yorkshire. Its culture, and perhaps its kings, were closely linked to the East Angles. The first king we know of was Ælle, son of Yffe, who was ruling at about the time Gregory became pope in Rome. He seems to have been succeeded by one Æthelric, who was slain when Æthelfrith of Bernicia conquered Deira in 604. Æthelfrith married Ælle's daughter Acha, probably to legitimise his usurpation, and ruled ably for twelve years. In 617 he was slain on the River Idle by Rædwald of the East Angles who placed Ælle's son Eadwine on the throne. Eadwine seems also to have ruled directly over the Bernicians, though we are not told if he had any family claim to do so. Before finding support from Rædwald, Eadwine had visited many kingdoms in his exile, including Mercia and the British kingdom of Gwynedd. In Mercia he had found a bride in Cwenburh, daughter of King Cearl. They had two sons, Osfrith and Eadfrith. Eadwine led a number of campaigns against the British, perhaps in an attempt to bring Bernicians and Deirans together in a common cause, and probably conquered Lancashire and Westmoreland for Deira as well as the British kingdom of Elmet. In c.625 he married for a second time. His new bride was Æthelburh of Kent, and she brought with her the Christian Bishop Paulinus. It was their hope that Eadwine would convert. At first he was cautious, but a year or so later he narrowly escaped being assassinated by the Gewisse. He planned a punitive expedition and swore that if he were successful he would convert. The campaign was a success and he kept his oath, sponsoring mass baptisms throughout the kingdom in c.627. In 632 he invaded and subjugated Gwynedd, but the following year its king, Cadwallon, accompanied by Penda of Mercia, invaded Deira and killed Eadwine and his son Osfrith in battle at Hatfield Chase. After this, Bernicia regained its independence and Eadwine's cousin Osric became King of the Deirans. Within a year, Cadwallon had killed him too. This effectively marked the end of the Deiran kingdom: although Osric's son ruled the territory as a Mercian protectorate between 644 and 651, its future lay with that of the Bernicians. Æthelburh fled back to Kent and sent her son Uscfrea and Osfrith's son Yffe to the King of the Franks for safety. They both died soon afterwards. Eadwine's other son Eadfrith went in exile to the Mercian court, where he was mysteriously killed.

THE KINGS OF THE BERNICIANS AND NORTHUMBRIANS

The Bernicians were a people apart among the Anglo-Saxons. They displayed little of the distinctive material culture or pagan funerary rites of their southern neighbours. Their rulers held court in fortified hilltop citadels, like the kings of the neighbouring Pictish and British peoples (the native tribes existing before the arrival of the Germanic invaders). The Bernicians had even borrowed the practice of tattooing from the neighbouring Picts. Were we reliant wholly upon archaeological evidence, we should probably not recognize them as Anglo-Saxons at all. But they were in no doubt that they were – and neither were their neighbours.

The original core of the Bernician kingdom probably lay along the line of Hadrian's Wall: indeed, they may have originated as a late Roman garrison of Germanic mercenaries. However, in the middle of the sixth century their king, Ida, seized and fortified the promontory of Bamburgh just south of the Tweed, and this became their royal centre. By the time of Ida's grandson Æthelfrith (593-617), the Bernicians controlled all of England north of the Tees together with the Tweed basin and Dumfriesshire. By the middle of the seventh century, they controlled Lothian, Stirlingshire and Lanarkshire as well as much of Ayrshire and Galloway. They also cast covetous eyes over Deira and increasingly exerted control there.

Æthelfrith is said to have conquered more territory from the Britons than any English king before him. He may even have been responsible for some naval raids carried out on Ireland and the Hebrides in the 610s. Bede, the Bernician historian, regarded the conquest of the Britons as the manifest destiny of the English nation and did not bother to chronicle it in detail. The one account of Æthelfrith's British campaigns that he gives us gleefully recounts the massacre of the British monks from Bangor-Is-Coed. The monks' demise demonstrates to Bede's satisfaction that the British Church did not find favour in the eyes of the Lord, and legitimised the relentless ethnic cleansing that the Bernicians practised in the course of their expansion.

After the interlude of Eadwine of Deira's rule over Bernicia (c.617-33), the sons of Æthelfrith returned from exile amongst the Gaels of Dál Riata and the Picts. Eanfrith, with his Pictish bride, lasted less than a year: he was cut down by Cadwallon of Gwynedd, whom he foolishly believed to be his ally. Within months his brother Oswald had avenged him, slaying Cadwallon near Hexham. Oswald (634-42) was the son of Eadwine's sister Acha and was also able to persuade the Deirans to take him as king. He was a Christian, and had spent most of his youth amongst the Gaelic rulers of Argyll and Antrim. Indeed, Domnall Brecc, King of Dál Riata, may even have aided his return to Bernicia. It was even claimed that, before his battle with Cadwallon, Oswald had a vision of St Columba, the founder of the famous monastery at Iona. In any event, following his victory, Oswald invited a mission from Iona, under Bishop Aidan, to Bernicia and gave them part at least of the island of Lindisfarne to found a monastery. Aidan could speak no English and Bede tells us that when the bishop went out preaching, King Oswald himself translated for him. The mission was a great success and churches and monasteries sprang up throughout Bernicia and Deira. Within two years of becoming king, Oswald married Cyneburh, daughter of Cynegils, the Gewisse king. It may have been at the same time that Cynegils converted to Christianity, for Oswald was his godfather as well as his son-in-law.

Oswald's reign lasted less than a decade. He carried his conflict with Cadwallon's ally Penda of Mercia deep into enemy territory and was slain in battle at Maserfeld (perhaps Old Oswestry in Shropshire). A third son of Æthelfrith, Oswiu, inherited Oswald's mantle but was not able to hold on to Deira. He was somewhat younger than Oswald and may have had a different, non-Deiran, mother. Instead, the Deirans, with the backing of Penda, took Oswine, son of Osric, to be their king. For the first part of his reign, Oswiu held his peace north of the Tees. He was probably consolidating Bernician rule in areas taken from the Britons by Oswald and may have extend the frontier a little himself. We know he had a British wife, Raegnmeld, during the early part of his reign. Shortly after Oswine's accession, however, Oswiu married Eanflæd, Eadwine's daughter, whom he had fetched from Kent. She bore him two sons, Ecgfrith and Ælfwine, and when it was clear that they would survive infancy he made his move against Oswine. Oswine attempted to raise an army but lost his nerve and went into hiding, where he was murdered by one of his own men. Eanflæd, who was his cousin, persuaded Oswiu to found a monastery in penance for this killing.

Rather than attempt to rule the Deirans himself, Oswiu set up Æthelwald, Oswald's son, who had Deiran royal blood, as king. Penda of Mercia seems to have been engaged in warfare with the East Angles at this point and was unable to protect his protégé Oswine. Having successfully slain King Anna in 654, however, he turned his attention northwards. To Oswiu's surprise, Æthelwald went over to Penda, and Oswiu fled northwards to his fortress of Giudi (thought to be Stirling Castle). Besieged here, he paid off Penda, who was accompanied by thirty kings and princes including the Kings of the East Angles, Gwynedd and Powys. The distribution of Giudi, when Penda shared out the Bernician treasure that had been handed over to him, became legendary amongst the Britons. Keeping his bargain, Penda turned south and headed back towards Mercia. Oswiu, however, felt the need to recover his lost face and together with his eldest son Alhfrith he gathered a Bernician army and pursued Penda southwards. They caught up with him at the river Winwaed, somewhere near Leeds. Penda's army was destroyed. Only two of the royal princes escaped: Cadfael 'Battle-dodger', the King of Gwynedd (who broke camp the night before the battle), and Æthelwald of Deira, who decided to sit out the fight. Æthelwald saved his life but lost his throne. Alhfrith took the kingship of Deira (655-c.667).

By this time the English were for the most part professing Christianity. The conversion had, however, taken place as a result of several missions. The Italian mission to Kent and the Gaelic mission to Bernicia were the most prominent. Although there were no theological disagreements between the different missions, there were certain organizational peculiarities. In particular, the Church of Iona and its offshoots adhered to a method for calculating the date of Easter that had been superseded in most other areas. Most of the Deirans, including Queen Eanflæd, calculated Easter according to the new system, while the Bernicians, together with the Bishop of Lindisfarne, who had jurisdiction in both kingdoms, held to the traditional method. In about 660, King Alhfrith invited the Frankish Bishop Agilbert, who had recently left his see amongst the Gewisse, to minister to the Deirans. Under Agilbert's authority, the new dispensation became authorized in Deira, and this seems to have created friction between Alhfrith and his father King Oswiu. In 664 the two dates of Easter were so far apart that Oswiu and his wife between them had to experience a Lenten period that was almost double the prescribed length. A synod was held at Whitby in which the two dispensations were debated. Eventually, Oswiu opted for the new dispensation and re-unified the see (both Agilbert and Colmán of Lindisfarne then left, and a compromise candidate took over). By opting for the Deiran practice, Oswiu seems to have outflanked an attempt by Alhfrith to obtain greater autonomy for the southern kingdom. Alhfrith seems to have maintained himself as King of Deira for a little longer, for he sent St Wilfrid to be consecrated by Agilbert after the latter had become Bishop of Paris (c.667). Eventually, however, he rebelled against his father and was replaced as King of Deira by his half-brother Ecgfrith, who was a grandson of Eadwine.

When Oswiu died, he was succeeded as King of Bernicia by Ecgfrith, while Ecgfrith's younger brother Ælfwine became King of Deira. After Ælfwine was killed in battle against the Mercians in 679, the Deiran kingship reverted to Ecgfrith, and from that time on the two kingdoms remained united and became known as Northumbria. On Ecgfrith's death in battle against the Picts in 685, it seemed that the Bernician royal house had come to an end; but a bastard of Oswiu's, Aldfrith, was found studying on Iona and he returned to Northumbria to take up the kingship. Aldfrith (686-705) was famous as a scholar in the Gaelic world and there survives a body of Old Irish verse attributed to him. After the death of his sons, the line descended from Æthelfrith did indeed come to an end, and much of the rest of Northumbrian history is an incoherent catalogue of internecine strife between noblemen with a more or less distant claim to the kingship. Something of a golden age occurred under King Eadbert (737-58), whose brother was simultaneously Archbishop of York. After Eadbert retired into monastic retreat, however, the chaos returned.

It was during one of these periods of civil war (between 862 and 867) that the Danish Great Army led by the brothers Ingwær, Healfdene and Ubba arrived in Northumbria. They killed the leaders of both factions, Osberht (848-67) and Ælle (863-7), and imposed their own nominee Ecgbert (867-73). Following the reign of Ricsige (873-6), the kingdom was divided, with Deira falling to the Danish leader Healfdene (876-8) and Ecgberht II succeeding to Bernicia. The fact that this split occurred along the old lines suggests that the union of 679 had not been entirely successful. Confusingly, both the Danish and the English portions were called Northumbria in contemporary sources, but modern convention names them after their chief royal centres, York and Bamburgh. Ecgbert II was succeeded by Eadwulf II (d. 913) who was followed by his son Ealdred (913-34). On Ealdred's death, Æthelstan, 'King of the Anglo-Saxons', invaded and ended the royal aspirations of the rulers at Bamburgh.

THE KINGS OF THE MERCIANS

The origins of Mercia, on the middle and upper Trent, are unknown. Its name means 'the march', or border, but whether this is a northern or a western march is unclear. The first king we hear of is Cearl, but only in as much as he was Eadwine of Deira's father-in-law. We do not even know what relationship existed between Cearl and the next known Mercian kings, Eawa and Penda, sons of Pybba. Eawa was killed at Maserfield in 642, in the same battle as Oswald of Bernicia, but we do not know which side he fought for. Was he the predecessor of his brother Penda? His rival? Or did they share the kingship? It is after Maserfield, when Penda is very much in charge (642-55), that we begin to understand the Mercians and their regional hegemony.

'Old Mercia' was surrounded by kingdoms that have almost no independent history and which were gradually absorbed into Mercia. The only known King of the Middle Angles, Peada son of Penda (d. 656), was the son of a Mercian king. The first known King of the Magonsaete, Merewalh, was also said to be Penda's son. The relations of the Kings of the Hwicce with the sons of Pybba are not clear, but they were clearly under Mercian dominion from their first appearance in the record in the 660s. The rulers of the Lindesfarona ('Lindsey') had their own independent dynasty but were usually under Mercian overlord-ship. As in the North, conquest in the seventh century did not usually lead to complete absorption of territory but to the placing of a kinsman or retainer into the kingship of the conquered territory. Some areas like Middle Anglia may have had an independent history, but others, such as the territory of the Magonsaete, probably originated as Mercian colonies in British lands.

After Penda's death and three years of rule by Oswiu of Bernicia (655-8), Mercia once more became a dominant force under Penda's son Wulfhere (658-c.675). Wulfhere success-fully expanded southwards, extending Mercian dominion over the East Saxons and conquering much of the Thames basin from the Gewisse. In this latter region, he seems to have established a short-lived sub-kingdom of Suthrige ('Surrey'). He ravaged the Isle of Wight and gave it to the South Saxons on condition that they became his vassals and accepted Christianity. Wulfhere was succeeded by the last of Penda's sons, Æthelred (674-704). Æthelred married Osthryth, daughter of Oswiu of Bernicia, but hostility to the Bernicians in his kingdom was such that she was murdered by his retainers in 697. He endowed the church of Worcester in the kingdom of the Hwicce and eventually resigned to become a monk at Bardney in Lindsey. Their patronage of monasteries in their subject-kingdoms indicates how secure the Mercian kings felt in their hegemony.

Following the brief reigns of Wulfhere's son Coenred (704-9) and Æthelred's son Ceolred (709-16), the kingship passed from the descendants of Penda to Æthelbald, grandson of Penda's brother Eawa. From Æthelbald's long reign (716-57) we have a plethora of documentary evidence but no good chronicle account. In one charter Æthelbald styles himself 'King of Britain', the first ruler ever to do so. His coinage circulated in Kent as well as the Midlands. Curiously, Æthelbald was eventually murdered by his own retinue, though how he had offended them is unrecorded.

After a brief period of civil war, an obscure cousin of Æthelbald's, Offa, emerged as king. Offa (757-96) began to centralize the Mercian hegemony and in his time most of the tributary kingdoms were reduced to provincial status, their rulers being termed *ealdormen* rather than kings. Sometimes this required the elimination of the native royal lines, but sometimes men accepted the reduced status as the price of survival. At some point in the middle of his reign, Offa lost territory on his western frontier to Eliseg, King of Powys, and it was probably this event that led him to construct his famous Dyke. Although this is often said to stretch from coast to coast, recent research suggests that only the central portion, the border with Powys, was built at this time. Offa himself seems to have preferred the southern portion of the Middle Anglian kingdom as a place of residence: he endowed or re-founded St Albans and was buried in Bedford. He may perhaps have originated in this area, but it is just as likely that it was the proximity of London, the main port in his empire, that drew him here. Watling Street, the Roman road that runs from London through St Albans and past the Mercian royal centres of Tamworth and Lichfield, was the spinal column of the kingdom.

From about 765 until 776, and then again from 784 until his death, Offa was in direct control of Kent. Relations with Canterbury were not good, however, and in 786 Offa persuaded Pope Hadrian I to raise Lichfield to archiepiscopal status. Hadrian's letters address Offa jointly with his wife Cynethryth, the only Anglo-Saxon queen to have coins issued in her name. Her prominence may indicate that the marriage brought together two rival branches of the royal house. When Offa's son Ecgfrith died childless within months of becoming king, the scholar Alcuin interpreted the event as divine justice. He claimed that Offa had decimated the royal family in order to secure Ecgfrith's succession and that it was fitting it should come to nothing.

Ecgfrith's successor, the distantly related Coenwulf (796-821), proved to be a very effective king. On Offa's death both the East Angles and the Cantware had raised up independent kings. In 798 Coenwulf invaded Kent, seized the king and put his own brother Cuthred into the kingship. Having taken control of Kent, he ended the schism in the Church by reducing Lichfield to the status of an ordinary bishopric (803). When Cuthred died in 807, he took Kent directly under his rule. At an unknown date he also re-asserted his rule in East Anglia. In 816 he invaded North Wales and in 818 he devastated Dyfed. He died in 821 at Basingwerk, near the Welsh border, probably while planning another campaign. Coenwulf's brother Ceolwulf (821-3) continued the Welsh wars, destroying the fortress of Degannwy in Gwynedd and totally conquering Powys in 822. Ceolwulf's successors, Beornwulf (823-5), Ludeca (825-7) and Wiglaf (827-40), were not so fortunate. In 825 Egbert of Wessex defeated the Mercians in North Wiltshire and regained control of the Thames basin. In 826 East Anglia broke away and in 829 Egbert temporarily conquered Mercia altogether. The short reigns of these kings indicate that there was also civil strife.

✠ Ego Aethilbalt dño donante rex nons olum Marcersium sede tocinium
prouinciarum quae generale nomine Sutangli dicuntur proremedio
animae meae etrelaxatione piaculorum meorum aliquam terrae par
ticulam idest x. cassatorum uenerando comite meo Cyniberhtte.
adconstruendum coenubium inprouincia cui ab antiquis nomen in
ditum est Husmerae. iuxta flauium uocabulo Stur. cum omnibus ne
cessariis adeam pertinentib. cum campis siluisq. cum piscariis pratisq
inpossessionem ecclesiasticam benigne largiendo trado. Itaut quam
diu uixerit potestatem habeat tenendi acpossidendi cui cumq. uoluerit
uel eo uiuo uel certe post obitum suum relinquendi. Est autem supra
dictus ager incircuitu, exutraq. parte supra nominati fluminis
habens exaquilone placa siluam quam nominant Cynibre. exocci
dentale uero aliam cui nomen est. Moerheb. quarum pars maxima
adpraefatum pertinet agrum. Siquis autem hanc donationem uio
lare temptauerit sciat se intremendo examine tyrannidis ac
praesumptionis suae dõ rationem terribiliter redditurum.
Scripta est haec cartula anno abincarnatione dñi nīhūxpi septin
centissimo tricessimo ui indictione quarta

✠ Ego Aetdilbalt rex Britanniae propriam don̄ . . . . ipsi subscripsi.
✠ ego uuor episcopus consensi etsubscripsi.
✠ ego uuilfridus episc. iubente Aethilbaldo rege subscripsi.
✠ ego Aethilric subregulus atq. comes gloriosissicu principis Ethilb
    huic donatione consensi etsubscripsi.
✠ ego Ibe acsiindignus abbas consensi etsubscripsi.
✠ ego beardberht frater atq. dux pre fati regis consensi etsubscripsi
✠ ego Ebbella consensum meum acomodans subscripsi
✠ ego Onoc comes subscripsi.
✠ ego Oba consensi etsubscripsi
✠ ego Sigibed consensi etsubscripsi
✠ ego Bercol. consensi etsubscripsi
✠ ego Ealduuft consensi etsubscripsi
✠ ego Cusa consensi etsubscripsi
✠ ego Dede consensi etsubscripsi

11. An extract from a charter of Æthelbald.

The last great Mercian king was Burgred (852-74). He allied himself with the West Saxons and fought off the Vikings. He married Æthelswith, daughter of Æthelwulf of Wessex, in 853, and in the same year the two kings invaded Wales. In 865 Burgred seems to have extended his dominion as far as Anglesey, but in 868 the Danish Great Army came south from Northumbria and wintered at Nottingham in Old Mercia. A joint siege of the Vikings by Burgred and his West Saxon brothers-in-law encouraged the Vikings to go elsewhere, but they returned in force in 873 and the following year Burgred resigned his kingship to go on pilgrimage to Rome. His successor Ceolwulf II (874-9) was regarded by the West Saxons as a 'foolish king's thegn' and is generally viewed as a pro-Viking quisling. He was not without his moments: in 878 he defeated and slew Rhodri, King of Gwynedd. Nevertheless, the Vikings gained control of the eastern portion of the kingdom. Ceolwulf II's fate is not known, but he was succeeded by Æthelred (879-911), the last Mercian king. Early in his reign Æthelred suffered a crushing defeat at the hands of Anarawd, son of King Rhodri, and lost many of the lands conquered in North Wales by his predecessors. He was initially more successful in South Wales, but the rulers there appealed to Alfred of Wessex for protection. Æthelred married Alfred's daughter Æthelflæd in c.884, and in 886, when Alfred captured London and southeastern Mercia from the Danes, he received these back as a fief. The price was high, however, for from then on Æthelred was generally regarded as 'Lord' rather than 'King' of the Mercians, and Alfred's authority ran throughout both kingdoms. Æthelred, and after his death his widow, now concentrated on driving the Vikings out of the northeast of the kingdom. When he died, Æthelflæd ruled Mercia for her lifetime, but on her death Edward of Wessex annexed the kingdom.

THE KINGS OF THE GEWISSE (WEST SAXONS)

The early history of the Gewisse is difficult to reconstruct. This is partly because there are no good southern chronicles surviving from the early period and partly because their history was extensively rewritten in the age of Alfred. In the sixth and seventh centuries they seem to have had many kings simultaneously and we should perhaps think of them as being like the West Angles, a confederacy of provinces ruled by a number of kings from the same dynasty. When Eadwine of Deira attacked the Gewisse in 626 he killed five kings, but at least two who had borne the title before his attack survived. Unification seems to have occurred in the late seventh century, perhaps under Cædwalla (685-8) or Ine (688-726). The original territory seems to have been the middle Thames basin and, the Gewisse's first bishop was installed at Dorchester on Thames in c.635. Their earliest kings, Cerdic (c.538-54), Cynric (c.554-81) and Ceawlin (c.581-8), had British Celtic names, which may mean that the kingdom originated as a sub-Roman unit heavily reliant upon Saxon mercenaries.

In the mid-seventh century, the Gewisse suffered a great deal from interference from Penda of Mercia. Penda's son Wulfhere had an even more traumatic effect on the Gewisse, conquering much of their Thames valley homeland. The bishopric was transferred from Dorchester, now lost to the Mercians, to Winchester in the 660s and the kingdom became refocused on recently acquired territories in Hampshire and Wiltshire. While affairs in the North went badly for the Gewisse, they continued to expand westwards into the lands of the Britons, reaching the Bristol Channel in the 650s and conquering southern Dorset in the 680s. Ine fought against the British King Geraint in Somerset in the early eighth century.

With unification came a change of terminology, as 'West Saxon' gradually supplanted 'Gewisse'. Cædwalla (685-8) conquered the Isle of Wight and killed off most of the rival dynasts, while Ine (688-726) used his long reign to consolidate the kingdom and to establish the Church on a firmer footing. Both these kings resigned their kingship to go to Rome. The consolidation of the kingdom and the gradual accretion of more British territory led to the West Saxon kingdom becoming the largest unitary kingdom in the South. But bad experiences in the seventh century meant that eighth-century kings did not tend to pick fights with the Mercians. At the time of the visit of the papal legates to England in 785, Cynewulf of Wessex (757-86) was the only southern king other than Offa of Mercia whom they noticed. Cynewulf seems to have generally been on good terms with Offa but was not a subject in the way other rulers were. Cynewulf was murdered whilst on a love tryst in 786 and his successor Beorhtric (786-802) became an even closer co-worker of Offa, marrying the latter's daughter Eadburh. Beorhtric began to adopt certain Mercian styles for his charters and was also the first West Saxon to mint silver pennies after the Mercian fashion. He is said by Asser (King Alfred's biographer) to have accidentally been poisoned by his wife, who was trying to murder a retainer. Queen Eadburh then fled with the royal treasure to the court of Charlemagne, the Frankish ruler who in 800 was crowned Emperor. Charlemagne made Eadburh an abbess, but she was turned out after being caught having an affair and eventually died in poverty at Pavia in Italy.

Beorhtric was succeeded by Ecgbert (802-39), whose father may have been the Ealhmund who was briefly King of Kent in one of the rebellions against Offa. Ecgbert had been driven out of Wessex by Beorhtric and Offa after contending for the kingship some years earlier and had lived as an exile at the Frankish court. On his assumption of the kingship he may have instituted the shiring of Wessex: the idea of having the kingdom divided into regular sized blocks with a royal appointee at the head of each, based in an urban or quasi-urban settlement, looks very like the system of counts and counties used by the Franks. In 825 at Ellandun (now Wroughton) in Wiltshire, Ecgbert defeated an invading Mercian force under King Beornwulf. As a result of this victory, he seems to have taken Kent, Surrey, Sussex and Essex out of Mercian lordship. These territories were given to his son Æthelwulf to rule as a sub-kingdom. In 829 Ecgbert drove Wiglaf of Mercia out of his kingdom and ruled all the English south of the Humber. Although Wiglaf regained his kingdom in 830, the kingdom of the East Angles slipped out of his control, and since its next three kings, Æthelstan (c.830-45), Æthelweard (c.845-55) (both known only from their coins) and Edmund (c.855-69) have names borne by the descendants of Ecgbert, it is possible that this too became a West Saxon sub-kingdom. In 838 Ecgbert also fought against the Britons of Cornwall, who had allied with the Vikings, and defeated them at the Battle of Hingston Down. This is the last evidence of Anglo-British conflict in the Southwest. Ecgbert died in 839 at a great age.

Æthelwulf (839-58), Ecgbert's son, took the kingship of the West Saxons and passed his own south-eastern sub-kingdom on to his eldest son Æthelstan (who had perhaps ruled East Anglia hitherto). Æthelwulf, in the face of increased Viking pressure, entered into alliance with the Mercian Kings Beorhtwulf (840-52) and Burgred (852-74). In 855 he went on pilgrimage to Rome but, unlike his predecessors, he returned, and with a new wife, Judith, daughter of Charles the Bald, King of the Franks. On his departure for Rome, Æthelwulf had divided his kingdom between his sons Æthelbald, who received Wessex, and Æthelbert, who received the Southeast (Æthelstan was already dead). When Æthelwulf returned, Æthelbert turned his kingdom over to his father, but Æthelbald refused. King Æthelwulf refused to fight his son and accepted this situation. On his death, Æethelbert took over the Southeast again, but Æthelbald, the senior, married his stepmother. He himself only lasted another two years, and in 860 Æthelbert (860-5) re-united Wessex and the Southeast. He faced increasing Viking activity but died peacefully and was buried, like his brother before him, at Sherborne. A further brother, Æthelred (865-71), now took over the kingdom. In his time the Great Army came to Britain and Æthelred led the West Saxon forces northwards to help his brother-in-law Burgred of Mercia. In 871 the Great Army turned south and fought against the West Saxons in a number of battles. In some of these the Christians prevailed, and in others the pagans. On 15 April 871, King Æthelred died and was followed into the kingship by the last remaining son of Æthelwulf, Alfred.

THE KINGS OF THE ANGLO-SAXONS

ALFRED THE GREAT (871-899)

Alfred, together with his son Edward and grandson Æthelstan, is one of the chief contenders for the title 'First King of England'. At the beginning of his reign, the prospects of such great claims seemed remote. A Viking army occupied part of Wessex, and Alfred was soundly beaten in his first battle. Believing discretion to be the better part of valour, he paid the Vikings off and they left Wessex. Alfred thus had breathing space in which to consolidate his rule. But in 876 a Viking force landed at Wareham and, after negotiating and breaking a treaty, moved on to Exeter. The enemy then moved off to Gloucester and from there, in January 878, made an unexpected winter attack on Alfred at Chippenham. With a small following, Alfred fled into the Somerset levels and hid on the Isle of Athelney, supporting himself by ravaging the surrounding country-side. (It was during this period that, according to later legend, Alfred took refuge anonymously in a peasant household and, distracted by his cares, was reprimanded by his unwitting hostess for failing to notice that her cakes were burning.)

In the spring of 878, however, the West Saxons were heartened when Oda, Ealdorman of Devon, won an unexpectedly decisive victory at Countisbury, killing Ubba and 1,200 of his followers. Ubba was the last survivor of the three brothers who had led the Great Army to England in 865. Rallied by this victory, Alfred gathered an army from the western shires and confronted the Danish force occupying Wiltshire at Edington. After resoundingly beating them on the field and besieging the survivors for two weeks, he forced them to come to terms. Their leader Guthrum gave hostages to Alfred and received baptism, taking the name Æthelstan. His army then crossed back into Mercia and camped at Cirencester for a year before moving on to East Anglia in 880, where Guthrum/Æthelstan took the kingship. In the same year the army that had dominated the Southeast from a base at Fulham left Britain for the Frankish realm. Alfred was now master of all that his father had ruled.

From 880 Alfred had the upper hand in his dealings with the Vikings. He organized the burghal system, which established fortified centres evenly spaced across his kingdom. From these, most of the medieval towns of the South developed. He also re-organized the levy system so that only half the militia (the *fyrd*) would answer any one call and half would remain in reserve, thus allowing him to keep his army in the field for far longer at a stretch (the second half of the army relieving the first when their tour of duty was over). He also brought in Friesian shipwrights and sailors to build a fleet that could meet Danish ships at sea. In 886 he besieged and captured London and the territories on the north bank of the Thames. These had been

Mercian before the coming of the Great Army, and Alfred now restored them to Æthelred of Mercia on condition that the latter recognize him as lord. From this time Alfred seems to have begun to use the title 'King of the Anglo-Saxons' and to have had his coins minted across both Wessex and Mercia. The southern Welsh rulers, the Kings of Brycheiniog, Gwent, Glywysing and Dyfed, also put themselves under his protection – although interestingly their fears were not of the Vikings but of Æthelred of Mercia and Anarawd of Gwynedd. Eventually even Anarawd himself came to Alfred's court and swore allegiance to the king, presumably before 894 when he ravaged the provinces of Ceredigion and Ystrad Tywi with English help and installed his brother Cadell as king there.

Alfred's programme of national reconstruction was not confined to political and military reforms. He also patronized learning and gathered at his court scholars from all over England and the neighbouring regions, including Bishop Asser of St Davids (who was to write his biography), Grimbald, a Frank who helped set up a school system for young noblemen, and John the Old Saxon who became abbot of the monastery Alfred founded at Athelney. The king instituted a programme of translation into English of texts most useful for his nobles and churchmen to know. These included Gregory the Great's treatise *On Pastoral Care*, the *Consolation of Philosophy* by Boethius, St Augustine's *Soliloquia* and the first fifty Psalms, all these perhaps translated by the king himself. Under his auspices, Gregory's *Dialogues*, Orosius's *History Against the Pagans* and probably Bede's *Ecclesiastical History of the English People* were also translated. Remarkably for an early medieval ruler, Alfred believed that his secular officials should be literate and learned, and he seems genuinely to have attempted to produce an educated mandarin class.

Alfred's last great literary work was the commissioning of the *Anglo-Saxon Chronicle*, a history of the English, giving prominence to the West Saxons but trying to reconcile all the regional traditions. Copies of this chronicle were distributed about the kingdom and kept up to date at different centres. This first recension may have been distributed as early as 892, although one version of the surviving Chronicle has material up to 896 that is likely to reflect Alfred's own views very closely. Interestingly, the *Anglo-Saxon Chronicle* gives a version of the West Saxon royal pedigree including, for the first time, the name of Scyld Scefing, the ancestor of the Danish kings. Alfred's appropriation of this ancestor probably reflects his desire to be seen as the rightful ruler of the Danes resident in England. Alfred also began the building of the New Minster in Winchester, which he seems to have intended to be both monastery and palace, on the Frankish model. Although he made some other grants of lands to churches, it seems likely that he also appropriated Church land in strategically sensitive places in order to endow warriors. His law code also expanded royal authority and his insistence that his own son Edward, rather than one of his nephews (whose fathers had, after all, been kings before him), should succeed show that he was not the selfless hero-king of popular myth.

Alfred married Ealhswith, the granddaughter of a Mercian king, in 868 and she bore him five children who survived childhood. These were Æthelflæd, who married Æthelred of Mercia, Edward, his heir designate, Æthelgifu, who became abbess of Shaftesbury, Ælfthryth, who married Baldwin II of Flanders, and Æthelweard. Alfred died in 899 and was buried at Winchester.

EDWARD THE ELDER (899-924)

Alfred's will clearly signalled that he intended to be succeeded by his eldest son, Edward. One charter from 898 describes Edward already as king. This may indicate that he was given a sub-kingship whilst his father was still alive. His succession, however, was not uncontested.

Clockwise from top   12. Coin of Ecgbert, King of the West Saxons (802-39).
13. Coin of Æthelwulf, King of the West Saxons (839-58), Ecgbert's son.
14. Coin of Æthelstan, son of Æthelwulf and brother of Alfred.
15. Coin of Eírik Blood-Axe, Norwegian King of Northumbria (d. 952).
16. Coin of Æthelred, King of the West Saxons (865-71), son of Æthelwulf and brother of Alfred.

Æthelwold, son of King Æthelred, Alfred's predecessor, made a play for the kingship. As part of this attempt he abducted a nun (possibly Alfred's daughter Æthelgifu) from a monastery and 'married' her, and took control of Wimborne in Dorset. Edward led an army to Wimborne and although Æthelwold escaped, the nun was recovered. How serious this attempt to seize the kingdom was, or how long it took to suppress it, is not clear, but it is noteworthy that although Alfred died in October 899 Edward's inauguration, at Kingston upon Thames, did not take place until June 900. This is the earliest record we have of the use of Kingston as the site for inaugurations and its position, where Wessex, the southeastern sub-kingdom and Mercia all meet, may be suggestive that this was a new ceremony associated with the idea of the unified 'kingdom of the Anglo-Saxons'.

Edward's inauguration probably coincided with his second marriage, to Ælfflæd, daughter of Æthelhelm, Ealdorman of Wiltshire. She bore him two sons and six daughters. His first union had been with a woman of unknown antecedents named Ecgwynn, who bore him one son, Æthelstan and, perhaps, a daughter. It is possible that Ecgwynn had died by 901, but it is equally likely that marriage to Ælfflæd was the price of Ealdorman Æthelhelm's support in the civil war, and that Æthelstan's mother was set aside for political considerations. Edward needed all the support he could get, for in 902 the pretender Æthelwold returned in alliance with Eohric, the Danish King of East Anglia, and invaded the kingdom of the Anglo-Saxons. The insurgents were chased back into East Anglia and, in a bloody battle at Holme in 902, both Eohric and Æthelwold were slain. These events secured Edward's kingship.

In 910 a large Viking force, drawn from Northumbria and the settlements established around the Irish Sea following the Norse expulsion from Dublin in 902, invaded English Mercia. Edward, together with his sister Æthelflæd, cut off the army as it returned home and engaged it between Wednesfield and Tettenhall in the Northwest Midlands. The resulting battle was a complete victory for the English, with all three of the Viking kings, Healfdene, Ingwær and Eowils, being killed. The following year the English harried Northumbria. However, Æthelred of Mercia (who had been ill for some time) died, and Edward claimed back London, Oxford and the lands granted to Æthelred by Alfred in 886.

The acquisition of southeastern Mercia opened up Edward's frontier with the Danish-held lands of the East Midlands and East Anglia. Over the next five or six years, through a combination of military activity and purchase for cash, Edward recovered most of the territories east of Watling Street. The East Angles finally accepted his rule in 917. When his sister Æthelflæd died in 918 the Mercians chose her daughter Ælfwynn to succeed her, but within a year Edward had brought an army into Mercia and removed her to Wessex. In 920 Edward received the submission of Rægnald, who now ruled Danish Northumbria, Ealdred, King of northern Northumbria, and Owain of Strathclyde and Constantín, King of Scots. What this meant in real terms is debatable, but from now on Edward's kingdom was to be the most formidable in Britain. Edward also consolidated his conquests by expanding the burghal system into the East Midlands and shiring these territories.

At the height of his power Edward set aside his second wife Ælfflæd, who had borne him eight children, and married for a third time. His new wife was Eadgifu, daughter of Sigehelm, Ealdorman of Kent, who had been killed at the Battle of Holme. Eadgifu bore Edward two sons, Edmund and Eadred, and two daughters, Eadgifu and Eadburh. Ælfflæd retired into the nunnery at Wilton. It is possible that the wave of ecclesiastical reform that was beginning to sweep through England at this stage, as evidenced by the creation of three new West Saxon sees at Wells, Ramsbury and Crediton, caused Edward to end his second marriage. It is more than likely that he and Ælfflæd were related within the prohibited degrees as laid down by the reformers. Edward died at Farndon in Cheshire, apparently after suppressing a revolt by Idwal of Gwynedd and the men of Chester.

THE KINGS OF THE ENGLISH

ÆTHELSTAN (924-939) 15 yrs

On Edward the Elder's death, his eldest son by Ælfflæd, Æthelweard, seems to have been chosen to succeed him in Wessex. The Mercians, however, chose his first child Æthelstan, Ecgwynn's son, who had been fostered at the court of Æthelred and Æthelflæd. Whether the half-brothers would have accepted the division of the kingdom or fought it out with one another was never put to the test. Æthelweard died within a fortnight of his father and Æthelstan was proclaimed 'King of the Anglo-Saxons and the Danes'. He was not conse-crated at Kingston upon Thames until 4 September 925, however, which may suggest that some opposition continued.

In 926 Æthelstan secured his northern border by marrying a sister, Eadgyth, to Sihtric, King of York (921-7). Sihtric is said to have repudiated Eadgyth (who became a nun at Polesworth in Mercia), but in any case he himself was dead within the year. Æthelstan seized the opportunity to annex Danish Northumbria and on 12 July 927 he held a meeting at Eamont Bridge, on the borders of Cumberland and Westmorland, with the northern kings, Constantín, Owain and Ealdred. At about the same time the various Welsh kings also submitted to him: King Hywel of Dyfed in particular became a frequent attendee at the English court and was often accorded precedence among the secular magnates. From 931 Æthelstan's Chancery began to use titles such as 'King of Albion' or 'King of Britain'. His coins also bear the legend *rex totius Britanniae* – 'King of all Britain'. Within a few years Æthelstan was even interfering in the succession disputes of kingdoms beyond the sea. In 936 his nephew Louis d'Outremer was imposed on the Western Kingdom (France) and Alan Twisted-Beard, who had grown up in exile in England, was made King of the Bretons. At about the same time, Æthelstan also helped his foster-son Hákon to oust his brother, Eírik Blood-Axe, from the Norwegian kingship. Closer to home, however, his interference in dynastic succession was storing up trouble for the future.

Eadwine, brother to Æthelweard and half brother to Æthelstan, made a bid for the kingship in 933, perhaps with aid from the clerical establishment at Winchester. The pretender drowned at sea between England and Flanders and it was rumoured to have been no accident. In 934, Ealdred of Bamburgh died. He had maintained good relations both with Edward and Æthelstan and with Constantín, King of Scots. At his death, the succession at Bamburgh was disputed, perhaps with pro-West Saxon factions vying against pro-Scots factions, and this resulted in Æthelstan mounting a huge northern expedition, leading one of the largest armies yet seen in Britain northwards beyond the borders of his realm. He visited the tomb of St Cuthbert, at Chester le Street, and had the saint's body clothed in garments made by his sisters. Then, having gained the saint's support, he led his fleet and army north of the Forth into the kingdom of Alba. He besieged Constantín at Dunottar, just south of Aberdeen, and forced him into submis-sion. That Christmas, Constantín kicked his heels at Æthelstan's court in the South; but he was not to forget his humiliation.

In 937 Constantín, together with his son-in-law Olaf Guthfrithsson, King of Dublin and the Isles, and probably with help from Owain of Strathclyde and Idwal of Gwynedd, invaded Mercia. Eventually they were defeated at the Battle of Brunnanburh (location unknown) and fled, leaving many dead including Constantín's son. Despite his victory, Æthelstan's losses were very heavy and there is some evidence that his power waned. Hywel of Dyfed ceased to be noted as present at court and Eírik Blood-Axe may have taken up residence in York. Æthelstan died on 27 October 939, at Gloucester and was buried at his favourite monastery of Malmesbury. Whilst Æthelstan was a member of the West Saxon royal house, it has been argued that his success was partly a consequence of his close identification with Mercia. In view of the obvious dynastic imperative, it is curious that he is not known to have married or had any children.

EDMUND (939-946)

Edmund, the son of Eadgifu, Edward the Elder's third wife, succeeded his brother Æthelstan and was consecrated at Kingston upon Thames on 29 November 939. Within a few months, however, Olaf Guthfrithsson returned to Britain and, driving Eírik from York, invaded northern Mercia, apparently with the aid of Archbishop Wulfstan of York. Olaf and Edmund came to terms, the former taking everything north and east of Watling Street and the latter retaining Wessex, the Southeast and western Mercia. The following year, Olaf died whilst ravaging Lothian. His cousin Olaf Sihtricsson succeeded him but was driven out in favour of Rægnald Guthfrithsson. Edmund took advantage of these internal squabbles to seize back Mercia and East Anglia and to attack and kill Idwal of Gwynedd, who had supported the Vikings. In 944 he was able to win back Northumbria. In 945 he ravaged Strathclyde and 'let' it to Mael Coluim, the Scots king. What this means is uncertain: Strathclyde retained its own king, Dyfnwal, although his sons, hostages at the English court, were blinded. From a shaky start, Edmund was beginning to show himself as a worthy successor to his brother. Unfortunately he was murdered whilst trying to save one of his servants from an assault at the royal villa of Pucklechurch in Gloucestershire. He was twenty-five years old. As well as his military achievements, Edmund had been an enthusiastic supporter of the Benedictine reform that was spreading across England at this time, appointing St Dunstan to the abbacy of Glastonbury.

Edmund married twice. Ælfgifu, the mother of his sons Eadwig and Edgar, predeceased him and was buried at Shaftesbury, where she was held to be a saint. His second wife, the daughter of the ealdorman of Essex, bore him no children.

EADRED (946-955)

Edmund was succeeded by his brother, Eadred, who seems to have preferred the title 'King of the Anglo-Saxons, Northumbrians, Pagans and Britons'. In political terms, his reign seems to have been a struggle for control of Northumbria. In 947 the Northumbrians swore oaths of allegiance to Eadred, but within a year they took Olaf Sihtricsson as their king. By 950 they had accepted Eírik Blood-Axe back. Eadred ravaged Northumbria, burning Ripon, and seems to have won the loyalty of Oswulf of Bamburgh. In 952 Oswulf led Eírik into a trap on Stainmore and had him killed. Northumbria would no longer have its own kings. Eadred was a sickly man and

Clockwise from top   17. A passage from the *Anglo-Saxon Chronicle* recording the victories of Æthelred and Alfred at Ashdown in 871. Translation is as follows: *In this year the* [Viking] *army came to Reading in Wessex, and, three nights after, two jarls rode up when the earl Ethelwulf met them at Inglefield and there fought against them and gained the victory; and one of them was there slain, whose name was Sidroc. Four nights after this King Æthelred and Alfred his brother led a large force to Reading and fought against the army, and there was great slaughter made on each side; and Earl Athelwulf was slain, and the Danes held possession of the battleplace. And four nights after, King Æthelred and Alfred his brother fought with all the army at Ashdown.*

18. Coin of Edward the Elder (899-924).

19. Coin of King Alfred (871-99) minted at London.

OMNIS CHO RVS ANGELO

ONNIS CHORVS PROPHETARVM

increasingly withdrew from public life. He died without children and was buried in Winchester.

EADWIG ALL-FAIR (955-959)

Edmund's son, Eadwig, was dissolute and impatient. He fell out with the powerful Abbot Dunstan over his sexual preferences and exiled him. He also confiscated all the property of his grandmother Eadgifu, who had remained prominent at court for the previous quarter century. He promoted new men, perhaps descendants of Æthelred of Wessex (d. 871) and kinsmen of his wife Ælfgifu, in an attempt to free himself from the establishment created by his father and uncles. In 957, perhaps as a result of these tensions, the kingdom was split. Eadwig retained the title 'King of the English', but his younger brother Edgar, who, at twelve, had just come of age, was accorded the title 'King of the Mercians and the Northumbrians'. Edgar recalled Dunstan and persuaded Archbishop Oda to annul the marriage of Eadwig and Ælfgifu on grounds of consanguinity.

EDGAR (957-975)

From Eadwig's death in October 959, Edgar ruled a re-united kingdom of the English. Edgar restored his grandmother to her lands and status and threw himself wholeheartedly behind the monastic reform movement. Righteous in the eyes of the Lord he may have been, but he was no soft touch. In 969, for unknown misdemeanours, he had Thanet ravaged by his soldiers; and his obituary in the *Anglo-Saxon Chronicle* notes that his one fault was that he was 'over-fond of pagan men', probably an allusion to his maintenance of a Scandinavian mercenary force such as later kings were known to have.

Edgar had three sons by three women. His eldest son Edward (by either Wulfthryth of Wilton or Æthelflæd Eneda) may not have been legitimate since, in a charter issued in 966, the infant Edmund, his second son, is designated *legitimus clito* whilst the older half-brother is simply *clito*, 'prince royal'. Edmund died in infancy but had a younger full-brother Æthelred. Their mother was Ælfthryth, the widow of Æthelwold, Ealdorman of East Anglia.

In 973 Edgar appears to have had a second consecration. This was held at Bath, the most impressive set of Roman ruins in Britain, and may have been an 'imperial' coronation. Immediately after the ceremony, Edgar sent his fleet around Wales to Chester where he received the submission of a number of insular kings including Cinaed of Alba, Mael Coluim of Strathclyde and perhaps even the Irish King Domnall of Leinster. A significant participant was Maccus son of Harald who had recently begun to compete for the leader- ship of the Vikings in Ireland and the Isles. 973 also saw a thorough reform of the coinage. During Edgar's reign England seems to have been entirely free from attack by its neigh- bours and this was probably due, in part, to his reputation as a warrior. Unfortunately, however, he died in 975, before either of his surviving sons reached manhood.

EDWARD THE MARTYR (975-978)

Edgar's oldest son Edward succeeded him. From the beginning of his reign, there was some support for his younger brother, but Æthelred was very much a minor and was unable to press his claim. Interestingly the eastern ealdormen and the western churchmen supported

Opposite   20. A manuscript illumination of Christ from the Æthelstan Psalter, a ninth-century prayer book traditionally associated with King Æthelstan.

Edward, while the western ealdormen and the eastern churchmen supported Æthelred. Edward was eventually accepted by all parties, but in March 978 he was murdered whilst visiting his brother at the villa of Corfe, in Dorset. Later writers blamed his stepmother for the murder, but it is more likely that it was a private initiative by some of Æthelred's household who like the idea of being king's men.

ÆTHELRED THE UNREADY (978-1016) 3 lot yrs -

Æthelred was the longest reigning member of his dynasty since Ine (d. 726), and for much of his reign he was a successful ruler who strengthened the English State. Unfortunately, his final years were riven by foreign invasion and civil strife and his reputation has suffered accordingly. Æthelred was about twelve when he became king, and for the first six years of his reign he was counselled by Bishop Æthelwold of Winchester and his mother Ælfthryth. In 984 Æthelwold died and Ælfthryth seems to have left the court. It is likely that the king, now in his twenties, was eager to assert his independence. Over the next few years he seems to have appropriated much land from the Church, but from 993 his mother was back in his counsel and a more stable period of rule followed. This, however, coincided with the resumption of Danish raids, which were small-scale affairs in the 980s but a much more serious threat from the 990s.

Unlike most of the Viking activity of the tenth century, the attacks of the 980s and 990s were not the work of groups resident in Britain and Ireland but of newcomers from Scandinavia. The Scandinavian nations were undergoing a process of unification and conversion to Christianity in this period, and to a large extent the new raiders were unsuccessful competitors in domestic squabbles who had been driven overseas. Æthelred chose to deal with the invaders by paying them off. The monetarization of the economy and the increase in effective taxation and revenue through the courts during the previous century encouraged him to think that payment was a better deal than fighting. Between 991 and 1012, more than £134,000 was paid out in Danegeld. Many of the individual Viking leaders, like Olaf Tryggvason who was paid off in 991, kept their word and did not return; but once word got out that silver could be had for the asking, the attacks simply increased. In 1002 Æthelred tried to solve the problem by organizing an act of genocide against Danes living peacefully in England. Unfortunately for him, one of those slain was the sister of Svein Fork-Beard, King of Denmark, who then began to prosecute a national war against the English.

In 1012 Æthelred changed his policy: he abandoned the raising of tribute to pay off the Danes and adopted a regular tax, the Heregeld, in order to maintain a Scandinavian (mostly Swedish) fleet as a permanent military force that could be used against both external and internal enemies. This tax was levied every year until at least 1051. The first commander of this fleet was Thorkel the Tall, the Viking commander implicated in the martyrdom of Ælfheah, Archbishop of Canterbury, in the very same year in which he was hired. The long war against Svein is difficult to follow since both English and Scandinavian commanders seem to have kept changing sides. One particularly malign figure was Eadric Streona ('the acquisitor'), Ealdorman of Mercia from 1007. Although his treachery was instrumental in allowing the Danes the final victory in the war, Svein's son, Cnut, had him executed as a warning against traitors. One could be forgiven for imagining that the endemic treachery of the period actually created a certain sympathy between the principals of the opposing factions.

Despite the political chaos of Æthelred's later years, English culture flourished. A legislative programme was set in motion under the auspices of Archbishop Wulfstan, as was the composition and translation into English of hagiographical works and other educational aids by scholars such as Ælfric and Byrhtferth. To some extent both the failures and the successes of Æthelred's reign pay tribute to the creation of the Old English State, which had reached a level of structural coherence which enabled it to function even if the political leadership was in flux. The age of empires rising and falling according to the dynamism of particular dynasts was long gone.

Æthelred was temporarily ousted by Svein in 1013 but returned the following year, after Svein's death. By the middle of 1014, however, his heir apparent, Æthelstan, was dead, and by 1015 Æthelred and his oldest surviving son, Edmund, had fallen out. Svein's son, Cnut, continued to keep up the Danish pressure. When Æthelred finally died in April 1016, nothing was certain.

EDMUND IRONSIDE (APRIL-NOVEMBER 1016)

Edmund, the son of Æthelred, struggled to hold the kingdom together following his father's death in 1016, but was betrayed by Eadric Streona and defeated in battle by Cnut. He made peace with the Danish king, dividing the country with him. Less than five weeks later he was dead and his family fled overseas.

CNUT THE GREAT (1016-1035)

On Edmund's death both factions, worn out by years of warfare, recognized Cnut as king. Cnut was the son of Svein by his Polish wife, and had almost certainly been brought up a Christian. He had also spent some time in England during his father's campaigns and had a long-standing relationship with an English noblewoman, Ælfgifu, daughter of Ælfhelm, Ealdorman of (southern) Northumbria. On his accession, which was marked with a continental-style coronation rather than the traditional inauguration at Kingston, Cnut married Emma of Normandy, Æthelred's widow. (She wisely sent Æthelred's children overseas for safekeeping.) He seems to have maintained his relationship with Ælfgifu, however, as she later turns up as regent of Norway on his behalf. Cnut purged the old regime of its least trustworthy or most self-sufficient members, such as Eadric Streona and Uhtred of Bamburgh, but kept the trustworthy like Archbishop Wulfstan. An agreement was reached in 1018 between the Danish and English notables, aimed at a return to the stability of Edgar's reign. During the early 1020s Cnut issued a series of law codes, probably drafted by Wulfstan. In as many ways as possible, Cnut seems to have stressed continuity with his English inheritance.

Following the death of his brother Harold (c.1018), Cnut became King of Denmark and subsequently spent much of his reign in Scandinavia. He sporadically controlled Norway, which he placed under Ælfgifu and her son Svein, and conquered Gautland (now southern-central Sweden). Back in Britain in the mid 1020s, Cnut, with the help of Richard of Normandy, patched up the war in which Uhtred had engaged with Mael Coluim of Alba, probably establishing the Tweed as the border. In 1027 he felt secure enough to go to Rome on pilgrimage and to attend the coronation of the Emperor Conrad II. By 1031 he was back in England and travelled north to take the submission of the northern Kings Mael Coluim and MacBethad, rival claimants to the kingship of Alba, and Eachmarcach, King of the Isles.

21. Coin of Edmund (939-46).

22. Coin of Eadred (946-55) minted at Norwich.

23. Coin of Eadwig (955-9) minted at York.

24. Coin of Edward the Martyr (975-8) struck at Stamford.

25. King Edgar: a conventional representation of a crowned king, from an Anglo-Saxon manuscript.

By forcing peace on Mael Coluim and MacBethad, he neutralized the threat presented by a unified Scotland.

Cnut's government of England relied upon powerful earls such as Siward of Northumbria, Ealdred of Bamburgh, and Leofric of Mercia (he kept Wessex for himself), and this is often presented as an Anglo-Danish innovation. In reality, such 'super-ealdormanries' had been around since at least Æthelstan's reign. The true novelty of Cnut's reign was the introduction of the Scandinavian term 'earl', which makes it easier for historians to distinguish the great provincial viceroys from the ealdormen of single shires. Equally, the Scandinavian mercenary troops in the royal household now had a specific term applied to them, *huscarls*, but were probably an institution that had been around for the best part of a century. The bilingualism of the Anglo-Danish court created the possibility of more nuanced semantics of government, but it did not radically change government.

Cnut, like Edgar, seems to have been able to mix genuine piety with ruthlessness and realism. The famous story of his trying to turn back the waves, which first appears in a twelfth-century history, was originally aimed at flattering courtiers. On being told by sycophants that even the waves obeyed him, Cnut is said to have trooped everyone down to the beach to demonstrate that this was utter nonsense. Cnut died at Shaftesbury in Dorset in November 1035: he was not yet 40. His son Svein, titular King of Norway, had predeceased him by a year but he was survived by Svein's brother, Harold, and a son by Emma called Harthacnut.

Harold Hare-Foot (1035-1040) and Harthacnut (1035-1042)

What Cnut intended for his empire is not clear. Later writers claimed that his son by Emma of Normandy, Harthacnut, was to inherit the whole, but this may reflect ecclesiastical opinions about Harold's legitimacy and the ultimate success of Emma's son Edward and her Norman kinsmen. The grandson of a Mercian nobleman who had ruled Northumbria, Harold was acclaimed king on Cnut's death by Leofric, Earl of Mercia, while Godwine, Earl of Wessex, proclaimed himself for Harthacnut, then in Denmark. Initially the parties agreed to a divided rule, but Harthacnut was delayed in his return to England by warfare in Scandinavia with Magnus of Norway. Nevertheless Archbishop Æthelnoth refused to consecrate Harold, perhaps because of his illegitimacy. In 1036, his stepmother, Queen Emma, despairing of Harthacnut's ever returning, sent to Normandy to her surviving sons by Æthelred. Edward led a fleet across the Channel to ravage Hampshire, and his brother Alfred landed on the south coast and was received by his mother and Godwine. Earl Godwine switched his allegiance at this point and handed Alfred over to Harold, who had him imprisoned at Ely and blinded. He died shortly afterwards. Godwine probably realized that through his wife he was kin with Harthacnut, but that he had no blood ties with Æthelred's sons. This failed coup by Emma led to Harold annexing the South and driving the queen overseas. In 1039 Harthacnut led a Danish fleet of sixty ships to Flanders, where he joined his mother and prepared for an invasion. The following spring, however, Harold died at Oxford and was buried in Westminster. When Harthacnut landed, he had his brother's body dug up and thrown into a fen. The following year, in 1041, Edward returned from Normandy and was sworn in as king alongside Harthacnut. They shared the same court. Within a few months, Harthacnut died whilst attending the wedding of Osgod Clapa. He left no children. Whilst Harold

ÿþþan wæs se þridda dæg pharaones gebyrdtid · þa worhte he mi-
celne beorscipe his cnihtum · gemang þam ða geþohte he þæra
byrla ealdor · and þæra bæcestra · and he gesette þæra byrla mægyster
to þære note þe he ær hæfde · þone oþerne he het hon · on gealgan · Ða
wæs iosepes soþfæstnys afandod · and þeah hwæþere þæra byrla
ealdor forgeat iosepes ærende ·

[Æ]fter twam gearum pharao mætte þæt he stode be anre ea · and him [þ]-
uhte þæt he gesawe gán up of þam flode seofon fægre oxan · and swiþe [f]-
ætte · and hi man læswode on morigum lande · him þuhte eac þæt
he gesawe cuman oþre seofon oxan up of þære ea · þa wæron fule
and swiðe hlæne · and hi eodon be þære ea ofrun on grenum stowum · and a-
-ton þa fættan oxan · and fræton hi · Ða awóc farao and slep eft ·
and him mætte oþer swefn · Him þuhte þæt he gesawe seofon
[e]ar weaxan on anum healme · fulle · and fægere · and he geseah
oþre seofon · lyþre · and forscruncene · Ða fræton ealle þa fæge-
ran · Ða awóc pharao of slæpe ::

H
[anno] uiii an[nis]
ẏsaac in [b]
[...]us natus o[...]
ripis

Sciendū qđ añ mortē · ẏsaac · xii · annis uēdit⁹ ē ioseph

xiii ·
Tredecim · annis fuit ioseph
[i]n egipto antequam ingrederetur
[d]omū pharaonis ·

had kept the standing fleet at sixteen ships, Harthacnut raised in to sixty, and this led, inevitably, to high and unpopular taxation.

EDWARD THE CONFESSOR (1041/2-1066) 25yrs-

The reign of Edward the Confessor has been obscured by the certain knowledge of historians that he would fail to provide an undisputed heir. This failure, however, cannot have been clear for most of the reign: even in its last months there must have been a likelihood that he would live long enough to see his great-nephew Edgar reach an acceptable age, for Edward can only have been in his early sixties by January 1066, when the boy was already fifteen.

Edward's accession went very smoothly. As the son of Æthelred II and Queen Emma, he had a strong dynastic claim and powerful political backing. He had been nominated by Harthacnut and inducted into the kingship whilst his brother was still alive, and his mother and Earl Godwine stood by him. He also had the backing of his cousin, Duke William of Normandy. Edward was probably about thirty-eight when Harthacnut died. In 1045 he took Godwine's daughter Edith to wife. This marriage marks the beginning of the rise of Godwine's family to supreme power in the land and the cutting of other ties. In 1043 Queen Emma had been deprived of her wealth and confined in Winchester, and the following year Gunnhild, the daughter of Mieszko II of Poland, was expelled from the country. Taken together, these three events concerning women may reflect the rise to dominance at court of Earl Godwine. Edward became king while still unmarried and under the influence of his mother. It is quite possible that Gunnhild, Cnut's niece, who had been married for the first time in 1030, was considered as a potential bride who would allow Edward to bring some Danish royal blood into his family. By removing Emma and Gunnhild, Godwine cleared the way for his own daughter to become queen.

The marriage between Edward and Edith was to store up trouble for the kingdom. By 1051 they were still childless, and although later hagiographers claimed that Edward's piety led to celibacy it is more likely that one of them was infertile. Edward desperately needed to set Edith aside and find a new wife: but how was he to do that without offending Godwine? His friendship with Earl Godwine's family was already causing embarrassment. Godwine's oldest son Swein had been made Earl of Southwest Mercia and in 1046, while returning from an expedition against Gruffudd ap Rhydderch, King of South Wales, Swein abducted the Abbess of Leominster and kept her as a concubine before casting her off. Swein was outlawed but fled first to Flanders and then to Denmark, where his cousin, another Swein, had just made himself king. Probably on the Danish king's advice, Swein returned to England in 1049 with eight ships, seeking forgiveness. Edward was advised against making peace by Godwine's second son, Harold, Earl of East Anglia, and Beorn Estridsson, who held an earldom in the North Midlands. Shortly afterwards, however, Swein met Earl Beorn in Sussex and asked him to mediate with the king. Since they were cousins, Beorn trusted Swein and rode off with only three companions. They went not to the king but to Swein's ships, and Beorn was carried off to Devon and murdered. Godwine and his family distanced themselves from Swein's outrageous behaviour and the outlaw fled back to Flanders.

Opposite   26. An image of a crowned king, conventionally identified as Æthelstan, in an Old English manuscript of the early books of the Bible.

The following spring, 1050, Godwine persuaded the king to disband all but five of his mercenary ships. Once the shipmen had gone their way Swein returned from Flanders and Earl Godwine forced Edward to reinstate him in his earldom. Edward turned for help to his new archbishop, the Norman Robert of Jumièges, and to Count Baldwin's over-mighty and rebellious subject, Edward's brother-in-law, Eustace of Boulogne. In 1051, Eustace tried to seize Dover from Earl Godwine, and when the earl refused to acquiesce Edward had the whole family outlawed. Harold and Leofwine, Godwine's sons, went to Diarmait, King of Leinster, while the father and the rest of the family went to Count Baldwin in Flanders. The following year Godwine mounted an expedition from Flanders. At the same time, however, Harold came from Dublin with a great fleet and ravaged the West Country and rendezvoused with his father on the Isle of Wight. The combined fleet then came up to Southwark. Archbishop Robert fled back to Normandy and the king was forced to restore Godwine and retrieve Edith from the nunnery to which she had been sent. Within months, however, Earl Swein, who had gone to Jerusalem as a penance, and Earl Godwine were dead. Harold succeeded as Earl of Wessex.

In 1054 Bishop Ealdred of Worcester was sent to the Continent to hunt down Edward's nephew, Edward the Exile, a son of Edmund Ironside who had grown up in Kiev. Suspiciously, Edward the Exile died within days of his return in 1057, but he did leave a young son, Edgar, who became the expected successor. When King Edward died in January 1066, aged about sixty-two, Edgar 'the Ætheling' was only about fourteen, and the country was not prepared for a minority. During the crisis of 1051 Edward seems to have promised the kingdom to his cousin William, Duke of Normandy, but on his deathbed he offered it to Earl Harold – though whether as king in his own right or as regent for Edgar is not clear. Had Edward lived a year or two longer, Edgar's succession would probably have been ensured.

HAROLD GODWINSSON (JANUARY-OCTOBER 1066)

Following his father's death, Harold seems to have genuinely won the respect and affection of the English by vigorous campaigning against Gruffudd of Gwynedd during the years 1055-63, and by fair-mindedness, including siding with the Northumbrian thegns against his younger brother Tostig. He had also won the friendship of William of Normandy in 1064 when he had joined him on a military expedition to Brittany. He was not, however, of royal descent, so his kingship could not go uncontested, it is even likely that, while visiting William, he had promised to promote the latter's claim, even if only under pressure.

Anxiety about Harold's claim may explain why he was crowned in Westminster Abbey on the day after Edward's death. William of Normandy was not the only threat on Harold's horizon. Although Earl Swein had died on his way back from pilgrimage, Harold had had further trouble from his brother Tostig. Tostig had been made Earl of Northumbria in 1055, but by the end of 1064 he had alienated the local aristocracy to such a degree that they drove him out and chose Morcar, brother of Earl Edwin of Mercia and brother-in-law of Harold, as their earl. Harold realized that Tostig had demonstrated his incompetence for leadership and came to terms with the rebels. Tostig was outlawed and went to Flanders, to the court of Baldwin V whose sister he had married. Baldwin's daughter was married to William, and for a while it looked as if Tostig would support the Norman claim. But something went wrong. William may not have trusted Tostig, or may even have been

27. A charter of Æthelred the Unready.

28. Part of the Bayeux Tapestry where Harold Godwinsson is seen reporting back to Edward the Confessor. The previously upstanding Harold is here shown hunched and disfigured, suggesting perhaps that he already intends to break his oath to William the Conqueror.

Overleaf   29. Edward the Confessor, Westminster Abbey.

uncertain what move to make himself. Tostig then led his own fleet across the Channel and raided the coast before setting off to his cousin Svein in Denmark. Svein, for whatever reason, chose not to challenge Harold, so Tostig moved on to Norway where he found a more sympathetic audience at the court of King Harald Hardraada. In the summer, Harald of Norway led a fleet to Orkney and thence down the coast of Scotland, entering the Humber at the beginning of September.

Harold of England had been expecting the threat to come from William, whom he knew to be preparing a fleet. The Norwegians defeated the northern earls at Fulford, outside York. Days later, Harold arrived from the South with the main army and, taking the enemy by surprise, defeated and killed the Norwegian king at Stamford Bridge. His audacious forced march north had, however, left the south coast undefended, and by the time he returned William of Normandy had established a beachhead at Hastings. On 14 October 1066 Harold's tired army was annihilated by William; and the king, most sources agree, died with them. Harold's sons, all illegitimate, fled to Ireland. Anglo-Saxon England was over.

2

THE HOUSE OF NORMANDY
1066-1154

DAVID BATES

The Norman Conquest ushered in a new era in the history of England. From 1066, England was ruled by the descendants of Rollo, a Viking leader who had earlier won lands for himself in north-western France and set up the land of the Northmen – or the duchy of Normandy, as it had become by the time that Duke William arrived in his newly claimed kingdom in 1066. For much, though not all, of the period down to 1204, Normandy and England, though always treated by their rulers as distinct territories, were run as a coordinated empire under the control of a single ruler. Even after the loss of Normandy in 1204 and the subsequent renunciation of their rights to the duchy in 1259, the kings of England would continue to hanker after their old patrimony: Henry V was to present his conquest of Normandy in the fifteenth century as a conscious revival – and reversal – of the events of 1066. The closer contact with the Continent generated by the Norman Conquest created a new elite and new influences in England; for three hundred years thereafter, 'English' kings would operate in an international courtly context that was almost entirely French, and the Old English vernacular, which had served as the language of written government and literature for the Anglo-Saxons, was superseded by Latin and by an increasingly distinct French dialect referred to as Anglo-Norman. Thus was England brought, through force and persuasion, more directly into contact with the political and cultural world of the European mainland.

WILLIAM I (1066-1087)

The future King William I was born in late 1027 or early 1028 at Falaise in Normandy. He was the son of Robert 'the Magnificent', Duke of the Normans from 1027 to 1035, and Herleva, a woman whose origins have been much debated by historians; the most likely suggestions, which are based on differing interpretations of twelfth-century sources, are that she was the daughter either of a tanner or of an undertaker from Falaise. Although Robert and Herleva's relationship was never formally consecrated, William, the only male offspring

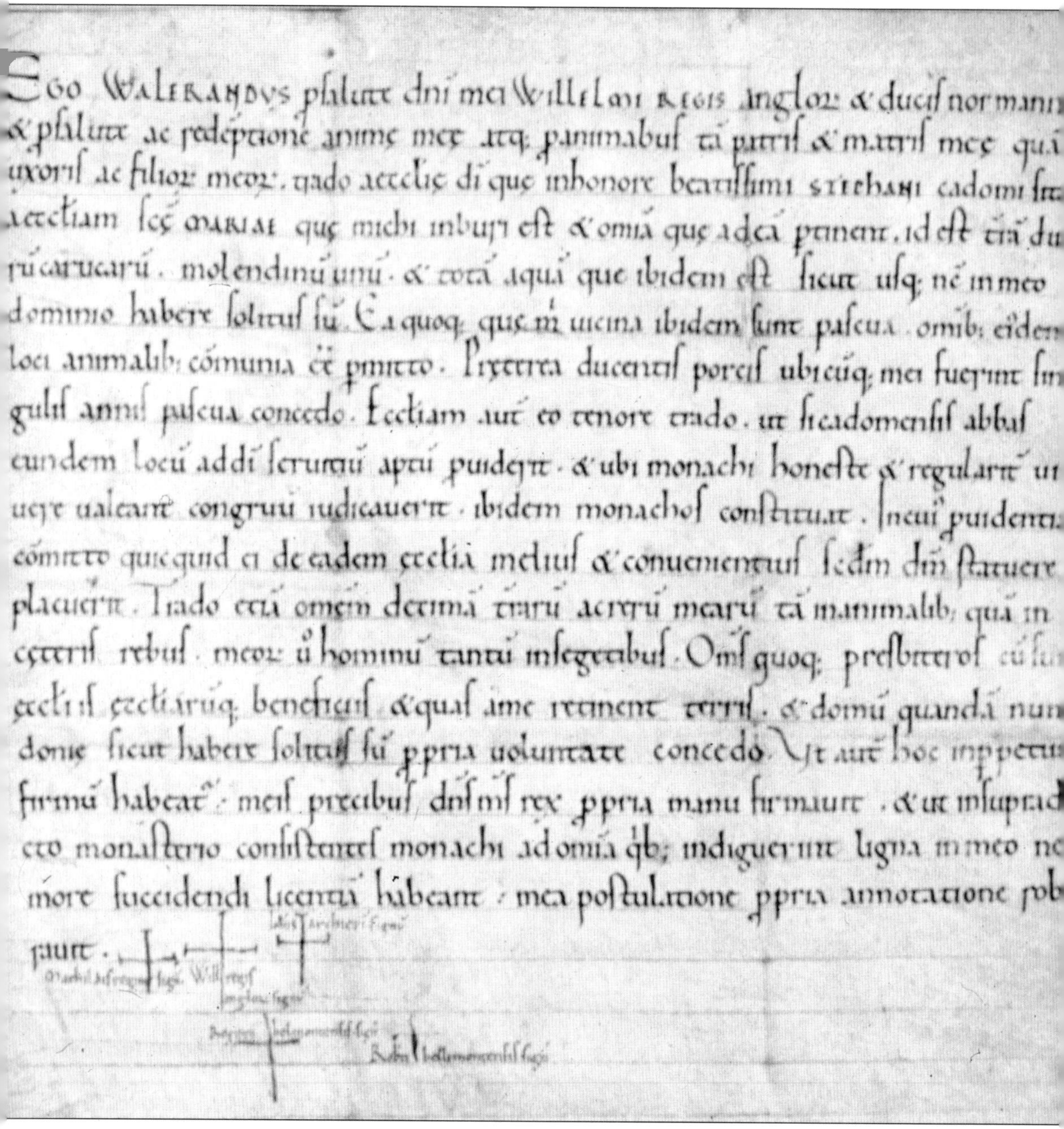
Ego Walerandus p salute dni mei Willelmi regis anglor & ducis normannor
& p salute ac redeptione anime mee atq; p animabus tam patris & matris mee quam
uxoris ac filior meor: trado aecclie di que in honore beatissimi stephani cadomi sita
aecclesiam scę mariae que michi in buris est & omnia que ad eam ptinent. id est terram duarum
carrucarum. molendinum unum. & totam aquam que ibidem est sicut usq; nc in meo
dominio habere solitus sum. Ea quoq; que mihi uicina ibidem sunt pascua. omnibus eiusdem
loci animalibus comunia esse pmitto. Preterea ducentis porcis ubicumq; mei fuerint sin
gulis annis pascua concedo. Ecclesiam aut eo tenore trado. ut si cadomensis abbas
eundem locum addi seruitium aptum puiderit. & ubi monachi honeste & regulariter ui
uere ualeant congruum iudicauerit. ibidem monachos constituat. In cuius prudentia
committo quicquid ei de eadem ecclesia melius & conuenientius secundum dm statuere
placuerit. Trado etiam omnem decimam tam agrorum meorum tam in animalibus quam in
ceteris rebus meor. uel hominum tantum in segetibus. Omnis quoq; presbiteros cum suis
ecclesiis ecclesiarumq; beneficiis & quas ante retinent terris. & domum quandam nun
donis sicut habere solitus sum ppria uoluntate concedo. Ut aut hoc imppetuum
firmum habeatur: meis precibus dns mis rex ppria manu firmauit. & ut in supradi
cto monasterio consistentes monachi ad omnia quibus indiguerint ligna in meo ne
more succidendi licentiam habeant: mea postulatione ppria annotatione robo
rauit.

31. An original diploma of William the Conqueror for St Stephen, Caen, granting land at Bures St Mary (Suffolk). The crosses of those confirming the diploma are autograph. William's is the middle of three on the top row.

of the duke, must from the beginning have been recognized as a potential successor. In January 1035, when Robert was about to set off on the pilgrimage to Jerusalem on which he died, William was designated as his heir. Accepted by both the chief nobles of Normandy and his overlord, the French King Henry I, William duly became duke in November 1035 before he had reached the age of eight. He had a tutor, which presumably indicates that he received some sort of literary education, but it is extremely unlikely that he could either read or write. After his father's death, his mother, who married a minor member of the Norman aristocracy, remained important, and the two sons of this marriage, Odo, the future Bishop of Bayeux, and Robert, who became Count of Mortain, were later treated with exceptional favour by their half-brother.

The duchy of Normandy, whose beginnings were the result of Viking settlements around the town of Rouen and the River Seine in the late ninth and early tenth centuries, had become a formidable power in northern France by the time of William's grandfather, Duke Richard II (996-1026). The paganism of Richard's Viking ancestors was also very much a thing of the past, with Richard enjoying a remarkable reputation as a Christian prince. The creation of the duchy of Normandy must, however, be seen as part of a wider process of change taking place within what we now know as France, as royal power retreated to a small region around Paris and large territorial principalities and smaller lordships emerged as effective units of power. With its Viking background and its continuing links with the North, Normandy played a significant, but ambivalent, role in the politics of the increasingly severe Scandinavian attacks on Æthelred the Unready's England. An event with profound consequences was the marriage of Richard II's sister, Emma, to King Æthelred in 1002. As Æthelred's regime floundered, Emma and her children, including the future King Edward the Confessor, sought refuge in Normandy in 1013. Thereafter Edward and his siblings grew up in France and were regular and welcome guests at the court of the Norman dukes.

With factions fighting to control the young duke and localized conflicts breaking out between many of the great aristocratic families of Normandy, William's position in Normandy was not truly secure until after his victory at the Battle of Val-ès-Dunes, near Caen, in 1047 when, with considerable help from Henry I of France, he defeated his cousin, Guy, Count of Brionne, who was trying to take over the duchy. After 1047, William became involved in the conflicts between the major territorial principalities of northern France, assisting Henry I in 1049 in a campaign against the then dominant prince, Count Geoffrey Martel of Anjou. In 1051, however, the balance of power in northern France shifted radically into a pattern that was to last for the rest of William's life, as Henry and Geoffrey formed an alliance against him. Quite why this happened is unclear. Edward the Confessor's promise of succession to the English kingdom, which was communicated to William in 1051, must have caused alarm. His marriage to Matilda, the daughter of the powerful Count of Flanders, which was mooted in 1049, and which took place in 1050 or 1051, may also have signalled an alliance that threatened the balance of power and most certainly indicated that the young William had arrived on the political scene.

William's increasing dominance over Normandy and northern France was the indispensable foundation for the later conquest of England. Invasions of Normandy organized in 1053-4 and 1057 by King Henry and Count Geoffrey were repulsed. Henry's and Geoffrey's deaths in 1060 meant that William no longer faced serious rivals in northern France, since Henry's successor was a child and Geoffrey's death was followed by a succession dispute. In 1063-4 William made his first major conquest, taking over the county of Maine to the south of Normandy on the basis of a supposed promise of the succession, which had to be implemented against strong local opposition. Within Normandy, William's younger half-brothers were raised to positions of great importance and a remarkable level of co-operation developed between William and a small group within the Norman aristocracy, of whom William fitz Osbern, Roger de Montgomery and Roger de Beaumont were the most prominent. The Norman Church also thrived at this time with William's encouragement, as monastic foundations, many of them as recent as the 1030s and 1040s, prospered, and new cathedrals were built in the Romanesque style. Increasingly prominent within the Norman Church was the renowned theologian and lawyer Lanfranc, an Italian who had initially sought solitude at the new Abbey of Le Bec, but who emerged from the late 1040s as the duke's chief ecclesiastical adviser. Lanfranc's Europe-wide contacts made him a superb diplomat and representative. He was at the heart of the negotiations by which the papacy acquiesced in William's marriage (which supposedly fell within the then prohibited degrees of consanguinity) in return for the founding of the two great abbeys at Caen, the churches of which can still be seen. In the 1050s and 1060s Matilda produced at least nine children, including William's heir in Normandy, Robert 'Curthose', and the two future Kings of England, William (II) and Henry (I).

The designation of William's eldest son Robert as his heir in or before 1063 indicates that the duke was already anticipating the hazards of an invasion of England. Although William was able to extract oaths from Earl Harold, during the latter's visit to Normandy in 1064 or 1065, that appeared to provide support for William's title to the English throne, this proved to be more effective as propaganda than as a practical guarantee, because Harold was crowned King of the English on the basis of a death-bed designation by Edward. William's despatch of a mission to secure papal approval for the projected invasion indicates a careful attention to issues of legitimacy and morale typical of his career. In spite of the eloquent legal case constructed after 1066 by William's apologist William of Poitiers, the truth of the matter is that, in an age where rules of succession were extremely unclear in the event of failure in the direct male line, anyone who could claim designation by, and kinship to, the previous king, and acceptance by the nobility, had a chance. William's conquest of England was in the last resort an act of brilliant opportunism rather than the fulfilment of a legally justified right.

William had assembled an army and a fleet composed of warriors from all over northern France in the estuary of the River Dives by July 1066. In September, they moved to Saint-Valéry-sur-Somme in Ponthieu and on the night of 27-28 September they crossed to Pevensey. Harold's absence fighting King Harald Hardraada of Norway's invasion in northern England at the Battle of Stamford Bridge (25 September) allowed William an unimpeded crossing. His victory at the so-called Battle of Hastings (at modern-day Battle in Sussex) on 14 October came after a hard-fought battle that lasted almost all day. It is likely that the English army, which consisted exclusively of infantry, was starting to flag in the later stages, and that Harold's death late in the battle proved decisive. The Norman victory should ultimately be attributed to the way in which discipline was maintained and that sections of the cavalry were able to carry out feigned retreats that disrupted the English line. Harold's attempt to take William by surprise – with the result that his army lacked archers – was also crucial. After Hastings, William's army carried out an intimidatory march through Sussex, Kent and Surrey, circling round London, where Edgar the Ætheling, grandson of King Edmund Ironside, was briefly proclaimed as king. William steadily received the submissions of the leading English earls and prelates and was crowned in Westminster Abbey, under conditions of high security, on 25 December.

Although the period from 1066 to 1070 saw an attempt to rule a genuinely Anglo-Norman kingdom, the period was notable for a series of campaigns that finally completed the subjugation of England in 1072. At first, many Englishmen remained in office as earls, bishops and sheriffs. William's earliest writs and charters stress that he was Edward the Confessor's designated heir and that every Englishman who remained loyal would hold his ancestral lands. The notion that the law remained the law of Edward the Confessor's day was the basis on which many legal disputes were settled and the very foundation of Norman rule. The Normans who had fought in the campaigns of 1066 and afterwards were required to do appropriate penances to expiate their sins. The revolts of English nobles such as the brothers Edwin, Earl of Mercia, and Morcar, Earl of Northumbria, were, however, followed inexorably by the confiscation of lands and offices and their transfer to William's followers. The most spectacular of William's campaigns was the savage devastation of northern England in the winter of 1069-70, the so-called 'harrying of the North'. Also in 1069-70, invasions despatched and, eventually, led by the King of Denmark, Svein Estrithsson, were kept confined to eastern England and ultimately persuaded to depart on terms. It was also necessary to campaign in the West of England in 1068 and on the Welsh border in 1070. The final resistance within England was overcome in 1071, when the Lincolnshire thegn, Hereward the Wake, a man around whom legends gathered rapidly, was defeated in the Isle of Ely. In 1072 William marched north to Scotland, forcing King Malcolm III to accept his lordship and to give hostages. Malcolm also agreed to expel the English pretender Edgar the Ætheling from his court, thereby renouncing support for further English resistance to William. In general, the efforts of William's many English and British opponents had lacked coordination, enabling him to crush each one in turn. That the conquest had been completed against so much opposition indicates how deeply unpopular William's acquisition of the kingdom initially was. The year 1070, when William was crowned for a second time by cardinals sent by Pope Alexander II – an event without precedent in English history, and when several English bishops and abbots were deprived of office – marked the point of no return. Thereafter the ruling elite of William the Conqueror's England was almost exclusively French. It looks as if William in due course abandoned all serious attempts at conciliation, becoming after 1072 an irregular visitor to his kingdom and giving up his efforts to learn the English language.

In 1066 Normandy had been left under the supervision of Matilda and a group of nobles. In the next few years, while William was occupied with wars in England, the duchy was often under her rule or, nominally, that of their eldest son Robert. Over time, with the revival of the French monarchy under Philip I and of the county of Anjou under Fulk Rechin, problems of a familiar type began to re-emerge around the Norman frontiers. In 1069 a local revolt overthrew Norman control over the county of Maine and in 1070-1 a quarrel broke out among Matilda's relatives in Flanders. In the short term the situation in Maine proved to be irretrievable until William was sufficiently released from English preoccupations to lead an expedition in 1073. An ill thought-out military expedition into Flanders led to the death of one of William's chief lieutenants, William fitz Osbern, in 1071. Within Normandy there existed latent contradictions involving the role of Robert Curthose, who, if some difficult evidence is correctly interpreted, was apparently seen as a sort of second duke. The last twelve years of William's life were notable for the range of difficulties he faced on both sides of the Channel. Since, as far as we know, he visited England only four times, in 1075-6, 1080-1, 1082-3 and 1085-6, spending around eighty per cent of his time in Normandy, it looks as if

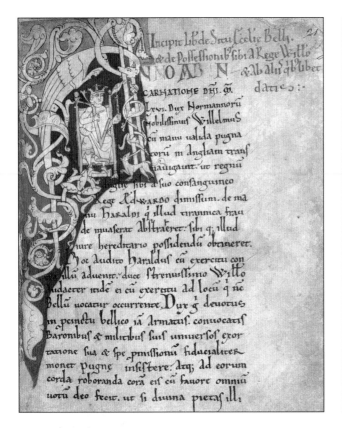

Clockwise from top left   32. The chronicle of Battle Abbey recounts the history of the monastery founded on the battlefield of Hastings by William the Conqueror, supposedly at the place where King Harold was killed. The manuscript dates from the early twelfth century. The illuminated letter represents William.

33. A representation of William the Conqueror in an early thirteenth-century cartulary/chronicle of the Abbey of Abingdon.

34. The Bayeux Tapestry, commissioned by William's half-brother, Bishop Odo of Bayeux, and almost certainly made in England, depicts events from Harold's journey to Normandy to William's triumph in the battle of Hastings. This scene shows the battle of Hastings in 1066. The Norman cavalry and densely packed English infantry clash. The portrayal of a sole English archer is often seen as indicating that Harold's hurried march to Hastings required him to leave crucial troops behind.

he saw his problems in France as much the more severe. He was brought to England in 1075 by the so-called 'revolt of the three earls', which was followed in 1076 by the execution of Waltheof, the last Englishman to hold an earldom. Interestingly, Waltheof's tomb became a centre of a pilgrimage, suggesting that, after the failure of armed resistance, English resentment at the conquest was transformed into the veneration of the defeated as saints and heroes.

Unquestionably the most disruptive event of all during this period was the quarrel between William and his eldest son Robert, which broke out in late 1077 or early 1078. This came to a head in a pitched battle in 1079 outside the castle of Gerberoi on Normandy's south-eastern frontier, at which William was wounded by his own son. A settlement in 1080 proved only to be temporary, and in early 1084 Robert went into exile again, remaining there until his father's death. The quarrel not only disrupted whatever arrangements William was planning for the succession, but also caused stress within the royal family; the fact that Robert's second exile occurred very soon after his mother's death in November 1083 may well indicate that she had previously held the family together. The way that these and other events were exploited by William's enemies throughout northern France and Britain was especially damaging. Not only did Robert Curthose obtain direct assistance from King Philip I, but so too did Ralph de Gael, one of the rebels of 1075, who fled to Brittany and set himself up in the castle of Dol near the Norman frontier in 1076, enabling King Philip to inflict one of William's few military defeats. It is surely not a coincidence that in 1079, when William's problems with his son were at their greatest, King Malcolm of Scotland broke the agreement of 1072 and raided northern England. William's return to England was followed by the restoration of the previous *modus vivendi* through an expedition into Scotland led by Robert Curthose. Also very disruptive was the breach between William and his brother, Bishop Odo of Bayeux, in late 1082 or early 1083, because of Odo's amazing plan to travel to Rome and buy the papacy for himself. So strong was William's disapproval that Odo was imprisoned for the rest of the king's life. William's strategy for controlling his dispersed cross-Channel realm was thrown into some disarray, for, just as he had relied on Matilda and Robert to take care of Normandy during his absences in England, so he had used Odo as his regent in England. In 1081 William made his only known visit to Wales, undertaking a pilgrimage to St Davids and undoubtedly exacting tribute from the Welsh princes. In 1083 another revolt broke out in Maine and received support from the Count of Anjou.

William's concern to fulfil the then traditional ruler's role as protector of the Church is very evident. He was a very generous patron, making numerous gifts to monasteries throughout northern France; and just as the Caen abbeys had been founded to expiate his possibly sinful marriage, so he founded Battle Abbey on the site of the Battle of Hastings. The visit of the cardinals in 1070 was followed by the appointment of Lanfranc to the archbishopric of Canterbury, an event that marked the start of a much more coordinated Norman approach to the affairs of the English Church. William supported Lanfranc both in asserting Canterbury's primacy over the other English archbishopric, York, and in holding a series of councils designed to reform the English Church. While William made his presence felt in all serious matters affecting the Church, his overall attitude was conservative and pragmatic and his prime concerns were the maintenance of royal and ducal authority and the salvation of his soul; the legislation of Lanfranc's ecclesiastical councils, for example, drew on recent Norman precedent, rather than the ideas that were becoming prevalent at Rome. It is in this context that the fracturing of the harmonious collaboration between William and earlier popes occurred after 1073, when the more radical Gregory VII became pope. Gregory's objective of reducing lay involvement in the Church was clearly in conflict with William's paternalistic notions; yet at the same time the pope recognized William's virtues and never pushed matters to an open breach. Events such as William's refusal to do fealty to the papacy in 1080, for example, should not be seen as bitter arguments between two hostile parties, but as resistance to what William and Lanfranc saw as undesirable innovation: the same letter that resisted the fealty freely acknowledged that the payment known as Peter's Pence was owed. Although Gregory VII's position as pope became increasingly parlous because of his quarrel with the German King Henry IV, William and Lanfranc never abandoned him for Henry's anti-pope, and their ambivalence after his death towards any papal claimant was undoubtedly occasioned by genuine moral anxiety.

England was threatened with another invasion from Denmark in 1085. William made elaborate preparations, involving particularly heavy taxation and the billeting of troops brought from France. At a court held at Gloucester at Christmas, he launched the survey that produced Domesday Book. The genesis and method of completion of this monumental survey, quite without equivalent in the history of early medieval western Europe, have been a source of controversy among scholars for generations. Its debt to existing English systems of assessment for tax and military service and to the local courts of shire and hundred is beyond doubt. Its prime purpose was undeniably to record resources and therefore to assist the levying of tax, but the interest shown by the commissioners in local customs and land disputes undoubtedly indicates a wider concern with the complexities of William's newly acquired kingdom and the redistribution of land. After taking an oath from all his chief land-holders on 1 August – the so-called Salisbury Oath – William crossed the Channel to deal with an invasion of southern Normandy by King Philip I. Advancing down the Seine into the region between Normandy and Paris known as the French Vexin in July 1087, he was thrown forward on to the pommel of his saddle while devastating the town of Mantes, sustaining painful internal injuries. Carried back to Rouen, he was installed in the priory of Saint-Gervais outside the city for peace and quiet. He died there on 9 September. During his last days he made arrangements for the succession, acknowledging the rebellious Robert's prior claims to Normandy and sending his second surviving son William to England to take the kingdom. The rationale behind this division is not explained by any of the surviving sources: indeed, there are hints both that William intended entirely to disinherit Robert and that he had once intended him to have both Normandy and England. It is probable that William was ultimately following a Norman tradition whereby the succession was organized by a ruler once the onset of death was obvious and whereby landed provision was made for all male members of the ducal kindred.

A hypothetical reconstruction, based on a single thighbone surviving in William's tomb in the Abbey of St Stephen at Caen, suggests that he was approximately 1.75 metres tall, an exceptional height for the period. Many of the literary sources indicate that he was physically imposing and extremely strong. He became very fat in his later years. The obituary in the *Anglo-Saxon Chronicle*, written by an anonymous Englishman with no reason to like William, speaks of the great power of his kingship and the peace he preserved, as well as of his piety and generosity to the Church. The manner in which he strove to legitimize his conquest speaks of a man with a well-developed sense of the importance of law and propaganda, and his religious patronage, of someone who fully shared the eleventh-century belief that atonement through good works was necessary to salvation. His English crown-wearings, his love of ceremony, and the remarkable buildings such as the White Tower of London and the castle and two abbeys at Caen, indicate a sense of the importance of display. A figure of European importance, he was invited to intervene in the tangled politics of both the German kingdom and in Italy on behalf of Pope Gregory VII – and was hard-headed enough to turn both down. His greatest personal faults were cruelty and greed. He was also passionately devoted to hunting and reserved large areas of land solely for that purpose, such as the New Forest in Hampshire. Unusually for a medieval aristocrat, and indeed an English king, he was a loyal husband and was not sexually promiscuous even before marriage.

William the Conqueror's historical importance depends ultimately on how the Norman Conquest, often thought to be one of the great turning-points in English and British history, is interpreted. When placed in the broader context of Britain's history, however, 'the Conquest' is but one among many. Furthermore, the notion that William was Edward the Confessor's designated heir underpinned a theoretical and, in many instances, a practical continuity. William's kingship differed little from that of his predecessors and built on the strength of the pre-1066 monarchy. Below the uppermost levels of the aristocracy, English men and women continued to be important in local societies, and English remained the language of the vast majority of the people. William's preoccupations in France and his lengthy absences from his kingdom meant that he was heavily dependent on others for the maintenance of order; his arm was, however, a long one and, despite Domesday Book's evidence for a great deal of local disorder, his authority was generally respected. The settlement of a new aristocracy with different customs and ideas on property and social relationships led eventually to change and the stronger ties with Normandy intensified England's already well-developed contacts with northern France. Scandinavian kings ceased to attempt to conquer England, although they were to remain a strong presence in the North and West of Britain for a long time to come. A major, but of course unintended, consequence of William's conquest was that English kings for centuries to come regarded it as their right and duty to intervene in the politics of the French kingdom.

William's achievement, in presiding over the successful occupation and takeover of the English kingdom, was immense. A violent man and a skilful politician, the scale of his achievements is truly remarkable. His role in the Norman Conquest should, however, be placed within a larger process. The Norman advance continued under his sons. William's limited objectives in his dealings with Wales, Scotland and, indeed, northern England, left a great deal for the next generation to accomplish. Mighty king that he was, he could not in the end subdue the innate structural political problems inherent in the societies of both Britain and northern France. His death was followed by war among his sons and the partial collapse of Norman hegemony in northern France. Although he exploited the instabilities of unclear succession practices to bring off a great conquest, the same type of endemic instabilities within his own family plagued his last years and threatened his achievement after his death. His Norman and English predecessors were constantly at the mercy of neighbouring powers. He kept all of them at bay with considerable success, but his sons had still to deal with them after he had died.

WILLIAM II (1087-1100)

The third son, and in all likelihood the fifth child, of William the Conqueror and his wife Matilda, William was born in, or shortly before, 1060. Although he became King of England on his father's death in 1087, it is doubtful whether his prospects had always been promising. The Norman

Clockwise from left   35. Fifteenth-century depiction in stained glass of William the Conqueror, St. Mary's Hall, Coventry.

36. Seal of Battle Abbey, founded by William the Conqueror after his victory there. It was said that the altar was located on the exact spot where Harold fell.

37. William Rufus and Henry I enthroned. These are purely conventional pictures of kings, not portraits of these two kings in particular. They were painted more than 100 years after the kings reigned.

Conquest of England in 1066 transformed his life and that of many others, and the death of one of his two elder brothers between 1069 and 1074 made him more prominent. His eldest brother Robert Curthose was, however, his father's designated successor in Normandy and, as far as we know, the possibility that William might succeed his father in England was not made clear until William the Conqueror, on his death-bed, despatched William to England with a letter addressed to Archbishop Lanfranc of Canterbury instructing him to crown the young William. His coronation took place with minimum delay on 26 September.

Before becoming king, William seems always to have been loyal to his father and was not tempted to side with Robert Curthose, who took issue with his father's unwillingness to give him any power in Normandy and was in exile for much of the last decade of their father's life. Charter evidence suggests that William spent much time at his father's court, and that Robert and William were regarded as more significant than their younger brother, Henry (the future Henry I). Even if Robert may have expected to succeed to Normandy and England, it is certain that William would not have gone unrewarded. The practice of assigning acquired property to younger sons was common among the Norman aristocracy at this time, and it had long been normal for a Duke of Normandy to make territorial provision for more than one son. There is no direct evidence that the nickname 'Rufus' was used during his lifetime. It was, however, regularly used by the great Anglo-Norman historian Orderic Vitalis, who was born in 1075 and who wrote most of the passages that describe William's reign in the 1120s and 1130s. Its basis was William's red hair, which turned blonde as he grew older, and his red complexion. He was also short and plump.

A great warrior, William was a more colourful and rumbustious character than either his father or his brother Henry. A recruiter of knights from many lands and a noted figure of chivalry, he epitomizes the military qualities of male society in the Middle Ages. Almost all the histories written in his lifetime or after his death condemn his lifestyle as immoral and his court as a place of extravagant fashion and licentious behaviour. He was probably homosexual, and he certainly never married. He quarrelled bitterly with St Anselm, Archbishop of Canterbury (1093-1109), and was a notorious blasphemer whose oaths and obscenities seem to have fascinated as well as appalled the clerics who wrote about him. He was also very ready to use the Church's wealth to finance his wars. The vivid stories that survive suggest a rather uncouth bully, but also an intelligent man with a strong sense of the royal dignity. He ruled effectively and consolidated Norman government in England, as well as advancing Norman power into Wales and towards Scotland. In spite of William's power being initially confined to England, the politics of the cross-Channel Anglo-Norman realm were a major preoccupation throughout his reign. From the start, relations with Robert Curthose were fraught, with both seeking to make gains at the other's expense, and their younger brother Henry, who was more often the ally of Rufus, feathering his own nest as best he could. Because of England's superior resources and Robert's rather purposeless character, William tended to gain strength and influence as his reign progressed. The aristocracy, many of whom had estates in both Normandy and England, had an interest in stability, but most must have recognized that this could be achieved either through co-operation between the brothers or the triumph of one of them. Dual loyalty must have been a strain for all concerned.

Within six months of William's coronation, a large coalition of the major magnates of Normandy and England, including the Conqueror's two half-brothers, Bishop Odo of Bayeux and Count Robert of Mortain, began a revolt intended to make Robert King of England and rejoin the two territories under the same ruler. Although revolts broke out in all parts of his kingdom, William concentrated his attention on the chief rebels in the Southeast of England, while successfully preventing the rest from concentrating their forces. A fleet controlling the

Channel kept Robert in Normandy. William's support came chiefly from the sheriffs of England and he is known to have made considerable use of English troops. Over time the various rebels submitted and came to terms with the king, with the revolt being brought to an end when Bishop Odo's forces in Rochester Castle surrendered in July. Of the rebels only Odo, who lost all his English lands and was banished from the kingdom for ever, was severely punished. Having secured his power in England, William established a foothold in eastern Normandy in 1089-90 by purchasing the support of several major magnates, and even provoked a revolt in Rouen, the duchy's chief town, in 1090. He invaded Normandy in January 1091, but rapidly reached an agreement with Robert, after which they embarked together on campaigns in Normandy, Wales and Scotland designed to consolidate their respective authorities around the borders of their territories. The collaboration tended to benefit William because little attention was given to overcoming the local conflicts in Normandy, which Robert had been unable to quell, and because no effort was made to recover Norman power in Maine, which had disintegrated after the Conqueror's death. With Robert accusing his brother of providing him with insufficient help, their co-operation ended acrimoniously in September 1091. William again invaded Normandy in 1094, but does not seem to have achieved a great deal.

In March 1093 William fell seriously ill at Gloucester and believed himself to be dying. While ill, he agreed to appoint Anselm, abbot of the Norman monastery of Le Bec, to the archbishopric of Canterbury, which the king had kept vacant since Lanfranc's death in 1089 in order to divert the revenues into the royal treasury. We have a detailed, vivid and thoroughly biased account of events from Anselm's chaplain, the Englishman Eadmer. It is to Eadmer, for example, that we owe the dramatic story of William forcing the ring of office on to Anselm's finger, and the account of Anselm's prophecy that these events had yoked together a tired old sheep (Anselm was sixty years old) and a wild, unbroken bull, to the detriment of all. A great philosopher and a very religious man, Anselm in theory had all the desirable qualities for an archbishop. In practice, the two men proved temperamentally unsuited and to be rigid on matters that each identified as issues of principle. Anselm's criticisms of the immorality of the royal court, his insistence on maintaining his allegiance to Pope Urban II, to whom he had professed obedience in Normandy while William Rufus had maintained his father's and Lanfranc's policy of not deciding between the two popes claiming to rule Christendom, and William's refusal to allow him to hold the sort of ecclesiastical council which had been frequent in Lanfranc's time, all led to a rapid and irreconcilable deterioration of personal relationships.

Eadmer's account of the great set-piece debate at the Council of Rockingham in February 1095 is marvellous theatre. Anselm, needing a pallium from the pope to exercise fully the office of archbishop, confronted the king and the assembled bishops and magnates and argued that his earlier acknowledgement of Pope Urban made it obligatory for the kingdom's welfare that the king should now recognize him as well. In thus choosing to place obedience to the pope above obedience to the king, Anselm infuriated William beyond tolerance. Other quarrels followed and the archbishop went into exile in November 1097. In spite of the drama, however, the dispute should not be seen as an out-and-out conflict between secular and ecclesiastical principles. William Rufus appears to have enjoyed the support of all the English bishops throughout the dispute, Pope Urban II made considerable efforts to seek a compromise, and Anselm in numerous ways showed himself ready to assist the king after the manner of his predecessor, Lanfranc. It is just that certain issues proved irresolvable. William's wild behaviour and stubborn adherence to what he believed to be his royal prerogative, his irreverent manner and disrespect for ecclesiastical authority proved unacceptable to a high-minded archbishop who, in turn, irritated the king enormously.

38. The White Tower of London is the keep of the castle begun in the last years of William the Conqueror's reign and finished under his son William II. Along with Chepstow and Colchester castles, the Tower is the most substantial military building to survive from William's time.

39. Coin of William II struck at Leicester.

After reaffirming the earlier agreement made between William the Conqueror and Malcolm III in 1091, William's great achievement in 1092 was to regain Cumbria from the King of Scots. This was followed by the construction of a castle at Carlisle. He campaigned twice in Wales in support of the Norman magnates who were advancing their power, and, although the invasions were not especially successful, his reign was notable for a considerable expansion of Norman control in South and West Wales by aggressive barons. After Malcolm III's murder at the hands of the Norman Earl of Northumbria in 1093, William sent troops to Scotland both in 1094 and 1097 to assist Malcolm's sons Duncan and Edgar against their uncle. There were stories that he intended to launch an invasion of Ireland. In 1095 he overcame a serious baronial revolt led by the same Earl of Northumbria, Robert de Mowbray, this time punishing the earl's suspected supporters severely. From 1096, he was also responsible for Normandy when Robert Curthose mortgaged the duchy to him in order to take part in the First Crusade. He followed this by re-establishing Norman power over much of Maine and resuming the attack on the French Vexin in which effort his father had been mortally injured in 1087. During this period William became a true Anglo-Norman ruler as his father had been, and as his brother Henry I was to be after 1106.

A notable builder, William completed the White Tower of London, which had been started in his father's time, and himself oversaw the construction of Westminster Hall, both of which substantially survive. Of the latter, probably one of the largest halls then standing in Europe, William is said to have remarked that he would have liked it to have been twice as big. His government has a reputation for rapacity and efficiency. The document known as Henry I's Coronation Charter, for example, accuses William of a range of extortionate activities, such as the unjust exploitation of reliefs and wardships. There are stories of churches having to strip altars of precious metals in order to pay his taxes. The charter evidence allows us to discern more clearly than in William the Conqueror's time a small group of administrative servants around the king, responsible for effecting his decisions. Chief among these was Ranulph Flambard, an obscure Norman priest who became Bishop of Durham in 1099, and a man whose activities provoked extensive complaints from several monastic chroniclers. In general, William Rufus's rule should be viewed as a continuation of his father's and a step towards the greater emphasis on bureaucracy that was typical of Henry I's reign.

What Rufus might eventually have achieved is a moot point since, on 2 August 1100, he was killed in a hunting accident in the New Forest in his fortieth year. Death was instantaneous, and there was no time to perform the last rites. His body was taken to Winchester Cathedral for burial. With Robert Curthose still on the return journey from the Crusade, their younger brother Henry, who was with the hunting party, rushed to Winchester to seize the royal treasury, and then to Westminster where he was crowned king on 5 August. Historians have frequently suggested that Henry or others had a hand in William's death. Hunting accidents were, however, common in the Middle Ages, and no contemporary source suggests that Rufus's death was anything other than an accident.

HENRY I (1100-1135)

The youngest of the nine known children of William the Conqueror and his wife Matilda, Henry was born in 1069. He apparently grew up in England and must therefore have been

Opposite   40. Henry I and his family tree. Below Henry I is a picture of a sinking ship. Henry's only legitimate son, William, was drowned in 1120.

Cui successit henricus frater
eius 7 regnauit annis xxxvi
hic erat pastor feraz 7 custos
nemoz fuit 4 sapiens 7 stre
nuus Dux normannie que
uertius ambrosius leonem iusticie
in historia Regum noiauit ffecit qz em
iudicium 7 iusticiam in terra Duxit qz
vxorem generosam 7 optimam de
nobili genere anglorz 7 Britonu p
quam multum sibi confederauit reg
num scilicet filiam pncipis sui Alba
nie vita 7 monibz oznatam soeozem
scilicet Alexandri principis sui scocie
7 dauitis scocie qui postea fuit pnceps
Albanie. Cui vero Rex henricus psa
tus sedit honorem de huntingdon
cum matilda cognate sua que erat
vxor prius pmi simonis de scenliz
comitis de huntingdon 7 norhamp
ton cum custodia puerorz suorz et dic
concordes ad inuicem scinde effecti
fuerunt qua prestus Alexander ven
sicauit sibi iure hereditario corona
7 monarchiam tocius Regni presta
dicto verus heres 7 iustus de iure boni
Regis Edwardi vltimi. Alexander qz dm
sup omnia silauit qz scdm ecclsiam in
multis p loca ffecit qz bonu in ghtu
totius malum qz deseruit vocabitur
matild Regina optima ¶Obiit vo
predictus henricus in normannia
apud d youns. sepultus enim fuit
in Anglia apud Redinges in Alba
thia quam construxerat. matilda
vero Regina predicta sepulta fuit
in Anglia apud Westmonasteriu
quius anime ppicietur deus.

Normania nati pelago peunt ac
filia que remanet impiale te

Henricus pimus genuit

Willm
qui periit
in mari

Ricm
qui piit
in mari

matild
dam im
peatice

Ricardi
q obiit

henria
Regis se
cundi

separated for long periods from his parents, who are known to have spent much of their time in Normandy. Henry was once considered to have been exceptionally learned, but modern scholarship has shown this reputation to be mostly a creation of the fourteenth century. At his father's deathbed in September 1087 he was given the large sum of £5,000 to maintain himself, while his eldest brother Robert Curthose succeeded his father as Duke of Normandy and his other older brother William Rufus became King of England. He used £3,000 of his money to purchase the districts of western Normandy known as the Cotentin and the Avranchin from Robert very soon after their father's death and supported the duke against his more powerful younger brother until 1091, while carving out a considerable lordship for himself. Driven out of Normandy by his two brothers in 1091, he installed himself at Domfront on the southern border of the duchy, beyond Robert's authority. In 1094 he became a firm ally of Rufus, participating in several of his campaigns, and moving to and fro across the Channel with William's court when he took over the duchy in 1096 after Robert Curthose's departure on the First Crusade. On 2 August 1100 he was a member of the hunting party in the New Forest in which William was accidentally killed.

Henry moved with remarkable speed after his brother's death, seizing the treasury at Winchester on 3 August and having himself crowned King of England at Westminster on 5 August. The sheer rapidity of his *coup* has led to suggestions that he had masterminded William's murder. This is, however, unlikely: not only do all contemporary sources consider the death to have been an accident, but the timing was also not particularly good for Henry, with his elder brother Robert on the return journey from crusade. Henry speedily sought to legitimize and strengthen his rule by issuing a Coronation Charter promising to abandon unacceptable aspects of his brother's rule, and by recalling Anselm, the Archbishop of Canterbury with whom Rufus had quarrelled, and who had been in exile since 1097. In November 1100 Henry married Edith (henceforth Matilda), the sister of Edgar the Ætheling, the Englishman briefly proclaimed as king in London after the Battle of Hastings, and the daughter of Malcolm III, King of Scots. This alliance with one of the most direct surviving descendants of the pre-Conquest English kings was an attempt to reinforce symbolically Henry's right to be king. Although ultimately a usurper, Henry had done a great deal to consolidate his power by the time that his brother Robert invaded England in July 1101.

Henry I was seen by contemporaries, and is judged by most modern historians, to have been an extremely successful king. Eventually taking over Normandy from Robert and also dominating Wales and Scotland to an extent that his father and brother had never done, his reign looked even more like a golden age of peace to twelfth-century historians writing with the benefit of hindsight during the subsequent civil war between his nephew Stephen and his daughter, the Empress Matilda. Like his brothers before him, Henry was determined to rule the paternal inheritance of Normandy and England and therefore spent much of his time in Normandy, preoccupied with many of the same strategic problems as his father before him. Nicknamed, the 'Lion of Justice' by some contemporaries, he has an enduring reputation for effective, and possibly innovative, rule. Short and corpulent, he was known to prefer diplomacy to war and to seek to achieve his ends by bribery and influence rather than force. A great recruiter of knights from all parts of western Europe, he kept an extensive military household that formed the core of all his armies. Sexually promiscuous in his younger years, he fathered over twenty illegitimate children. After the death of his only legitimate son William in 1120, however, he lacked a direct male heir and had to develop various stratagems to try to ensure the acceptance of his daughter, the Empress Matilda, as his successor. A famous comment by a contemporary described Henry as a successful ruler, but one who was permanently worried that all might unravel.

Robert Curthose's invasion of England led in early August 1101 to a settlement which acknowledged Henry's kingship in England; in all probability, neither the brothers nor their magnates wished to risk the uncertain outcome of a battle between evenly-matched forces. After this, Henry proceeded steadily to undermine his brother's authority in Normandy, confiscating the English lands of some of Robert's most prominent supporters, such as Robert de Bellême and William, Count of Mortain, and meddling in Norman politics to disrupt Robert's power and build up alliances. Invading the duchy in 1104, he defeated the politically weakened Robert at the Battle of Tinchebrai in Southwest Normandy in 1106. Robert was thereafter kept in captivity until his death in Cardiff Castle in 1134. Henry's rule over Normandy was, however, frequently disturbed. Robert's son, William Clito, born in 1102, became the focus for the schemes not only of Henry's enemies in northern France, such as the French King Louis VI and Count Fulk V of Anjou, but also of a significant section of the aristocracy of Normandy which tended to have relatively little land in England and which, with good reason, saw Robert Curthose and William Clito as the duchy's rightful rulers. 1111-13, 1116-19 and 1123-4 were particularly difficult years. During the last two of these periods, extensive rebellions within Normandy combined with invasions from outside, and in 1118-19 Henry briefly faced invasion from the three strongest powers in northern France, the King of France and the Counts of Anjou and Flanders. It was at this time that he suffered the biggest military defeat of his life at Alençon at the hands of Count Fulk in December 1118.

Henry consistently sought to divide his opponents by diplomatic means. In the case of Count Fulk of Anjou, he arranged a marriage alliance in 1113 between his son and heir, William, and the count's daughter, Matilda. In the case of King Louis VI, Henry made terms in 1115 and 1120 by agreeing that William should do homage to the French king for Normandy, thereby hoping to legitimize his own rule through his heir. How ruthless Henry's diplomacy could be is best illustrated by the way in which he persuaded the pope to forbid a proposed marriage between William Clito and another daughter of Count Fulk, on the grounds that the couple, whose blood relationship was of course exactly the same as William's and Matilda's, were related within the prohibited degrees. Unsurprisingly, Count Fulk was furious. Another diplomatic tactic of Henry's was to arrange marriages between his illegitimate daughters and the holders of lordships around the borders of Normandy.

When necessary, Henry did fight battles, defeating, for example, Louis's invasion of Normandy at Brémule in 1119. All Henry's schemes were, however, devastated shortly after-wards by the death of his son in the wreck of the White Ship in November 1120, when a ship carrying members of many members of Anglo-Norman aristocratic families hit a rock in the Seine estuary and sank, taking almost all its passengers to the bottom. With his wife Matilda having died in 1118, Henry immediately married the young Adeliza of Louvain in 1121. In the absence of a son, Henry recalled his one surviving legitimate child, the Empress Matilda, from Germany in May 1125 after the death of her husband the Emperor Henry V, and on 1 January 1127 secured an oath from his chief magnates and clergy that she would be his heir in England and Normandy. In June 1128 the twenty-five-year-old Matilda was married to Count Fulk's fourteen-year-old son Geoffrey, in a repeat of an old diplomatic tactic of Henry's designed to give strong northern French support to his daughter's cause. The threat he feared did not, however, materialize since William Clito, apparently set to become Count of Flanders, and therefore to become a truly formidable opponent for Henry, was killed in battle six weeks after the marriage. The last years of the reign were shrouded in uncertainty, since to the anxieties caused by the potential succession of a woman to England and Normandy were added the fact that she was married to a long-standing enemy of Normandy. Henry's relationship with his daughter was always fractious. At the time of his death, they had quarrelled badly.

England remained peaceful throughout Henry's reign. With the king spending so much time in Normandy, arrangements to maintain routine royal authority were required. Up until 1120, Henry relied on his family, most notably his wife Matilda, just as William the Conqueror had relied principally on his brother Odo. We can, however, discern more clearly than in previous reigns the presence of a group of individuals specifically charged with the oversight of royal finance and justice. At its head was Roger, a priest first associated with Henry in the Cotentin before he became king, who was made Bishop of Salisbury in 1102. Between 1123 and 1126, with Henry once more occupied in Normandy and his first wife and son dead, Bishop Roger acted formally as regent. In general, Henry's rule in England showed a strong desire to emphasize its continuity with the pre-Conquest period. This was, for example, a period when substantial collections of Anglo-Saxon law, such as the so-called *Leges Henrici Primi* (a tract whose actual connection with the king and his court cannot be established) and the *Textus Roffensis* (a product of the bishopric of Rochester) were compiled. Queen Matilda was a noted patron of historical writing, encouraging, for example, William of Malmesbury to write his history of the English kings (*Gesta Regum Anglorum*), the first extensive account of English history since the days of Bede. Any assessment of Henry's reign that stresses its originality must take careful account of this powerful wish to forge links with the past. A further feature of Henry's rule was the stress on display and ritual. While abandoning the formalized pattern of three annual crown-wearings established by his father, Henry continued to hold great assemblies of magnates with whom he regularly conferred.

Several contemporary writers commented on the domination that Henry exercised over the princes of Wales. His two military interventions, in 1114 and 1121, were intended to achieve a formal recognition of overlordship and were thus, like the campaigns of his father and brother, no more than demonstrations of power. He was, however, able to insist that even the most powerful of the Welsh princes, such as Gruffudd ap Cynan of Gwynedd, paid tribute, recognized his overlordship and attended his court. There is a sense in which the princes of Wales were treated in exactly the same way as the noble subjects of the English Crown. Henry also intervened more directly in the territories in South and West Wales conquered during William Rufus's reign, using opportunities provided by political forfeitures or the absence of heirs to take over land for himself, or to install notably loyal subjects.

As far as the Scottish kingdom was concerned, Henry initially followed the same policy as Rufus, by providing support to his brothers-in-law, Kings Edgar (1097-1107) and Alexander I (1107-24). At the same time, he developed a much closer relationship with their youngest brother, who was brought up at Henry's court and made Earl of Huntingdon in 1113, and who succeeded to the kingdom of Scots as David I in 1124. David's reign is notable for the controlled introduction of Normans and other French, and of new up-to-date religious orders, such as the Cistercians and Premonstratensians, into the kingdom of Scots. Remaining an English magnate as well as King of Scots, David played a prominent part in English affairs, attending, for example, the court at which the oath to recognize the Empress Matilda as Henry's heir was sworn. Although Henry's success in dominating the Welsh and neutralizing the King of Scots is manifest, it needs to be kept in mind that in Wales the frontier between the lands occupied by the Normans and French and those retained by the Welsh was a tense and highly militarized one, and that David, for all the displays of friendship, did not abandon any of the Scots' claims to Cumbria, taken away as recently as William Rufus's reign. Henry's achievement was to overawe his neighbours with the great financial and political might of the English kingdom and to consolidate his hold on the English side of the disputed frontiers through the installation of new lordships.

Henry I's treatment of the Church in England and Normandy and his personal religious attitudes were never censured by contemporaries, in the way that his brother had been. In 1100 he rapidly recalled Anselm from exile, and in 1102 showed himself solicitous of the archbishop's wish to hold a council of the English Church. He nonetheless quarrelled with Anselm over the subject of the lay investiture of bishops and abbots, with Henry insisting on his customary right to invest both with ring and staff, the symbols of their office, and Anselm taking a stand on his obedience to papal decrees specifically forbidding the practice, which he had heard during his period of exile in 1097-1100. Anselm's second exile lasted from 1103 to 1107, during which time the archbishop, the king and the papacy engaged in extensive diplomatic activity to try to reach a settlement. The final resolution, the so-called Concordat of London (1107), involved Henry abandoning the ceremony of lay investiture, but retaining (through the right to take homage) oversight of elections to bishoprics and abbacies.

The settlement typifies the sort of jurisdictional dispute which became much more common in twelfth-century Europe, as the Church in general placed a stronger emphasis on the distinctness of ecclesiastical affairs. In this area, Henry's reign is characterized by a number of episodes in which traditional royal powers clashed with changing religious attitudes, and in which a negotiated settlement tended to be achieved which saved face for all concerned. A fine example is the visit of the papal legate, John of Crema, to hold a council and carry out a tour of inspection of the English Church in 1124-5. Henry was prepared to permit a more intrusive papal involvement in return for support against William Clito. Henry, a generous religious patron, founded the Cluniac abbey at Reading as a mausoleum for himself and favoured some of the newer religious orders that were emerging in the early twelfth century, such as the Augustinian canons and the nuns of Fontevraud. Overall, Henry comes across as a typically pious twelfth-century layman. Unsurprisingly, his generosity to the Church increased in the later years of his life. A famous story which appears in the chronicle of John of Worcester told of Henry's fear of an uprising of the three orders, the warriors, the clergy and the peasantry, against his rule, and the increased almsgiving which resulted.

Henry's reputation for innovative government is based both on arguments for social change and on the development of more efficient, rational and literate methods. At the heart of the former is the belief that individuals of relatively humble aristocratic birth were advanced to play a central role in royal administration. The trend is exemplified by the regular role played by Bishop Roger of Salisbury and others and by a famous passage, often quoted out of context, from the contemporary history of Orderic Vitalis to the effect that Henry 'raised men from the dust' and placed them over members of long-established families. In general, however, it appears that, while the presence of the administrative group is undeniable, Henry's basic policy was to maintain a traditional aristocracy into which he advanced his own protégés. These protégés tended, as in all medieval kingdoms, to be drawn from the king's own kindred: in addition to the case of King David I, already mentioned, there are the even more spectacular ones of Henry's illegitimate son Robert, who was made

Earl of Gloucester, and his nephew Stephen, who received the forfeited estates of one of Robert Curthose's supporters, William, Count of Mortain, as well as many other lands. The administrative servants, while enriched through well-selected marriages, never advanced to the same level of wealth or influence. Institutional changes, exemplified by the appearance of the Exchequer, an abacus that counted the king's revenues at the two annual audits at Easter and Michaelmas, and the pipe roll, a written record of this account, were certainly important. It must, however, be emphasized that the revenues collected and the rights exercised were traditional ones. The existence of the one pipe roll that has survived from the reign, that of 1129-30, may again create an illusion of greater innovation than in fact took place. The same is also true of the despatch of royal justices into the shires of England recorded in the pipe roll and other sources. More evidence may indicate more activity, but, beyond any doubt, the visitations had not yet acquired the systematic character of the later twelfth century.

Henry I died in Normandy on 1 December 1135, supposedly after eating a surfeit of lampreys: he had over-indulged himself on fish. His reign must be set in the context of the early stages of the movement known as the Twelfth-Century Renaissance and the changes in government should be interpreted in the context of the increasingly literate methods and concern with law and jurisdiction that go with it. Equally, however, it should be seen as building on the great power of the Old English monarchy, preserved and developed by his father and brother. All this must in turn be placed against the background of the cross-Channel realm established by his father. Active government was stimulated, at least in part, by the necessity of raising money for war and diplomacy and the profoundly disruptive consequences of the succession dispute with Robert Curthose and William Clito. Henry's last years were difficult ones because of anxieties over the succession and quarrels with his daughter and heir. At the time of his death he had been on bad terms with the Empress Matilda and her husband for some months, a situation that allowed his nephew Stephen to seize the English kingdom in much the same way that Henry had done thirty-five years earlier. Henry's responsibility for the civil war and local disorder that followed his death has been endlessly debated by historians. In truth, his rule was one that relied to a large degree on brute force and personal alliances. As so often happened in the medieval period, the removal of the lynchpin of strong kingship was followed by political and social breakdown.

STEPHEN (1135-1154)

Probably born in 1096, Stephen was the third son of Stephen, Count of Blois and Chartres, and Adela, the youngest known daughter of William the Conqueror. It is almost certain that the marriage of Adela and Count Stephen was arranged by William the Conqueror to consolidate an alliance with a territorial principality on the River Loire and thus to gain support for his frequent wars against the King of France and the Count of Anjou. Adela apparently retained a strong sense of loyalty to her paternal family, is known to have had a tapestry depicting the Battle of Hastings in her bedchamber, and, from a date shortly before 1113, sent Stephen to be educated at Henry I's court. Stephen's elder brother Theobald, who succeeded to the counties of Blois and Chartres and also of Champagne, was a constant ally of Henry I's. Accumulating lands through Henry's favour, Stephen had become one of the wealthiest landholders in England and Normandy by the time of his uncle's death on 1 December 1135. His fortune had been further increased by his marriage in 1125 to Matilda, heiress to the county of Boulogne, a territorial lordship to the north-east of Normandy whose holders had acquired vast lands in England after the Norman Conquest. His

Clockwise from top 41. The illustration shows a specimen of King Stephen's second seal. The earliest surviving impressions of English royal seals date from the time of Edward the Confessor. 42. Although not a direct portrayal of any of the Norman kings, this representation of a king in a late eleventh-century astronomical manuscript is important as one of the few images of kingship to survive from that date.
43. A representation of King Stephen with a hawk in a fourteenth-century manuscript. Like other such representations, it was not intended to be a likeness.

brother Henry, who had become a monk of the famous Burgundian abbey of Cluny, had also installed himself in England and became Abbot of Glastonbury in 1126 and Bishop of Winchester in 1129, probably making him the wealthiest churchman in England.

On hearing news of Henry I's death, Stephen, who was at Boulogne, crossed to England, with his brother's assistance seized the treasury at Winchester, and persuaded the Archbishop of Canterbury to crown him on 22 December 1135. Although his actions bore a very close resemblance to Henry I's thirty-five years before, there was a major difference in that, whereas Robert Curthose had no specific claim to the English kingdom beyond being the Conqueror's eldest son, Stephen and all the other chief magnates had taken an oath in 1126, subsequently repeated, that they would accept Henry's daughter, the Empress Matilda, as his heir. This oath came back constantly to haunt Stephen. In 1135 he argued both that Henry had exacted the oath under duress and that the old king had changed his mind on his deathbed. Throughout his reign, it was very much to his advantage that his coronation was accepted by all as constitutive, and that, as a result, he was always acknowledged as king even by his enemies; Matilda in consequence was usually called 'the Empress' or 'the Countess of Anjou' and, in 1141-2, when she appeared close to victory, 'Lady of the English', but never queen. By 1139 the papacy had also decided in Stephen's favour. It was nonetheless possible for anyone who chose to oppose Stephen to use the oath as a justification for supporting Matilda.

In 1135-6 the barons of Normandy, who had initially invited Stephen's brother Theobald to become duke, accepted Stephen when they heard that he had taken England. His court held at Oxford at Easter 1136 was attended by most of the great magnates, including Earl Robert of Gloucester, Henry I's illegitimate son, who was eventually to become the Empress Matilda's most powerful supporter. At the same court, urged on by his brother Bishop Henry, Stephen pronounced his support for Church reform and renounced excessive royal interference much more openly than any of his predecessors had done. There were nonetheless already reasons for concern. The King of Scots, David I, had invaded northern England in December 1135, ostensibly in support of his oath to his niece, but with equal probability to regain Cumbria and other territories taken from his kingdom by William Rufus. The Empress Matilda meanwhile had established a base in southern Normandy at Argentan whence her and her husband's armies could harass the duchy.

The events of Stephen's reign have been much discussed by historians. Contemporary chronicles tell numerous tales of violence and local disorder, of weak kingship and the breakdown of justice. A famous and influential passage in the Peterborough Chronicle provides a lurid tale of castle-building, local tyranny and torture; for its anonymous author, these were 'the nineteen years when Christ and his saints slept'. The confident English historiography of the nineteenth century identified the period as a time when the forces of feudal disorder – that is, the aristocracy bent on increasing its own power – took advantage of weak kingship to do just this. The terminology of 'Anarchy' was coined by the influential scholar John Horace Round, with profound consequences for most subsequent interpretations. The last forty years have seen a reaction against these views. There has been a recognition of the scale of the problems which Stephen faced: that, unlike any of his Norman predecessors, he had to deal with not only a disputed succession but also a powerful rival with a base in Normandy and England and allies to the south and north in Anjou and Scotland. It has also been appreciated that aristocratic behaviour was determined by a complex mixture of loyalty, opportunism and self-protection, rather than any drive to dismember a strong monarchy. In short, events in England and Normandy should be seen not as anarchy, but as a civil war. In addition, the vulnerability of the power of the previous Norman rulers in Britain and

44. Representation of Baldwin fitz Gilbert encouraging his troops to the right during the Battle of Lincoln (1141) at which King Stephen was captured. The drawing is in a manuscript of Henry of Huntingdon's *Historia Anglorum* which dates from the early thirteenth century.

45. Coin, struck at York, of Stephen's elder son, Eustace, who died in 1153.

northern France was devastatingly exposed. Stephen may not have been the greatest of medieval kings, but he was certainly courageous and determined in the face of very great odds.

For two years, all seemed to go reasonably well. A rapid march north early in 1136 led to a settlement with David I and a campaign later in the year led to the capture of Exeter and the defeat of Baldwin de Redvers, who had taken up the Empress Matilda's cause. Meanwhile Matilda's husband, Count Geoffrey of Anjou, had been unable to make any progress in Normandy. Stephen's visit to Normandy in 1137 was not, however, a success. Quarrels broke out within his army and, while the campaign was not a failure, it did not achieve the vital strategic goal of dislodging Matilda from her base in the south of the duchy. In May 1138, Earl Robert of Gloucester formally defied Stephen and espoused his half-sister's cause. His behaviour was justified at the time by the historian William of Malmesbury, who presented Robert's initial adherence to Stephen as necessary expediency. His motives may in fact have been more complex, influenced undoubtedly by the increasing importance at court of the Beaumont twins, Waleran, Count of Meulan and Robert, Earl of Leicester, and by Stephen's failure to provide protection against a great Welsh revival that threatened all the Norman settlers in Wales and, specifically, Robert's estates in South Wales. Robert's defection placed a number of important strongholds, including Caen, Bayeux and Bristol, beyond Stephen's control. In July 1138 David I again invaded northern England, only to be defeated at the Battle of the Standard near Northallerton on 22 August by an army led by Archbishop Thurstan of York.

Stephen's actions throughout this period do occasionally raise doubts about his competence. In 1138, with Earl Robert still in Normandy, he surrounded Bristol Castle, but then abandoned the siege to campaign with considerable success as far north as Shrewsbury against other rebels. As in Normandy in 1137, he failed to deliver what may have been the knockout blow. In June 1139 Stephen acted against Bishop Roger of Salisbury and his nephews, two of whom were bishops of Lincoln and Ely. All were very powerful men, with the ageing Bishop Roger having been Henry I's right-hand man. His attack on them may well be indicative of the sort of divisions at court that had influenced Earl Robert to switch to his sister's cause. Stephen may well also have had good grounds to suspect their loyalty: the fact that all three possessed extensive secular interests is not in doubt, but the arrest and imprisonment of churchmen raised complex moral issues. Stephen seems to have emerged from the episode little weakened in the short term. Yet he had undoubtedly lost some of the moral high ground gained by his early cultivation of the Church. The arrest of the bishops also highlights a change in the organization of English government. Henceforth Stephen installed earls in each shire with responsibilities that were primarily military – a notable decentralization of responsibility from the days when kings had resolutely controlled the appointment of sheriffs.

The landing of the Empress and Earl Robert at Arundel on 30 September 1139 marked the beginning of the civil war in England. Stephen's decision to allow the Empress Matilda and Robert to travel from Arundel to Bristol looks like a mistake, and was indeed thought to be one by many contemporaries. A vigorously prosecuted siege of Arundel could once more have brought the business to a conclusion. Advised by Bishop Henry, however, Stephen took the view that allowing all his enemies to concentrate in western England would allow him to finish them off. In practice, matters proved to be more complex. While Stephen's party was much the stronger, the support that the Empress attracted in various parts of the kingdom proved to be a consistent distraction from the main task. A further invasion of northern England by David I required that further concessions be made to him. One among these apparent sideshows proved to be of decisive importance when Earl Ranulph of Chester, one of the most powerful of all

Anglo-Norman magnates, declared for Matilda and seized Lincoln castle. When Stephen's forces tried to dislodge him, they were attacked on 2 February 1141 by an army mustered by Ranulph and the Earl of Gloucester. Stephen showed great personal bravery, but was captured and imprisoned at Bristol. In the aftermath, his party disintegrated, with even his brother Bishop Henry transferring his allegiance to the Empress.

Matilda, however, found it impossible to push her cause through to the logical conclusion of a coronation. In the first place, there was the problem of what exactly to do with Stephen, an anointed king. No one seems to have contemplated deposing him; it was suggested that he might become a monk. Secondly, there was the obviously luke-warm nature of much of the support that the Empress attracted; the generous gifts she made did produce an entourage, but not loyalty. Ignominiously thrown out of London by a riot in the city (she had to leave behind an unfinished dinner), her forces attacked Winchester where Bishop Henry had made a demonstration of support for his brother. Stephen's wife Matilda, a resilient and effective support for her husband, then arrived with an army that routed the Empress Matilda's troops and captured the Earl of Gloucester on 14 September 1141. The two illustrious prisoners were then exchanged in November. Stephen's cause had suffered not just because of his defeat, but because so many magnates had shown themselves ready to sail with the prevailing winds of fortune. At the same time, the defences of Normandy were collapsing and the Empress Matilda's husband was moving inexorably towards the conquest that he completed in 1144-5. The many magnates with cross-channel estates now faced seemingly irresolvable conflicts of loyalty.

In England between 1142 and 1147, much of the fighting took place in the Thames Valley. Stephen made considerable gains, but, with no significant pitched battles being fought and most of the warfare consisting of sieges, he achieved no decisive advantage. Probably the closest he came to victory was in December 1142 when the Empress, surrounded in Oxford castle, made a dramatic escape in disguise across the snow. By 1147-8, Stephen's cause did appear to be growing superficially stronger, with Earl Robert of Gloucester dying on 31 October 1147 and the Empress Matilda leaving England for Normandy for good in early 1148. Appearances were, however, once again deceptive. Through the 1140s Stephen was in the process of losing the positive and very necessary support of the Church. This change was manifested in various ways. A disputed election to the archbishopric of York in 1141 had led to the election of a candidate favoured by Stephen and Bishop Henry, but opposed by local Cistercian abbots and, with them, by Bernard, the great Cistercian abbot of Clairvaux, and Pope Eugenius III. In consequence, there were in effect two Archbishops of York between 1148 and 1151. Also in the 1140s, Stephen was losing the support of the Archbishop of Canterbury, Theobald, who increasingly became an active supporter of the Angevins. The upshot of all this was that when, in 1151, Stephen tried to have his son Eustace crowned during his lifetime, the Church refused to do so. The continuation of Stephen's dynasty had been effectively blocked.

At the same time, the attitudes of many great magnates became increasingly neutral, if not hostile. One good example is provided by Earl Ranulph of Chester. Apparently loyal to Stephen after 1141, he did little to provide active support and concentrated on building up his own power in the North Midlands. In 1146 Stephen had him arrested at court by a trick, and imposed harsh terms. This display of apparently effective authoritarian kingship of course ensured that Ranulph supported the Empress Matilda's party from then onwards. A second example is provided by the Beaumont twins, Count Waleran of Meulan and Earl Robert of Leicester. Strong supporters of Stephen up until 1141, Waleran transferred his support to the Empress and moved his base to Normandy and France, while Robert, ostensibly a supporter of Stephen, looked after his English lands. In this case, family interest, rather than political loyalty, was clearly the predominant consideration; their objective was to preserve the family's cross-Channel landed interests and eventually join the winning side. After the Empress's withdrawal from England, her son Henry (the future King Henry II) became the effective leader of her party. Knighted by King David I of Scotland at Carlisle on 22 May 1149, he became Duke of Normandy in early 1150, and Count of Anjou when his father died on 7 September 1151. Historians will endlessly debate how far the fact that Matilda's gender was a disadvantage. It is probable that it was a considerable one in male-dominated age. In military terms, her husband's adamant refusal to cross to England and provide direct military support was another serious weakness. But from 1151, Stephen's chief opponent was male, able to bring to bear the full resources of a northern French territorial prince, and possessed of a legitimacy that Stephen's heirs could not enjoy.

Peace terms were eventually agreed by the so-called Treaty of Winchester (a convenient short-hand for a more complex process of settlement) of November 1153. At the heart of the settlement were the stipulations that Stephen would remain king for his lifetime and that Henry would be his successor. Stephen's near-capitulation had been brought about by a series of events which had made Henry's power steadily greater. The death of Stephen's queen, Matilda, on 3 May 1152 was followed by that of their son, Eustace, on 17 August 1153. Twice after Henry's return to England in January 1153, his and Stephen's armies had confronted one another, at Malmesbury in (probably) February and at Wallingford in August. On both occasions, their followers had simply refused to fight a pitched battle and had in effect forced Stephen and Henry to negotiate terms. Since 1151 Stephen had shown typical energy, constructing a coalition of northern French princes to try to expel Henry from Normandy, going as far as trying to arrest the English bishops if they persisted in their refusal to organize Eustace's coronation, and seeking to the end to fight the one decisive battle that might have given him victory. It was ultimately the war-weariness of the leading magnates that brought about a settlement. After the treaty, Stephen still acted with great vigour, making a great display of effective kingship. It was of course possible for him still to hope that, in spite of the fact that he was approaching sixty years of age, his cause might prevail through an accident to Henry. However, in October 1154, he was taken ill at Dover, dying there on the 25th. He was buried alongside his wife and eldest son at the Cluniac abbey of Faversham (Kent), which he had founded.

Stephen was an energetic king who determinedly fought his opponents over many years. His abilities as a soldier were praised by contemporaries and have rarely been criticized by modern scholars. He was to a considerable degree the victim of forces beyond his reach, of the power-bases that his enemies enjoyed in Anjou and Scotland, and, in a different context, of the Cistercian influence over the papacy. It is hard to judge his actions, since the frequent unfortunate outcomes of, for example, the release of the Empress Matilda from Arundel or the arrests of Bishops Roger of Salisbury or Earl Ranulph of Chester might in other circumstances have turned out to be strategically brilliant or displays of ruthless and effective power. The simple fact that so much turned out badly might, however, suggest that Stephen was ultimately a man who failed to convince others of his abilities. The effectiveness of his government in the areas under his control has been reappraised in recent years and he is generally seen as holding on to royal rights and power. Henry II, in France at the time of Stephen's death, returned to be crowned King of England on 19 December 1154, reuniting the kingdom with Normandy and combining both into the much larger collection of territories usually known as the Angevin Empire. The effectiveness of his rule in England demonstrates his debt to Stephen's dogged efforts.

3

THE HOUSE OF ANJOU
1154-1272

S.D. CHURCH

Although Henry II, who came to the English throne in 1154, was through his mother a member of the House of Normandy, his father's ancestors were the counts of Anjou – the Angevins – and it was with this dynasty that Henry, his sons and grandson, strongly identified. Their regime strengthened the links between England and the Continent by extending the territorial interests of the monarchy from its existing base in Normandy, through Anjou, Maine, Touraine and Poitou in central France, as far south as the duchy of Aquitaine. In the British Isles, too, this was a period of expansion: the lordship of Ireland was claimed by Henry II and added to the list of royal titles by King John. Ironically, though, the loss of all the continental possessions, save Aquitaine, under John and Henry III meant that by 1272 England was becoming increasingly nationalistic in its outlook, fearful of foreign influence and determined to exclude that influence from the government of the land. The Angevins also had a dynamic influence on the political, legal and administrative institutions of the English State, generating traditions of rule that could, in moments of crisis, be used to constrain the Crown itself. At the start of this period, kings ruled above the law; but by its end, the law was beginning to govern the actions of kings.

HENRY II (1154-1189)

In a charter addressed to all his earls, barons and liegemen, both French and English, and issued shortly after his coronation (19 December 1154), Henry, King of the English, Duke of the Normans and Aquitainians, and Count of the Angevins, affirmed his intention to return England to the state it had been in Henry I's day. This was no idle promise. In the years following his accession, Henry II transformed his country from one riven by civil war to one that was united under royal control.

In the first months of the reign, Henry turned to men of experience to help him rebuild the mechanisms of royal government. The Archbishop of Canterbury, Theobald of Bec, for example, played a central role in getting Henry established in England. It was Theobald who recommended to Henry the thirty-six-year-old Thomas Becket, who became his chancellor early in 1155. In the domain of royal finance, Henry brought out of retirement Nigel, Bishop of Ely, the former treasurer of Henry I. Nigel's expertise was in the Exchequer, the main debt-collecting agency of the king and thus central to the restoration of royal authority in England. Linked to the Exchequer was the role of the sheriff. In Stephen's reign, local control had been wrested from these appointed (and dismissible) royal officials and taken by men with hereditary titles. It was essential that Henry II take back control of the localities by appointing his own men to the office of sheriff. To this end, in 1155, he replaced twenty-one of the twenty-four sheriffs in post at the start of his reign.

The result of this two-pronged policy of rebuilding the workings of the Exchequer and of replacing the sheriffs was striking. By the Exchequer year 1158-9 (the financial year then ran from Michaelmas, 29 September), revenue claimed by the Exchequer from the proceeds of that year's debts reached £25,500, according to its record of outstanding debts, the pipe roll. This figure compares very favourably with the £26,500 claimed from new sources in the year 1129-30, the only year for which we have comparable evidence for the reign of Henry I. Within four years of taking the throne, therefore, Henry (and Henry was essential to this process) had restored stability to the financial administration of England.

The reconstruction of royal finances went hand-in-hand with other reforms implemented by the new king. Among the most important of these were the reassertion of control over royal castles and the destruction of unauthorized (or adulterine) castles. Henry also reformed the English currency. Since the tenth century, English kings had enjoyed a monopoly over the production of coinage in the realm. In the post-Conquest period, the mints of England situated in the towns and cities of the realm, came to be monopolized by certain powerful families. In 1158, Henry dismissed every single one of these moneyers and, moreover, fined them for the privilege of their dismissal. In their place he put new men who were to produce the new silver penny, known to modern historians as the *Cross-and-Crosslets* or *Tealby* type. It was an extraordinary move and one that could be undertaken, as one historian has put it, 'only by a king certain of his power'. It was the final stamp on his reassertion of royal rule and he could now turn his attention to his other territories.

The first of the three sons resulting from the marriage of the Empress Matilda with Geoffrey le Bel, Henry had been born on 4 March 1133. As the grandson of King Henry I and the son of the Empress, he was able to claim England and Normandy. He was also heir to his father's county of Anjou. And when he came to the throne in 1154, he was already much more than ruler of England. In 1150, just before Henry's seventeenth birthday, his father resigned the duchy of Normandy into his hands. On his deathbed a year later, Geoffrey also designated Henry as his successor to Anjou. This was a grant that was meant to be temporary, to stand until such time as Henry won England, when the land of Anjou was to descend to Henry's younger brother, Geoffrey. Henry, however, was not a man to let go lightly any land of which he had possession. And in 1152, Henry secured perhaps the greatest coup of his young life: the marriage to Eleanor, heiress to the duchy of Aquitaine and discarded wife of the King of France, Louis VII.

Such extraordinary success for this young man (he was only twenty-one in 1154) encouraged in him a relentless expansionism, mostly at the expense of his supposed overlord, the King of France. In 1159 Henry was to be found in Toulouse, pressing his claim to the county as the husband of Eleanor. It is this focus on Toulouse and on the continental lands of Henry that brings into stark relief the issue of how we should view Henry II. He was, of course, King of the English, and this was his highest title. Hence, in his grants of land and in the letters he sent, he was 'Henry, by the grace of God, King of the English, Duke of the Normans and Aquitainians, and Count of the Angevins'. The titles are ranked in order of seniority (king outranks duke, but duke is superior to count). And yet Henry's father was an Angevin, Henry himself was born in Le Mans (at that time an Angevin city), and he spent his early years in the county of Anjou. Henry's mother, moreover, was a granddaughter of William the Conqueror. By no means was Henry an Englishman: in fact, he was anything but an Englishman. He was a continental prince with continental origins and continental interests. Not surprisingly, therefore, the Continent was the place where he was to spend the majority of his life.

There is one event, however, for which Henry is justly infamous and which had its focus on England, and that was his part in the murder of Archbishop Thomas Becket on the evening of 29 December 1170. The immediate cause of Becket's death was the response of four of Henry's knights to Henry's wild outburst: 'What miserable drones and traitors have I nourished and prompted in my household, who let their lord be treated with such shameful contempt by a low-born clerk?' (This is more accurate than the better known 'Who will rid me of this turbulent priest?': the angry Henry II was less of a wordsmith than those who were captivated by his actions.) The wider context of Becket's murder, however, was the conflict between Church and State that emerged out of the papal reform movement of the eleventh century championed by Pope Gregory VII. The reformers wished to remove the Church from the 'tutelage of kings'; indeed, their aim was to elevate the Church to a position above all secular things. As Cardinal Humbert, one of the intellectual giants of reform, put it, 'The priesthood is the soul, the kingship the body... just as the soul excels the body and commands it, so too the priestly dignity excels the royal... kings should follow churchmen.' In Becket, papal reform found a new champion who was prepared to push this doctrine to the limit. Most famously, he confronted Henry over the issue of criminous clerks. Henry wanted those convicted in Church courts, once they had been divested of their clerical status, to be handed over to the secular authorities for punishment. Becket's view was that the 'clergy should have no other king than Christ' and should, therefore, only be subject to his law.

Henry II saw Becket's position as a direct attack on his authority as king. There was, however, also a personal edge to the conflict between him and his archbishop. Becket had been Henry II's loyal chancellor, and, while he was chancellor, he had given no indication of his reformist bent. Indeed, Henry might have been forgiven for thinking Becket would be a typical curial archbishop, a man who would give unwavering loyalty to his king. Becket was not just a representative of a reform tradition that was anathema to all secular rulers; he was also a former ally and friend who had turned to bite the hand that had fed him. Irritatingly, too, Becket was not a constant man. One moment he accepted Henry's proposals, the next he changed his mind and rejected them. This he did at Clarendon in 1164, much to the annoyance of his allies and his enemies alike. In the end, Becket courted disaster, almost as if he wanted to dare Henry to put an end to the conflict. Returning to Canterbury from exile in France on 1 December 1170, he entered his city 'like Christ on Palm Sunday'. He refused to lift sentences of excommunication already in place and added new sentences for those who had attacked Canterbury's lands during his absence. Henry II was driven to distraction: hence his infamous outburst and the consequences that followed – the murder of Thomas Becket in Canterbury Cathedral.

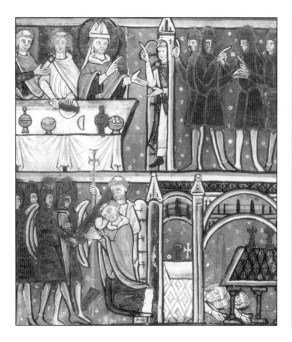

Clockwise from top left 47. Becket's murder, from a manuscript of John of Salisbury's *Life of St Thomas Becket.*
48. Henry II doing penance at the shrine of Thomas Becket, stained glass panel in the Bodleian Library, Oxford. Beckett's shrine in Canterbury Cathedral was the most popular English destination for pilgrims.
49. Seal of Henry II.

Did Becket achieve his aims? Well, he got martyrdom – if, indeed, we can suppose that was what he wanted. (Within a few years of his death his tomb was the focus of one of the most important cult centres in western Christendom.) And he certainly had Henry humbled. In 1174 the king came to Canterbury as a penitent pilgrim and was flogged before the shrine of the martyr. But the struggle for which Becket had given his life, namely the emancipation of the Church from royal domination, did not end in 1170. Henry II and his successors would continue to interfere in the affairs of the Church by having their own men appointed to ecclesiastical positions, by leaving bishoprics and abbeys vacant in order to enjoy their revenues, and by intervening at all levels in the administration of the English Church. And even in the case of benefit of clergy (the right of someone in holy orders to be tried in an ecclesiastical court, and the issue over which Henry and Thomas clashed most fiercely at Clarendon in 1164), the secular courts still regulated practice. The murder of Becket was just one of the many struggles between Church and State that occasionally came to the fore throughout the Middle Ages.

Eleanor and Henry II had in total eight children. The daughters all made marriages which expressed the breadth of Angevin political interest and the extent to which families of note wished to be associated with the house of Anjou. It was the surfeit of sons that Henry and Eleanor produced, however, which was to provide the greatest threat to Henry's control over his lands. While it was a truism that no medieval king could have too many sons in order to ensure the succession to his lands, it was also equally axiomatic that no medieval king could afford to have these sons waiting in the wings for too long. The wise medieval king died before his heirs became too restless.

In an attempt to avert the potential problems caused by having adult sons looking for a role, Henry sought to pull the teeth of rebellion by granting them separate spheres of authority where they might practice the art of ruling. To that end, in 1169, Henry made provision for the inheritance of his lands after his death. Henry, the eldest surviving son, was to have the heartlands of Henry II's dominion: Anjou, Maine, Normandy and England; Richard was to have Aquitaine; and Geoffrey was to have Brittany. (John, then just two years old, was excluded from this settlement.) On 24 May 1170, in imitation of the Capetian royal practice, Henry II had the young Henry crowned King of England. In June 1172, Richard was formally installed as Duke of Aquitaine. And although Geoffrey was not made Duke of Brittany until 1180, he had in 1169 received the homage of the Breton barons. But while in theory the act of naming his heirs might have worked, in practice all Henry succeeded in doing was giving his sons bases from which they could muster support for their own ambitions.

The first of the rebellions that Henry was to suffer came in 1173-4. Encouraged by King Louis VII of France, the rebellion came as close as any to unseating Henry II from his throne. Moreover, at the centre of the web of intrigue against Henry lay his queen, Eleanor of Aquitaine, almost certainly the instigator of her sons' treachery. Quite why Eleanor took such an extraordinary step has tantalized historians for generations. She had been left as *de facto* ruler of Aquitaine, with her son Richard at her side and with almost no interference from Henry II, between 1170 and the outbreak of rebellion. The answer to her defection probably lies in the fact that when, in February 1173, Count Raymond of Toulouse did homage for his lands to Henry II and the Young King, the event signalled to Eleanor (who claimed Toulouse as part of her inheritance) that Aquitaine was to be permanently subordinate to an Angevin king. This was not a situation that any Aquitainian could take lightly; Aquitaine had long seen itself as being independent of all outside control, and Eleanor was an Aquitainian to her core.

The initial impetus for rebellion was Henry II's plans for his youngest son, John. In assigning John certain castles, Henry II unsettled the terms of the 1169 agreement. Most aggrieved was the Young King, who, urged on by King Louis of France, demanded the immediate transfer of at least a part of his inheritance: he wanted Anjou, Normandy or England. Henry II refused, so outright war between Henry, his sons and his wife ensued. It was, as one contemporary commentator put it, 'a war without love'. But despite the huge forces arrayed against him, Henry II, with a combination of wealth and guile, won out. In the course of the war, he captured Queen Eleanor; and while, at the end of 1174, he made peace with his sons and their supporters, he could not bring himself to forgive Eleanor for her treachery. She was to be kept in captivity at Henry's pleasure in an English prison: a southern belle in a northern cage and a permanent hostage for her sons' good behaviour.

Henry was to face other rebellions from his sons. In 1183, Henry and Geoffrey once again turned against their father, this time by attacking Richard in Aquitaine. They were aided in their rebellion by the new King of France, Philip II 'Augustus' (1180-1223), who had continued his own father's policy of sowing the seed of enmity in the Angevin family. Only the Young King's premature death brought the revolt to an end. But even in this tragedy there were more causes for dissension. Henry II assumed that the provisions for the inheritance to his lands meant that Richard would now step into the Young King's place as heir apparent to the core of Henry's patrimony. Richard, however, had other ideas. He was certainly unwilling to give up Aquitaine. John was given his father's blessing to attack Richard, and Geoffrey of Brittany joined in the fight with their older brother. Geoffrey's death in a tournament in 1186 did nothing to lessen the tensions between Henry II and Richard. By 1189, Henry II had been driven to the point of despair. Forced by Richard to acknowledge him as his heir to all his lands, Henry died on 6 July 1189, a broken man.

Perhaps Henry II's greatest legacy was in the realm of royal justice. In the view of modern historians, Henry II has a very real claim to be the founder of English Common Law. It was Henry who first planned and put into effect the regular countrywide visitations by justices acting in his name (events called 'eyres') that were to bring regular royal justice to the localities. Moreover, the justices who sat on these eyres were royal appointees with the authority to preside over the court *and* to make judgments: hitherto, judgment had been given by local men, according to local custom, though admittedly within the bounds of certain norms. Furthermore, royal justice was now available in the localities for those who wanted it without the immediate presence of the king: eyres were regarded as sittings of the king's court, and so delivered judgment as good as if the king had made it himself. The Common Bench (later known as Common Pleas), too, has its origins in Henry II's reign within the Exchequer. Although the Exchequer was in origin a financial institution, it quickly came to be seen as a court where other judgments might be passed. The Exchequer was especially useful in this regard, because, unlike the king, who was itinerant, it was settled at Westminster and so might more easily be found by litigants. Henry II also instituted a number of important writs that enabled litigants to remove cases from the seigniorial courts (that is, courts of local lords) and the ecclesiastical courts that dominated twelfth-century England. Building on a set of legal norms that had existed before his reign (norms that allowed litigants to predict the outcome of some cases in some courts with a degree of certainty), Henry II's reforms created the beginnings of a single legal system for England.

It was also in the reign of Henry II that three remarkable treatises were produced that were to be amongst the most important of England's contributions to the great flowering of learning known as the Twelfth Century Renaissance. In the first text, known as the *Dialogus de Scaccario* ('The Dialogue of the Exchequer'), Richard fitz Nigel, Henry II's treasurer, described for his audience the detailed workings of the Exchequer. The *Dialogus* is therefore the first civil service departmental handbook to be written in England. The second text, known as *Tractatus De Legibus et Consuetudinibus Regni Anglie* ('The Treatise on the Laws and Customs of the Kingdom of England'), often shortened to *Glanvill* after its presumed author, Ranulph de Glanville, Henry II's justiciar, provided a textbook for those training in the law or who had business at the royal courts. And in the third text, known as *Policraticus* (a made-up word meaning 'The Statesman's Book'), the scholar John of Salisbury gave the first serious thought to the nature of the State and of government since the early fifth century. Each of these books was much more than a simple manual. In the words of R.W. Southern, 'each one aspired to invest the routine of government with an intellectual generality… [and] they provide glittering testimony to the growing claims of secular government such as we could find nowhere else in Europe.' In England, Henry bequeathed to his sons one of the most sophisticated bureaucratic states in twelfth-century Christendom.

RICHARD I (1189-1199)

If Henry II was not an Englishman, then neither was his son Richard I; although he was born at Oxford on 8 September 1157, his parentage and his upbringing made him a continental prince to his core. His father was a descendant both of the Dukes of Normandy and of the Counts of Anjou; his mother, Eleanor of Aquitaine, was a scion of one of the most famous families in medieval France. She was a patron of courtly literature and her native tongue was a very different form of French than that spoken by her husband – or, indeed, by most of the men with whom Henry surrounded himself. Aquitaine itself was, moreover, and had been for generations, independent of either the idea or the reality of a unified France. The Dukes of Aquitaine looked southwards for their politics, their language and their culture, as, indeed, did the aristocracy. Few, if any, Aquitainians can be found in Henry II's court, except when Henry was actually in the region exercising ducal authority. This was a separate world from the rest of the Angevin continental lands; and it was the world into which Richard's mother brought him as her heir in 1169. In June 1172, aged just fourteen years, he was formally invested as Duke of the Aquitainians; by 1174, he was running the show on his own, his mother now languishing in an English gaol after the rebellion of 1173-4 to be finally released on her husband's death in 1189. Richard, it seems, was an extraordinarily successful Duke of the Aquitainians, bringing the region very much under his domination. It was here, too, that he learned the military skills that were to be so vital to him as king and crusader.

While battles in the Middle Ages were rare events, when they did occur they could be decisive. The Battle of Hattin on 4 July 1187 was one of those occasions when the course of history was changed. On that fateful day, the chivalry of Jerusalem was cut to the ground and the way was left open for the combined Muslim power under the leadership of Saladin to put an end finally to the hundred-year Christian occupation of the Holy Land. On 2 October 1187, Jerusalem itself fell; and by January 1188, the Christian hold on Palestine was restricted to just three coastal cities: Tyre, Tripoli and Antioch. The reaction in the West to the imminent loss of Outremer (the land beyond the sea) was immediate. Richard himself was the first northern

European prince to take the Cross, doing so in the autumn of 1187; others quickly followed him, including, in January 1188, his overlord, Philip Augustus, King of France. The news of Richard's decision clearly annoyed his father; Henry was a man with a practical mind who was more interested in maintaining his own lands than seeking glory elsewhere. To Richard, however, the lure of crusade was irresistible, with its opportunity for participating in the greatest enterprise open to any man or woman in this world or, indeed, the next. Jerusalem was the centre of the spiritual and the real world, and there could be no greater cause than its recapture for Christ. With his father's death in July 1189, Richard was free to organize his affairs and to turn his attention to the greatest adventure of his life: the Third Crusade.

Richard left for crusade in the summer of 1190, having put in place a series of measures designed to keep his lands intact during his absence. In the southern part of his lands, his position was to be secured by the promise of his marriage to Berengaria, daughter of King Sancho VI of Navarre (which took place in Cyprus on 12 May 1191). The marriage was a political one, designed to set up an alliance against Count Raymond V of Toulouse, who alone among the princes of France had not taken the Cross. Evidently he intended to profit from Richard's absence. But as well as solving a potential problem, the marriage caused another one – or, more accurately, brought another problem to a head. Since January 1169, Richard had been betrothed to Alice, daughter of King Louis VII of France; though he had promised often to marry her, the marriage ceremony had never come to pass. With his marriage to Berengaria of Navarre, Richard had created in Philip Augustus, Alice's brother and now King of France, a mortal enemy. Philip was humiliated, and a humiliated Philip was a very dangerous man indeed. Both kings were intent on their journey to the Holy Land on a mission to rescue Jerusalem from the Muslims, and for the moment they could agree to be allies for the greater purpose. But this could only be a temporary respite from the inevitable storm.

Having wintered in Sicily, separately with Philip ahead of Richard, the two kings set sail for the East. En route to the Holy Land, Richard stopped off at Cyprus and brought the island under his control. It may well be, as one historian has recently argued, that Richard recognized the significance of Cyprus to the long-term future of the Christian occupation of Palestine. It is unlikely that so great a strategist as Richard would have overlooked such an obvious point, and unlikely, too, that he conquered the island by 'accident' or in a fit of pique, despite what the king himself said in a letter reporting the events leading up to the conquest. Having conquered it, Richard then sold the island to the Templars, thus demonstrating that his aim was indeed to bring Cyprus in as a resource for the survival of the Christian occupation of Palestine.

Richard arrived at Acre in the Holy Land on 8 June 1191. The city had fallen to Saladin in July 1187 and had been under siege from Guy of Lusignan, King of Jerusalem, since August 1189. In that time Acre came to represent the very essence of the Christian fight against the Muslims. Should Acre withstand the siege, then all would be lost; should Acre fall, then it might be possible to reverse the gains made by Saladin in the wake of Hattin. Fortunately for the crusaders, Acre was captured on 12 July as a result of the combined efforts of the forces of Richard and Philip Augustus. The way was now open for the reconquest to begin, but first Richard was confronted by the shocking news that King Philip intended to return home, the task that they had set themselves hardly begun, let alone completed. Richard was now in sole charge of the Third Crusade, but he must have wondered what tricks Philip would get up to while his attention was focused on the Holy Land. And when he eventually did return home, it took Richard the rest of his life to undo the harm that Philip did during his absence from his lands. But, at the moment there was a crusade to conduct.

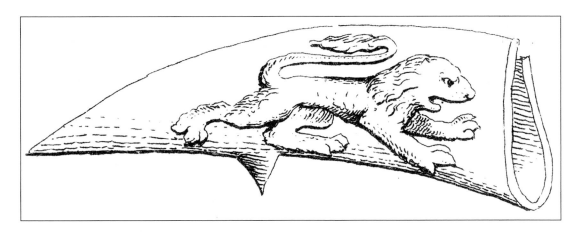

Clockwise from top 50. The coat of arms of Richard I.
51. Two Templars on a horse from the *Historia Anglorum*. The sharing of the mount of a warrior
signifies their humble beginnings.
52. Richard I as depicted in the *Abingdon Chronicle*.

On 25 August, Richard's army began to move towards Ascalon, the place that would be the key if Jerusalem were to be held. He kept the sea on one flank, while fighting off skirmishing Muslim soldiers on the other. At Arsuf on 6 September, Saladin drew up his forces to meet the Christians. This was Richard's first ever experience of battle. During it he gained a reputation not just for being brave, but also for being in the right place at the right time to rally the troops. It was a famous victory and the Muslims retreated in some disarray. The battle over, the crusaders resumed their progress to Ascalon. On 10 September, they arrived at Jaffa only to find that Saladin had ordered its destruction. During the following few days, Saladin had Ascalon levelled, too, through fear that if Richard took that city the way would be open to Jerusalem.

Fortunately for Saladin, however, Richard was in charge of a crusading army, one that was, by and large, motivated by a desire to undertake an armed pilgrimage to Jerusalem to fulfil the terms of their vows and then to return home. Mostly these men and women were not on a campaign of conquest and would not have, therefore, focused on the strategic issues relating to the recapture and, more significantly, the holding of the Holy City. Pressured by the majority of his army to leave Ascalon to its fate and focus on Jerusalem, Richard decided to re-fortify Jaffa. He also continued negotiations with the Muslims, something he had done since his first arrival in Palestine, constantly trying to learn of their plans and to use all means to achieve his ends. It was also at Jaffa that he contemplated an attack on Egypt, long seen as the key to unlocking the mighty Muslim coalition arrayed against the Holy Land.

The move towards Jerusalem was a gradual one in which Richard rebuilt fortresses that Saladin had destroyed so as to secure the supply lines to Jerusalem. By 12 December, Saladin was forced to let his army disband for the winter leaving the land to the crusaders. In early January, Richard planned the siege of Jerusalem but then decided, on the advice of locals, that it would be an impossible task. The decision was a heavy blow to those who had come all this way to be at the very centre of their spiritual and temporal world. Richard's army again moved towards Jerusalem in the summer of 1192, but, as in January, caution got the better of him and he turned back before laying siege to the city. It was a decision that not only caused grief amongst the crusaders; it also had an adverse impact on Richard's reputation in the West. He was ever perceived as the king who had got to the very point of laying siege to Jerusalem and had turned back not once but twice. All Richard could do was to negotiate passage for those who wished to see the Holy City (he himself did not go) before preparing to return to his lands in Europe. On 9 October 1192, Richard set sail; the Third Crusade (in the words of one historian 'his crusade') was over.

The journey home, however, was not going to be an easy one. Moving quickly, Richard left many of his forces behind him; he was now vulnerable to attack from those who had reason to resent him. Unfortunately for Richard, there were many such men and, despite the fact that he still enjoyed the protection of the Church as a crusader, when he reached Europe he was hunted down and eventually captured in a 'disreputable house' (perhaps no more than a poor man's dwelling rather than a place of ill-repute) in Vienna. The man who captured him was Duke Leopold of Austria (humiliated by Richard at Acre) who then sold Richard on to the Emperor Henry VI of Germany.

Philip Augustus, while himself trying to get hold of Richard, or at least to ensure that Richard was never released, turned to Richard's brother, Count John, and in January 1193 invested him with Normandy, Anjou, Maine and Aquitaine. John crossed to England and announced that his brother was dead and that he was now the rightful king. Fortunately for Richard, no-one believed John, and Eleanor of Aquitaine and Walter of Coutances, Archbishop of Rouen and, since October 1191, the head of Richard's administration in England, rebuffed the pretender, fortified England against him, and set about raising the money for their king's release. It was to be a king's ransom: 150,000 marks, or £100,000, which was equivalent to four years of ordinary crown revenue from England, and perhaps more than a year's revenue from the whole of the Angevin lands. On 4 February 1194, Richard was released from captivity; on 13 March, he landed in England where he re-established his presence in the land and re-asserted his royal authority. By 2 May, he was ready to return to the Continent where he spent the remainder of his life attempting to undo the damage done by Philip Augustus and Count John.

In Normandy, Philip Augustus had made tremendous gains during Richard's period in captivity, capturing over thirty strategically important castles in the duchy. Richard's absence had enabled the French king not only to capture Norman territory, but also to put great pressure on the marcher barons to transfer their allegiance from Richard to him. Philip was able to provide an alternative source of lordship and justice for the disaffected in Norman society. But now Richard was back, King Philip was on the defensive and had lost the support of Count John: the latter sought and gained his brother's forgiveness, and now entered royal service as one of Richard's commanders. The French king sued for peace, Richard refused, and the war between them became even fiercer than before.

Richard's problem, however, was that he did not just have Normandy with which to deal. Like his father before him, Richard was master of a huge continental empire, which meant that his presence was required in many places. Philip, on the other hand, could concentrate his forces on Normandy. It was not long, therefore, before Richard had to turn his attention southwards. In June 1194, he took the castle of Loches on the Touraine-Berry border. In July, Richard was in Aquitaine subduing the Angoumois; meanwhile, Philip continued to stir up trouble in Normandy, forcing Richard to re-focus his attentions there. By January 1196, Richard had recaptured large tracts of Norman land taken by Philip. The next step was to reconquer the Norman Vexin. To this end Richard began the process by which one of the most extraordinary castles of the Middle Ages would be built: it was to be called Château-Gaillard ('impudent castle', a name given by Richard himself and referring, presumably, to the fact that building on the site had been specifically forbidden by treaty with Philip Augustus) and was to stand on the rock of Les Andelys overlooking the River Seine. In the summer of 1196, work began on the castle and at the same time he fortified the Isle of Andelys and began construction of the town that was to become Petit-Andelys. This was to provide Richard with a launching pad to begin the process of re-acquiring the Norman Vexin; the building work was completed in just two years. From here Richard could attack Philip's castles; and from here, too, he could conduct a war by water.

As well as fortifying Les Andelys, Richard also brought about an event that has been described as a 'diplomatic revolution'. For forty years the Angevin kings, through the claim of Eleanor of Aquitaine, had been conducting an incessant war against Toulouse. In 1196, Richard brought this impasse to an end by giving up his claim to the county. It was a decision that must have irked his mother greatly (she was still very much alive and in 1196 in retirement at the Abbey of Fontevraud). But it meant that Richard no longer had to fight in the South and in the North; he could now focus on his real enemy, Philip Augustus of France. By 1198, there was a formidable alliance behind Richard, and the French king was in full retreat. It could not be long before Paris itself fell to the Lionheart.

Then disaster struck: on 26 March 1199, outside the walls of Chalus-Chabrol, Richard was hit on the shoulder by a crossbow bolt. The wound turned gangrenous, and at Chalus on 6 April Richard died. He was a king at the height of his power, in charge of a collection of lands whose might rivalled anyone's in western Christendom. He was at Chalus-Chabrol prosecuting a war against the Viscount of Limoges and not, as some thought, simply chasing after treasure-trove. But whatever the case, the Lionheart was dead and men began to scramble for his inheritance.

What of that inheritance, and why had Richard not seen fit to provide for himself an heir of his own body? What exactly was his relationship to Berengaria? Was Richard, as some historians have argued, homosexual, and therefore unable or unwilling to do what a king ought for the provision of the succession? The answer to the third question is most easy to give: Richard, in the view of his most recent and most effective biographer, was certainly not gay. The questions raised about his sexuality are later misconceptions (they date no earlier than the eighteenth century), brought about by a willingness to think badly of Richard and to de-contextualize the actions of a twelfth-century European king. As for his relationship with Berengaria, it seems to have been distant and cool. The soldiers on his crusade liked to believe that Richard loved his queen, but then they would. The reality was that Richard, out of necessity and choice, spent little time with his wife. He certainly neglected the business of providing heirs, though since he had an illegitimate son, named Philip, we should assume that he was capable of siring children. Perhaps Berengaria was unable to conceive; she certainly never had children and remained, after Richard's death, an unmarried widow. By 1197 it must have been clear that the marriage was barren; and in that year Richard nominated his brother John as his successor.

John (1199-1216)

In 1197, John's position as successor to his brother, Richard I, may have been assured; but until that point, the youngest son of Henry II and Eleanor of Aquitaine was very much out of the frame. As W.L. Warren, who wrote the definitive modern biography of King John, noted, 'fourth sons, even of a king, are among the more insignificant of God's creatures'. Just two years old at the time of the Angevin dynastic settlement of 1169 (he was born on 24 December 1167 at Oxford), John was excluded from its terms: hence his later sobriquet of 'Lackland'. In 1172, Henry II tried to rectify his error and provide for his youngest son by allocating him the castles of Chinon, Loudun and Mirebeau, the traditional holdings of minor members of the Angevin comital family. The result was the internecine 'war without love' of 1173-4. The death of John's eldest brother, the Young King, in 1183 presented another opportunity for Henry to provide for John. If the settlement of 1169 had established the principle that the eldest son should succeed to the heartlands of Henry II's lands, then surely now Richard should step into the young Henry's shoes as king-, duke- and count-in-waiting, leaving Aquitaine available for the endowment of John. Henry II may have thought that there was a principle underlying his actions in 1169, but Richard was not inclined to accept it. He had been invested as Duke of Aquitaine and intended to keep the duchy – as well as stepping into his brother's shoes as the heir apparent to England, Normandy and Anjou. Not once but twice, then, John's brothers, and in particular Richard, had intervened in his inheritance prospects to his own detriment. It is little wonder that John himself felt no compunction in trying to benefit from Richard's misfortunes when the opportunity arose.

The only substantial piece of land over which Henry had some claim, and in which he appeared able to exercise his will concerning the inheritance, was Ireland. In the 1150s, Nicholas Breakspear (the 'English Pope'), who presided over the Church as Adrian IV (1154-9), issued the bull *Laudabiliter*, which gave Henry II papal authority to bring Ireland under his control. Henry, however, had other priorities, and only in 1171 did he feel inclined to do anything about his claim; and then his invasion of that year had more to do with the success being enjoyed by the English men who had followed the adventurer Richard, Earl of Clare (known to history as Strongbow), to Ireland the previous year. In the face of the might of the King of the English, all submitted.

It was this land that (perhaps as early as 1176, and certainly by 1177) Henry had in mind for John, though of course the prince was too young at this stage to take charge of Irish affairs personally. By 1185, however, John was eighteen and, since Aquitaine was not available to him, Ireland beckoned. John seems to have had little regard for the rights of the established Irish lords, and sent them into open rebellion. In the context of the twelfth-century thought-world inhabited by John, his actions were justified: the Irish were, according to 'civilized' men such as Gerald de Barri (Gerald of Wales), barbarians, and to John this meant they could be treated with contempt and distain and their lands distributed to his followers at will. This naive approach by the young prince was, however, very unwise. The native Irish united against John, who also encountered resistance from the most powerful representative of the Anglo-Norman baronage, Hugh de Lacy. Within eight months of landing at Waterford, John was home again; their new master impressed neither the native Irish nor the Anglo-Norman lords.

Some historians have suggested that John should have been grateful for Ireland and not got involved in plots to gain more than his share of the Angevin inheritance. In their view, John showed himself treacherous by his actions toward both his father and his brother Richard. But Richard was no angel: he had certainly rebelled against his father and had acted in a way in which a dispassionate observer might equally call treacherous. During the final years of Henry II's life, Richard had been in league with Philip Augustus to ensure his inheritance, despite the fact that what he claimed was not unambiguously his to inherit. And one could also argue that Richard, in the wake of the death of the Young King Henry in 1183, had denied John what some would have seen as his legitimate inheritance. In 1191, moreover, Richard nominated the four-year-old Arthur of Brittany, the son of his brother Geoffrey and Constance of Brittany, as heir should he die on crusade. If John was treacherous, he had something to be treacherous about; and if John was 'selfishly' seeking his own preferment to the Angevin lands, then Richard in particular had shown the way. Of course, in the end, Richard won the struggle. In 1189, he succeeded to all his father's lands. His reputation among his contemporaries, therefore, was assured. Public opinion did not look kindly on John's actions in the lead-up to his father's death; he, after all, came out of the affair with nothing.

Or rather, not quite nothing: for Richard was off on crusade, and, in order to secure his dominions at home, he had to make sure that his youngest brother was unlikely to rebel during his absence. As well as putting in place structures to ensure the continued security of his newly acquired inheritance, Richard also gave John lands that he hoped would be enough to satisfy his ambitions. John was made Count of Mortain in Normandy and married to the heiress of the earldom of Gloucester, Isabella. In England he was given control of five counties and six major honours, catapulting him into the ranks of the baronial elite. All this, however, was granted on the condition that he should remain out of England during Richard's absence on crusade.

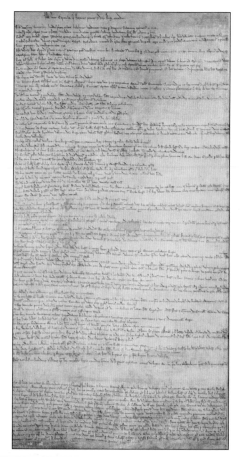

Clockwise from top left 53. King John and his dog from Peter of Langtoft's *Chronicle of England*. This manuscript was probably written and illuminated during the reign of Edward II.
54. Articles of the Barons, 1215.
55. Papal Bull of Pope Innocent III 1215 in which the Pope released King John from his promise to observe Magna Carta. The name 'Bull' comes from *bulla*, the lead seal used by the pope to seal documents.

John, of course, did not remain out of England. Nor did Richard's grant stop his youngest brother from pursuing his own interests: it was, after all, the Angevin way to seek one's own preferment. John caused enough trouble in 1191 to have Richard's custodian in England, William de Longchamp, Bishop of Ely, removed from office. In 1193, having received news of Richard's capture, he also did his best to gain his brother's lands, but without success. In order to gain the lands he desired, John in the end had to await the failure of Richard's marriage to produce an heir and the eventual destination of the flight of a crossbow bolt. In 1199 Richard was dead, and in the best tradition of heirs apparent, Count John made straight for the Angevin treasury at Chinon to secure the financial resources that would make a reality of his standing as Richard's heir. It was an inheritance that needed making, for it was not immediately obvious that John would succeed to all Richard's lands. There were some parts of the Angevin lands where Arthur, John's twelve-year-old nephew, was more favoured. This was certainly the case in Brittany; it was also so in Anjou, Maine and Touraine, though John's support in England and Normandy was extensive. Arthur also had the endorsement of Philip Augustus; so if John was to succeed, he needed to defeat a formidable coalition of the French king, Arthur of Brittany and the magnates of those lands that had declared for Arthur. It is a testament to John's skill that he achieved this feat.

In England, the succession was straightforward: here William Marshal, Archbishop Hubert Walter of Canterbury, and Geoffrey fitz Peter the justiciar secured the support of the magnates for John. In Normandy, too, John's accession was assured by the fact that Arthur was a Breton: the Bretons were the traditional enemy of the Normans. And, in Aquitaine, John's inheritance of the duchy was made certain by the support of his mother, Queen Eleanor. In the first months of his reign he managed to bring the rest of Richard's lands under his control by a series of negotiations and campaigns. By the end of September 1199, Arthur was prepared to sue for peace.

From this high point in the autumn of 1199, however, John's position deteriorated. Arthur, not surprisingly given his attempt to usurp (at least in John's eyes) the Angevin inheritance – and not surprisingly, too, given the Angevin reputation for exacting brutal retribution from their enemies – fled to the court of Philip Augustus. Now in the hands of the French king, Arthur became a pawn in Philip's long-term plans to destabilize the Angevin Empire. Arthur could always be held over John as a potential rival to the Angevin continental lands. Aware of this fact, John found it necessary to concede the terms of the Treaty of Le Goulet (22 May 1200). Philip recognized John as Richard's sole legitimate heir, but exacted a high price. John was required to perform the act of homage for his lands in France and to hand over to Philip a 'relief' of 20,000 marks (£16,667). The relief was the payment made to one's lord for permission to enter into one's inheritance; the act of exacting that relief demonstrated that the lord had real power over the inheritance. While Henry II and Richard I had performed homage, they had never paid relief; the treaty therefore demonstrated that John held his continental lands only on the sufferance of King Philip. Just as importantly, John was persuaded to give up the grand coalition that Richard had been building against Philip. This left him fatally exposed when the French king turned against him in the spring of 1202.

The immediate cause of King Philip's move against John in 1202 was his treatment of one of his own vassals. John had been married to Isabella of Gloucester since 1189, though they had no children. In 1199, John had the marriage dissolved and, in August 1200, he married Isabella, heiress to Angoulême. In theory this was a brilliant match for King John. The Counts of Angloulême were virtually independent rulers of the Angoumois, a stretch of land that separated Poitou from Gascony. It was a key area for the Angevin kings, and it had occupied more than its fair share of attention from Henry II and Richard I. The marriage, then, brought the Angoumois into the Angevin orbit. But it also had another benefit: it deprived Hugh IX of Lusignan of the territory. Hugh, as well as controlling Lusignan, had his position as Lord of La Marche recognized by John in January 1200. Within a few months of receiving La Marche, Hugh was betrothed to Isabella, and it looked as though he would soon be in control of a belt of territory cutting the Angevin lands in two. In marrying Isabella, therefore, John killed two birds with one stone: he gained control of an important county vital for contacts with the south, and he deprived a difficult man of control of most of the county of Poitou. For John, the marriage also had a collateral benefit: it seems that he found the young Isabella very attractive.

In marrying Isabella, John seemed to have found the solution to a number of problems. In reality, however, he had stirred up a hornet's nest. Hugh took his complaint to the court of John's overlord, King Philip of France. Philip at first dealt with the matter gingerly, but when in the summer of 1201 John accused the Lusignans of treason against himself and his brother, they appealed again. On this occasion, Philip took his opportunity to order John to do justice to the Lusignans. John refused, and Philip ordered John to appear before his court at Paris, John refused again, and Philip declared John's continental lands forfeit. Philip now had a justification for his proposed invasion of Normandy. In the wake of the declaration against John, Philip invested Arthur of Brittany with all of John's continental lands except Normandy, which the French king intended to keep for himself.

The fate of John's inheritance depended on the turn of events in Normandy. The duchy was the linchpin of the empire: if it fell, so too would John's control over all his continental domains. But why *did* Normandy fall in 1204? Undoubtedly the fact that the empire was composed of many peoples with many languages, and even more laws and customs, made it difficult for any one man to hold it together. So long as the King of France was ineffectual, it did not matter that the only thing that held these lands together was the person of the Angevin ruler. But when the King of France became strong, then the empire came under severe pressure. That pressure had been intense during Richard's absence, but his timely return and his undoubted qualities as ruler made it possible for him to regain the lands taken by King Philip of France. John, however, was not a man of such mettle.

Every medieval king had one or two instants in his reign when it became necessary to gird the loins and leap into the abyss to face valiant death or everlasting glory. The way in which a monarch handled these occasions determined the future direction of his reign (and, indeed, posterity's judgment on his success or failure). In 1204, John had one of those crucial moments and was found wanting. After what was a terrible year for his cause, and when everything seemed to be going against him, he returned to England in December 1203 to 'take counsel from his barons'. By the time he had made provision for his return, at the beginning of March 1204, Château-Gaillard had fallen to King Philip and the way was now open to Rouen, which in its turn capitulated on 24 June. Normandy was now in the possession of a French king for the first time since Rollo and his Viking followers had settled in the region in the second decade of the tenth century. John should have been in Normandy providing a focus for the campaign: Richard I would have been, and so too would Henry II. The fact that by March 1204 John had already spent a month longer in England than Richard spent in his kingdom in the last five years of his reign is the most damning indictment: King John was not where he was needed most.

The loss of Normandy changed the nature of Angevin rule. It meant that England, for the first time in fifty years, experienced the full and unflinching attention of its monarch. Fifty years was a long time in the development of the mechanisms of government. In 1154 the Exchequer lay in ruins, justice was mostly a local matter, sheriffs were yet to be fully brought under royal control, and the monarchy was weak. In 1204, the Crown was very powerful indeed. Not only did Angevin kings espouse a theory of monarchy that placed them just below God and well above all others (including the law), but they had also developed the means to make this power real and effective. With John permanently in England, determined to rule the realm in person, and certain, too, of his triumphant return to the Continent to re-possess his rightful inheritance, the pressures of Angevin monarchy began to increase.

The Angevin kings had long used England as an important source of money to finance their wars; but with the loss of their continental holdings, England and Ireland became the only available sources of revenue. The pressure was now on to raise the money required to sustain John's supporters and allies and to pay for the impending campaign of re-conquest. In the period between 1204 and 1211, by squeezing money out of his subjects through direct taxation and by taking full advantage of his rights of lordship, John quadrupled his annual takings at the Exchequer from roughly £22,000 to £83,000. To put these figures in context, in 1207, John had stored in his castle treasuries something between a sixth and a fifth of all the circulating money in England; and by 1213 that proportion had risen to almost a half of all circulating money. The effect of this policy of storing huge amounts of money was deflation in the English economy. The lack of money also made it even more difficult for men to meet their debts to the Crown. Times were very hard for the English ruling elite in the early years of the thirteenth century.

Despite Thomas Becket's martyrdom in the cause of the liberty of the English Church, Angevin kings still expected to appoint their own men to episcopal sees. It was a brave, perhaps even foolhardy, ecclesiastical electorate that stood against Henry II, Richard I or John in the appointment of its spiritual head. Nonetheless, in 1205, the monks of Christ Church, Canterbury, decided that they would elect as Archbishop of Canterbury their sub-prior Reginald, rather than the man John had insisted they elect, John de Gray. Realizing their precarious position, the group of monks went to Rome with Reginald to enlist Pope Innocent III's help. John mustered his supporters and sent a new delegation of monks from Canterbury. Innocent advised the monks to elect a compromise candidate, Stephen Langton. John, however, refused to allow Langton into England to take up his see, and a titanic struggle ensued.

In March 1208, Innocent III placed England under an interdict. There were to be no church services, except the baptism of infants and the confession and absolution of the dying. The interdict changed the normal rhythm of life, as the regular services of the Church came to a stop. John, however, failed to bow to the power of the interdict, and Innocent decided to excommunicate the king in November 1209. A sentence of excommunication was the most severe punishment the Church could place on one of its communicants. Spiritually, it meant certain damnation; but it was in the secular sphere that it had its most immediate impact, for it placed John outside of the protection the Church and it salved the consciences of those who might seek to depose him. But even this sanction did not bring John to heel; his reconciliation with the Church of Rome had to await baronial discontent at home and the threat of invasion by King Philip. In 1212 John's negotiations with the papacy became more earnest, and in May 1213 he agreed terms with Innocent: Stephen Langton was to be accepted into England, reparations were to be made for the moneys taken by John during the interdict, and England and Ireland would henceforth be held as fiefs of the pope. In July 1214, the interdict was finally lifted.

The irony of the date of this final reconciliation with the Church was that it came at the same time as John's fate on the Continent and in England was sealed. On 27 July 1214, on a field outside the Flemish town of Bouvines, the combined forces of John's allies were met and defeated by King Philip of France. John's intention had been to confront Philip on two fronts, one in the North, led by the German Emperor Otto of Brunswick, the other in the South, led by John. John, however, failed to moblize at the appropriate moment, and his allies were left to face defeat on their own. King John, though not present at the battle, returned to England to face concerted and coherent resistance to his rule.

There had been rebellions in the past, many of them so serious that they came close to unseating the ruling monarch; these earlier revolts had at their centre an alternative person to whom the rebels could look. In 1215, however, the rebellion coalesced around a document demanding governmental reform. That document was called Magna Carta, and it marked an extraordinary moment in English history. The men who mustered under the banner of reform had many grievances, but their overriding complaint was that they objected to the arbitrary exercise of royal rights to raise revenue. For years, the Crown had extracted from the English barons military service or payments in lieu (fines called 'scutage'). By 1215 many lords would tolerate no more demands on their material resources. In part, then, the rebellion of 1215 was one of the king's debtors. There was, however, a more important issue at stake, and that was the idea that English kings should be subject to the rule of law. Meanwhile, one of the most contentious political sections was clause 61, which provided for twenty-five barons to supervise the king's actions and to bring him and his officials to account should they break the terms of the charter. It was this so-called security clause that especially infringed the king's traditional, and rightful, freedom of action.

The 1215 version of Magna Carta quickly became a dead letter. Within weeks, Innocent III had annulled the charter and preparations were quickly made for civil war. Throughout the autumn of 1215, John mustered his armies, mostly comprised of foreign knights who were brought in at great expense. By December 1215 John was in a position to fight the rebels, and by Easter 1216 he had reduced them to a few isolated outposts and the city of London. In May, however, John received a severe setback: Prince Louis of France, son of Philip Augustus, arrived in England at the head of a powerful force. For a while it seemed as though John's cause was lost, as many of the more significant men who had remained loyal until this point deserted what they thought was a sinking ship. By the autumn of 1216 John was back on the offensive, and it was beginning to look as though he might be able to improve his fortunes. In the midst of this revival, however, John contracted dysentery and, on 18 October 1216, died at Newark Castle in Nottinghamshire. Rarely has a ruler of England chosen such an unfortunate moment to die; it is partly, indeed, this tragedy of timing that accounts for the extraordinarily vituperative criticism of John's regime that immediately set in, and which continued until very recently to dominate historical judgments of his reign.

HENRY III (1216-1272)

Henry III was just nine years old when his father, King John, died. He was the first of five children born to John and Isabella of Angoulême. As heir to his father's lands in the British Isles and on the Continent, he seemed to be confronted by impossible odds. Normandy was

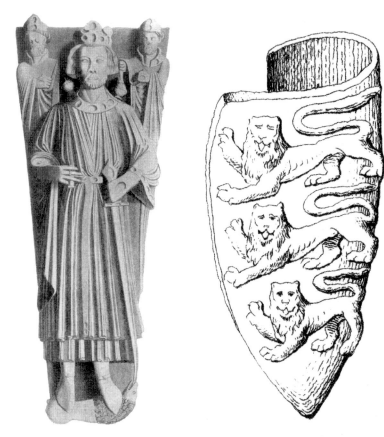

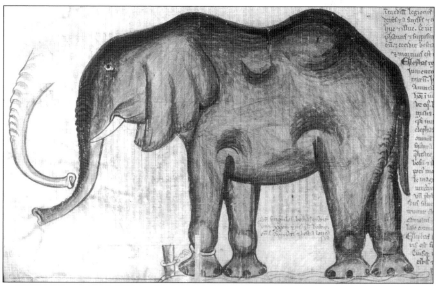

Clockwise from top left   56. Effigy of King John in Worcester Cathedral.
57. Coat of arms of King John.
58. Henry III's ten-year-old elephant, given to him by Louis IX of France in 1255. It lived in the
Tower of London.

lost, more than half England was under the control of the French, and royal finances were in a parlous state: to put it bluntly, Henry's government was broke, and had its back to the wall. It did, however, have one extremely important advantage: the boy Henry was not King John.

As an infant, Henry did not, of course, rule in his own right; he had appointed for him a guardian who ruled England as regent in his name. That man, until his retirement in 1219, was William Marshal, Earl of Pembroke. William was a true stalwart, a man for whom royal service was the very purpose of life. He had served, at the very highest levels, Kings Henry II, Richard I and John; and, despite having his loyalty tested to the very limit by John, he had never wavered. In return for this service, his royal masters had made William Marshal vastly rich. He was, moreover, a knight without peer in martial pursuits. In short, he was the perfect man to be Henry III's guardian.

One of William's first acts was to have Magna Carta reissued. The 1216 version of the charter was designed to bring the rebels to the negotiating table. It also attempted to include in its terms the wider community of the land. The reconciliation that it promised to bring about failed, at least in the first instance, because there were too many vested interests in keeping the civil war going. And with the might of the French monarchy (in the form of Prince Louis) present in England, the military situation was bleak. Only isolated victories served to bolster royalist moral. At Dover, for example, the justiciar Hubert de Burgh held out against the might of Louis's siege engines. Dover was 'the key of England', according to Hubert, and Louis needed to capture it; but despite inflicting heavy losses, at one point managing to undermine a part of the walls of the castle, Louis failed. As a near contemporary rather laconically put it, 'Louis departed to besiege smaller castles'.

The vital moment in the revival of Henry III's fortunes came on 20 May 1217, when William Marshal led the royalist forces against the part of Louis's army that was laying siege to Lincoln castle, still defended by the formidable woman, Nichola de Hay. It was a famous victory and proved a turning point in the war. In its wake, many rebels returned to the royalist cause and Louis was forced on the defensive. The final victory came as a result of a sea battle off Sandwich on 25 August. From this point onwards, events moved to a speedy settlement: Louis left England, suitably compensated for his losses, and the remaining rebels were reconciled with Henry. In November 1217, the peace process was sealed by a further reissue of Magna Carta. Relationships between the king and his magnates were now clearly defined, and limits were placed on the king's power. Magna Carta had taken root in the government of England. The restoration of royal government was, however, a long and arduous affair, taking many years and a change in regime to achieve. William Marshal retired in 1219, shortly before his death, to be replaced by the so-called triumvirate, consisting of the legate Pandulph, Bishop Peter des Roches of Winchester, and the justiciar and hero of Dover, Hubert de Burgh. The consolidation of royal power was only completed by the end of 1223, fully seven years after Henry III's accession.

Such a long period of minority government had profound effects on the attitudes of English men towards the running of government. No matter how powerful were the regent or the triumvirate, they still needed the consent of Great Councils (gatherings of the baronial and ecclesiastical elite of England) to their actions. Hence, when the minority government needed money to fund a campaign to defend Gascony in 1225, it had to turn to the Great Council for approval of a tax of a fifteenth on all movables in the land. The Great Council in its turn demanded that Magna Carta should be reissued. The 1225 issue of Magna Carta was specifically made to all the people of his realm, and it is this version of the charter that found its way into the statutes of England and the laws of Britain's former colonies, including the United States of America. By 1225, therefore, English kingship had radically changed: it was now widely accepted that there were certain limits to royal rule and that these limits were outlined in the charters. England now had a written constitution.

The problem with this written constitution was, however, that, with the 1215 security clause expunged, there was now no body that could ensure that its provisions were upheld. Once the king entered into his majority, he could attempt to rule much as his predecessors had done. There was one important thing, however, that Henry III could now not do without the assent of his subjects, and that was to levy taxes. As the concession for the fifteenth of 1225 had shown, English kings needed the consent of the Great Council to raise the extra revenue required for campaigning. And it was this need for more general taxation that laid the origins of the English Parliament.

Despite having been declared old enough to rule by Pope Honorius III in 1223, Henry did not begin the process of becoming master in his own house until 1232. Even then, he assumed power only as a result of a coup in which he and his Poitevin supporters ousted Hubert de Burgh. Despite a baronial reaction led by Richard Marshal in 1233, Henry III regained control in 1234 and ruled in his own right until the crisis of 1258. Remarkably, Henry seems to have governed during this period within the confines of Magna Carta. The king really did rule below both God *and* the law. So if Henry was such a model, charter-minded king, why did his reign experience crisis from 1258 to 1265? In order to answer this question, we have to look at Henry's personality and his continental interests.

Henry harboured ambitions to retake his patrimonial inheritance that his father lost in 1204. The expedition to Gascony in 1225 had succeeded in retaining this land for the king, but Poitou, Anjou and Normandy remained outside his control. Henry launched a campaign in Brittany in 1230, but this ended in failure. He turned, therefore, to diplomacy: if he could not beat the French king, Louis IX, in France, he would beat him elsewhere. Henry's marriage to Eleanor of Provence in 1236 was part of this strategy, since her family controlled the vital links between the Europe north and south of the Alps. And she was a well-connected lady, too, with uncles and cousins throughout Europe, whom Henry hoped to win over by gifts of large amounts of money. He also came to use these relations to help him govern England and to provide diplomatic links with other European rulers. These were the men whom contemporaries called the Savoyards.

The Savoyards were not the only foreign element Henry brought into his court. His mother, Isabella of Angoulême, had, in 1217, returned to her native land. In 1220, she married Hugh X of Lusignan. (She had been betrothed to Hugh's father before John had carried her off.) Isabella was an extraordinary woman: not only was she very fecund (she had five children by John and nine by Hugh), she was also a very active ruler of her lands. Two of the sons of Isabella and Hugh who came to England, William de Valence and Aymer de Lusignan, were given high office by their half-brother.

Henry's ambitions on the Continent were not limited to simply recapturing the family's lost lands. In 1255, he acquiesced to an invitation by the pope to send money and troops to the kingdom of Sicily in an attempt to install his son Edmund as its new king. Henry agreed to pay the pope over £90,000 (almost as much as Richard I's ransom) for the privilege of being allowed to try to conquer southern Italy; he agreed that he would personally be responsible if the campaign failed and that he would submit to excommunication if it did so; and he further agreed that, in the event of the failure of the expedition, the pope might put England under an

pres son regna henry le terz sun fiz. lvi. aunz. si
fuit de ix. aunz de age quant fuit corone. e en
ne fuit la bataylle de Euesham. ou fuit occys syr
ymund de munfort. e sun fiz henry. e syre hugh le d
enser e muz des barouns des cheualers de Engl
e puis mozust cel henri le roy e gist a Westmest

interdict. Furthermore, the conquest had to take place and the money paid to the pope within eighteen months of the date of the agreement. Henry's barons and prelates were appalled, and they told him so in no uncertain terms. In 1258, Henry III was an isolated monarch because of his imperial ambitions. It was in this context that he was constrained by Louis IX to agree to the terms of the Treaty of Paris of 1259, by which Henry agreed to give up his claims to all the traditional Norman and Angevin lands in northern and western France but to retain Aquitaine in return for paying feudal homage to the French Crown.

In the meantime, English politics had been plunged into crisis. A group of the king's courtiers, composed of English magnates, the Savoyards and a French man by the name of Simon de Montfort, turned on another group of courtiers, led by Henry III's Lusignan half-brothers. The first group had caught the mood of the moment, which was becoming increasingly nationalistic, and, because of their foreignness and the favour they had received at Henry's court, the Lusignans were on the receiving end of the hatred that engendered. Also on the receiving end of this chauvinism was the papacy, which was perceived as an intolerable intruder into English affairs. The Sicilian affair, moreover, as well as enhancing anti-papal feeling also confirmed what people increasingly had come to believe: that Henry III was not fit to govern.

1258 was, therefore, a palace revolution (led by men who had hitherto been close allies of the king) in which one faction ousted another from power; since the king heavily supported the loosing party, he lost power, too. At the Westminster Parliament in April 1258, the rebel magnates confronted their king, fully armed, it is said, and demanded the expulsion of those damnable foreigners, the Lusignans, and his acceptance of certain conditions. The fact that the revolt had at its heart a French man, Simon de Montfort, and that Henry III's Savoyard uncles were heavily involved in the upheaval, seems to have passed people by.

Simon de Montfort recognized that, if the reforms he and his associates proposed were to have any chance of going beyond the Westminster Parliament, he had to widen their appeal. Forming themselves into a commune (a sworn association bound in a common oath), into which they drew the king and his son Edward, they elicited support from the wider baronial community. The rebels drew up a list of what they saw as the shortcomings in Henry's rule, known as the Petition of the Barons. At Oxford in June and July, the commune drew up its most radical document, the Provisions of Oxford. It was here that they proposed the wholesale reorganization of the system of government in England. The Provisions established twenty-four men (twelve nominated by the king and twelve by the barons) who were to be responsible for the process of reform. In addition, the document named fifteen men (chosen by representatives of the twenty-four) who were to make up the King's Council (the body that would advise the king). Parliament, moreover, was to meet at fixed times throughout the year and not await the king's summons. The king's officers were to be appointed for year-long terms and were to be answerable for their actions to the king and the Council. In short, the Provisions of Oxford proposed the introduction of a constitutional monarchy.

Wondrous though it is to relate, these measures for the government of England actually lasted for two years. In the end, however, they foundered on Henry III's tactics and the disunity of the Council. In 1264 both parties, including the king and Simon de Montfort, agreed to submit their cases to the arbitration of King Louis IX of France at his court at Amiens. The result was the so-called 'Mise' (a settlement by agreement) of Amiens. In the context of the events of the last 110 years, the submission of an English king to the judgment

Opposite   59. Coronation of Henry III, 1216.

of a French king in order to settle a dispute with his English barons was an extraordinary event. Louis IX, on seeing the extent of the barons' demands, and seeing too the significance of the commune that effectively removed Henry III's power, judged in favour of his royal cousin: England was plunged into civil war.

After Amiens, events moved rapidly to Lewes where, on 14 May 1264, Simon de Montfort met and defeated the royal army. Henry III and his son Edward then holed themselves up in the nearby Lewes Priory, along with a large force of royalist knights. On the night of 14-15 May, negotiations between Simon and Edward took place that resulted in the Mise of Lewes. In this agreement, Henry promised to abide by the Provisions of Oxford, to expel foreigners and other traitors from the land, to forgive the rebel barons for their actions and to restore their lands. Henry further agreed that arbitrators should be established to look again at the Provisions and amend them as necessary, and that further men should be appointed to review the terms of the Mise of Amiens, which had proved so unsatisfactory to the rebels.

As a result of Lewes, the young Edward was in Montfort's hands, though Simon had to let the king go free. During the next sixteen months, Montfort governed England as a protectorate (an experiment that was not to be repeated until the seventeenth century), issuing his orders through the king. But despite all his attempts to legitimize his regime, he ruled in a way that was just as arbitrary as Henry had done. Simon's rule began to collapse once he lost control of Edward. On 18 May 1265, the heir to the throne made his escape and provided for the opponents of Simon's rule a figurehead and a military leader of proven ability. Edward's army trapped Simon and his followers at Evesham on 4 August 1265, where they defeated him, dismembered his body and had it displayed in its broken, gory form. With Simon's death, the period of the protectorate came to an end and opposition to Henry III lost its focus.

Between 1265 and 1270, Henry re-established himself so firmly on the throne that in that year he could afford to let his son and heir, Edward, go on crusade. By the time of his death, therefore, despite his many follies, Angevin monarchy was still strong, if slightly ameliorated by the events of the previous half-century. Henry III died on 16 November 1272 at the height of his power. He was buried close to the shrine of his special saint, Edward the Confessor, whose church at Westminster he had rebuilt: indeed, the gothic choir of Westminster Abbey remains to this day one of the major testaments to Henry's rather high-flown vision of divinely-appointed kingship. (Henry was probably the first king in England to claim the right to be able to heal scrofula simply by touching its victims or making the sign of the Cross over them.) Interestingly, however, he gave his heart to Fontevraud Abbey, deep in the traditional continental lands of his forebears, to lie with the bodies of Henry II, Eleanor of Aquitaine, Richard I, and Isabella of Angoulême.

4

THE HOUSE OF PLANTAGENET
1272-1399

W.M. ORMROD

It was the Angevin symbol of the sprig of broom, *planta genista*, that gave the House of Plantagenet its name; but while in origin the title might be supposed to date back to Henry II's assumption of the throne in 1154, it was not in fact used by the English royal family until the fifteenth century. To call the kings of England from 1272 to 1399 'Plantagenets' is therefore something of a fiction. There is, however, some justification for treating the rulers from Edward I to Richard II as a distinct group. First, although most of these kings attempted, in one way or another, to regain the French territories lost under King John and Henry III, they also gave much attention to the British Isles: this was the period in which the English monarchy not only clung tenaciously to its claims to the lordship of Ireland but also conquered Wales and attempted (and failed) to subdue the independent kingdom of Scots. It was during the late thirteenth and fourteenth centuries that the English monarchy therefore gave its first indications of a coherent ambition for the unification of the British Isles. Secondly, the loss of the overseas territories meant that, to pursue their wars, rulers were dependent on the resources of the kingdom of England, and had to enter into tax negotiations with their subjects through the newly evolving institution of Parliament. Finally, this was a period during which two kings – Edward II and Richard II – were forced to give up their thrones through their incompetence and tyranny. The latter of these depositions brought to an end the direct line of descent of the English crown and heralded the arrival of a new dynasty, the House of Lancaster.

EDWARD I (1272-1307)

The first king since the Norman Conquest to bear the Old English name of Edward was born on 17 June 1239, the first child of Henry III and Queen Eleanor of Provence. Edward and his younger brother, Edmund 'Crouchback', were both named in honour of Anglo-Saxon royal saints: Henry III's devotion to Edward the Confessor is well known, but he also had a strong attachment to the cult of St Edmund of East Anglia, centred at Bury St

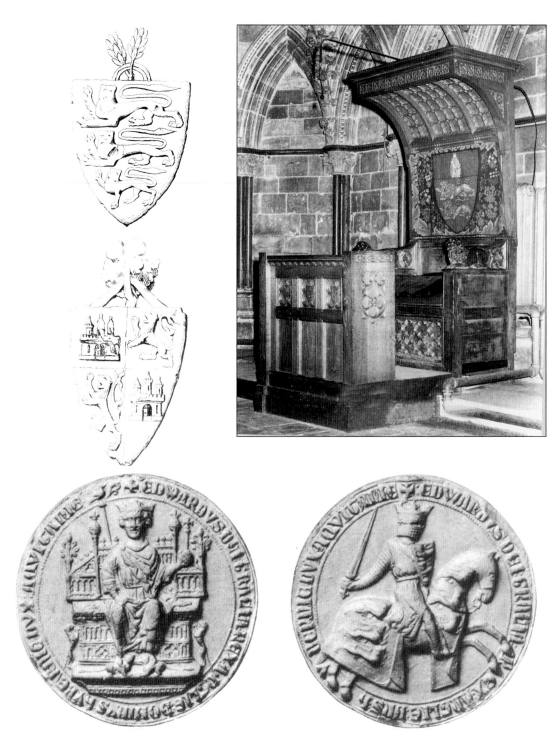

Clockwise from top left   61. The coat of arms of Edward I.
62. The throne of Edward I, Lincoln Cathedral Chapter House.
63. The seal of Edward I.
64. The coat of arms of Eleanor of Castile.

Edmunds. Edward was trained in the school of hard knocks: his emergence to manhood and public life coincided with Henry III's quarrel with the English barons, and Edward early earned himself a reputation not merely for the vigour and ruthlessness that would be a hallmark of his kingship but also for a tendency to shift his loyalties: he moved from being a supporter of Simon de Montfort's reform programme to being his bitterest enemy; and after the Battle of Evesham, in which the prince decisively defeated the opponents of the Crown, he was commemorated in verse as one who changed his allegiance in the same way that the leopard was then believed to change its spots.

It must have been something of a relief to the ageing Henry III when Prince Edward determined to join the Crusade launched by Louis IX of France. Edward arrived in the East only after Louis's death, and the expedition was already something of a spent force. But he remained in the Holy Land for the following two years, appealing periodically for further English support and being briefly reinforced with troops brought over by his brother Edmund, and managing to secure a truce with the Muslim leader, the powerful Sultan Baybars al-Bunduqdari, in May 1272. Edward's departure was then delayed by an attempt on his life by a Muslim assassin: a romantic tradition soon sprang up that the prince was saved from certain death when his wife, Eleanor of Castile (whom he had married in 1254), sucked the poison from his wound.

Whatever the truth of this story, Edward's recovery was certainly slow and his sojourn in the Holy Land consequently prolonged. It was shortly after he arrived in Sicily that he heard the news of his father's death in November 1272. Partly in response to the obvious delay that would now be experienced before the new king was crowned, the formal date of Edward's accession was fixed not, as previously, from the date of the coronation but from the day after the old king was alive and dead. With the new regime in England thus able to operate immediately in the new king's name, Edward evidently did not find it necessary to rush home. Instead, he stopped off en route at his main continental possession of Gascony, where he remained until his eventual arrival in England in August 1274.

England had been generally calm during the king's absence, but Edward's return heralded a widespread investigation of the infringements to royal rights that were thought to have occurred while direct royal supervision was lacking. These inquiries of 1274-5, extended to include general investigations of the activities of the Crown's agents in the localities, were drawn together into a set of records known as the Hundred Rolls (because the inquiries were held by calling together juries at the administrative level of the hundred). The Hundred Rolls represented the most ambitious and detailed survey of England since Domesday Book; this evidence, supplemented by a further set of inquiries in 1279, provided Edward's regime with the ammunition it needed to launch a major programme of reform. Over a period of some fifteen years, a tide of legislation flowed from the Crown, including the two Statutes of Westminster (1275 and 1290) and the Statute of Winchester (1285). Much of this reform was about providing new mechanisms of litigation and new methods of peacekeeping: the Statute of Winchester, for example, became the basis of the authority of the justices of the peace in the fourteenth century. But Edward I also sought through such official instruments to rebuild the authority of the Crown: the so-called *quo warranto* inquiries which had operated periodically since Henry III's time culminated in a formal statement of 1290 that all rights of jurisdiction exercised by the king's great subjects derived from (and were therefore depended on the continued favour of) the Crown.

The years before 1290 had equally dramatic consequences for the wider dominions of the English Crown. Edward's sojourn in Gascony in 1272-4 gave him a detailed understanding of the administration of his duchy of Aquitaine, and he revisited the region again in 1286-9, being the last English ruler to do so before the final loss of the lordship to France at the end of the Hundred Years War. Closer to home, he made a sustained attack on the parts of Wales beyond the Marches which had continued since the Norman Conquest to be ruled by quasi-independent native princes. The rise of the principality of Gwynedd during the thirteenth century and the assumption by its ruler, Llewelyn ap Gruffydd, of the title of Prince of Wales had been tolerated and legitimized by the regime of Henry III, and ratified in the Treaty of Montgomery of 1267. But when Llewelyn refused to do homage to Henry's successor, Edward asserted his right to take up arms against a rebellious vassal and launched a major campaign into the principality in 1277. At this stage it was not his intention to conquer Wales, but to subdue it: Llewelyn was forced to concede a large area of contested territory in Northwest Wales, but he was also released from the war indemnity initially imposed on him, allowed to retain his title, and even permitted to marry the daughter of Simon de Montfort (a controversial union that had partly caused his rebellion in the first place). It was only when Llewelyn's brother, Daffydd, led a rebellion against the English in 1282 that Edward determined on a policy of outright conquest. Proceeding along the coast of North Wales, Edward took Anglesey and forced Llewelyn back into Snowdonia. When Llewelyn attempted to move south, he was ambushed and killed in November 1282 at Irfon Bridge, near Builth. Prince Daffydd himself was captured in June 1283 and put to death as a traitor to the English Crown.

The most lasting memorial to the Edwardian Conquest of Wales is undoubtedly the great ring of castles built or rebuilt by Edward I – at Flint, Rhuddlan, Conwy, Beaumaris, Caernarfon, Criccieth, Harlech and Aberystwyth – to stand as strongholds and symbols of Plantagenet rule. But the Statute of Wales of 1284 also brought about huge changes, placing the former principality under the direct jurisdiction of the English Crown and English law. Further revolts in 1287 and 1294 were ruthlessly suppressed. In 1301 Edward chose to bestow on his eldest surviving son the title of Prince of Wales. Later tradition saw this either as an example of Edward's infamous duplicity (the story of a baby prince being presented to the Welsh as knowing no English is entirely bogus, but nevertheless revealing) or as an act of conciliation by an astute statesman. In reality, it simply confirmed the fact of military occupation and the now virtually unassailable exercise of English sovereignty.

Edward's experiences in Wales may have been formative in the development of a grander plan for the political unification of the British Isles. From 1290, his attention turned to Scotland. King Alexander III of Scotland had died in 1286, leaving as his heir an infant granddaughter, Margaret, the 'Maid of Norway'. By the Treaty of Birgham (1290), it was agreed that Margaret would marry the English king's son: although the two kingdoms would remain separate, they would thus be united, in the course of time, under a single ruler. The death of Margaret prevented the match and created a succession crisis, in which Edward I was invited to take the role of arbitrator. Seizing his opportunity, Edward decided in favour of John Balliol, but required him to pay liege homage to the English Crown in 1292. The Scottish Council of nobles objected to this unwelcome assertion of English suzerainty and resisted Edward's demands for military service. Edward's response was to enter the northern kingdom with force: in 1296 he marched via Edinburgh, Perth and Aberdeen as far north as Elgin, removed the Stone of Destiny from Scone, forced Balliol to resign his throne, and reduced the status of Scotland from a kingdom to a 'land' or dependent dominion of the English Crown. Thus far, it seemed that Scotland, like Wales, would inevitably bow to the sheer force of Edward's personality and the supposed invincibility of his military strategy.

This, however, was seriously to underestimate the strength and organization of the opposition to Edward's regime among the Scots. While Edward was in Flanders in 1297, a Scottish army under William Wallace imposed a decisive defeat on the Earl of Surrey at Stirling Bridge. The English responded quickly to the emergency: Edward returned home, moved his administration to York in the spring of 1298, and began what turned into a series of annual military campaigns lasting for the rest of his reign. Wallace was captured and executed – like Prince Daffydd, as a traitor to the English Crown – in 1305, and in the same year Edward I issued an ordinance for the government of Scotland, formally subordinating the territory to his own sovereignty, though allowing much of the existing system of administration and law to remain intact. But the emergence of a new contender for an independent Scottish throne, Robert Bruce, in 1306, revealed this settlement to be more theoretical than real, and left Edward's successor an embarrassing and bitter legacy of war that would have disastrous consequences for his own regime.

One of the reasons for Edward's failure in Scotland was that he could simply not afford the appropriate levels of investment, either in the hardware of castles or the software of garrisons. The crusade and the Welsh wars had already proved expensive, and the Scottish wars were a considerably greater drain on the resources of the Crown. Edward had exploited all his dominions to resource the conquest of Wales: in a remarkable programme of logistics, he had drawn money, manpower and victuals not just from the heartland of England but also from the outposts of his empire in Ireland and Gascony. It was therefore a very real, as well as a symbolic, loss to him when, in 1294, Philip IV of France occupied the duchy of Aquitaine and cut off the supply route to England. (The provision of Gascon wine to English aristocratic tables was also severely disrupted!) The excuse for Philip's confiscation of Aquitaine was Edward's refusal to attend the court of the King of France to answer for the deeds of various of his Gascon subjects who had become embroiled in a naval skirmish with sailors from Normandy. More generally and pertinently, however, Philip was aiming (just as Edward had done in Scotland) to test the rights and powers he claimed as feudal suzerain of Aquitaine under the terms of the Treaty of Paris established between Henry III and Louis IX in 1259.

Edward had never liked the terms agreed by his father, and had done his best to wriggle out of them both at the time and subsequent to his becoming king. He was also therefore angling for a fight by 1294, and saw it as a natural and rightful reaction that he should take up arms against an unreasonable feudal lord in defence of his duchy of Aquitaine. Nonetheless, the ensuing war took many people by surprise on both sides of the Channel, and even the kings cannot have predicted the scale either of the fighting or of the expense. Edward had to find over £750,000 to cover military expenditure (including lesser amounts spent on Wales and Scotland) during the French war of 1294-8, and royal finances simply could not take the strain: at the time of Edward's death in 1307, the Crown still owed in the region of £200,000. By 1298 both sides in the Anglo-French dispute recognized that a compromise needed to be reached: a truce was effected, and final terms were established in 1303. Although this settlement restored the status quo in relation to the feudal status of Aquitaine, it is worth noting that Edward I never renewed in person the homage that the English Crown continued to owe for the right to hold its lands in southern France.

The French war had a profound effect on domestic politics. Edward I's assertiveness had often been directed against, and tested on, members of the baronage, and many powerful men in England had personal grievances against the king. In 1297 there was a serious breach between the domestic administration and a group of disaffected lords led by the Earls of Hereford and Norfolk. Resurrecting some of the techniques of 1258-9, the opposition presented its grievances

Clockwise from top   65. A medieval king directing building work.
66. Prince Llewelyn being decapitated.
67. Persecution of the Jews.

in the name of the 'community of the land' and challenged directly the Crown's right to use a state of emergency to override the normal conventions of free negotiation over military service and taxation. Edward I sought to extricate himself from the situation by embarking for the Continent and claiming that he had never received a copy of the barons' complaints; but the emergency brought on by the English defeat at Stirling Bridge forced the administration to come to terms with the malcontents, and Edward eventually gave his consent to a legislative act that confirmed Magna Carta and additional clauses that defined and limited the Crown's rights to tax its subjects. However, the 'Confirmation of the Charters' of 1297 was greatly resented by the king, and in 1305 he conspired with a new pope, Clement V (one of his own Gascon subjects, and a former royal clerk) to release him from the sentence of excommunication set down for breaches of this law, thus allowing the way for the legislation to be ignored and annulled. This caused a good deal of discontent among the political community in England that rose to the surface again after the old king's death.

The last decade of the reign was therefore one in which Edward I turned from a dynamic and charismatic leader into an increasingly defensive and mistrusted old man. The change in the character of the regime is nicely demonstrated by Edward's use of Parliament. His reign is acknowledged to have been formative in the development of this institution, and during the period down to the 1290s its importance and popularity can be accounted for in terms of the special responsibility that Edward gave it as a court for the resolution of private grievances. By encouraging his subjects to use Parliament as a forum in which to petition for the exercise of royal grace in the righting of wrongs and the dispensation of patronage, and by guaranteeing that all petitions presented in Parliament would be answered (though not, of necessity, always favourably) before the relevant session ended, the king turned Parliament from a baronial 'talking shop' into an institution of relevance and utility to a large number and wide range of his subjects. The process of private petitioning in Parliament coincided with the regular summons of representatives of the shires and towns to attend at least those assemblies in which the Crown planned to negotiate taxes; these men often acted on behalf of their constituents in carrying petitions to Parliament. One consequence of this emphasis on petitioning, however, was that the baronage also began to see Parliament as a place in which their collective concerns – and those of the 'community of the land' – could be articulated and resolved. In 1300, the king actually chose not to collect a tax granted in Parliament because it was seen to bind him to the concessions that he had allowed in the so-called 'Articles upon the Charters'; and in subsequent years he tended to rely on the exploitation of his feudal rights rather than submit to the process of political negotiation over extraordinary subsidies in Parliament. An institution created very largely in his image had already begun to show its potential as a source of criticism and reform, and Edward I, who hated opposition of any kind, clearly did not like the trend.

This intolerance of nonconformity with the royal will was demonstrated at many levels through Edward's life. The chroniclers reported a number of acrimonious exchanges between Edward and his great men: in 1297, for example, he threatened to hang the Earl of Norfolk unless the latter obeyed the king's command to serve in the army being sent to Flanders. This violent temper could also be vented on members of the royal family: Edward threw his daughter Elizabeth's coronet into the fireplace during one domestic altercation, and is supposed to have torn out handfuls of his son's hair in his fury at the prince's relationship with Piers Gaveston. Edward could also, however, be notably sentimental. Eleanor of Castile, who bore him at least fifteen children, was a significant influence in his life: even if we acknowledge that he turned her death in 1290 into something of a public relations exercise, it is difficult to resist the sincerity of the king's statement that he had loved her in life, and would not cease to love her in death. Certainly, the Eleanor Crosses which he erected to mark the places where her body rested on its final journey from Harby in Nottinghamshire to London had an enduring impact on popular perceptions of the queen, turning her reputation from that of a rather grasping and spiteful woman into a quasi-saint. Edward cannot have enjoyed quite the same companionship with his second wife, Margaret of France, who was only about twenty at the time of her marriage to the sixty-year-old king in 1300. But he showed some attention for her welfare and comfort, no doubt grateful that his dwindling supply of sons (all but one of the boys born of the first marriage died in childhood) was re-stocked when two princes, Thomas and Edmund, were born of this match.

Edward I has always enjoyed a high reputation among historians of England. Dubbed the 'English Justinian' in the seventeenth century, he is still regarded as having had a formative influence on the institutions and constitution of the English State. Elsewhere his reputation is more controversial: in Wales and Scotland, not surprisingly, he is sometimes still viewed as a public enemy. Indeed, the hackneyed nickname 'Hammer of the Scots' seems rather inappropriate in light of the subsequent failure of his attempt to take over sovereignty of the northern kingdom. At his death, on 7 July 1307 (an event that occurred while he was undertaking yet another campaign against the Scots), there were many people even in England who probably breathed a sign of relief at the passing of such a difficult man and challenging ruler. But there were also those who – either because they had been taken in by the Edwardian myth-making machine, or out of genuine admiration for the achievements of the man – commemorated his passing with a sense of sadness and pride. Edward was one of the first English kings consciously to identify himself with the mythical (though, for contemporaries, historical) figure of Arthur: in 1278, he and Queen Eleanor had even attended a fantastical ceremony at Glastonbury in which the putative remains of Arthur and Guinevere were re-buried before the high altar of the abbey church. The idea that Edward was a kind of reincarnated Arthur bit deep into the public consciousness, and created a peculiarly potent form of royal propaganda utilized by a number of his successors. In the catalogue of royal worthies successively re-written during the succeeding generations, Edward's name was a constant.

EDWARD II (1307-1327)

For those inclined to the view that childhood experience is formative in the development of the adult character, the example of Edward II provides an instructive, not to say tragic, case study. Edward was in fact the youngest of the fifteen (or more) children born to Edward I and Queen Eleanor. His one surviving older brother, Alphonso, who for ten years was heir apparent to the throne, died within a few months of Edward's birth, which occurred on 25 April 1284. (How England might have coped with a ruler called Alphonso is one of the many unknowns of history.) Since the young Prince Edward was rapidly provided with his own independent household, it seems that he spent comparatively little time either with his parents or with his five surviving sisters, Eleanor, Joan, Margaret, Mary and Elizabeth, the oldest of whom was in any case already twenty-five when he was born. The death of his mother when the prince was only six (followed hard upon by that of his grandmother, Eleanor of Provence, in 1291), and the preoccupation of his father in the years that followed with the wars in Scotland and France, must have made the young Edward peculiarly lacking (even by royal standards) in the emotional security that is today regarded as desirable for the psychological and social development of the young person.

68. Seal and counterseal of Margaret of France, second wife of Edward I.
69. Edward II, Edward III and the Black Prince as benefactors of St Albans.

It is not perhaps surprising, then, that when the prince was offered affection, he accepted it with an unquestioning eagerness. Edward I's marriage to Queen Margaret in 1299 – a woman much closer in years to her new step-son than to her husband – may have introduced a significant new influence upon the boy: we know that Margaret remained in England after Edward I's death and seems to have remained on good terms with the new king. But a much more powerful, and altogether more problematic, friendship arose between the young Edward and Piers Gaveston, the son of a Gascon lord who had made his way to England in search of patronage. In the Parliament held at Carlisle shortly before Edward I's death in 1307, the old king quarrelled publicly with his son over the latter's relationship with Gaveston. Prince Edward had the temerity to ask that Gaveston be invested either with the county of Ponthieu (an English royal possession in northern France) or the earldom of Cornwall (a title which, although not yet automatically held by the heir to the throne, was generally regarded as exclusive to members of the royal family). Edward I's answer to the problem was simply to send Gaveston to the Continent: until the old king's death, there was no prospect that his son's harmful friendship could be renewed.

It is hardly surprising, then, that one of the first acts undertaken by Edward II on his assumption of the throne later in 1307 was to recall Gaveston from exile and to invest him as Earl of Cornwall. The new king's coronation was deliberately delayed until after his wedding in 1308 to Princess Isabella, daughter of Philip IV of France (and niece of Queen Margaret). Yet at the coronation banquet, Gaveston appeared to usurp the new queen's rightful place alongside her husband. Isabella was only about twelve at the time – the minimum age set for the consummation of marriage – and those of her relatives present at the occasion were alarmed at her apparent vulnerability and potential predicament. Since the legalisation of homosexuality in the 1960s, many historians have stated explicitly what could previously only be implied: that Edward II and Piers Gaveston expressed their relationship physically as well as emotionally. But the matter is still contested. The contemporary chroniclers' statements that Edward *loved* Gaveston can, if one chooses, be read as the expression of that intensely emotional but entirely platonic relationship between members of the same sex considered perfectly 'normal' before the advent of Freudian psychoanalysis. One recent interpretation, indeed, casts the friendship in a medieval tradition of 'adoptive brotherhood' and sees the contemporary hostility to Gaveston as arising not from contempt for the act of sodomy but from a real political concern that Edward was seeking to make Piers England's 'second king'. Beyond these ambiguities, one thing is clear: that Gaveston was seen by the political elite as a problem that could not be tolerated and had to be removed.

Calls for Gaveston's return into exile therefore proved one of the political constants of the early years of Edward II's reign. When these were coupled with demands for administrative reform and growing anxiety over the king's inadequacy in responding to the emergency in Scotland, they proved impossible to resist. Edward I's annulment of the Confirmation of the Charters had generated a loss of faith in the Crown's commitment to good governance. Meanwhile, the investiture of Robert Bruce as independent King of Scots in 1306, and his immediate challenge to the English on both sides of the northern border, had created an urgent need for military action to which Edward II seemed notably deaf: there were no royal expeditions to Scotland between 1307 and 1310, and the winter campaign of 1310-11 simply highlighted domestic political problems, as a number of the magnates excused themselves or refused to serve. In 1311 a commission appointed by the Crown to produce a programme of reform issued the so-called New Ordinances, an elaborate system of checks and balances designed to impose restrictions on the king's prerogative and requiring him to seek consent to a range of activities – including the dispensation of major patronage, the declaration of war and the conclusion of peace – from the baronage formally assembled in Parliament. The most relevant clause of the Ordinances, and the one in which most of the nobility were really interested, was that demanding (once again) the exile of Gaveston. Edward II had little choice but to accept the Ordinances and to deny himself access to the man whom he trusted above all others. But in 1312, Edward attempted to recover the initiative and ordered Gaveston to return to England. Alarmed and angered, a number of the barons marched upon Scarborough in Yorkshire, where Gaveston had taken up residence at the castle in the hope of withstanding a siege. He was constrained to surrender and was taken southwards to a mock trial at Warwick Castle and to a traitor's death, by decapitation, at Blacklow.

The president of the Ordainers, and the ringleader in the ambush and murder of Gaveston, was none other than the king's first cousin, Thomas, Earl of Lancaster. The death of Piers created an implacable hostility between the royal relatives, compounded by Lancaster's notoriously stubborn efforts to have the Ordinances properly observed long after their central purpose had been fulfilled. Lancaster was a reluctant and not altogether able political leader, and after 1312 a number of his erstwhile supporters, encouraged by signs of good intent on the king's part, returned to court and to royal service. The rallying of allies did little, however, to assist Edward against the Scots: the campaign of 1314 resulted in unmitigated disaster at Bannockburn, where, for the first time since Edward I had taken charge of the war in 1298, an English army was roundly defeated in pitched battle. Although Bannockburn had comparatively little strategic significance, its effect on morale was very considerable. The Scots saw it as affirmation of divine favour on Robert Bruce, and undertook a series of negotiations to secure papal recognition of his kingship culminating in the celebrated Declaration of Arbroath of 1320. The English, meanwhile, saw Bannockburn as the beginning of the end: although Edward II upheld his father's policy of refusing to acknowledge Bruce's kingship, he not only made a truce with the Scots in 1323 but also subsequently reneged on virtually all his responsibilities to defend the North of England from continued cross–border raids: the material and psychological damage suffered by his subjects during the Scottish incursions of the 1310s and 1320s had a fundamentally negative impact on Edward II's reputation as protector of his people.

In spite of the stronger sense of loyalty provoked among at least some of the baronage by the emergency following the defeat at Bannockburn, the later 1310s produced few signs of lasting political reconciliation in England. Indeed, by 1320 there were alarming signs that the Gaveston phenomenon was about to be resurrected, this time in the persons of Edward II's new favourites, the father-and-son team of the two Hugh Despensers. The younger Hugh became royal chamberlain in 1318, thus controlling access to the physical presence of the king and, in effect, determining the ability of the king's subjects – even, indeed, of his wife – to secure patronage and influence policy. The young Hugh Despenser married one of the co-heiresses of the Earl of Gloucester (who had died at Bannockburn) and through her built up a large landed interest in the Welsh Marches based on the lordship of Glamorgan: the great stronghold of Caerphilly stands today as testimony to Hugh's extraordinary wealth and power. In July 1321, in a conscious reiteration of their action against Gaveston, the barons demanded the exile of the Despensers. And when Hugh the younger returned to the king's side a few months later, the stage was set not merely for an organized vendetta against the king's favourites, but for outright civil war.

In November 1321 both the king and Thomas of Lancaster prepared themselves for military action. The dispute with the Despensers ranged widely over the country: the first signs of armed conflict arose at Leeds Castle in Kent, and during the winter of 1321-2 the

king and his favourites undertook a sustained – and successful – campaign to root out opposition in the West Country and South Wales. Support for Lancaster was already waning, and
Edward II was careful to advertise the fact that his cousin was supposedly negotiating with
the Scots for assistance against the English Crown – an accusation of treachery that seriously
damaged the earl's political reputation. When Lancaster tried to move northwards, possibly
to lay in for a siege at his fortress of Dunstanburgh in Northumberland, he was ambushed
at Boroughbridge, north of York, on 16 March 1322. Six days later, Thomas of Lancaster was
declared a traitor and put to death at his own castle of Pontefract.

The execution of the king's cousin marked the start of an extraordinary programme of
vengeance by the Crown against its erstwhile enemies, and the ferocious and arbitrary nature
of the ensuing bloodbath had a profound impact on political society. Six of Lancaster's major
supporters were put to death at York on 23 March. Following a Parliament held in that city
in May 1322, the king formally annulled the Ordinances and thus symbolically restored
himself to full power. Needless to say, the main beneficiaries of the redistribution of honours
following the collapse of Lancaster's opposition were the Despensers themselves. Hugh the
elder became Earl of Winchester, while his son amassed both an enormous landed estate and
a huge accumulation of liquid wealth.

The executions following the Battle of Boroughbridge had left the remaining noble families
feeling cowed and vulnerable, and it was not easy to organize effective resistance to the
Despensers: Parliament, which Lancaster and his allies had seen as a controlling force upon the
Crown, counted for little during the arbitrary regime of the mid-1320s. In the end, it was the
queen herself who would take the lead in opposition. Isabella had been in no position to
influence politics during the ascendancy of Gaveston. By the 1320s, however, she had grown to
womanhood and had accomplished her dynastic responsibility by bearing her husband at least
four children, the eldest of whom, Prince Edward (born in 1312), was emerging into adoles-
cence. Isabella was clearly a woman of intelligence and ambition who, even without the problem
of her husband's favourites (not to mention his sexuality), would probably have felt somewhat
thwarted by his lack of personal dynamism and political acumen. This sense of frustration may
have been intensified by the fact that the queen's father, Philip IV of France, had intended her
marriage as a means of bringing the Plantagenets into a closer, and more dependent, relationship
with the French royal house: Isabella was apparently encouraged to believe that her position as
a Princess of France was just as important as that of Queen of England.

During the middle years of her husband's reign, Isabella's influence with her birth family had
proved most useful as a means of promoting peace between England and France. But when war
broke out in 1324 on the pretext of a squabble over jurisdiction in the Agenais (part of the
territory claimed by the English as incorporated into the duchy of Aquitaine under the terms of
the peace settlements of 1259 and 1303), her influence in her adopted land was called into
question, and she even had to suffer the embarrassment of being treated as an alien and having
her lands sequestered for the greater security of her husband's realm. It is not surprising that
when, in the spring of 1325, she was offered the opportunity to visit her brother, Charles IV, and
negotiate a settlement to the (rather half-hearted) war, the queen seized the opportunity to
escape from an intolerable personal predicament.

The peace terms worked out as a result of Isabella's embassy involved Edward II performing
liege homage to his French brother-in-law for the lands he held beyond the Channel. It was the
Despensers themselves who, possibly anxious for the king's personal security, seem to have
worked out a compromise deal by suggesting that his heir should perform the required homage

instead. But by despatching the thirteenth-year-old Prince Edward to the French court, Edward II blundered badly. Isabella made it clear that neither she nor her son would return to England until the Despensers were removed from power. It was during her time in France that Isabella entered a liaison with Roger Mortimer, one of the disaffected English nobles who had fled to the Continent following the Battle of Boroughbridge. There is little doubt that their relationship was more than a political vehicle: Isabella seems to have found in Mortimer the physical and emotional passion that was lacking in her husband. Both, however, were also driven by ambition, and soon hatched a plot to invade England, with the presumed intention of overthrowing the Despensers by armed force.

Isabella and Mortimer landed on the coast of Essex on 24 September 1326 with a small band including, vitally, the young Prince Edward. They made their way to London, which was known to be hostile to the king, and distributed a manifesto calling for the removal of the Despensers from the king's company. Edward II had already taken fright and fled from the capital, seeking refuge in the younger Despenser's lordship of Glamorgan. There was an alarming collapse of public order in London, where the emergency created opportunities for mindless acts of violence and looting: the Bishop of Exeter, one of the king's adherents, was dragged from his horse and murdered by an angry mob. So far, however, there was no public statement that the king himself was under threat: the rebellion mounted by the queen and her lover was still theoretically loyal to his regime. When they arrived at Bristol, Isabella's party had Prince Edward proclaimed keeper of the realm, on the grounds that the king had left, presumed to be en route for Ireland. Although the action was of dubious legality, it gave the queen's party the legitimacy they needed to assume the government of the realm. The elder Despenser surrendered and was declared a traitor and executed; and during the following months the remainder of the king's party were captured and put to death, with the younger Despenser being subjected to a particularly detailed (and inventive) series of accusations in his judgment of treason at Hereford on 24 November.

By this stage, the king himself was also at the mercy of the rebels. Edward had escaped as far as Neath, hoping to get to Ireland where he perceived himself to have supporters. For some reason, however, he backtracked, and was ambushed at Llantrisant in November, presumably while trying to make his way to Caerphilly Castle. While Parliament sat at Westminster in January 1327, a deputation claiming to act in the name of the estates of the realm visited Edward II in captivity at Kenilworth, and constrained him to abdicate the throne in favour of his eldest son, whose reign was formally announced on 25 January. The anomaly of the former king's position was self-evident, and it was no particular surprise when his premature death was announced as having taken place at his prison of Berkeley on 21 September 1327. While the inevitable – and fanciful – tales circulated about his survival, the new regime gave them little credence, and the presence of the royal family at the ex-king's funeral at Gloucester Abbey, together with the erection of a handsome tomb in his memory, effectively put an end to the possibility of a future pretender.

Edward II remains an enigma. Contemporaries tried to explain his inadequacies as king by pointing out the eccentricities of his behaviour. Rather than indulging in courtly pastimes, he was said to enjoy unsophisticated sports such as swimming and rowing and the rustic crafts of hedging and ditching. His death was supposed to have been brought about by a parody of the sin of sodomy: a hot poker was forced into his anus. Most of this comment and scandal mongering, however, occurred after Edward's death, and may have been as much a justification of events as a reasoned statement of reality. In his own time, the king was known as a tall, athletic

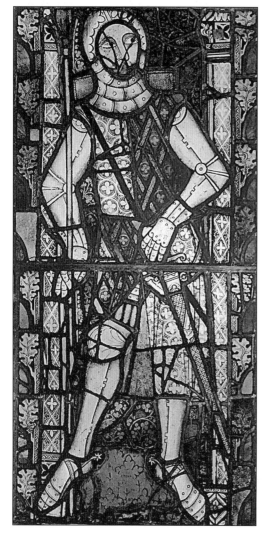

Clockwise from top   70. Practice at the archery butts.
71. Coat of arms of Isabella of France, Queen of Edward II.
72. Coat of arms of Edward II.
73. Hugh Despenser the Younger, from a window in the clerestory of Tewkesbury Abbey, *c.*1334.

man, whose good looks were seen as a mark of divine favour. Modern scholars have pointed out that, in addition to his four children by Isabella, he had at least one illegitimate son – though whether this tells us anything in itself about his sexuality is dubious. It is somewhat ironic that the emphasis placed by Edward's immediate successors on the legitimacy of his monarchy actually had the effect of changing Queen Isabella's reputation from that of saviour to that of traitor: her Frenchness, her adultery, and her transgression of the traditional submissiveness of wives, combined to turn her into a controversial and sometimes contemptuous figure.

EDWARD III (1327-1377)

The future Edward III was born at Windsor on 13 November 1312, the first child of Edward II and Queen Isabella. The baby boy became Earl of Chester by right of his birth, but he was never given the title earlier created for his own father, that of Prince of Wales. Edward's childhood is poorly documented: the only thing clear is that, within months of his birth, he was separated from both his parents and given his own household, which moved around the country quite independently of those of the king and queen. What would now be regarded as an extraordinary and most unfortunate isolation was at least mitigated by the fact that Edward's younger brother, John of Eltham, and his sisters, Joan and Eleanor, spent at least some of their own childhood in his company. It may not be a coincidence that, whereas Edward had only rather formal – and at times strained – relations with his father and mother, he showed some concern and affection for his siblings: the royal household accounts show that the then king suffered bad dreams at the news of the premature death of Prince John in 1336.

Edward of Windsor entered public life during the negotiations for an Anglo-French peace at the end of the War of 1324-5. Edward II agreed that the English ruler should give homage to the King of France for his lands in Aquitaine, but decided to have Prince Edward perform that homage on his behalf in order to avoid the demeaning spectacle of an anointed King of England doing obeisance to a French monarch. In 1325 Queen Isabella was therefore charged to take the young prince to Paris for the performance of the necessary ceremonies. Once there, however, Isabella refused to return home and, recognizing that her son was a potential key to the kingdom of England, prevented his own departure too: Edward II wrote a number of letters to his wife and son expressing his vexation at their delay in coming back to England. The king's concern was compounded by the fact that Isabella was clearly using Prince Edward as a bargaining counter to gain continental allies: whereas Edward II had concentrated on the idea of making a marriage alliance with one of the Spanish kingdoms, Queen Isabella turned her attention to the Netherlandish county of Hainault, and promised that her son would marry Philippa, daughter of Count William, in return for military aid against her estranged husband. A troop of Hainaulters was thus prominent among the forces that accompanied Isabella and her lover, Roger Mortimer, on their arrival in England in 1326. Prince Edward was with them too, and was kept close by throughout the events that followed: his father's flight into the Welsh Marches allowed Isabella an excuse to proclaim her son keeper of the realm, and the capture of Edward II and his forced abdication of the throne permitted the announcement of the formal succession of Edward III in January 1327.

By artificially accelerating the natural order of the succession, Isabella and Mortimer had brought to the throne a youth of fourteen years. There was no rule in medieval England as to the age at which a boy-king might take up power: the convention that the tenants-in-chief of the Crown had to wait until they were twenty-one to assume their estates did not apply to the kingdom itself. The solution of an interregnum and formal regency, as worked out during the minority of Henry III, was deemed unsuitable, and the fiction was maintained that the new king was in charge of his own regime. In reality, however, power was exercised by the queen and her lover, whose extraordinarily self-serving regime ironically proved as divisive and dangerous as the one it had overthrown. They rushed to secure diplomatic settlements both with France and with Scotland, and in the process agreed to terms that even Edward II would have found intolerable: the Treaty of Edinburgh of 1328 acknowledged, for the first time since 1296, that Scotland was an independent kingdom with its own ruler. The elevation of Roger Mortimer to the unprecedented tile of Earl of March in 1328, and the squandering by the queen of the war reparations paid by the Scots under the terms of 1328, indicated that Isabella and her lover were both selfish and reckless in their stewardship of royal government.

The young king had good cause to feel personally frustrated, as well as publicly humiliated, by his mother and her paramour. His new young wife, Philippa, whom he married at York in 1328, was denied coronation until her first pregnancy necessitated her elevation to full queenly status in 1330. In the same year Edward felt sufficiently beleaguered that he wrote to the pope to say that the only royal messages sent to the holy see that would actually express his own wishes would be those bearing the address *pater sancte* (holy father) written in the king's own hand. (It is this correspondence that thus provides us with the earliest extant example of English royal handwriting.) Finally, the young king's chance came on the night of 19 October 1330, when he and a group of close friends ambushed Mortimer at Nottingham Castle. The following day the king formally announced his assumption of full power. In an act carefully designed to assure the nobility of his good intent towards them, Edward had his mother's lover declared guilty of treason not in some kangaroo court but in Parliament. As for Isabella, she was accorded the respect due to a dowager queen: the tradition that Edward III imprisoned her at Castle Rising in Norfolk is unfounded, and this was merely one of the residences she inhabited during a long period of retirement ending with her death in 1358.

Edward III was a man of energy and conviction who, for all his supposed compromises to the power of the English throne, actively pursued two policies during a long a productive reign. First, he was determined to restore the prestige of the monarchy after the political disasters of the 1320s. The reputation of the throne had rarely been lower than in 1330, and the new king was aware that the only effective way of recovering security and confidence was through an active accommodation with the great men of his realm. This vision also partly explains Edward's second main policy: the pursuit of war in Scotland and France. In 1332 a group of northern magnates, frustrated at the loss of lands in Lowland Scotland under the terms of the treaty of 1328, took up arms in support of Edward Balliol, the son of Edward I's earlier nominee for the throne of Scotland. In 1333 Edward III agreed to provide them with official support, and won a resounding victory at Halidon Hill. The infant David II, who had succeeded Robert Bruce in 1329, was forced to flee to France, and Edward Balliol was installed as King of Scots and required to perform liege homage to the King of England.

Throughout the mid-1330s, Edward III gave much time and energy to the establishment of the Balliol monarchy. But by 1336 it was apparent that this intervention was also putting considerable strain on Anglo-French relations. Philip VI of France insisted that any resolution to the long-standing diplomatic dispute over the Plantagenet possessions on the Continent would have to involve the recognition of the Bruce family as legitimate rulers of Scotland. Edward was probably keen for a fight, and in March 1337 he created six new earls and the first English duke (his eldest son, Prince Edward, Duke of Cornwall) as a publicly declared re-

Clockwise from top   74. A king handing a writ to a messenger.
75. Edward III performs homage to King Philip VI of France.
76. The Black Prince defeats John II of France at Poitiers.
77. David II of Scotland with Edward III.

stocking of the English aristocracy in preparation for war. While a number of the older nobility were at best ambivalent about another military commitment beyond the Channel, Edward's success in engaging the military class in his personal enterprise looked set to generate rich dividends for the Crown.

The opening stages of what was later dubbed the Hundred Years War were, in the event, a problem for Edward. His programme of purchasing alliances with the rulers of the Low Countries and Germany committed England to astonishingly high levels of taxation. The only result of the long period of 'phony war' between 1337 and 1340 was Edward's assumption, early in 1340, of the title of King of France. There was some justification for the move. His mother's brother, the Capetian Charles IV, had died without a direct heir in 1328, and the French throne had passed to the latter's Valois cousin, Philip VI. Edward could claim to be closer to the direct line of Capetian succession, and the later notion that descent through the female line debarred him (the Salic Law) was not considered an impediment at the time. But it was also well understood in England that Edward took the new title for tactical reasons, in order to secure the alliance of the Flemish, who were under the jurisdiction of the throne of France. As a result, when the title was announced in England, Parliament promptly required the king to confirm that the two realms over which he now claimed to rule would be kept strictly separated, and that the English would never be subject to him or his successors in their capacity as Kings of France. Within a few months, indeed, Edward's virtual bankruptcy forced him into a humiliating truce. When he returned to England at the end of 1340 he was in no mood to apologize, and instead attempted to punish his chief adviser, John Stratford, Archbishop of Canterbury, for what the king saw as the negligence of the home administration. The nobles took fright at the arbitrary manner in which Edward proceeded, and in 1341 required Edward to promise that the Lords temporal and spiritual should have the right to free trial before their peers in Parliament. For a short while, Edward's policy of reconciliation and reconstruction appeared to be ruined.

In the event, the crisis of 1340-1 proved less significant than some had hoped. Stratford was marginalized, and a new group of loyal ministers, led by William Edington, Bishop of Winchester, took over the offices of government. The renewal of the Scottish and French wars in the 1340s also provided the nobles with new opportunities for glory and gain. While the country remained concerned about the burden of the king's demands for money and manpower, there was little that could be done in practice to challenge the king's right to expect support for the pursuit of his claims in France. In 1346-7, three great victories demonstrated God's evident blessing on Edward. At Neville's Cross, near Durham, David II of Scotland was defeated and captured. Meanwhile, Edward's own campaign through northern France had already generated his spectacular victory over Philip VI at Crécy, and the English army went on to take the town of Calais, after a long siege, in the summer of 1347. Edward returned home heavy with honours and celebrated his success in a round of high-profile pilgrimages and tournaments culminating in the foundation of the Order of the Garter at a celebration held in Windsor Castle in 1348.

The outbreak of the Black Death in 1348-9 seemed at first to be a great crisis for the English Crown: the war had to be suspended, and the king and royal family had to flee the capital to avoid an epidemic that may have killed as much as forty per cent of England's population. In fact, the plague had the effect of drawing together the political classes in defence of their proprietary rights, and they naturally looked to the Crown to support them in restoring normality. The result was the issuing of new laws that attempted to prevent agricultural workers and artisans from taking advantage of the labour shortage to demand higher wages, and the rapid

78. Shield with arms of Edward III from the tomb of the Black Prince in
Canterbury Cathedral.

Clockwise from top left   79. Edward III grants Aquitaine to the Black Prince.
80. The coat of arms of Edward III.
81. Edward III and his family. Left to right: Thomas of Woodstock, Duke of Gloucester; Edward
III; Philippa of Hainault; Edward, the Black Prince. This drawing was traced from wall paintings
discovered accidentally in 1800 behind a coating of wood panelling in St Stephen's Chapel,
Westminster, and which were walled up again immediately after copies and tracings had been
made. The paintings were lost in the fire that consumed Westminster Palace in 1834.

emergence of a new magistracy, the justices of the peace, to enforce this and other economic legislation. As a result, Edward found that the elite strongly supported his own plans for the renewal of the French war, and Parliament continued to grant regular taxes for the support of the enterprise in France. Prince Edward, who had already won renown for the bravery he showed on the field of Crécy, undertook a major expedition through southern France in 1355 and met with the forces of John II (the son and successor of Philip VI) at Poitiers in 1356. Once again, the French suffered a humiliating defeat; and on this occasion both their king and a large a number of his senior commanders were taken prisoner. John II was treated as an honoured guest by Edward III when the prince brought him back to England; but the absence of its head was a disaster for the Valois government, and in 1358 there was a major outbreak of disorder in northern France dubbed the Jacquerie.

The possession of David II and John II was both a powerful weapon and a diplomatic embarrassment for Edward III. In order to capitalize on his captives, he would have to recognize their rights to the thrones of Scotland and France, and thus give up his more grandiose notions of a great Plantagenet empire stretching from the Isles to the Pyrenees. Pragmatism apparently prevailed, especially after an unsuccessful progress through northern France in 1359-60 convinced Edward that he could never really hope to be crowned King of France at Rheims. Under the terms of the Treaty of Berwick (1358) and the Treaty of Brétigny (1360), Edward agreed to accept very substantial ransoms for David and John. The Anglo-French settlement required him to renounce his claim to the French throne; but it also promised to give him full sovereign control over his own continental dominions in Ponthieu (including the new acquisition of Calais) and in Aquitaine. Edward eagerly took up the terms that suited him, and in 1362 invested his eldest son as Prince of Aquitaine, taking homage from him in just the same way that Charles IV and Philip VI had earlier received it from him. Unfortunately, neither John II nor his successor Charles V was able to effect the transfers of territorial sovereignty that went with the new agreement, and in the meantime Edward held off from making a final renunciation of his title of King of France. As a result, after nearly a decade of sometimes tense but continuous truce, the terms proposed in 1360 were withdrawn and the French war re-opened in 1369.

The final phase of Edward III's reign was a sad postlude to an otherwise remarkable success story. Many of the king's contemporaries were dead, and the concentration of royal patronage upon members of the royal family (Edward had five sons who grew to manhood) left the king increasingly isolated in political and personal terms. Although Edward remained ready to take up arms, he was prevented from proceeding to France in 1369 by the death and funeral of Queen Philippa, and in 1372 by the non-cooperation of the winds and tides. It was believed that power and influence was increasingly being exercised by a group of unscrupulous courtiers led by Lords Latimer and Neville and the king's mistress, Alice Perrers. Following a temporary truce with the French in 1375 and the king's descent into chronic illness, the political community undertook a long and humiliating analysis of the state of misgovernment in the realm: in the course of the so-called Good Parliament of 1376, the Commons made their first recorded appointment of a speaker to represent their complaints to the Crown, and used their nominee, Sir Peter de la Mare, to present their collective accusations against various courtiers and financiers, thus inventing the process of parliamentary impeachment. The threat to the security of the succession from the death of the Black Prince, the king's partial recovery and resumption of public life, and the threat of an imminent French invasion all had the effect of turning support back to the Crown, and during the winter of 1376-7 many of the acts of the Good Parliament were undone. But while loyalty to the old king, and to his grandson and heir Prince Richard, was unwavering, there was much speculation about the political ambitions of the king's third son, John of Gaunt, who was thought to be about to usurp the throne.

Edward III died at Sheen on 21 June 1377, and was buried, with great pomp, at Westminster Abbey in a tomb adjacent to those of his esteemed ancestors and decorated with miniature figures of his numerous sons and daughters. Edward's achievement was not easily assessed either by his contemporaries or by subsequently historians: the reign was long, had begun and ended ignominiously, and seemed to have been preoccupied with what, in hindsight, seemed like reckless and unrealizable ambitions abroad. But the valuable continuity and stability provided by Edward's personal rule was certainly appreciated in his own and subsequent generations: it was only in the sixteenth century that Henry V replaced him as England's greatest royal hero. Edward's single-minded pursuit of the cult of chivalry had its ludicrous side: the dressing-up and play-acting associated with the royal tournaments of the period have a worrying air of unreality to a modern audience. But Edward also had a formative influence upon what might be called the royal style: his major rebuilding work at Windsor Castle during the 1360s created a secular counterpart to Henry III's work at Westminster Abbey that publicly presented the English monarchy as one of the richest, most powerful and most revered dynasties in the known world.

RICHARD II (1377-1399)

The child who became King Richard II of England in 1377 had been born at Bordeaux ten years earlier, on 6 January 1367. He was the second son of the Black Prince and Joan of Kent. His older brother, Edward of Angoulême, died in childhood: it is an interesting mark of family piety that Richard II was later to have his brother's remains disinterred and brought to England for re-burial at the royal foundation of King's Langley. Richard himself was probably named in honour of one of his father's chivalric heroes, Richard the Lionheart: one of the tapestries that the Black Prince bequeathed to his son at his death in 1376 was a depiction of Richard I's crusading encounter with Saladin. Such a heady mix of royal history and chivalric legend seems to have had some impact on Richard II, who in his adulthood demonstrated considerable interest in his lineage and in the deeds of his predecessors.

Richard's premature accession raised some of the same problems that had attended the beginning of his grandfather's reign. Although the succession of a child was not challenged, it was widely believed in England that the new king's uncle, John of Gaunt, had designs upon the throne. Gaunt was not included in the series of Councils appointed between 1377 and 1380 to assist in the government of the realm until such time as the young Richard could assume full power. It is possible, however, that Gaunt's position as the premier nobleman in England and a possible heir presumptive to the throne simply made it inappropriate that he should be nominated to the Council, and that his influence was freely acknowledged at least in court circles. Another influence during these early years was the king's mother: Princess Joan, though not involved in public politics, took on some of the functions of a queen prior to her son's marriage, and indeed assisted, in the manner of the times, in the negotiations for his nuptials. Joan, who has gone down in history as the 'Fair Maid of Kent', was a colourful and controversial figure: supposedly one of the great beauties of her age, she had been married twice before she wedded the Black Prince; and the Hollands, Richard's older step-brothers, were to become a contentious influence at his court.

82. Richard II and Henry Bolingbroke.
83. Richard II's Irish campaign from Jean Creton's *History of King Richard.*

Richard II was only fourteen when England was rocked by one of the greatest political and social upheavals of the Middle Ages, the Peasants' Revolt of 1381. A series of inequitable and unpopular subsidies (the infamous poll taxes of 1377-80), culminating in a series of intrusive inquiries into tax-evasion during the summer of 1381, sparked a widespread and seemingly coordinated outbreak of resistance and violence in Essex and Kent; and in many other parts of the country – the Home Counties, East Anglia, and Yorkshire – the disturbed conditions were taken as an opportunity and excuse for the pursuit of local vendettas. When the rebels of Essex and Kent marched on London, the king's government went into a kind of paralysis. The chancellor and treasurer could think of nothing more to do than to set in for a siege in the Tower of London, and suffered the vengeance of the mob for their apparent indifference to calls for reform by being dragged from this royal fortress and ritually murdered.

The chroniclers represented the young king as the only effective and dynamic player in the crisis, though whether this genuinely represents an exercise of political judgement on Richard's part can be doubted: his advisers, and his mother, may have appreciated that the best way to quell the ferocity of the riots then raging in the city of London was to arrange a carefully-staged meeting between Richard and the rebels. At Mile End on 14 June, Richard agreed to the demand for an abolition of serfdom; but at Smithfield on the next day the leader of the insurgents, Wat Tyler, overreached himself. His radical demands, including the removal of all feudal lordship and the disestablishment of the Church, alarmed the king's entourage, and his familiarity with Richard offended courtly sensibilities, with the result that the Mayor of London, William Walworth, took action to defend his sovereign and ran Tyler through with his sword. The revolt rapidly dissipated, and the government set about a ruthless policy of suppression, with the king undertaking a military-style campaign through the Home Counties in pursuit of former rebels. Although the mood was to change, and reconciliation was to be the order of the day from the time of the November Parliament of 1381, Richard and his subjects were to convince themselves that the whole episode marked him out as a man with a mission.

With such heightened expectations of the monarchy, it was all the more aggravating when the young Richard failed to live up to his early promise. By the mid-1380s, English politics focused on two interconnected issues: the wars with France and Scotland, and the expenses of the royal household. The French war ground to a halt in 1384, but the truce was unpopular with the English aristocracy, who still hankered after the great days of victory under Edward III. In 1385, when the truce ended, the threat of the old Franco-Scottish alliance raised its head, and Richard was finally persuaded to take up arms and lead an army to the northern border. The campaign achieved little, and was remembered principally as the occasion on which the king bestowed a number of new noble titles on his followers, including, most controversially, Michael de la Pole, the son of a merchant financier, who was made Earl of Suffolk. It was the influence of de la Pole and another of the king's close friends, Robert de Vere, Earl of Oxford (later Duke of Ireland), that caused Parliament to become increasingly suspicious about what it saw as the reckless extravagance of the court: in an attempt to ensure that public funds were not diverted into private excess, the Parliaments of the mid-1380s set conditions on a number of taxes, requiring the king to go to war in person before the subsidies were paid.

The growing sense of concern over the Crown's military and fiscal policies came to a head in the Parliament of 1386, where de la Pole, in his capacity as royal chancellor, made a demand for a new tax of unprecedented proportions. The king's youngest uncle, the Duke of Gloucester, led a deputation to meet with Richard, who had decided not to attend the session in person: when they encountered the king at Eltham and asked for the dismissal of de la Pole, Richard reportedly replied that he would not bow to the demands of Parliament even to dismiss the lowliest scullion from his kitchen. In response to a pointed reminder about the fate of Edward II, however, he had to concede. The Commons promptly took advantage of de la Pole's disgrace to impeach him; and Parliament appointed a commission of high-ranking nobles and bishops (including the king's uncles of York and Gloucester) to control the administration for a year and to carry out what were perceived to be the urgent inquiries and reforms that would restore order to the processes of government.

The events of 1386 had an extraordinary impact on Richard II: arguably, he never forgave those who (as he saw it) usurped his prerogative powers in that year. During 1387 he called together the royal judges on two occasions and put to them a series of questions about the legitimacy of the new commission. They answered, predictably enough, that Parliament and the lords had no right to infringe the king's rights in this way; and they added – much more contentiously – that those who had conspired in the setting up and preservation of the extraordinary Council deserved to be treated as traitors. The lords predictably took fright at this unwarranted threat to what they saw as their own political rights and duties, and tried to counter-claim Richard's actions by making an appeal of treason against de la Pole, de Vere and three others of the king's close associates. There was a call to arms, and the leaders of the aristocratic opposition – Gloucester, Arundel, Warwick, Nottingham and Derby – defeated a royalist force led by de Vere at Radcot Bridge on 20 December 1387. When they visited the king in the Tower of London a few days later, there is some suggestion that they formally deposed him, but reinstated the hamstrung Richard when they could not decide on a successor. If the story is true (and remembering that Gloucester was the king's uncle, and Derby his first cousin), then it demonstrates a striking and significant difference between the events of 1326-7 and those of both 1387 and, subsequently, 1399: whereas Edward II could conveniently be replaced by his direct heir, Richard II had no children, and the royal family was clearly divided on who ought to succeed him.

The accusations of treason made by the five lords appellant were heard in the Parliament that opened at Westminster in February 1388, an assembly that appropriately became known as the 'Merciless Parliament'. All five of the appellees were condemned, though only two of them – Robert Tresilian and Nicholas Brembre – could be found and put to death. Playing on the apparent willingness of the House of Lords to support the opposition's attack on royal advisers, the Commons then impeached four other courtiers, including the king's erstwhile tutor Simon Burley, and had them publicly executed: Richard's young queen, Anne of Bohemia, and a number of other members of the royal family, tried to plead for Burley's life, but the thirst for blood was out and could not easily be assuaged. The king himself was forced to accept a new group of councillors to be constantly with him and whose consent would be required for all royal actions. The Merciless Parliament ended with the tense formality of the renewal both of the king's coronation oath and of the lords' oaths of allegiance.

This idea of a new start to a kind of second reign encouraged Richard II to take up a number of novel strategies during 1388-9. Both in Parliament and in the country he made conscious attempts to gain the support of the gentry, and thus to build up a new power base for the Crown independent of the high nobility. He also entered into serious negotiations for peace with France, which, although fraught with diplomatic difficulties, released him from the crushing burden of expenditure on war and thus freed him from some of the political constraints imposed by Parliament. It was around this time that Richard also began to petition the pope for the canonization of his great-grandfather, Edward II, on the grounds that the latter had given his life in defence of a royal title to which he had been called by God: although such requests attracted little serious attention,

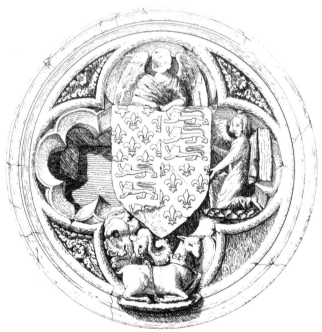

84. Death of Wat Tyler in 1381 from Jean Froissart's, *Chronicles.*
85. The coat of arms of Richard II.

Richard was clearly hoping to invalidate the argument that he might be removed from the throne on the precedent of 1327. Finally, on 3 May 1389 the king declared himself to be of age and sufficient to rule on his own: while some may have thought that, at twenty-two, the king had been distinctly slow to realize his own rights, the action was really meant as a means of disavowing the attempts of 1386-8 to place the Crown under the supervision of noble Councils. Richard would now rule independently, a sovereign monarch in his own realm.

The history of the years 1389-97 is difficult to characterize: historians are divided between those who see this as a period of political reconciliation and those who argue that Richard was simply awaiting the opportunity to have his vengeance on the former lords appellant. Much of the king's energy during this period went into the negotiation of a lasting peace with France. Richard was eager to put an end to the Hundred Years War, which he regarded as deeply damaging to his regime in England: he was also taken up, latterly, by the notion that the end of the war would allow the rulers of Europe to unite in a new crusade. As so often, however, the talks foundered on the issue of Aquitaine. Although the French were prepared to concede on some of the disputed territories on the borders of the duchy, they insisted that it should be held in liege homage, and suggested that the King of England might grant Aquitaine to John of Gaunt and his descendants, thus creating a permanent split between English Crown and its dependency. This solution pleased neither the English Parliament nor the Estates of Gascony, and in the end Richard's plans for a final settlement failed, although he did secure a twenty-eight-year truce in 1396.

Richard's marriage to Anne of Bohemia in 1382, while it had little diplomatic or dynastic success, had evidently proved to be fulfilling in personal terms: the king and queen spent much of their time together, and at his palace of Sheen Richard created a special set of private apartments for the couple where they could withdraw from the cares of state and the public life of the court. Anne's death in 1394 removed an important check on the royal temper: when Richard re-married, under the terms of the Anglo-French settlement of 1396, his new bride, Isabella of France, was only an infant, and could not be expected to take on either the public functions associated with queenship or the role of personal mentor to her king. It is sometimes argued that Richard was deranged by Anne's death: he lashed out at the Earl of Arundel when the latter showed less than due respect by arriving late at the queen's funeral. On the other hand, Arundel was one of the former appellants, and any offence that he showed to Richard was likely to be taken as an opportunity by a king who clearly found it difficult to forgive and forget. In recent years, Richard's mental health has come in for further discussion: it has been suggested that by the time he reached the age of thirty he had developed schizophrenic or narcissistic tendencies, with the result that he was unable to differentiate between reality and fantasy and became obsessed with the possibility of challenges to his throne. It is equally possible, however, that his supposedly manic behaviour after 1397 represented a carefully thought-out strategy, and that the so-called 'tyranny' of his last years was intended systematically to re-build the majesty of his position and the sense of obedience that he wished to instil in his subjects.

In 1397 Richard ordered the arrest of Gloucester, Arundel and Warwick and their trial in Parliament. The assembly was carefully stage-managed: the special corps of Cheshire archers that Richard had developed into a personal bodyguard was set around Westminster Hall, with instructions to shoot at the least sign of attempted disruption to the king's plans. A group of lords who owed their recent elevations to the king's patronage (the 'little dukes', as one chronicler later disparagingly called them) made appeals of treason against the three former appellants, in deliberate – almost mock – imitation of the events of 1386. Arundel was condemned to death; Gloucester, it was reported, had already died (there are reasonable grounds to assume that he had been murdered by Richard's friends); and Warwick, who put up a great show of histrionics when declared guilty, was spared his life but sent off to be held in close custody on the Isle of Man. Ironically, one of the other former appellants, the king's cousin Henry of Bolingbroke, Earl of Derby, was one of the beneficiaries of the resulting redistribution of patronage, now becoming Duke of Hereford. But in 1398 the king's wrath fell on him too, when, as a result of a dispute between Hereford and the Duke of Norfolk, Richard chose to banish both parties from the realm, Norfolk for life and Hereford for a term of ten years. Crucially, Richard specifically allowed that, should his uncle John of Gaunt die during Bolingbroke's period of exile, the latter would be allowed his rights to the title and estates of the duchy of Lancaster. But when the hypothetical became real with his uncle's death in February 1399, Richard refused to stand by his promise and put the duchy into royal custody. Although the decision is often seen as indicative of Richard's lack of political judgement, it was also the only thing that the king could do to prevent his principal enemy from becoming the most powerful lord in England.

Having supposedly resolved the issue of the Lancastrian inheritance, Richard II set off for Ireland. It was his second visit to the lordship, which he was determined to bring back under the effective control of the English Crown after several generations of neglect. Contrary to the king's calculations, Henry of Bolingbroke seized this opportunity to return to England and claim his rightful succession to the duchy of Lancaster. Richard had no alternative but to fight for his throne, and, crossing to Haverfordwest, made his way to North Wales to meet up with the forces that his ally the Earl of Salisbury was supposed to be rallying to his cause. But few men were prepared to risk their lives for a king who had become a liability, and Richard was taken under custody to Chester and thence to the Tower of London. Bolingbroke, who had advertised his grievances in terms of his rightful claim to the Lancastrian estates, now saw that the throne itself was within his grasp, and prevailed upon Richard to abdicate. In Parliament at Westminster on 30 September, a series of charges was laid against Richard II, on the basis of which his right to the throne was annulled and he was declared deposed.

Richard spent the last months of his life in prison, latterly at the Lancastrian stronghold of Pontefract. The circumstances of his death in 1400 remain unclear: some sources say that he starved himself to death, others that his gaolers deprived him of food, and others that he was murdered. Given the anomalous position of a deposed king, the vulnerability of Henry IV's title and the ham-fisted attempts to restore Richard's rule, it is not unreasonable to suppose that the new regime had a hand in the ex-king's death. Even after his burial at King's Langley, however, rumours continued about Richard's survival and preparations for a return to power. When Henry V later disinterred the body and re-buried it in the double tomb that Richard had earlier commissioned for himself and Anne of Bohemia at Westminster Abbey, he was not only undertaking a symbolic act of political reconciliation but also putting paid, once and for all, to the troublesome tradition of a surviving Richard II.

5

THE HOUSES OF LANCASTER & YORK
1399-1485

A.J. POLLARD

The years between the deposition of Richard II in 1399 and the defeat of Richard III at Bosworth in 1485 marked one of the most complicated, not to say chaotic, periods in the history of the English monarchy. Because Richard II's supplanter, Henry IV, was also the claimant to the duchy of Lancaster held by his deceased father, John of Gaunt, he and his son and grandson are known as the rulers of the House of Lancaster. In 1461, however, the last of the Lancastrian kings was deposed by a distant cousin, Edward IV, the son of the Duke of York, whose dynasty is therefore referred to as the House of York. The struggle between the Lancastrians and the Yorkists was written up by Tudor historians as one of unprecedented acrimony and bloodshed, and has been referred to since the nineteenth century as the Wars of the Roses. In reality, these events were probably no different than the civil wars generated by the dynastic struggles between Stephen and Matilda and between Henry II and his squabbling sons. Ironically, it was the heightened expectations that the political community had developed towards royal authority and the rule of law that caused Englishmen in the late fifteenth century to consider their predicament as intolerable: their predecessors in the twelfth century had simply taken quarrels over the throne as a fact of life. This is not to say that England did not suffer as a result of the Wars of the Roses; but the threat of civil war was never welcome, and the majority of the aristocracy realized, at least after 1471, that the stakes were simply too high to allow them to pursue personal vendettas under the cloak of political unrest. What really shook the political traditions of England after 1469 was the spectacle of kings fighting for, and losing, their crowns on the field of battle, and the implication that, in the absence of any clear rule about the succession, it was force rather than right that could determine the selection of a king.

THE HOUSE OF LANCASTER: HENRY IV (1399-1413)

When Henry Bolingbroke landed at Ravenspur at the beginning of July 1399, he did not intend to make himself king. His purpose was the recovery of his duchy of Lancaster confiscated by his

Clockwise from top   87. The empty throne. The moment between Richard II's abdication and
Henry IV's accession as imagined in a fifteenth-century manuscript of Creton's *Metrical History*.
88. The coat of arms of Henry IV.
89. Henry IV's second wife, Joan of Navarre's coronation at Westminster Abbey,
26 February 1403, from the Pageant of Richard Beauchamp.

cousin, Richard II, and quite possibly to assume the government of the realm in the king's name in his capacity as Steward of England. So complete and swift was his victory, so overwhelming the support he seemed to have received, however, that soon after Richard II was in his hands, on 15 August, he decided upon the course of deposition and usurpation. A rapid search was ordered for the best possible title to be found, and Parliament was summoned to Westminster on 30 September. On the eve of the Parliament, Richard was persuaded to abdicate. This was accepted by the assembly, and Bolingbroke stepped forward to claim the empty throne. He was unanimously declared king, the assembly was dissolved and recalled as a Parliament in his name on 6 October, and seven days later he was crowned as King Henry IV.

Henry was unable to find a sure title for his throne. He explored the possibility of claiming that his ancestor as Duke of Lancaster, Edmund Crouchback, had in fact been the eldest son of Henry III and thus the rightful heir; but a thorough search of the chronicles could not prove this. As an alternative, he gave three grounds for his action: he was descended in the right line of blood of Henry III; God had sent him to recover the throne; and the kingdom was on the point of collapse. He significantly avoided making a claim through the unbroken male descent from Edward III on the grounds of a settlement made by his grandfather in the last year of his reign. He also steered clear of any suggestion of election by Parliament. By this route, he kept open the English claim to the throne of France, dependent on descent through the female line, and made no compromise on the prerogatives of the Crown. But the title was flawed and left his dynasty vulnerable to a counter-claim from the descendants through the female line of the children of Edward III's second son, Lionel of Clarence. Indeed, the childless Richard II had considered nominating his grandson, Roger, Earl of March as his heir in 1398. Roger's descendants were to harbour an alternative and (as they argued) legitimate claim to the throne throughout reigns of Henry IV, Henry V and Henry VI. Despite its success, the House of Lancaster was never able to rid itself of this flaw.

Henry IV possessed many of the qualities expected of a medieval king. Born in 1366 or 1367, he was of royal stock, the son of John of Gaunt, Duke of Lancaster, and Blanche, co-heiress of Henry of Grosmont, Duke of Lancaster. A man of letters, a patron of poets and a keen musician, he had been a famous jouster, had crusaded in eastern Europe and been on pilgrimage to Jerusalem, and was renowned for his magnanimity and generosity. He came near to living up to the highest contemporary ideals of virtue and honour. Moreover he had four sons (from his first wife, Mary Bohun, who had died in 1394) to continue the dynasty. He had been a magnate in his own right on the basis of his wife's inheritance of half of the earldom of Hereford. He was also an experienced politician, who had been deeply involved in the aristocratic opposition to Richard II, being one of the lords given the name 'appellant' for their actions against the king in 1388. Had he come to the throne in uncontroversial circumstances, he may well have enjoyed a peaceful and prosperous reign. Yet the new king was soon overwhelmed by a series of crises, which during seven years not only came close to sweeping him away but also threatened the very unity of the kingdom.

The first rebellion occurred in January 1400, led by the displaced courtiers of Richard II. It was easily crushed but probably sealed the fate of the deposed king, who died in Pontefract Castle. In September a rebellion began in Wales, which, from local beginnings, under the control of Owain Glyn Dŵr soon consumed the whole nation. At first the king himself sought to bring the rebels to heel, campaigning in Wales for successive years. But Henry's armies could not cope with the guerrilla tactics of the Welsh. Ultimately he had to settle for containment by strengthened border garrisons and a slow war of attrition under the command from 1404 of his eldest son, Henry, Prince of Wales. Nevertheless, this did not prevent Glyn Dŵr from setting up his own independent government, recognized abroad by England's enemies, and in receipt of French military assistance. Wales was not finally pacified until 1409.

At the height of the Welsh uprising, Henry faced a second and more serious baronial revolt led by Sir Henry Percy, 'Hotspur'. Hotspur was the son and heir of the Earl of Northumberland. He and his father had been key supporters of the usurpation and had been liberally rewarded by the new king. The earl had been given his head in his territorial ambitions in Scotland; Hotspur had been given command in North Wales and in the county of Chester, where Richard II had built up a personal following. In the summer of 1403, disenchanted with the new regime, Hotspur, supported discretely by his father and Glyn Dŵr, rose in the name of the infant Edmund, Earl of March. The king acted swiftly. He met and defeated Hotspur at the bloody Battle of Shrewsbury on 21 July. Two years later the Earl of Northumberland himself rebelled, in alliance with Glyn Dŵr and Archbishop Scrope of York. Northumberland escaped to Scotland, but Scrope fell into the king's hands and was executed. In 1408 Northumberland made a last forlorn effort to depose Henry but was defeated and killed at Bramham Moor in Yorkshire.

At the same time as the war in Wales and the rebellion of the Percys, Henry IV waged a war against Scotland, the climax of which was the victory won by the Percys at Homildon Hill in 1402. The French too sought to take advantage of England's divisions. Not only did they assist Glyn Dŵr, they also attacked Calais and English possessions in Gascony in 1403, 1405 and 1406. Moreover, from 1400 an unofficial war was waged at sea, which reached a climax in 1403 and 1405 with French raids on Plymouth, the Isle of Wight and Dartmouth, and English counter-raids on the coasts of Picardy and Normandy.

The costs, direct and indirect, of waging war on all fronts were huge. Moreover the war in the Channel, and the piracy it spawned, seriously disrupted overseas trade. The financial crisis that rapidly engulfed the regime was exacerbated by the king's own profligacy, the high cost of his household, and the annuities that he dispensed to his supporters, not to mention the generosity of the dower provided for his second wife Joan of Navarre, who arrived in England early in 1403. Unsurprisingly, financial crisis led to frequent conflict with the Parliaments that Henry called to grant taxes. In 1401 Parliament secured a reform of the administration; in 1404 it insisted on the appointment of treasurers of war to oversee expenditure and the formal appointment of the king's councillors charged to ensure good government; and in 1406, after a prolonged Parliamentary stand-off which lasted from 1 March to just before Christmas, the Crown was forced to put the government of the realm, and especially the management of its finances, into the control of a special Council.

The survival of the regime through all these crises owed much to Henry's own decisiveness, his persistence and determination. It also owed much to the strength and depth of his support. Henry came to the throne at the head of the mighty affinity created by his father, John of Gaunt, which served him loyally at court and in the country. He could also count on his ally from Richard II's days, Thomas Arundel, Archbishop of Canterbury, and on his half-brothers the Beauforts (the children of John of Gaunt's liaison with Katherine Swynford, legitimized by Richard II), especially Henry, Bishop of Winchester. The new king was also a man who was prepared to listen to criticism and to engage in debate. He had come to the throne as the representative of the appellant tradition that had opposed what was perceived as Richard II's tyranny, and had demanded a kingship more

Opposite   90. Music composed by Henry IV or Prince Henry, 1410-15. The name 'Roy Henry' ('King Henry' in French) appears at the top of the page in red ink. This probably means that the music was composed by Henry IV or the young Henry V before he became king.

responsive to the concerns of the nobility. It was this style of kingship that he put into practice, especially in his relationship with Parliament. Henry engaged in parliamentary and conciliar debate, was prepared to make concessions, and accepted compromise. Neither an experimenter in parliamentary monarchy (as the great Victorian historian, William Stubbs, proposed), nor (as has been more recently suggested) a vulnerable ruler forced to make humiliating concessions to a hostile Commons, Henry IV was a pragmatic politician who understood from his own experience the need to reach agreement with his subjects.

In 1406, however, Henry was forced to step back from centre-stage because of the collapse of his health. Hostile contemporaries perceived his illness, reported to be leprosy, as a divine punishment for the execution of Archbishop Scrope. It is likely, however, that the king suffered the first of a series of strokes or heart attacks in April 1406. He was unable to attend the second session of the 1406 Parliament, in which Archbishop Arundel acted as his spokesman. One reason for the prolonged wrangling that followed was the king's continuing incapacity. Subsequently, although he intervened from time to time, the government of the realm was to remain in the hands of the Council until the end of the reign, led at first by Arundel.

Arundel's government, assisted by the end of war with Scotland, the pacification of Wales, internal divisions in France and the recovery of trade, was able to bring the finances of the realm under control. Yet as the dynasty became more established, so also factionalism emerged at court. The king's eldest son, Prince Henry, was anxious to play a more prominent role. At the end of 1409, he and his Beaufort allies were able to oust Arundel. For two years they dominated the Council, but were in their turn removed at the end of 1411 when the king stirred himself to restore Arundel and to bring his second and favourite son, Thomas, to the fore. The rivalry between the two groups was intensified by differences over foreign policy. Civil war in France offered an opportunity for intervention. Prince Henry favoured an alliance with the Duke of Burgundy and campaigning in northern France, Arundel and Prince Thomas an alliance with the Orléanists and a strengthening of the English position in the Southwest. In 1412, Thomas, now Duke of Clarence, led a successful march from Cherbourg to Bordeaux. Before the expedition set sail, Prince Henry made a protest in strength, demanding an audience with his father. A reconciliation was achieved, but the Prince of Wales had given notice that he was not to be excluded for long. Within a year he was able to take up the reins of power, for on 20 March 1413 the long expected death of the stricken king finally occurred. Henry IV was buried in Canterbury Cathedral next to the tomb of St Thomas Becket, where his widow, Joan had a monument raised to both him and her.

The growth of factionalism in the last six years of Henry's life has been frequently emphasized; less often noted is the underlying strength of the regime, which enabled it to survive the collapse of the king's health and consequent strains. This was because the shared commitment of the king's family and his supporters was greater than their differences and because Henry himself, however grudgingly, accepted the need to step back from day-to-day involvement. He was a man who, if never loved by his subjects, won their respect. Historians have been ambivalent about him. In Tudor times he was disparaged as the unprincipled and ambitious deposer of a true king. But in the nineteenth century he came to be seen as a monarch before his time, standing up for liberty against tyranny and for constitutional monarchy against absolutism. He was a more complex and more medieval figure than these extremes imply. The usurpation was a hard-headed political calculation taken after careful thought about the alternatives. Henry's kingship, while seeking to give nothing away of the royal prerogative, was consistent with his principles as a subject in opposition. Henry IV's reign was exceptional in the extent to which a medieval king was willing to rule in partnership with his subjects; it was not a style to be repeated by his successors.

Previous Page 1. Edgar.
This page 2. Cnut and Emma.
Opposite 3. Edward the Confessor as depicted in a wooden screen, *c.*1500, of St Catherine's Church, Ludham, Norfolk.

4. The coat of arms of William I and Matilda of Flanders.

5. The coat of arms of William II.

6. The coat of arms of Henry I and Matilda of Scotland

7. The coat of arms of Stephen and Matilda of Boulogne.

8. The coat of arms of Henry II and Eleanor of Aquitaine.

9. Princess Nest achieved some notoriety as a mistress to many lovers – including Henry I – earning herself the sobriquet 'Helen of Wales'.

10. Richard I and Saladin. This fourteenth-century imaginary encounter was a commonplace in legends about the Lionheart.

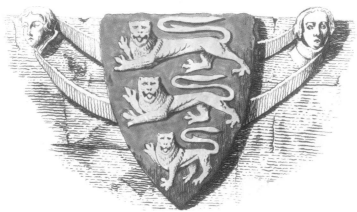
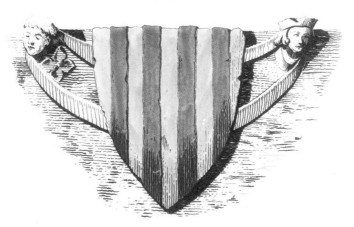

11. The coat of arms of Berengaria of Navarre.
12. The coat of arms of John and Isabella of Angoulême.
13. The coat of arms of Henry III.
14. The coat of arms of Eleanor of Provence, Henry III's queen.

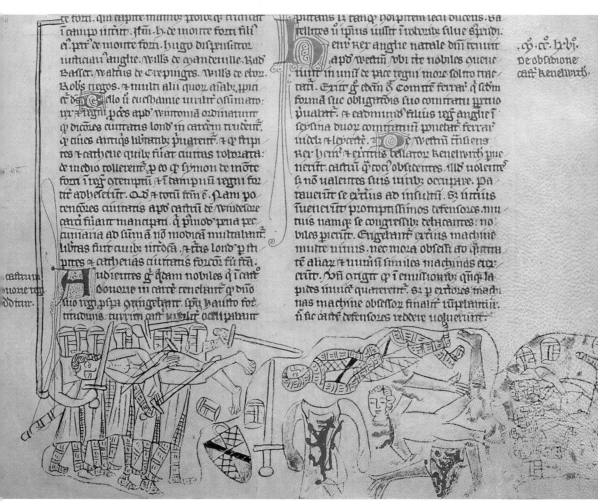

15. Bracton, *On the Laws and Customs of England*: Edward I surrounded by
soldiers and lawyers.
16. Simon de Montfort's death and mutilation.

17. Edward III as patron of the Order of the Garter.

18. Henry V as Prince of Wales receives a copy of the advice book called *Regiment of Princes*, the message of which he well understood, from the poet Thomas Hoccleve.

Opposite   19. Sir Nigel Loring in Garter robes.

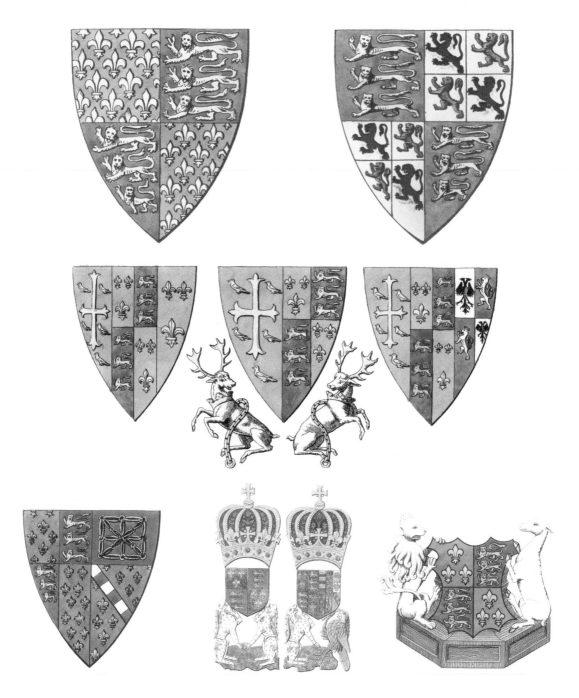

20. The coat of arms of Edward III.
21. The coat of arms of Phillippa of Hainault, queen of Edward III.
22. The coat of arms of Isabella of France, Richard II's second queen and Anne of Bohemia, his first.
23. The coat of arms of Joan of Navarre, Henry IV's queen.
24. The coat of arms of Henry VI and Margaret of Anjou.
25. The coat of arms of Edward V.

26. Henry VI as depicted on a wooden screen, *c.*1500, of St Catherine's Church, Ludham, Norfolk.

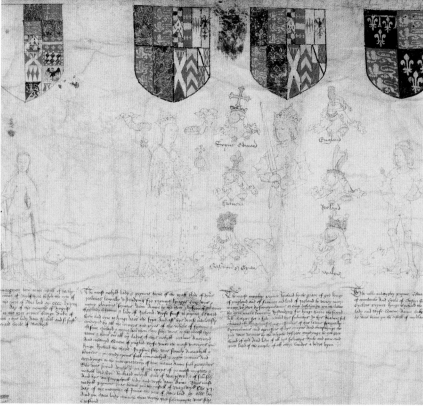

27. The saintly child. The twelve-year old Henry VI at prayer before the shrine of St Edmund, from the dedicatory manuscript of John Lydgate's *Life*.

28. Richard III and his queen as depicted in the Rous Roll, with a eulogy of the king and a paean of praise for the queen, composed while they were still alive.

29. The coat of arms of Henry VII.
30. The coat of arms of Elizabeth of York.
31. The coat of arms of Henry VIII.
32. The coat of arms of Elizabeth I.

33. Mary Queen of Scots in widow's dress.

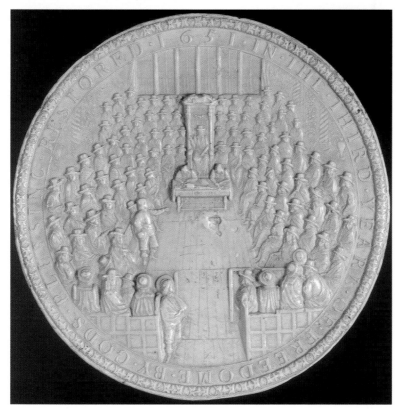

34. James II from the Guild Book of Barber Surgeons of York.
35. William and Mary from the Guild Book of Barber Surgeons of York.
36. After the execution of Charles I the great seal of state was changed to reflect the new political atmosphere. Out went the representation of the enthroned monarch with orb and sceptre and king in armour riding a horse and in came an engraved map of Britain and a picture of the House of Commons. This is the second version of this seal first used in 1651. It reads 'In the third yeare of freedome by Gods blessing restored 1651'.

37. The coat of arms of Charlotte of Mecklenberg, wife of George III.
38. The coat of arms of George III.

Henry seems to have found personal happiness with his second wife and queen, Joan of Navarre, the dowager Duchess of Brittany, whom he had met once or twice during Richard II's reign. Three years younger than Henry, she married him, by proxy, in April 1402. Joan had nine children by her first husband, eight of whom survived into adulthood. Henry himself had seven children (six of whom survived) by his first wife, Mary Bohun, who died in 1394, aged only twenty-five, after the birth of the last. Henry's daughters Blanche and Philippa married respectively Ludvig, the heir to Emperor Rupert II, and Eric IX, King of Denmark. In spite of all this fecundity, and the fact that Joan was still only thirty-five when she came to England in 1403, she and Henry had no children of their own. After early opposition to the size and composition of her household, Joan did not figure in public life. From 1406 she possibly concentrated on the care of her ailing husband. Later she suffered at the hands of her stepsons. In 1419 Henry V accused her of sorcery, placed her under house arrest and seized her dowry. Shortly before he died, he relented and restored her. But his youngest brother, Humphrey, Duke of Gloucester, also extorted some of her possessions in the next reign. She lived on in retirement at King's Langley and then Havering until her death in 1437, when she was buried next to Henry IV at Canterbury.

HENRY V (1413-1422)

The confident young man who succeeded to the throne on 20 March 1413 was born at Monmouth in 1386 or 1387, the son of Henry Bolingbroke, Earl of Derby, and Mary Bohun. At his birth and during his education until his early teens there was no expectation that he would become King of England. Because of the sophisticated cultural interests of his father, he received a literary and musical as well as a chivalric education. At the end of 1398, when his father was banished by Richard II, he was taken into the care of the king's household. In the king's company when Richard sailed to Ireland in 1399, he was subsequently placed under guard at Trim when Bolingbroke invaded England in July. Once his father had seized power, he was brought back to England and almost immediately promoted to the dignity of Prince of Wales and its associated titles. While still well under age, and formally in the care of his father's nominee, he was, because of the rising of Owain Glyn Dŵr, quickly thrown into affairs as the nominal commander of English military operations in Wales; involvement became actual on the field of Shrewsbury in July 1403, during which, at the age of sixteen or seventeen, he was wounded in the face. Once recovered, he seems to have assumed full responsibility for the conduct of the war in Wales from his base at Hereford. By the end of 1406, the Welsh revolt having been stemmed, he began to appear in Parliament and to sit on the royal Council in Westminster. However, he continued to campaign in Wales, probably in command in the field for the first time, in the sieges of Aberystwyth in 1407 and 1408 and of Harlech in 1408-9, which finally brought the rebellion to an end.

The experience of war in Wales, especially from 1403 to 1409, in which he had recovered his own patrimony from the self-proclaimed rival Prince of Wales, Owain Glyn Dŵr, was not only to be a formative apprenticeship in the effective organization and prosecution of war, but also for him, as the heir to a usurper, a lesson in the need, where necessary, to use force to make good the rights to which he laid claim. Henry's experience in the remaining years of his father's reign was also to shape his kingship. A young man impatient to exercise power and unwilling to accept second place, he discovered, as a subject and the prime mover, how faction could destabilize government; he learnt (and manipulated) the ways of Parliament; he built up a dedicated personal following among the English nobility; and he became well-versed in foreign affairs. When he became king, Henry V was thus, like his father, a man of considerable military and political experience.

ere shewes howe at the batell of Shrovesbury: betwen kyng Henr
nd S. Henr Percy / Erle Richard there beyng on the kynge party
tably & manly behaued hym self / to his grete laude & worship
ich batell was slayne the said S Henr Percy and many other
yn. And on the kynge party there was slayne in the kyng cute
ief of other the Erle of Stafford. Erle Richardes Auntes sn
any other in grete nombre on whose soules god haue mcy

The new king quickly made his intentions clear. Contemporaries commented that he was as another man, who had left his fractious past, later to be glossed as a dissolute youth, behind him. While his followers as Prince of Wales, especially the members of his half-family, the Beauforts, became prominent, he set out to reconcile all the political nation, not only estranged Lancastrians such as his own brother, Thomas, but also the heirs of those who had been attainted for their support of Richard II, and, eventually, in 1416 the Earl of Northumberland. His was to be a government of national unity. He immediately launched a programme of financial reform and embarked on a campaign to impose law and order, which had deteriorated in the last years of his father's reign. This began at the very top when he disciplined two of his own personal followers, Lord Furnival and the Earl of Arundel, and was taken further in a major judicial tour of the Midlands, which he himself supervised in the summer of 1414.

The temper of the new reign was perhaps most clearly revealed in the handling of the Oldcastle affair. Sir John Oldcastle was a companion in arms from the wars in Wales. He was an avowed Lollard, a member of the heretical movement, which, foreshadowing the Protestants of the sixteenth century, espoused revolutionary doctrines which threatened the whole existence of the established Church. Oldcastle was the historical model for Falstaff, the misleader of Henry's fictionalized youth. But in fact, Henry the man was less tolerant of Lollardy than his father had been. He summoned Oldcastle to his presence in an attempt to persuade him to abandon his beliefs. The obdurate heretic was handed over to the Church and condemned to death. However, he escaped and, it was later alleged, planned to raise rebellion and depose the king. Groups of Lollards did indeed converge on London to protest. Eighty or more were promptly arrested, most of whom were summarily executed. Oldcastle himself remained at large. Whether or not this represented an armed uprising against the king, Henry took full advantage to blacken Lollardy as treasonable and to drive it underground.

Henry's purge of Lollardy, sustained by the tightening of the laws against heresy in the subsequent Parliament and backed up by his own promotion of liturgical reform, was an aspect of his severe Christian orthodoxy. Henry himself took a leading role in efforts to end the Schism that had split Christendom under two rival popes, personally instigated monastic reform in England, and founded his own religious houses. His own personal life, until he married in 1420, was dedicatedly chaste. His piety was part of his perception of kingship. He was a man who, from the very beginning of the reign, fashioned himself as the personification of the ideal monarch: the defender of mother Church, the fount of justice, and the paragon of chivalry. It was in the last respect that he was to make his greatest and most lasting impact on his kingdom.

Henry was only gradually drawn into full-scale revival of the war in France, but it was to become his great obsession. The deep division in France between the Burgundian and Armagnacs for the domination of the kingdom presented him with an irresistible opportunity to advance English claims. By playing one side against the other, he progressively increased his demands from concessions of territory until he laid claim to the throne itself. He became committed to war in 1414, when he began massing equipment, gathering transports and raising taxation. The expedition was almost ready to sail at the end of July 1415 when a plot against the king's life, led by a disgruntled Earl of Cambridge in the name of the reluctant Earl of March as heir to Richard II, was revealed. The conspirators were quickly despatched and the expedition delayed for only a few days. The initial objective was the capture of Harfleur at the mouth of the Seine, achieved after a longer and

Opposite   91. A depiction of the Battle of Shrewsbury, 21 July 1403, from the Pageant of Richard Beauchamp, a near contemporary chronicle of the life of one of the most important medieval nobles.

more difficult siege than expected, on 22 September. Having garrisoned the town, Henry then set off on a risky march to Calais. His weary and depleted force was intercepted by a fresh and confident French army. Remarkably, at the battle fought in the mud at Agincourt the greatly outnumbered English army destroyed the French with very few casualties. Henry returned in triumph, his foray into France having sealed his and his dynasty's grip on the throne.

This, however, was but the beginning of Henry's ambitions. He began to plan, diplomatically, financially and logistically, for a full-scale invasion. Harfleur was held against a French counter attack, the victory of Henry's brother, John Duke of Bedford at sea in the mouth of the Seine having relieved the beleaguered town. The Emperor Sigismund was won as an ally, in promise for support in his efforts to end the Schism. The neutrality of the Duke of Burgundy was secured. And new subsidies were voted by an enthusiastic Parliament. On 1 August 1417, the largest and best-equipped army to have invaded France since the reign of Edward III landed at Touques, on the coast opposite Harfleur, prepared for the systematic conquest of Normandy. It took only two years for Henry to achieve this remarkable feat, culminating in the six-month siege of Rouen, which surrendered in January 1419. Henry's success was partly due to his command of logistics and thorough planning, partly to his inspiring leadership, and partly to the division among his enemies who completely failed to oppose his progress.

By the summer of 1419 Henry was ready to negotiate peace with whoever in France would give him the best terms. In a hectic round of negotiations with Duke John of Burgundy (who for a while controlled the person of the ineffective king, Charles VI) and the sixteen-year-old dauphin (who was in the Armagnac camp), he found that neither side was ready to make significant concessions. However, the assassination of the Duke of Burgundy by the Dauphin Charles at Montereau on 10 September transformed the situation. By the Treaty of Troyes (21 May 1420) between Henry and Philip, the new Duke of Burgundy, it was agreed that Henry would marry Charles VI's daughter, Catherine, and was recognized as heir to Charles VI and Regent of France until his new father-in-law's death. In this treaty with one of the great powers of France, Henry undertook to bring the French kingdom under the control of the Crown to which he was now acknowledged by his ally to be heir.

Henry returned to England early in 1421. His stay was short, only long enough for the coronation of the queen, a meeting of Parliament to confirm the treaty, and a tour of the kingdom to raise much needed reinforcements. Hearing news of the defeat and death of his brother Thomas, Duke of Clarence, at Beaugé, he cut short his tour and returned as rapidly as possible to France, campaigning as far south as the Loire in an effort to bring the dauphin to battle. This proving futile, he settled for the slow strategy of territorial consolidation by the siege of Meaux, which, in dauphinist hands, disrupted communications between Paris and the duchy of Burgundy. Dysentery afflicted the English camp as the winter dragged on; one victim was the king himself. After the eventual fall of the town on 22 May, Henry retired to recuperate. But his health continued to fail, and he died at Vincennes, outside Paris, on 31 August 1422. His body, embalmed, was brought home in solemn and unhurried style to be buried in great state in Westminster Abbey on 7 November where, over his tomb, a magnificent chantry chapel was built. He failed by two months to achieve his ambition of making himself King of France, for Charles VI died on 21 October. Fortunately for his dynasty, however, Queen Catherine had given birth to a son, Henry, on 6 December 1421.

Henry's nineteen-year-old queen, understandably, made little impact on her new countrymen before her husband died. After his death, however, she had a crucial role to play in the child's upbringing until he reached the age of seven, when he was a removed to a male establishment. Her personal life caused concern. Rumour spread that she was not chaste, and her name was linked in particular with the young Edmund Beaufort, the Bishop of Winchester's nephew. In 1427-8 an unusual act was passed forbidding anyone to marry an English queen without conciliar assent. It is not known whether there was fire as well as smoke in this affair. By 1432 at the latest, and possibly as early as 1429, she had secretly married an esquire of her household, Owen Tudor, possibly to make legitimate the birth of the child she was carrying, the suspiciously named Edmund, later Earl of Richmond. She had three further children unquestionably fathered by Owen before becoming terminally ill and withdrawing to Bermondsey Abbey, where she died on 3 January 1437, still only thirty-six.

Henry V's meteoric reign was remarkable. He was the most spectacularly successful of English warrior kings. And, despite the fact that he was absent from England for all but five months of the last five years of his reign, he never loosened his grip on his realm. Government was left in the hands of Councils under the presidency of his brothers, first John, Duke of Bedford, and then Humphrey, Duke of Gloucester. A stream of letters from the saddle or camp, several on quite trivial matters, kept his councillors and officers on their toes. Henry still insisted on the enforcement of justice, imposed his authority on erring nobles, and continued to push through his programme of ecclesiastical reform. He was also (and paradoxically, considering his pursuit of his claim to France) the first self-consciously English king, vigorously promoting the English language and that most English of saints, George. He inspired the respect of all and the devoted loyalty of his nobles, but insisted on obedience and subservience. When Henry Beaufort, Bishop of Winchester, his kinsman and trusted councillor, accepted a cardinal's hat and legatine powers from the pope without the king's leave, he was forced to retract and submit. The sheer dynamism and force of Henry's personality impressed friend and foe alike. An obituary notice minuted by the Council that took over the government of the realm on his death recorded that he was 'the most Christian warrior of the Church, the sun of prudence, the exemplar of justice, the most invincible king and the flower of chivalry'. Historians over the centuries have also been unanimous in singing his praises: one influential twentieth-century scholar, K.B. McFarlane, pronounced him the greatest of all English kings.

And yet Henry and his achievement were not all that he and his admirers have claimed. There were disturbing undercurrents to his rule. He was rapacious, increasingly as the prosecution of the war consumed him. He was not above exploiting the technicality of the law to seize the property of several noble widows. In particular, he pursued trumped-up charges of sorcery so that he could deprive his stepmother, Queen Joan, of her dower to help pay for the fighting. Possibly refused a grant of taxation in 1421, he resorted to loans which one contemporary described as extortion. Driven perhaps by an incipient paranoia about the legitimacy of his title to the throne, he was high-handed with the law of treason both in the summary trial of the conspirators of 1415 and in his pursuit of the dissident Sir John Mortimer in the last year of his life. There are indications that he was impatient with the constraints of Parliament upon him: he sought in his first Parliament to make the speaker his own agent; he amended a statute after it was enacted; and it was probably his ambition to secure a grant of annual taxation from Parliament without the need of renewed assent. There was more of the style of Richard II, whose body he had solemnly reburied in Westminster Abbey at the beginning of the reign, than of his father in his kingship. It is indicative that when ratifying the Treaty of Troyes, the Commons secured an assurance that he did not intend to introduce French law into England.

The Treaty of Troyes itself, presented as the achievement of a permanent peace, was no such thing. By it, Henry made himself a party to continuing civil war in France, a war he was unlikely

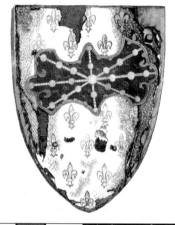

Clockwise from top   92. Letter of Henry V in his own hand, referring to the safe-keeping of prisoners captured at Agincourt, dated *c*.1419.

93. A lively sea battle during Henry V's Agincourt campaign, probably that which took place in August 1416 in the mouth of the Seine estuary, from the Pageant of Richard Beauchamp.

94. Badge of Henry V from MS Vincent 152 at the Herald's College.

95. Shield of King Henry V from his chantry chapel in Westminster Abbey.

to win. Whereas before he had been able brilliantly to exploit his position as an independent party to advance his own objectives, thereafter he and his successor were sucked into the vortex of French politics. Like other territorial aggressors in history who have been initially irresistible, he was so carried away by his own success that he lost sight of the possible. It is hard to believe, had he lived and continued to pursue the war as obsessively, that he would not, sooner rather than later, have come into conflict with his subjects who were already less enthusiastic about the war than they had been. As it was, he left for his successor an almost impossible legacy in France that was in time to play its part in his dynasty's eventual nemesis.

HENRY VI (1422-1461, 1470-1471)

Henry VI, the only child of Henry V and Catherine of Valois, was born at Windsor Castle on 6 December 1421. Nine months old when he inherited the throne of England, he also inherited the Lancastrian title to the throne of France before his first birthday. A Council under the presidency of his father's younger surviving brother Humphrey, Duke of Gloucester, as protector of the realm, took over the reins of government in England; Humphrey's elder brother, John, Duke of Bedford, became regent of France. The minority Council in England, which included several lords and clerics with experience stretching back to the later years of Henry IV, was much inspired by the memory of Henry V and dedicated itself collectively to the preservation of his inheritance until the king was old enough to take up the personal rule of both his kingdoms. Business was to be as before; in effect the reign of Henry V was to continue in commission.

Of course, a Council could not rule as a king, let alone a dead one. It was dominated by a triumvirate: the Dukes of Gloucester and Bedford, and Henry Beaufort, Bishop of Winchester (soon to gain his cardinal's hat). Conflict emerged almost immediately between Gloucester and Beaufort. By 1425 they were almost at blows, and periodically over the next ten years rivalry between them reached dangerous proportions. It was left to the Duke of Bedford to make peace between them, especially in 1425-7 and 1433-4. Bedford did not always see eye to eye with Gloucester, especially over the conduct of the war, and found an ally on the English Council in Beaufort. On the other hand, Bedford was intensely conscious of his brother's dignity and thus ensured that Gloucester never lost face. What is remarkable is not that there was tension, but that for over fifteen years it was contained; in the last resort Gloucester and Beaufort held back for the greater good of the realm.

It is not surprising that the Council had difficulty keeping the peace in England. Many conflicts arose within the ranks of the greater aristocracy. But by dint of resorting to arbitration where an adult king would have imposed judgment, by requiring subjects to take oaths, and by other novel means, the Council kept the worst possible abuses of the law at bay. In one region, the borders with Scotland, it even improved on the record of Henry V. The campaign against heresy was sustained; and, after a further rising in 1430, Lollardy was kept firmly underground. The Council kept the Crown solvent, if only by a whisker. While at first the war was funded from French revenue, after 1429 the English Parliament was called upon to renew taxation. A thorough retrenchment in 1433 maintained credibility, but by 1437 the royal finances were in a parlous state.

The war itself was waged relentlessly. Bedford won a victory at Verneuil in 1424 almost as decisive as Agincourt. Until 1429, although the Valois claimant to the French Crown, Charles VII, could not be brought to heel, the area under Lancastrian control was steadily extended. But significant ground was lost after the failure before Orléans, and the combined blows of the rapprochement between Burgundy and Charles VII at the Treaty of Arras and

Bedford's death within a week in 1435, left little more of Henry V's conquests in hand than the duchy of Normandy.

For all this, when Henry VI approached his sixteenth birthday at the end of 1437 his councillors could justifiably feel that they had done as well as could have been reasonably expected. The kingdom of England was at peace, the Crown was solvent, and the duchy of Normandy was still in Lancastrian hands. The transfer of power was already in hand in 1437 when the king's prerogative in matters of his personal grace were restored to him. For a further five years, policy continued to be determined by the advice of a transitional Council, but from 1443 or thereabouts the king was deemed to be enjoying his full powers. The process was unclear, prolonged and apparently conflict-free because Henry VI had grown into a man quite unlike his father and utterly indifferent to the exercise of power.

The boy king had received a comprehensive training for his future role. Until 1428 he was in the care of his mother. At the age of seven he was moved to the tutelage of the Earl of Warwick, the most renowned soldier of his generation, who was charged with the king's education in languages, literature, courtesy and chivalry: a miniature suit of armour and a toy sword were made for the young boy. From an early age, Henry was introduced to public affairs. Before he was two he was brought ceremonially to occupy his throne at Parliament; two years later he was paraded through London in a display calculated to reassure public opinion at the height of the quarrel between Gloucester and Beaufort. Henry was already accustomed to ceremony when he was crowned, first as King of England, on 6 November 1429, and then as King of France, in Paris, on 16 December 1431. He began to be briefed about public affairs in 1433, and was brought into some decision-making the following year. He started to attend the Council after his fourteenth birthday at the end of 1435, and thereafter his own name was attached to some grants.

By 1437, however, his personality was worryingly apparent. Henry was a young man who turned his back on war and the chivalric ethic; by temperament and inclination he was more suited to the cloister, to be a monk not a soldier. Devoted to the Church, he was misogynist and prurient. He modelled his life on the unworldly Carthusian ideal. His one significant public interest was educational benefaction: he founded Eton College (as a seminary for priests) and King's College, Cambridge, in 1440, well before he was twenty. He was – not surprisingly, given that he had known nothing else – a young man highly conscious of his kingly state. But in governing and in warfare he had no interest whatsoever; in decision-making he was merely vacillating; and in dispensing pardons and distributing patronage he was feckless. It soon became widely known that the king was a soft touch, and he was publicly characterized as childlike or simple. It is possible, indeed, that Henry was a complete cipher who left all to his advisers and made no attempt to assert his own will. It is unlikely, however, that he played no role at all in formulating policy: it was probably his personal wish, for example, to see peace made with France. While the more partisan elements of his rule at home are likely to have been the responsibility of others, it was natural to blame the king in whose name all actions were taken. By 1444 his despairing councillors sought to impose some restraint on the king's profligacy, but to little avail. In all respects except his piety, there could not have been a sharper contrast with his father.

The first consequence of Henry's supine rule was the emergence of faction at court. By 1443 a group around the person of William de la Pole, Earl of Suffolk, had taken power. It has been argued that Suffolk sought high-mindedly to fill the vacuum left by the king's indifference, but there is no reason to suppose that he and his followers were uniquely disinterested. In fact, Suffolk and those attached to him lined their own pockets during the 1440s. They were also responsible for the destruction of the heir presumptive to the throne and their principal opponent, the Duke of

Clockwise from left 96. Engraving of Cardinal Henry Beaufort's tomb in Winchester Cathedral.
During the 1430s he controlled the government of the young Henry VI.
97. Catherine of Valois does her duty. The Birth of Henry VI from the Pageant of Richard Beauchamp.
98. The coronation of Henry VI as King of England in 1429 from the pageant of Richard Beauchamp.

Gloucester, in 1447. This is not to deny that, personal interest apart, they did not do the best they could for the king. Yet the finances of the Crown collapsed and towards the end of the decade there was an alarming deterioration in public order, the worst excesses being laid at the government's door. As far as foreign policy was concerned, Suffolk dutifully sought to find a way to peace with France. In 1444 a truce was sealed at Tours, according to the terms of which the king was to be married to a French princess, Margaret of Anjou. The earl was probably not responsible for the king's capricious promise in 1445 to cede Maine to the French, although he had to shoulder the burden of implementing the decision. Further attempts to find a more lasting peace foundered on the question of Maine. When war broke out again in 1449, disaster followed. By August 1450 all Henry V's conquest had been lost.

The outcry among the political classes led to impeachment proceedings against Suffolk in 1450. Suffolk was pardoned by the king, but subsequently murdered on his way into exile. Shortly afterwards, popular revolt in the southeastern counties under Jack Cade almost brought the kingdom to its knees. In the aftermath of the upheavals of 1450, new figures emerged on the scene. The chief beneficiary was Edmund Beaufort, Duke of Somerset, the late cardinal's nephew, who, returning from the Continent, became the king's new principal minister. He was opposed by Richard, Duke of York, the king's cousin and, after Gloucester's death, the would-be heir presumptive. York was Lieutenant of Ireland. He also hoped to profit from Suffolk's fall. Presenting himself as the spokesman for the common weal and by birth the king's natural adviser, he tried by various means, all abortive, to force himself on the government. Somerset, secure in royal favour, withstood this challenge and restored effective rule, perhaps even coaxing the king into more active involvement. However, all was undone by the sudden collapse of Henry's mental health in August 1453.

For almost eighteen months, Henry VI remained in a virtual coma, withdrawn completely into himself. After six months of confusion awaiting the king's recovery, the royal Council appointed Richard of York as protector of the realm. Thus by fortuitous means York secured the prominence he had vainly sought since 1450. York's protectorate was crisis-ridden. He had to deal with major disturbances in Yorkshire triggered by a violent quarrel between the families of Neville and Percy. He had entered into an alliance with the Nevilles, especially the young and dynamic Richard, Earl of Warwick, and his solution to their quarrel with the Percys was inevitably partisan. Henry Percy, Earl of Northumberland, was driven into the arms of the Duke of Somerset, whom York sought to bring to trial for treason. When the king recovered his wits at the end of 1454, and York stepped down, Somerset was restored to favour. The rivals were set on a collision course. In the centre of St Albans in May 1455 the Yorkists overwhelmed the court adherents, the Duke of Somerset and the Earl of Northumberland being deliberately sought out and killed by their enemies. Once more York took up the reins of power, but from the slaughter at St Albans sprang the Wars of the Roses.

The king was in a sorry state. He had recovered his sanity, but his health was permanently impaired; at the end of 1455 a second protectorate was briefly established. Whereas before he was disinclined to attend to affairs of state, after the end of 1454 Henry was incapable of sustained effort. The circumstances could not have been worse: had he remained completely incapacitated a permanent conciliar government could have been established; as it was, he was able to express his views, but was no more than a figurehead around which factions swirled amid a deepening crisis. After the death of the Duke of Somerset, Queen Margaret emerged as the focal point of those with access to the king and opposed to the Duke of York. Just like Edward II's wife Isabella before her, Margaret of Anjou has received a bad press as a 'she-wolf of France', but largely because the historical tradition was created by Yorkist propagandists. Until 1455, Margaret had fulfilled her conventional supportive role. Moreover, she had done her duty in producing an heir, Edward, their only child, born late in 1453. It was only gradually, and with growing concern for the future of her son, that she took on the role of defending her husband's throne, and not at the forefront until after the failure of a concerted effort at reconciliation in the spring of 1458.

By the summer of 1459 the kingdom was facing civil war. For eighteen months between September 1459 and March 1461, and through six battles, first one side and then the other had the upper hand. York and his allies finally abandoned the strategy of seeking to rule through force in the king's name in the autumn of 1460, when the duke boldly laid claim to the throne himself. Although he himself was subsequently defeated and killed at the Battle of Wakefield, his eighteen-year-old heir seized the throne as Edward IV, which he secured by his victory on the field of Towton at the end of March 1461.

Control of the person of Henry VI, through whose name the realm continued to be ruled until March 1461, was vital through all the conflict. By then, however, he was but a puppet, dismissed airily as a mommet by one of York's allies. The queen, however, had managed to recover his person after her victory at the Second Battle of St Albans in February 1461 and after Towton she was able to take him and their son away to safety in Scotland. For three years she fought on from a toehold in Northumberland. Eventually she and her son took refuge in France, leaving the deposed king in the care of loyal Lancastrians in northern England. In 1465 his whereabouts was betrayed and he was escorted to safekeeping in the Tower. His life was spared primarily because his adolescent son was alive and well in exile, and his cause revived as the new king's regime fell apart. In 1470 the Earl of Warwick, Edward IV's right-hand man in 1461, changed sides: it was this political vacil-lation that caused another change of monarch, and earned Warwick the nickname of 'Kingmaker' in subsequent generations. Having come to terms with Queen Margaret, Warwick ousted Edward and restored Henry VI. Warwick governed during this brief readeption; Henry himself, after the humiliations of the last decade, was a broken man, bewildered by what was happening in his name and pitied by his subjects.

The end came in May 1471. Edward IV recovered the throne, defeating and killing Warwick and then the Lancastrian Prince of Wales successively at the Battles of Barnet and Tewkesbury. While the tenacious Queen Margaret was to end her days in penniless and grief-stricken exile, the death of Prince Edward had the effect of making Henry VI totally expendable. On the night of 21 May, he was put to death on the orders of King Edward. The official story was that he had died of melan-choly, but when his body was laid out for display it was seen to bleed. Henry was buried without ceremony at Chertsey Abbey. Soon a vigorous cult grew up around this saintly man who had preferred in his life to be nearer to God than to be sullied by temporal concerns. Edward IV tried to suppress the cult; Richard III sought to harness it to his own cause by removing the body to St George's Chapel, Windsor; and Henry VII tried in vain to have his predecessor, whose heir he claimed to be, canonized.

While Henry VI never won the respect of his subjects as a king, he was admired in his lifetime for his personal qualities. That is one reason why there was such reluctance to depose him, and even at first to kill him. His failure, then, was not merely the result of his political incompetence. His father's impossible legacy also played a part: by crowning the young Henry VI as King of France, his advisers may have thought to fulfil the father's vision, but in reality simply made it more difficult to find an honourable peace. The cost of sustaining the war crippled an England already weakened by a severe economic recession. Even so, the dynasty itself need not have failed: Henry, like Edward II before him, had a son to succeed. Ultimately, Henry VI was undone by the flaw in his inherited title. His father had banished it from immediate memory, but had not eradicated it. It came back to haunt the son and his advisers, and then to become a reality through the frustrated ambition of Richard of York, the heir to the Mortimer claim to the throne. Thus the Lancastrian dynasty turned full circle on the wheel of fortune. Because of the flaw in the title, it was not just the king, but the dynasty itself, that was overthrown in 1461.

THE HOUSE OF YORK: EDWARD IV (1461-1483)

On 4 March 1461 the eighteen-year-old Edward, Duke of York, occupied the throne of England as the self-proclaimed legitimate heir to Richard II, established through parliamentary recognition of his father, Richard of York, as heir to the throne in November 1460 and justified on the grounds that Henry VI had forfeited the throne by breaking that accord. Edward had been born in Rouen on 28 April 1442 when his mother the Duchess Cecily (Neville), youngest daughter of the first Earl of Westmorland and Joan Beaufort, was residing there with her husband, then the English Lieutenant of Normandy. What little is known of his upbringing suggests that it was conventional for a member of the greater aristocracy. He was first reported in public affairs as a twelve-year-old in the company of his father, by which time he had been created Earl of March. By the time he was seventeen he was fully engaged, fleeing from the Yorkist rout at Ludford to Calais in the company of his Neville kinsmen, the father-and-son Earls of Salisbury and Warwick. Here he rapidly came under the influence of the dynamic Warwick, who had little time for the residual Lancastrian loyalty and tortured consciences of his father's generation. Edward fought his way through the Battles of Northampton and Mortimers Cross before rallying a wavering Warwick after a defeat at the Second Battle of St Albans. Within three weeks of taking the throne, Edward triumphed over the forces of the Lancastrians at Towton. Although youthful, he had proved his mettle in battle, and had emerged as an inspiring leader of a faction in the midst of civil war. A tall, handsome, charming and (in contrast to his dithering father) decisive young man, he promised a new beginning for the realm.

That the promise failed to materialize was the result of several factors. One was that it proved difficult to eradicate Lancastrian resistance. It took three years to subdue the far North of England; and it was not until 1468 that the last resistance in Wales, focused on Harlech Castle, was overcome. Moreover, while Henry VI fell into the king's hands in 1465, his queen, and above all his son Edward, Prince of Wales, escaped to France to form an alternative government in exile. So long as the Lancastrian cause retained political credibility, a significant number of the English peerage hedged their bets. Secondly, Edward's own power base was narrow. The Yorkist cause had only ever been supported by a minority of the peerage. The Yorkist affinity, from which emerged key figures such as Lords Hastings, Herbert and Howard, was not as extensive as the Lancastrian network of support. Edward was overly dependent on one family, the Nevilles: Warwick and his brothers George (Bishop of Exeter, soon to be Archbishop of York) and John (who rose to be Earl of Northumberland). Warwick in particular was indispensable in the early years, shouldering much of the defence of the realm and the burden of diplomacy. Thirdly, the peace and prosperity promised by royal propaganda proved stubbornly elusive. Economic slump persisted, worsened by a trade war with the Netherlands; popular unrest erupted in the early 1460s and again at the end of the decade. And finally, there were Edward IV's own shortcomings. Decisive in war he may have been, but he was indolent and easy-going in peace. His inclination towards mercy and reconciliation, unlike Warwick's vicious vindictiveness, led him to misjudge some of his past opponents. He was also willing to allow others too much influence, which led to the growth of factionalism at court. Inexperienced in politics, he remained too long in awe of the mighty earl who had assisted him to the throne, and was then inept in escaping from his shadow.

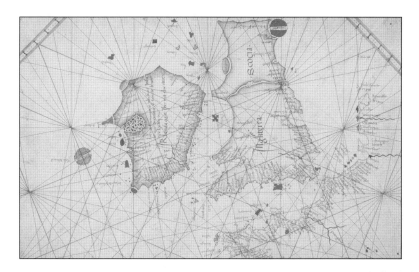

99. International trade, for which the British Isles were mapped for Italian merchants in 1473, revived under Edward IV.

100. Edward IV and his consort Elizabeth in the north window at Canterbury Cathedral. This was a gift to the church from Edward in *c.* 1480.

The rift with Warwick began in 1464, with the king's secret marriage to Elizabeth Woodville, a widow who, had she not stood her ground, might otherwise simply (and, as contemporaries thought, more suitably) have become Edward's mistress. Edward kept Warwick in the dark over the clandestine marriage for several months. When it became public, it was also soon apparent that it would result in changes at court: Edward began to gather around him a new body of favourites, prominent among them being the queen's father, Earl Rivers. Warwick's influence waned as Rivers' waxed. Tension developed in particular in the arena of foreign policy. Between 1465 and 1467 the king encouraged Warwick to pursue a French alliance, while at the same time also conducting parallel negotiations with the Duke of Burgundy. While Warwick was fully aware of the parallel negotiations, the underhand and humiliating manner in which Edward finally opted for a Burgundian treaty, through the marriage of his sister Margaret to Duke Charles, greatly incensed the earl. Thereafter, despite attempts to repair the damage, Warwick and the king were set on course for a collision that would have disastrous consequences, in different ways, for both sides.

The final blow to Warwick's political and personal pride came when the king refused his consent to a marriage between the earl's daughter, Isabel, and Edward's younger brother George, Duke of Clarence. In the summer of 1469 the earl, having suborned Clarence, took matters into his own hands. He raised his followers in the North, who destroyed the king's forces at Edgecote. In the aftermath, several prominent courtiers, including Earl Rivers, were hunted down and murdered. The king was briefly the earl's prisoner; but it proved impossible for Warwick to rule in his name, and so a truce between them was agreed. In the spring of 1470 Warwick rose again, this time intending to depose Edward and install Clarence. But the plot failed, their troops were overrun and the two rebel lords fled to France. There followed a most remarkable volte-face, as Warwick came to terms with Margaret of Anjou to restore Henry VI. A wave of aristocratic and popular support carried him to London unopposed and effected the release of Henry from the Tower. Edward IV was forced to flee rapidly to Holland with but a handful of loyal associates, his disastrous reign apparently over.

Warwick immediately took steps to prepare the kingdom for the return of the Prince of Wales and his mother. In accordance with the terms of his treaty with Louis XI, who had brokered the reconciliation, he declared war on the Duke of Burgundy. In response, the duke, who had at first kept the tiny band of Yorkist exiles at arm's length, sponsored an invasion. Edward was able to make land in Yorkshire before the return of Margaret of Anjou. In a brilliant campaign, the decisive moment of which was his own reconciliation with Clarence, he brought Warwick to battle at Barnet on 14 April 1471 and there destroyed him. On the same day the Lancastrians landed at Weymouth. Edward caught their army at Tewkesbury on 4 May. The Lancastrian Prince of Wales was killed, sealing the fate of his father. Edward IV, almost miraculously, had recovered his throne.

It was his military prowess that saved Edward in 1471, just as it had rescued the Yorkist cause in 1461. The restored king embarked on his second reign in a far stronger position. The Lancastrian line had been extinguished, and most of its prominent supporters had been killed in battle. The majority of those who survived now made their peace with the regime, believing their cause to be lost. A few, especially the Earl of Oxford, endeavoured to continue the fight, rallying to an unlikely claimant to the throne in the person of Henry Tudor, Earl of Richmond, himself in exile in Brittany. Furthermore the Nevilles had been removed. Warwick had proved as formidable an opponent as he had been a stalwart ally. His power had derived from his wealth and armed following (especially in the North of England), his command of Calais (of which he had been captain since 1456, and from which he controlled the Channel), his high standing in France (with which he had established virtually independent diplomatic links in the 1460s), and his readiness to court popularity and to incite uprisings in his support. This last made him particularly dangerous, for he thereby posed a threat not just to the ruling dynasty, but also to the social order itself. It is just possible that in 1471 the political nation sighed collectively in relief at his demise.

Edward IV embarked immediately on a plan to invade France. His purpose, he declared, was to heal the wounds that had inflicted England by making war on its common enemy. For four years he worked to put together an alliance against Louis XI with the Dukes of Brittany and Burgundy, cajoled Parliament into raising taxes, and brought together a large and well-provisioned army. But the invasion, after so much effort, came to little. The Dukes of Brittany and Burgundy failed to take to the field, the king moved only cautiously into French territory, and he was soon engaged in negotiations with Louis XI. At Picquigny, terms were agreed, which included a commercial treaty, a royal marriage, and the payment of an annual pension to Edward. The English army returned ignominiously home. Nevertheless, Edward was able successfully to present his 'great enterprise' as a triumph of sorts, and the Treaty of Picquigny brought French recognition of the Yorkist regime.

In 1476 the now secure dynasty marked its newfound unity by the solemn reburial of its founder, Richard of York, in the collegiate church he had founded at Fotheringhay in Northamptonshire. The unity, however, was illusory. In 1477 the king and his brother George, Duke of Clarence, fell out again. The occasion was the king's veto of the duke as a candidate for the hand of Mary, Duchess of Burgundy, after the deaths of her father and of Clarence's duchess. In an attempt to demonstrate that he was still a force to be reckoned with, Clarence took the law into his own hands in pursuit of a belief that his duchess had been poisoned. The quarrel escalated. Clarence was condemned for treason by a pliant Parliament and executed in February 1478. It is not all certain that Clarence was guilty of any greater offence than perverting the cause of justice. He was the victim of his own incorrigibility and the king's frustration. After his judicial murder, it was clear to all that the king was fully in command of his kingdom.

At home, peace and prosperity at last returned. Prosperity derived fundamentally from European economic recovery and a revival in overseas trade. But royal policy assisted the recovery. A stable regime was maintained through the agency of a handful of Edward's closest associates, kinsmen and senior officers of the royal household, who exercised considerable power on the king's behalf in the provinces. Abroad, Edward sought to maintain the benefits of the Treaty of Picquigny, while at the same time not allowing France to destroy the independent duchy of Burgundy. In a tortuous cycle of diplomacy he was eventually the loser, forfeiting his pension and the French match and witnessing a rapprochement between France and Burgundy from which he was excluded. One reason was that he became entangled from 1480 in a war with Scotland, which seriously restricted his freedom of diplomatic manoeuvre. When he died in April 1483 after a short illness, and still only forty, there was an imminent prospect of renewed war on two fronts.

The king was buried in St George's Chapel, Windsor, a royal mausoleum upon which he had lavished considerable expense in the last years of his life. He died unchallenged in his kingdom. His commanding presence and affability were undiminished. But he had run to seed; he became exceedingly fat and gave himself over to a round of ceaseless pleasure. Renowned for his many mistresses, most notably Jane Shore, he fathered one acknowledged bastard, Arthur. His queen dutifully tolerated his infidelities and bore him ten children, the last in 1480, including two sons who survived their father. She has been maligned as a grasping and scheming woman, largely on the basis of hostile propaganda circulated first by Warwick and later by her brother-in-law, Richard III. There is no reason to suppose, however, that she was anything but a conventional queen. Thrust into the political world in 1483, she was out of her depth. Outmanoeuvred by Richard III, she later also forfeited the trust of her future son-in-law, Henry VII, and ended her days in forced and impoverished retirement in Bermondsey Abbey, where she died in 1492.

Edward's own historical reputation proved no less controversial. Two traditions emerged shortly after his death: one, first expressed by his French contemporary Philippe de Commynes, that he was a lazy playboy given to fits of tyranny; and the other, first developed by the anonymous author of a continuation of the Crowland Chronicle, that he was a strong and decisive monarch. Broadly, it is now agreed that Edward did not neglect the business of kingship. But the division has persisted through to the twenty-first century in a debate as to whether the king relied too much on too few and alienated others who were excluded, especially by his manipulation of the laws of inheritance for the benefit of his immediate family; or whether, by the constructive partnership he developed with the local elites, he brought the medieval practice of kingship to perfection. One view holds him ultimately responsible for the collapse of his dynasty shortly after his death; the other attributes that collapse entirely to the subsequent actions of his brother. Assessment of his reign relies mainly on the last years, which Sir Thomas More remembered nostalgically as a golden age. In this period, royal authority and solvency were restored after more than two decades of weakness and debt. Several historians have discerned in this the foundations of a new style of monarchy; others have been doubtful. But tragically, domestic peace proved short-lived and royal recovery was brutally interrupted. Within two months, Edward's twelve-year-old son was deposed and a new round of civil war engulfed the kingdom.

EDWARD V (APRIL-JUNE 1483)

Edward V, the most tragic of fifteenth-century kings, was never crowned and reigned for only seventy-eight days. He was born in the sanctuary precinct at Westminster Abbey on 2 November 1470, where his mother Elizabeth Woodville had taken refuge after his father had fled the kingdom. In June 1471, two months after Edward IV recovered the throne, he was created Prince of Wales, and a Council was nominated to administer his patrimony. Before he was three, in September 1473 he was removed from his mother's care, and established in an independent household at Ludlow, under the tutelage of his maternal uncle Anthony, Earl Rivers, and Bishop Alcock of Worcester. In time, considerable administrative powers were granted to the emergent Council in the Marches, of which he was the nominal head. He was, according to his father's instructions, educated in 'virtuous learning' and 'honest disports', with the learning, as later reports suggest, being influenced by the new humanist culture introduced from the Continent. From 1476 negotiations were conducted for the prince's marriage, but he was still single when on 9 April 1483 his father died and he became king, still only twelve years of age.

His kingdom was immediately overwhelmed by crisis as his father's principal supporters competed for control during his minority. Edward himself, and his younger brother Richard, were the principal victims of this murderous strife. While his coronation was rapidly fixed for 4 May, a plan of his maternal relations, the Woodvilles, to secure control was rejected by the royal Council. However, mere presidency of the minority Council was equally unacceptable to his paternal uncle, Richard, Duke of Gloucester, who seized Rivers and his principal companions as they escorted the king up to Westminster, took custody of the youth, postponed the coronation and installed himself as protector. For six weeks, Gloucester ruled in the name of the uncrowned king; but then, in the space of ten days in the middle of June, he took the throne for himself, claiming that the king and his brother were illegitimate. The two princes were removed to the Tower, where they disap-

Clockwise from top   101. Misericord carving of Richard III at Christchurch Priory.
102. Fifteenth-century portrait of King Edward V, standing to the left of Edward IV, from the
manuscript 'Of Dictes and Sayings of the Philosophers' at Lambeth Palace.
103. Coin of Richard III struck in London.
104. Coin of Edward V.

Clockwise from top left 105. The coat of arms of Edward V.
106. The coat of arms of Richard III.
107. Badge of Richard III from MS Vincent 152 at the Herald's College.
108. The coat of arms of Anne Neville, Richard III's Queen.

peared. Some human remains discovered in the seventeenth century, and reputed to be those of the young king and his brother, were interred in Westminster Abbey.

The dead Edward V was praised on the eve of his planned coronation and after his death as a paragon of virtue, but these plaudits were what one would have expected in the circumstances, and there is no telling what manner of king he would have made had he been allowed to live to enjoy his inheritance. Meanwhile, the fate of the Princes Edward and Richard has remained a mystery to this day. The moving story told by Thomas More that they were suffocated under their pillows is not to be trusted. However, informed opinion believed that they were dead by September 1483, and that the deaths had been ordered by the new king, Richard III. And that remains the safest conclusion to be reached. The deaths of two boys on the threshold of adulthood, ordered, it was believed, by the uncle who had taken them into his care, shocked a not easily shaken kingdom.

RICHARD III (1483-1485)

Richard III was born at Fotheringhay on 2 October 1452, the last child of Richard, Duke of York, and the Duchess Cecily. Little is known of his childhood, except that at the height of the civil war in 1459-61 he was sent for safe keeping with his siblings to the Netherlands. After the triumph of his eldest brother, Edward IV, he was created Duke of Gloucester and subsequently for four years was placed for his upbringing in the care of the Earl of Warwick. However, by 1469 he had returned to the king's household and remained steadfastly loyal to Edward IV throughout the succeeding crises. Richard shared exile with Edward in 1470-1 and distinguished himself on the fields of Barnet and Tewkesbury. He was lavishly rewarded after 1471, being granted the northern estates of the Nevilles, succeeding to the Kingmaker's offices in the North, and being allowed to marry Warwick's younger daughter Anne. Stepping into Warwick's shoes, in the next decade he both secured the North for the dynasty and made himself exceptionally powerful in the region, even to the extent that the king, to whom he remained close, was dangerously reliant on him. The war with Scotland, upon which Edward IV embarked in 1480, was largely Gloucester's doing; the reward early in 1483 of a future palatinate carved out of Cumberland and planned conquests in Southwest Scotland was an indication of his influence and ambitions.

Edward IV's death threw these plans into disarray. Gloucester's determination to depose his nephew and take the throne for himself was not long-standing. It is possible that he had already committed himself when he forcibly took Edward V into his possession at Stony Stratford and made himself protector against the wishes of the majority of the minority Council. Alternatively, he may not have reached his decision until he discovered that he could not extend his protectorate, and his unchallengeable control of the kingdom, after a coronation. In a brilliantly executed coup, not of all of which necessarily went to plan, he occupied the throne on 26 June 1483 and was crowned on 6 July. His path to the throne was assisted by the support of several noblemen who had harboured grievances against Edward IV, especially Henry Stafford, Duke of Buckingham, and by his exploitation of divisions in the ranks of Edward's closest associates.

Despite the ease with which he took the throne, Richard's reign was disastrous. His wrong-footed opponents within the Yorkist ranks re-grouped and raised rebellion in September 1483 in the name of Henry Tudor. Buckingham, for reasons difficult to discern, threw in his lot. The rebellion was crushed. But in its aftermath, to secure the southern counties that had rebelled, Richard became over-reliant on his own followers, especially a group of northerners whose presence caused further resentment and fresh disturbances. Richard had at first pressed on with war against Scotland, and had resorted to a war at sea to put pressure on Brittany to surrender

Henry to him. This failed. He made peace with Scotland in 1484, but overtures to Brittany were thwarted when Henry Tudor escaped to France. By the end of 1484, Richard was anticipating and preparing to meet invasion. When it came, he banked all on a decisive victory in the field. But he was overthrown and killed at the Battle of Bosworth on 22 August 1485. His body was buried without ceremony in the friary at nearby Leicester, and his remains were subsequently dumped in the River Soar when the friary was dissolved.

Of Richard III's queen, Anne Neville, whom he married in 1472, little is known. She was born in 1456, the younger daughter of Richard Neville, Earl of Warwick. She had already been married to the Lancastrian Prince Edward who died at Tewkesbury in 1471. She was described by an admirer as 'semely, amiable and beuteus'. She had one son, christened Edward, who was installed as Prince of Wales at York in September 1483. He died six months later, to the reported grief of both his parents. Queen Anne died in the spring of 1485 amid rumours, which the king was forced publicly to deny, that he had poisoned her. Richard III also fathered two illegitimate children by unidentified mothers.

There can be little doubt that by his actions Richard III destroyed his own dynasty, which did not survive beyond one generation. The self-destructive fratricidal strife of the Yorkists stands in marked contrast to the fraternal solidarity of the Lancastrians. Richard himself has become the most controversial of English kings. Neither the deformed hunchback nor the serial killer of later legend, he had many qualities recognized by his contemporaries. He was a man who took the chivalric ethic seriously; he displayed a strong personal piety; he sought to improve the administration of justice; and he acquired a high reputation in the north of England, where he built up a dedicated following. However, his actions in 1483, when he deposed the nephew whose care he had taken upon himself and ordered the killing without trial of those who stood in his way, permanently tarnished his reputation. The majority of his subjects never accepted the legitimacy of his rule; the belief that he had no right to be king, the awareness of which perhaps explains his increasingly desperate attempt to demonstrate his worth, significantly undermined his regime. He was never in his lifetime able to shake off the belief that he was responsible for the deaths of Edward V and his brother. And, in spite of a sustained campaign in the twentieth century to rehabilitate Richard III, this flaw in the morality and legitimacy of his regime remains for most historians the decisive element in his downfall.

6

THE HOUSE OF TUDOR
1485-1603

RICHARD REX

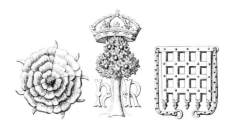

The argument that the Tudors brought peace, stability and prosperity to England after a century of infighting and disorder is a myth very largely of their own making: Henry VII, Henry VIII and Elizabeth I were all expert in the arts of what today is called propaganda, and much of the popular modern image of those rulers still derives from the messages they chose to impart to their subjects. To an extent, the Tudors were simply the beneficiaries of an economic and cultural dispensation that gave England new wealth, new ideas, and a new sense of its own identity during the sixteenth century. On the other hand, the greatest of the Tudors, Henry VIII and Elizabeth I, clearly helped to shape the government, religion and culture of their realm in a forceful, dynamic and expansive manner that demonstrated not only the long stretch of the arm of State but the real and considerable impact of personal monarchy. Most remarkably – and something often taken too much for granted today – the Tudor dynasty was the first successfully to establish both the principle and the practice of female monarchy: and if the experiment manifestly failed in the case of Jane Grey, and was at best of arguable success in the case of Mary I, it was spectacularly vindicated by the exceptionally durable and stable reign of Elizabeth I. Without the right of female succession, the Tudor dynasty would have failed in 1553, and might have gone down in history more in terms of the Lancastrian regime which, to a degree, it had earlier claimed to reinstate. The triumph of pragmatism represented in the failure of the male succession and the acceptance of regnant queens in itself articulated something of the new political culture that the Tudors had embraced and imposed upon the kingdom of England.

HENRY VII (1485-1509)

Henry VII was born at some distance from the English throne. His mother, Margaret Beaufort, was the great-granddaughter of John of Gaunt by his mistress, Katherine Swynford, and it was from her that Henry derived the dregs of Plantagenet blood that were his claim to the succession in 1485. His father, Edmund Tudor, was connected less directly but more respectably with

110. Seal of Henry VII: the king is portrayed seated on a throne with attributes of majesty.

111. Sir Thomas Lovell, who fought at Bosworth and was Henry VII's perpetual Chancellor of the Exchequer.

112. Henry VII.

royalty. He was the son of a Welsh gentleman, Owen Tudor, a minor officeholder in the Lancastrian court who won the hand in marriage of none other than Catherine of Valois, the young widow of Henry V. Henry VII made more of this connection than he did of his dubious descent from John of Gaunt: Henry V was still a charismatic enough figure to be worth invoking, even if only as a relative by marriage. The irony is that, were it not for the French Salic Law (which, though not recognized by the English, forbade female succession), Henry VII had a better claim to the French crown than to the English.

Henry was born on 28 January 1457, a few months after his father's death and a little before his mother's fourteenth birthday. His early years were overshadowed by the Wars of the Roses, and once Prince Edward of Lancaster (the only son of Henry VI) fell in the Battle of Tewkesbury (1471), Henry was packed off abroad for safety. As Edward IV consolidated his position in the 1470s, Henry's prospects seemed bleak. Edward had two sons and two brothers, and the nobility of England rallied behind him. Had it not been for Richard III, Henry could never have become king. It was Richard who cleared his path, splitting the Yorkist interest by calling the legitimacy of his two nephews into question, seizing the throne from them, and having them murdered.

Richard's squandering of the political resources carefully built up by his brother opened the door to Henry. His first raid, launched from Brittany in 1484, achieved nothing more than to provoke Richard to retaliate through diplomatic channels. But in 1485 he had another go. His mother, whose successive marriages had brought her considerable personal wealth along with a web of useful family connections, had agreed with Edward IV's widow, Elizabeth Woodville, that Yorkist supporters would back Henry Tudor on the understanding that he would marry Edward's daughter, Princess Elizabeth. Landing in Milford Haven on 7 August 1485, he moved north and east through Wales, gathering support. From Shrewsbury he marched across the Midlands, encountering Richard's army near Market Bosworth in Leicestershire on 22 August. Two forces from the north also converged on the scene: one under Henry Percy, Earl of Northumberland, and the other led by Thomas Lord Stanley (Margaret Beaufort's third husband and thus Henry Tudor's stepfather). In the ensuing battle, Stanley's decision to support Henry was no great surprise. But Percy's failure to commit himself to Richard decided the battle, while Richard's own reckless charge cost him his life and thus made Bosworth Field decisive.

Henry took possession of London, summoned Parliament, and backdated his reign to the day before Bosworth – thus legitimising the attainder of those who had fought against him. That vast majority of the peerage, who had studiously held aloof from the Bosworth campaign, thronged to the coronation on Sunday 30 October 1485. They were less enthusiastic in the following year, when Henry faced his first serious challenge: the appearance of a youth purporting to be Edward, Earl of Warwick (the son of Edward IV's brother George, Duke of Clarence), but better known to posterity as Lambert Simnel. Backed in Ireland by the Earl of Kildare, who induced the Irish Parliament to recognize the youth as 'Edward VI', and in England by John de la Pole, Earl of Lincoln, Simnel was perhaps no more absurd a contender for the throne in 1487 than Henry himself had been in 1485. But in the decisive battle at Stoke (near Newark) on 16 June, it was Lincoln who fell and the reigning king who survived. Simnel himself was captured and treated with unwonted clemency for a Tudor rebel: he was put to work in the king's kitchen.

This did not discourage Henry's enemies, and a few years later a similar plot was hatched around the person of Perkin Warbeck, who was touted for much of the 1490s as Edward IV's second son, Prince Richard of York, and was shuttled from one princely court to another as the kaleidoscope of diplomacy shifted around. In 1495 Warbeck made an unsuccessful attempt to land in Kent, and in 1496 King James IV of Scotland briefly took up arms on his behalf. Henry in turn planned a punitive expedition against James in 1497, only to find that he had to employ his army in putting down a rebellion provoked by the taxes that had paid for it. The ease with which the rebels, who rose in Cornwall and the West Country, reached the outskirts of London, showed how vulnerable the Tudor dynasty still was – although the royal army dispersed the rebels easily enough in the field. Warbeck himself landed in Cornwall hoping to exploit the situation, but was soon captured. In 1499 he was executed for having plotted escape.

The first half of the reign thus did nothing to calm the fears of a king who was deeply suspicious by temperament. He trusted few of his nobles and did little to restore their numbers, which had diminished sharply over his lifetime. Attainted peers were only slowly allowed back into favour, and few among Henry's own servants were promoted to the peerage: knighthood was the usual limit of their advancement. The lynching of the Earl of Northumberland in 1487 enabled Henry to erode Percy hegemony in the far North. Potential Yorkist claimants to the throne also fared badly. After a lifetime in captivity, the Earl of Warwick was executed in 1499 on trumped-up charges of treason, while Lincoln's younger brothers all fled the country sooner or later. Henry's suspicions were not confined to peers. Knights, gentry, and even wealthy merchants were, like peers, liable to punitive fines not only for real crimes but also for failing to fulfil anachronistic feudal obligations, and were often put under enormous financial bonds against possible repetitions of offences. All of this helped to keep the landed classes firmly under the king's thumb.

Henry's security policy merged imperceptibly with his fiscal policy. Clinging onto the crown lands (ampler now than at any time since 1066), increasing customs duties, and exploiting feudal rights such as wardship to the uttermost, Henry wiped out royal debt. Morally indefensible and legally dubious, his 'fiscal feudalism' freed him from dependence upon parliamentary taxes, which he disliked as a result of the rising of 1497. By such means he accumulated a vast treasure, which Francis Bacon, over a century later, reckoned at around £2,000,000. Not that Henry was mean. He spent lavishly on court entertainment and also on royal palaces, notably that of Greenwich. Yet this expenditure was not wanton. Display and magnificence were among the tools of kingship, helping to convince both Henry's own subjects and the ambassadors of foreign princes that the King of England's position was more secure than perhaps he himself felt.

In one respect Henry was an exemplary king. He provided adequately for the succession. His marriage to Elizabeth of York in January 1486 not only unified the houses of Lancaster and York but was a close and loving relationship. Prince Arthur was born later in the same year, followed by Margaret (1489), Henry (1494), and Mary (1496), as well as by other siblings who did not survive infancy. Henry VII's affections did not wander, and we know of no illegitimate children. Winning a daughter of Ferdinand and Isabella of Spain as a bride for his eldest son marked Henry's acceptance on the European stage. However, the marriage of Catherine of Aragon to Arthur, Prince of Wales, celebrated in November 1501, ended with the prince's death in April 1502. The death of Queen Elizabeth the following year was an even greater personal blow, and induced in Henry a brief crisis of conscience (evident in his appointment of his mother's spiritual director, the virtuous Dr John Fisher, as Bishop of Rochester in 1504) and a more lasting physical decline.

By the time he died, on 21 April 1509, Henry had squandered any personal affection he might have won as the bringer of peace and unity to the realm. The fate of his closest associates (Empson and Dudley, the agents of his fiscal oppression, were executed on spurious charges of treason in 1509) sums up popular revulsion from Henry's harsh and grasping regime. His reign has often been seen as inaugurating a 'New Monarchy' in England, replacing the traditionally dispersed power networks of the medieval baronage with the firmer grip of a king capable of imposing justice upon even the most powerful of his subjects. While the merits of this view are disputed, Henry VII certainly looks like what Machiavelli, writing a few years later, characterized as a 'New Prince' – a man who, having seized the throne, won the fear rather than the love of his subjects. John Fisher, chosen to deliver the funeral sermon, might have been supposed to provide a suitably uplifting message. But he damned with faint praise: the chief virtue he found in his late patron was that of repentance – his implied moral being that, if even Henry could repent, there was hope for anyone.

HENRY VIII (1509-1547)

The future Henry VIII was born on 29 June 1491, the second son of Henry VII and Elizabeth of York. Created Duke of York in 1494 (which explodes the myth, current since the seventeenth century, that he was intended for a career in the Church), this talented, athletic and temperamental man might have proved something of a handful to his elder brother, Prince Arthur, the firstborn, had he survived to wear the crown. But Henry's life was changed forever when Arthur died in 1502, shortly after contracting his ill-fated marriage to Catherine of Aragon. The death of their mother, Elizabeth, in 1503 left Henry as the sole surviving son – although at this stage, when he was not yet into his teens, it was still possible for loose tongues to debate the succession in terms which gave him little or no chance of securing it.

Henry's growth over the next few years into a handsome, well-built and personally charming young man set such wagging tongues to rest. He received an excellent education that gave him competence in half a dozen languages and an abiding interest in literature and scholarship. Desiderius Erasmus, the man who would soon be recognized as the greatest scholar of his age, was introduced to the young prince in 1499. Although his praise of Henry's accomplishments is tainted by flattery, it is revealing enough that Erasmus thought it appropriate to flatter the prince on his learning. Not that Henry's upbringing neglected the traditional aristocratic pursuits of riding, hunting, wrestling and the other skills which trained nobles for their allotted role as warriors. Adding the bravado and insouciance of youth to a well-built frame, Henry excelled at such martial sports.

When Henry's father died in April 1509, there was no longer any doubt about the succession. The leading Yorkist claimant, Edward de la Pole, was immured in the Tower of London, and Henry himself offered the best prospect of a change from the grim politics of his father's latter years. The late king's ruthless exploitation of his prerogative was effectively discredited by the execution of his most trusted agents, Edmund Dudley and Richard Empson. Henry VIII himself was not yet eighteen, hardly mature enough to rule with full autonomy in a society that saw twenty-one as the age of majority. His father committed him to the care of Lady Margaret Beaufort, but she followed her son to the grave within a few weeks. Henry was for the next year or two under the tutelage of a group of clerical advisers, notably William Warham (Lord Chancellor and Archbishop of Canterbury) and Richard Fox (Lord Privy Seal and Bishop of Winchester). Policy was unadventurous, despite the sense of a new beginning ushered in by the new reign.

Henry's own contribution to the sense of a new beginning was to fulfil the engagement that his father had imposed upon him, by taking Catherine of Aragon as his wife. The wedding in June 1509 was followed a few weeks later by the coronation, and these events set the tone for the more general sense of festivity during Henry's early years as king. With boon companions such as William Compton and Charles Brandon, he led a youthful court in hunting, dancing, feasts and masques. When Catherine gave birth to a son in January 1511, Henry's cup overflowed. The boy's death a few weeks later, though, was a bitter blow.

Henry's arrival at political maturity was marked by a decision to go to war. His reopening of England's ancient quarrel with France accompanied the gentle displacement of his father's clerical, elderly and pacific councillors by a new generation of royal henchmen. Pre-eminent among them was Thomas Wolsey, also a cleric, but highly ambitious, a man who appreciated that the path to advancement lay through making the young king's dreams of glory come true. Allied with Spain and the Papacy, Henry prepared for war with France. With his father's treasure and the readily proffered taxes of a realm that had enjoyed a long period of economic and demographic growth, he was in a strong position. The army that he took to France in 1513, equipped and shipped courtesy of Wolsey's logistical genius, was the largest since the days of Henry V. The circumstances, however, were not as favourable. France, a larger and wealthier kingdom, was now united under a strong monarch, and although Henry secured victory in the field (at the famous 'Battle of the Spurs', named from the rapidity with which the French fled) and occupied Thérouanne and Tournai, he was not able to revive the glories of his namesake.

The money soon ran out, and Henry was left stranded when the resources of his father-in-law, Ferdinand of Aragon, also dried up. Peace was made, and sealed by the marriage of Henry's younger sister, Mary, to the ageing Louis XII of France (whose death soon afterwards was attributed to the demands she made upon his constitution). France's new ruler, Francis I, led his troops over the Alps, gaining a victory at Marignano in 1515 that gave him control of northern Italy for a decade, and knocked England's potential allies out of the war. Thanks to Wolsey's diplomacy, however, Henry won the peace. The Treaty of Universal Amity which reconciled the warring parties of western Europe was signed in London in 1518, and Henry consoled himself for the cession of his conquests by basking in his role as peacemaker.

In the complexities of diplomacy that ensued, the rhetoric of peace masked a jostling for position. Even as Henry VIII talked perpetual peace with Francis I at that most splendid of summit meetings, which has gone down in history as the Field of Cloth of Gold (1520) because of the unparalleled luxury of its tents and temporary buildings, the King of England was also secretly negotiating a military alliance with the new Holy Roman Emperor, Charles V. Henry also found time the following year to write a book against Martin Luther, earning himself the title Defender of the Faith from a grateful pope and further consolidating the alliance against France. Hostilities resumed in the early 1520s, but despite ravaging swathes of northern France, English forces established no new footholds beyond the Channel. Meanwhile, in northern Italy, the Imperial army overwhelmed the French at Pavia in February 1525, capturing Francis I and decimating his nobility.

Unfortunately, Henry was no longer in any position to take advantage of his rival's discomfiture. A tax strike in the South and East, the result of more than a decade of unprecedentedly heavy taxation, left him without the resources to intervene. By this time, however, his attention was beginning to turn elsewhere. After fifteen years of marriage, Henry had only one surviving child, a daughter. And his wife, Catherine, was clearly past childbearing age. After all he had done for God by way of defending the Faith, Henry could scarcely understand how divine providence could have denied him a son. He found an explanation in the Bible. Leviticus forbade marriage to a brother's wife, and threatened any offending couple with childlessness. Since Catherine had previously been married to his elder brother, Henry's own marriage to her had been authorized by a papal dispensation. But now Henry began to doubt the value of the dispensation, and sought an annulment of the marriage that would free him to marry again. In normal times, this

Opposite   113. Henry VIII by Hans Holbein.

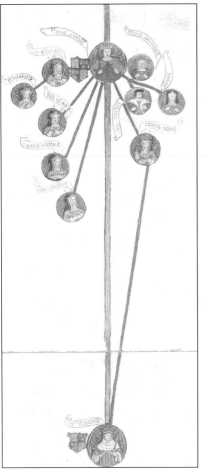

Left to right, top to bottom   114. Henry VIII and his wives from a sixteenth-century pedigree-chronicle.
115. Catherine of Aragon.
116. Anne Boleyn by Hans Holbein.
117. Jane Seymour by Hans Holbein.
118. Anne of Cleves by Hans Holbein.
119. Catherine Howard by Hans Holbein.
120. Catherine Parr.

should have been straightforward. Popes, especially grateful popes, were supposed to sort out the matrimonial problems of kings, and with a little ingenuity canon law (the law of the Church) could usually find some grounds to invalidate a marriage that had outlasted its usefulness.

This was to reckon without events in Italy. The victory at Pavia, which had brought France to its knees, had left Charles V master of Italy. In 1526 his troops sacked Rome, leaving even the pope at his mercy. Clement VII could not afford to insult Charles by granting a divorce that would be seen as a public disgrace for Catherine, who was the Emperor's aunt. Neither could he afford to alienate Henry VIII, one of the Papacy's most loyal supporters against the Protestant Reformation, by publicly denying him a divorce.

It was Wolsey who shouldered the burden of extricating his king from this impasse. He put together an alliance with the old enemy, France, with a view to liberating Italy and the pope from Imperial control. The lure for the French was the prospect of a marriage alliance with Henry, although while Wolsey was in France negotiating in 1527, Henry fell in love with Anne Boleyn, which added emotional zest to the political urgency of a divorce. After initial French successes in Italy, Clement despatched Cardinal Campeggio to England to preside with Wolsey over a tribunal to adjudicate on the king's marriage. Showing his habitual interest in things theological, Henry VIII himself had collaborated with the scholars who prepared his case for the court. But another crushing defeat for the French in northern Italy, this time at Landriano (21 June 1529), led to the immediate collapse of the tribunal in London, as Campeggio accepted Catherine's appeal and revoked the case to Rome.

By now Henry was utterly convinced of the righteousness of his cause. One of his scholars had pointed out, truly enough, that the threat of childlessness laid down in Leviticus really meant having no sons: so, despite the survival of his daughter Mary, Henry could now see his situation as living vindication of the biblical prohibition on marriage to a brother's wife. The revocation of the case to Rome, an obvious delaying tactic, was an intolerable affront, and it spelled the end for Wolsey. Nobles and courtiers long jealous of his pre-eminence howled for his blood, and Henry threw him to the wolves. Stripped of virtually all his lands and offices, Wolsey retreated to his archdiocese of York. His attempts to rebuild his position misfired, and in 1530 he was summoned to London to face accusations of treason. Fortunately for him, he died on the way.

Wolsey's fall did not bring the divorce any closer. Henry put pressure on his clergy to support his case; but as the king's infatuation with Anne Boleyn became common knowledge, so Catherine's position as the 'wronged woman' earned her widespread sympathy. In 1531 the king induced the clergy to recognize him, ominously if vaguely, as 'Supreme Head of the Church of England as far as the law of Christ allows'. In 1532, he forced them to allow him a right of veto over ecclesiastical legislation – a move that provoked Thomas More to resign the Lord Chancellorship, ostensibly on the grounds of ill-health. Meanwhile, a visionary nun at Canterbury, Elizabeth Barton, became the focus of opposition to Henry's divorce, uniting disaffected clergymen and nobles with a broader base of popular support won by her reputation as a wonder-worker, and predicting that he would lose his throne within six months if he divorced Catherine.

At the same time, Henry was giving ear to increasingly radical ideas about how the divorce might be achieved. The pope's jurisdiction in England was questioned, and the prospects of resolving the case locally were mooted. A local solution, however, could not be envisaged without the co-operation of the Archbishop of Canterbury, William Warham. Despite his healthy respect for Henry's temper (according to Catherine of Aragon, Warham's advice to her usually revolved around the ancient proverb 'the wrath of the prince is death'), the archbishop was also impressed by the prophecies of Elizabeth Barton, and was clearly not the man to defy the pope. It was Warham's death in August 1532 that therefore broke the deadlock. Henry's unlikely choice to succeed Warham was a relatively obscure scholar, Thomas Cranmer, who had first earned royal favour through scholarly labours concerning the divorce, and who was at this moment the English ambassador to Charles V in Germany. French support was secured at a summit meeting between Henry and Francis in France: Anne came too, and it may have been around this time that she and Henry began sleeping together. Shortly after Christmas she found herself pregnant, and there was a hasty private wedding. An act prohibiting appeals to Rome was rushed through Parliament to pave the way for Cranmer to hear the divorce case in April 1533 and thus to give the king his heart's desire. In lieu of a grand wedding, Anne was crowned queen on 1 June 1533.

The whole point of the 'break with Rome', which in retrospect was the crucial moment of Henry's reign, was to safeguard the divorce. As the pope delivered final judgement in Catherine's favour, and began proceedings to excommunicate Henry, the king set about consolidating his rather vulnerable position. Elizabeth Barton was arrested, and, once the six months of her prophecy had safely expired, was compelled to make a humiliating public recantation. The birth of a daughter, Elizabeth, to Anne Boleyn in September 1533 did not set the seal of divine providence upon the divorce in the way that the birth of a son would have done. So Henry had to resort to Parliament to resolve the succession. The Act of Succession (March 1534) not only recognized the claim of Elizabeth and any further offspring of the new marriage, but also demanded of every adult male in the land an oath upholding the new settlement. The terms of the oath were highly prejudicial to papal authority in the Church, but only a few refused it: Thomas More, John Fisher and some other clergymen, at the cost of immediate imprisonment. Compliance may have been encouraged by the execution for treason of Elizabeth Barton and her associates on the very morning that the oath was administered to the citizens of London (20 April 1534).

England's disengagement from the papacy was enshrined in the autumn of 1534 in the Act of Supremacy, which recognized Henry as 'Supreme Head of the Church of England'. Soon afterwards, another statute made it treason merely to deny the new royal title, and in the summer of 1535 a series of prominent victims under this legislation (including Fisher and More) reminded people about the wrath of the prince. There were relatively few executions, but even the lightest word against royal policy could land the unwary in gaol: the way in which alehouse gossip turns up in the government records of the 1530s shows us both how nervous and how effective the government was. Meanwhile, a preaching campaign of unprecedented scale was organized to justify the overthrow of nearly a thousand years of close association between England and the papacy.

Although Henry VIII was never swift to abandon familiar religious beliefs and practices, the ability of influential evangelicals at court to present religious change as the lawful exercise of the royal supremacy ensured that the unofficial advance of the Reformation would be matched by official changes to English religion. The new 'evangelical' teachings of those who would come to be known as 'Protestants' received a fillip from the break with Rome. Anne Boleyn certainly dabbled in these ideas, while Archbishop Cranmer had undergone a conversion to evangelical doctrines during his sojourn in Germany. Henry's rising chief minister, Thomas Cromwell, saw the political advantages of promoting these doctrines at home and allying with evangelical princes abroad in order to bolster the royal supremacy. As evangelical clergymen were those most zealous in preaching against the pope, they were given a freer hand in return for their support. Several were made bishops, probably thanks to the patronage of Queen Anne. Censorship of evangelical books and sermons broke down, while the overthrow of papal authority left canon law enfeebled and traditionalist clergy demoralized.

Clockwise from top   121. Scheme of the lost picture of the family of Sir Thomas More by Hans Holbein.

122. Thomas Cromwell by Hans Holbein.

123. Sir Thomas More by Hans Holbein.

The first success of the evangelicals was the dissolution of the monasteries, which began in 1536 as a shake-out of often under-funded and undermanned houses, yet ended in wholesale suppression, completed in 1540. At the same time, Henry was induced to curtail traditional manifestations of the cult of the saints. Pilgrimages were first discouraged then prohibited; the reporting of miracles and the display of relics were gradually done away with; and in 1538 England's most renowned shrines were closed down, yielding more booty for the crown. The most significant reform, though, was the official authorization of an English Bible, reversing more than a hundred years of censorship. Nothing did more to foster evangelical doctrines, although this outcome was far from Henry's intention.

These changes began to impress themselves upon public attention in 1536, sparking off the most serious challenge Henry ever faced: the Pilgrimage of Grace, a rising that brought together a range of fiscal, social, and political grievances under a religious banner (the flag depicted the Five Wounds endured by Christ on the Cross) and for a few months removed almost all England north of the Trent from royal control. But misplaced trust in the king's conservative religious instincts was the rebels' undoing. Reluctant to wage war against their king, they were dispersed by guarantees of pardon and hints that their complaints would be favourably considered. Soon afterwards the ringleaders were brought to London for trial and execution, while Henry's vengeance set men on gibbets throughout the North. Henry emerged from the crisis strengthened, more sure than ever of the approval of divine providence for both his assumption and his exercise of the royal supremacy.

Providence was soon to smile even upon the king's hitherto troubled matrimonial affairs. Anne Boleyn's failure to produce a son had left her vulnerable, and she had been brought down in the spring of 1536 on charges of serial adultery and even incest, which remain hard to credit. Adultery by a queen was treason, so Anne had been executed (along with her alleged lovers, including her brother George). Henry's eye had already fallen upon her successor, Jane Seymour, whom he married on 30 May 1536 (barely a fortnight after Anne's beheading). As Catherine of Aragon had died earlier that year, there could be absolutely no doubts as to the legitimacy of this marriage or of any offspring, and the deaths of both Catherine and Anne also paved the way for reconciliation between Henry and his elder daughter, Mary. Queen Jane became pregnant shortly after the dispersal of the Pilgrimage of Grace, and in October 1537 bore Henry a son, christened Edward a few weeks later, with Princess Mary acting as his godmother. Jane herself fell ill following the birth, and died within the month. Henry never forgot her. He made splendid provision for her funeral, and the new cathedrals he founded in the 1540s offered daily prayers for her soul. But grief at the death of his wife hardly dented his joy at the birth of a son.

Henry's more conservative tendencies resurfaced only towards the end of the 1530s, exacerbated by the emergence of 'sacramentarian' heresy: the denial of the real presence of Jesus Christ in the sacrament of the altar. Thomas Cromwell's policy of an alliance with German Protestant princes broke down over Henry's refusal to abandon traditional doctrines about the Mass. Abroad, a rapprochement between Francis I and Charles V was followed by the public excommunication of Henry VIII by Pope Paul III. A Catholic crusade against England seemed a real prospect, and Henry needed to demonstrate his essential religious orthodoxy. A prominent sacramentarian, John Lambert, was burned late in 1538, with Henry himself pronouncing the death sentence. In the spring of 1539 an act of Parliament endorsed Catholic doctrines on the Mass, the real presence, confession, and the celibacy of the priesthood – a smack in the face for Cromwell and Cranmer.

Cromwell sought to salvage his position by pursuing his Germanophile foreign policy and persuaded Henry to take as his fourth wife a German princess, Anne of Cleves. But Henry could not stand the sight of her: the marriage was not consummated and was hurriedly annulled. Cromwell's enemies, led by the Duke of Norfolk and the Bishop of Winchester, exploited Henry's loss of confidence in him by accusing him of heresy and treason. After the sort of show trial he had so often arranged for others, Cromwell was executed on 29 July 1540. The temporary victory of Norfolk and Winchester was sealed barely a week later by the king's fifth marriage, to Catherine Howard, a pretty young niece of the Duke's.

After the fall of Cromwell, religious change in England virtually stopped. However, almost nothing that had been done was actually undone, although some efforts were made to restrict private Bible-reading. Henry attached himself more and more to the rhetoric of the 'middle way', holding the ring for the two religious factions wrestling at his court. The evangelicals regained some ground, thanks to the indiscretions of the young queen. They produced proof of her infidelity, and she was executed in February 1542. Some relaxation of conditions for evangelicals resulted from the king's sixth and final marriage, to a young widow, Catherine Parr, on 12 June 1543. That same year Bishop Gardiner sought to destroy his great rival, the evangelical Archbishop Cranmer, by gathering evidence that the latter was fostering heresy in Kent. But Henry refused the bait, and Cranmer survived. A countercoup in 1544 sought to implicate Gardiner in treason, but he likewise survived, although his nephew and secretary, Germain Gardiner, went to the block.

The factional struggles of the 1540s did not threaten the stability of the realm now that the succession and the supremacy were secured. Nor did they distract Henry from a return to the priorities of his youth: war and glory. Border incidents with the Scots provoked a disastrous Scottish invasion late in 1542. The Scots were so heavily defeated at Solway Moss that James V's death a few weeks later was attributed to the news. Henry's eyes, though, were on France. Having launched a savage pre-emptive strike on Scotland early in 1544, when a force led by Edward Seymour (brother of the late Queen Jane) sacked Edinburgh, later that year Henry took another huge army over to Calais. But history repeated itself and Henry's grand alliance against France proved fragile. Charles V failed to march on Paris, and Henry's successes were limited to the capture of Boulogne – a poor enough return from an inordinately expensive campaign. The following year was devoted to repelling the French counter-action: a vast invasion fleet was met and beaten back off the Isle of Wight, in an engagement now better known for the loss of one of Henry's greatest ships, the Mary Rose. The preparations on land cost millions. Nevertheless, when Henry VIII addressed his Parliament in December 1545, it was as a victor and a saviour.

In 1546 Henry's declining health signalled that his reign was drawing to a close. Factional struggle intensified. The summer saw the conservatives in the ascendant. Anne Askew, a gentlewoman with connections to Catherine Parr and the court, was convicted of the sacramentarian heresy which Henry abominated, and the Lord Chancellor, Thomas Wriothesley, personally set his hand to the rack in his desperation to extract information that would compromise evangelical rivals at court. Anne, however, gave him nothing of value. By the autumn, the pendulum was swinging the other way. The Duke of Norfolk's son, Henry Howard, Earl of Surrey, was foolish enough to flaunt his Plantagenet ancestry by quartering the royal arms into his own heraldic bearings, an act easily portrayed as treason in the charged atmosphere of the dying king's court. The Howards' rivals pounced, and the duke and the earl were both charged with treason. Henry Howard was duly convicted (although only after the jury had received a personal message from Henry VIII to cut short their deliberations) and executed. The Duke of Norfolk himself

Left to right, top to bottom   124. Thomas Howard, Duke of Norfolk, by Hans Holbein.
125. Cardinal Wolsey.
126. Wooden carving of Catherine of Aragon, Cardinal Campeggio and Cardinal Wolsey in the choir stalls at Christchurch Priory.
127. Henry Howard, Earl of Surrey.
128. Archbishop Warham by Hans Holbein.

was in the Tower of London, and was saved from the same fate only because the king died before signing his death warrant.

All this meant that, as the end came, it was the evangelicals who surrounded the ailing king. Henry VIII, massively and unnaturally bloated by excess and disease, died on 28 January 1547. In his will, he endeavoured to provide collective government for his young son, nominating sixteen men to form a new Privy Council. But the disgraced Howards were excluded, as was their episcopal ally, 'wily Winchester', the shrewd Bishop Stephen Gardiner. Asked why he had omitted Gardiner, the king explained that while he, Henry, could manage the bishop, the latter would be able to run rings around the rest of them and would end up in sole command. Henry's anxieties about the future were accurate in everything except their focus. The exclusion of Gardiner delivered Edward VI into the hands of his uncle, Edward Seymour.

EDWARD VI (1547-1553)

The birth in 1537 of Prince Edward to Henry VIII's third wife, Jane Seymour, finally resolved the succession problem that had bedevilled English politics for a decade. Edward was full of hope and promise. A robust child, clearly his father's son (though without his father's awesome physique), he was precociously clever. From about the age of six, he became the beneficiary of perhaps the best education any child received in sixteenth-century Europe. England's most talented humanist scholar, John Cheke, was recruited from St John's College, Cambridge, to conduct the prince's formal schooling.

The intellectual movement we know as humanism was deeply committed to its own version of Plato's philosopher-king. Humanists believed that the key to good government lay in the education of princes, and countless textbooks on this subject (such as that published by Erasmus for the young Charles of Spain) bear witness to a touching faith in the moral power of education. Edward might have become the great test-case for the theory. As it is, we can see the education in all its glory, but not how it would have turned out. The theory was summed up by Cheke's friend Roger Ascham in his book *The Schoolmaster*. Its practice can be seen in the various essays and exercises by the young Edward that still survive today. It was based on a thorough grounding in Latin and Greek, acquired through a demanding regime of translation and retranslation into and out of the two languages. The most visible, though not the deepest, mark of Cheke's tuition can be seen in the fine italic hand that Edward learned to write.

The tender years of the king at his accession towards the end of January 1547 made it inevitable that there would be a struggle for power around him. Those nobles who were left in control of the young king by Henry VIII's will soon frustrated the old king's attempt to provide collective government for his son's minority. Edward Seymour, Earl of Hertford, the king's elder uncle, secured recognition as Lord Protector of the Realm and Governor of the King's Person. The only one who dared oppose him, Lord Chancellor Thomas Wriothesley, who had an equally low opinion of Seymour's political skills and religious commitments, was deftly outmanoeuvred and ousted from office. Edward Seymour rewarded himself and his allies with titles and lands. He became Duke of Somerset and gave his name to Somerset House in the Strand.

Somerset was not a success. Having made his fortune in Henry VIII's Reformation and his reputation in Henry's war with Scotland, his policy was more of the same. He pressed on with the grandiose but impractical scheme of compelling the Scots to hand over their sovereign, the infant Mary Queen of Scots, to be Edward's bride. Defeating the Scots in the field was relatively easy, but once Mary was whisked away to France, Somerset's policy was doomed. Continued military presence in Scotland was a pointless drain on resources. Clinging on to Henry VIII's solitary conquest in France, Boulogne, was another liability. Worst of all, Somerset became intoxicated with a sense of his own ability and authority, ruling more like a king than a minister, and relying on advisers within his own household rather than on the Privy Council. Nevertheless, his official position insulated him from criticism and attack. The only real threat came from his younger brother, Thomas, who shared Somerset's ambitions and abilities.

Thomas Seymour envied his brother and set out to rival him. He married Henry VIII's widow with indecent haste to cement his own ties with royalty, and took full advantage of the fact that the late king's younger daughter, Elizabeth, continued to live in Catherine Parr's household, treating the princess with a familiarity that today would probably land him on the register of sex offenders. After his wife's death in September 1548, his sights were on Elizabeth as his next bride. He also curried favour with the boy king, who was increasingly ignored and sidelined by his arrogant Protector. But Seymour's ambitions were too much for his brother, who in 1549 cut through the former's web of intrigue and destroyed him on charges of treason. Somerset's ruthlessness towards his flesh and blood did little to enhance his own chances of survival when the tide of events turned against him later that year.

Somerset's one momentous contribution to English history was the inauguration of a fully-fledged Protestant Reformation. Ironically, it was this that precipitated his fall. The new regime's commitment to the Reformation was proclaimed from the start of the reign. Thomas Cranmer's sermon at Edward's coronation urged him to emulate Josiah, the ancient King of Israel who had purged the temples of idols and published the Law of God among his people. No such call could have been made without the express approval of Somerset: it is a moot point, however, as to whether he was motivated more by ideological conviction or by the prospect of profiting further from the ecclesiastical plunder for which he, along with so many other noblemen, had acquired a taste under Henry VIII.

It was Archbishop Cranmer who really shaped the English Reformation. His *Book of Homilies*, published in 1547, presented a moderate version of Protestantism for parish priests to read to their flocks. Royal commissioners stripped churches of their religious imagery through autumn and over winter, and traditional ceremonies such as blessing candles at Candlemas and strewing greenery on Palm Sunday were banned. A Yorkshire parish priest, Robert Parkyn, left a nostalgic and moving account of the dismantling of the old order in these years. Meanwhile, Cranmer was at work on his masterpiece, the *Book of Common Prayer*, a uniform Protestant liturgy for the entire Church of England, to replace the old Mass. It was brought into effect on Whit Sunday (9 June) 1549, shortly after a law allowing priests to marry, in defiance of medieval custom.

The rebellion which this new liturgy instantly provoked in Devon and Cornwall threatened the entire regime. It sparked off a series of risings and rebellions across England, some inspired by religious conservatism, others stoked by inflation and poor harvests. Somerset's efforts at conciliation destroyed his credibility with the Privy Council, which was reinvigorated by the crisis. As powerful noblemen acted to suppress the risings with the aid of foreign mercenaries, they also conspired to strip Somerset of his special powers. A short, sharp struggle, during which he tried in vain to use his control of the king's person to rally popular support for his cause, resulted in Somerset's committal to the Tower.

It was John Dudley, then Earl of Warwick, who masterminded the overthrow of the Protector with a display of footwork even nimbler than that which had brought Somerset to power back in 1547. First he forged an unholy alliance with religious conservatives such as the ageing Lord Wriothesley, and then, having toppled the Protector with their aid, he rallied Somerset's supporters

Clockwise from top left   129. Thomas Cranmer by G. Fliccius.
130. Bishop Fisher, drawing by Holbein.
131. Lady Jane Grey by Lucas De Heere.
132. Edward Prince of Wales, later Edward VI, at the age of two, by Hans Holbein.

to himself by playing on their fears for the survival of the Protestant Reformation: indeed, as part of this complex manoeuvre he recalled Somerset to the Privy Council in February 1550.

John Dudley, though every bit as self-seeking and ambitious as Somerset, was a shrewder politician. His control of government was as complete as Somerset's, but he felt no need for the portentous title of Protector. Admittedly he promoted himself to be Duke of Northumberland, but his official position was Lord President of the Council. As such he created consensus and spread responsibility for his policies. He showed his appreciation of the intelligence and burgeoning maturity of the young king by involving him more directly in the business of government, letting him read and comment on state papers and bringing him to sessions of the Council. He worked at his relationship with the king as he worked at his relationship with other weighty political figures, where Somerset had simply presumed on the obedience due to his office. For the most part, his policies were cautiously conservative. He disengaged from war in Scotland and France, and endeavoured to restore some stability to England's shattered royal finances.

The two exceptions to Northumberland's conservatism were the greatest issues of the day: religion and the succession. Despite the upheaval of 1549, Northumberland allowed Cranmer to introduce a second version of the *Book of Common Prayer* in 1552. Churches were stripped bare in order to eradicate the memory and possibility of the Catholic Mass, and by the end of the reign parishes could boast little more than the plainest equipment needed to celebrate Cranmer's spartan liturgy. Northumberland and his cronies, still hungry for church wealth, began picking off the bishoprics. He himself did very well out of the lands of the Bishop of Durham.

Ambition and conscience happily coincided for Northumberland in his other bold move: the substitution of his daughter-in-law, Jane Grey, for Mary and Elizabeth in the line of succession when it became obvious in 1553 that Edward himself was on his deathbed. Yet if the scheme presumably originated with Northumberland, it enjoyed the full backing of the dying king, whose tutors and preachers had schooled him soundly in the new gospel of Protestantism. The boy who had personally berated Mary for her attachment to the Mass was only too willing to deny her the throne in favour of his godly cousin Jane. Although there was no time to call Parliament to sanction the plan, Edward signed up to it himself and commanded his household and government to do likewise. It was the one blow he could strike for the militant Protestantism that would have been his faith and his policy had he lived.

No doubt the king would in time have shouldered aside Northumberland. But there would have been no change in policy. There is no reason to think that he would have dispensed with the serviceable Cranmer, nor that Cranmer's Reformation was yet complete. The archbishop had prepared a Protestant revision of canon law, and even his second *Book of Common Prayer* still bore the mark of Cain: the evidence of its origins in the Catholic Mass. Cranmer would ultimately have disengaged it utterly from the medieval liturgy and probably also from the medieval Catholic calendar, Christmas and all. A Protestantism as uncompromising as that of Scotland or Switzerland and as militant as that of France or the Netherlands would have been the religion of England had Edward lived. But Edward died on 6 July 1553.

JANE GREY (JULY 1553)

The attempt to place Lady Jane Grey on the throne of England, doomed though it seems in retrospect, was not quite as lunatic a project as we might imagine. It resulted from two potent motives: Edward VI's determination to preserve the Protestant Reformation in England; and the Duke of Northumberland's scarcely veiled ambition to bring the English Crown into his bloodline, ultimately replacing the Tudors with the Dudleys. The plan had strong backing. The duke had manipulated his king and his colleagues in such a way as to put behind the succession of Lady Jane Grey the apparatus of the Tudor State. Mary Tudor's resolute refusal to conform to the Edwardine religious changes had left no doubt as to the fate of the English Reformation should she attain the throne. Northumberland, having married his youngest son, Guilford Dudley, to Jane Grey, urged upon Edward the unsuitability of Mary's younger sister, Elizabeth, perhaps playing upon the slurs that the Thomas Seymour affair had cast upon her loyalty and her virtue. Moreover, the easiest grounds on which to attempt Mary's exclusion, her illegitimacy, necessarily ruled out the succession of Elizabeth as well. The statutory exclusion of the Scottish Stuarts, whose claim derived from Henry VIII's elder sister, Margaret Tudor, left the descendants of his younger sister, Mary, known as 'the French Queen' thanks to her earlier and short-lived marriage to Louis XII of France. Mary's second marriage, a love-match with Henry VIII's boon companion Charles Brandon, had brought forth sons and daughters. But her sons died young in 1551 as students at Cambridge. Her eldest daughter, Frances Brandon, married Henry Grey, Earl of Dorset, and bore him three daughters: Jane, Catherine and Mary. It was the eldest of these girls – herself only fifteen at the time of Edward VI's death – whom Northumberland chose as his daughter-in-law and groomed as prospective queen.

Jane herself had little opportunity to develop or to display political skills. The nine days from Edward's death until her arrest were filled with Northumberland's increasingly frantic manoeuvres and the correspondingly evasive machinations of those whom he had induced to sanction his scheme. She made some gestures that suggest that she had a Tudor spirit. She let her husband Guilford know that she had no intention of making him king, thus bringing his father's wrath down upon herself. Had Northumberland won, she would have found it difficult to withstand him. But once his forces had melted away, her fate was sealed. Within two weeks she was in the Tower. Declared guilty of treason by act of attainder, the typically Tudor response to the risks of trial by jury, she was not in fact executed until 12 February 1554, and might have enjoyed Mary's eventual pardon had it not been for the comic-opera antics of her pathetic father, who threw in his lot with the Wyatt rebellion and, after its collapse, was at last found hiding in a hole in a tree-trunk on a neighbour's estate. Mary was well aware that Jane had no personal responsibility for the events of July 1553, and was inclined to mercy. But the shock of the Wyatt Rebellion led her to accept her Council's insistence on the death of the unfortunate girl. Jane met her death with dignity, showing more courage than her father-in-law, who desperately abjured two decades of growing commitment to the Protestant faith in an implausible bid for mercy. Although she formally died as a traitor, the manner of her death and her zeal for the Reformation won her a not undeserved place in John Foxe's *Book of Martyrs*. Had she been required to choose, she would rather have died than renounce her faith.

MARY I (1553-1558)

Mary Tudor is a somewhat neglected figure in the history of monarchy, given that she was the first woman ever to be crowned as Queen regnant of England. Born on 18 February 1516, the only surviving child of Henry VIII's first marriage, she was never in fact expected to succeed to the throne. In the fifteenth century Sir John Fortescue had regarded it as axiomatic that a woman could not inherit the throne, although she could transmit a valid claim; and Henry VII's accession during his mother's lifetime had endorsed Fortescue's conclusion.

Mary was expected to marry a foreign prince, and was educated for her future role. Her mother, Catherine of Aragon, took the advice of one of Spain's leading humanist scholars, Juan Luis Vives, in designing a suitable education which saw her master several languages and become skilled in playing the keyboards and singing as well as in the habits of physical exercise (riding) and piety which were required of a royal or noble lady. Had her life run according to plan, she might well have ended up presiding over some Renaissance court in the fashion of a Catherine de Medici.

We cannot tell how badly Mary was hurt by the destruction of her world in the late 1520s. As Henry's frustrated demand for a divorce turned into frank hatred for Catherine of Aragon, Mary was deprived gradually of the material comfort she had known and then, in 1533, was denounced publicly as the bastard fruit of an incestuous union. While her mother lived, Mary refused the oaths that would acknowledge her mother's dismissal, her own degradation, and the rights of the woman who had shoved them both aside. But once Catherine had died, Mary was on her own. Submission to her father's will was inevitable. Within months she wrote him a letter couched in terms of repentance and humility befitting an address to the Deity – the kind of letter that tells us more about the person who wanted to receive it than about the person who wrote it.

Whatever the personal cost of submission (and there is every reason to suppose that Mary grasped the theological implications of her father's claim to supremacy over the Church of England), it restored a degree of stability to her life. The execution of Anne Boleyn offered some consolation for ten years of misery, and the birth of Edward VI tempered the injustice of her own bastardy. Mary was welcome at Court. In 1543 she was restored to the succession, second only to her brother. Her father's will endowed her with substantial estates in East Anglia, mostly sequestered from the fallen Howards. Her royal blood, landed wealth and Spanish connections insulated her from the religious changes of her brother's short reign. Although Edward inherited his father's imperious instincts, a teenage boy could not cow Mary into submission as Henry had done in his pomp. The Mass continued to be celebrated in her household throughout Edward's reign, and England's would-be Catholics, still the vast majority of the population, looked to her for their future.

Yet in 1553, Mary's chances of succeeding her brother looked slim. In seeking to vindicate her claim against Jane Grey she faced the might of the Tudor State, which had already overthrown the monasteries, stripped the churches, and abolished the Mass, ripping the heart out of the old religion. All Mary had was her indomitable courage and the hopes of those who loved the Mass. No wonder the Imperial ambassador wrote off her chances in despatches to his master.

Retreating into her East Anglian heartland as rumours spread that the king was dying, Mary proclaimed herself queen as soon as news of his death was leaked to her. Summoning her loyal subjects, she pitched camp at Framlingham Castle in Suffolk, and watched her gamble pay off as men flocked to her standard. Northumberland's position deteriorated as rapidly as hers improved. He was compelled to take personal command of the paltry forces he could rally. As he made for Cambridge, where the Protestant authorities in the university greeted him with a spectacularly ill-timed display of loyalty, his erstwhile allies in London abandoned the enterprise. Northumberland's troops melted away as Mary's force headed to meet them, and the Duke himself was ignominiously reduced to proclaiming her accession before he was arrested as a traitor. Mary's bloodless victory turned into a stately progress towards London, which she entered amidst great rejoicing on 3 August. Symbolic figures of the old order, the ancient Duke of Norfolk and the Bishop of Winchester, were released from

Opposite   133. Portrait of Mary I, Queen of England.

the Tower, their places to be taken by the Duke of Northumberland and the Archbishop of Canterbury. The nobility of the land and the hierarchy of the Church turned up in droves for Mary's coronation on 1 October 1553.

Mary's was a reign of one policy: the restoration of Roman Catholicism in England. It commenced within days of her accession, and ceased only with her death. As soon as her victory was apparent, as we know from the joyous account of Robert Parkyn, the Mass was being offered once again in churches throughout the land – though Parkyn opened a revealing window onto the soul of Tudor England in his comment that this happened at the instigation of local lords and gentlemen. The Protestant religious legislation of Edward VI was undone in Mary's first Parliament, in October 1553. The antipapal laws of Henry VIII followed a year later, and England was formally reunited to the Roman Catholic Church in a ceremony of national reconciliation played out – again revealingly – in a parliamentary context. The papal legate, Cardinal Reginald Pole, presiding over a joint session of the Lords and the Commons on 30 November 1554, received a petition of repentance and in return absolved the nation as corporately embodied in those present.

The restoration of Catholicism under Mary is usually characterized in terms of the burning of Protestants, to the number of about three hundred – a story immortalized in John Foxe's *Acts and Monuments* (popularly known as his 'Book of Martyrs'). While Foxe's book, with its vivid illustrations, did more than the burnings themselves to brand Catholicism in the English mind as a religion of cruelty and oppression, we should not labour under any misapprehensions as to the scale of operations. Three hundred victims in just under four years represented a death-rate far in excess of that of the contemporary Inquisition in Spain. Nor should we forget those who fled the country rather than face death for their faith. About a thousand refugees are known, and there must have been many more. That said, Mary's policy enjoyed a measure of success. Dissent was largely silenced at home, and the vociferous polemics of the refugees abroad were little more than impotent rage. There is nothing in the history of Tudor England to confirm the modern superstition that censorship and repression never work.

Yet there was another story. Catholic teaching was promulgated in a new catechism and book of homilies produced under the aegis of Edmund Bonner, Bishop of London. In 1555 Cardinal Pole convened a council of the English Church that promulgated legislation embodying much of the reforming spirit of the Counter-Reformation. At the local level, the refurbishment and redecoration of parish churches was gathering momentum steadily, as was popular confidence in such traditional practices as Masses for the dead. The brief but successful restoration was presided over by a new generation of zealous Catholic bishops and churchmen who showed their mettle in their last-ditch struggle against Elizabeth's Protestant religious settlement early in 1559.

While Mary's religious policy enjoyed short-term success, its long-term future depended on a Catholic heir. For despite her half-sister Elizabeth's outward conformity to Catholicism, there was as little doubt about the younger princess's true sympathies as there had been about Mary's. Mary had to marry and bear a child. Given her generally old-fashioned view of the world, there was little prospect of her marrying one of her own subjects, however nobly born. So it was inevitable that she should seek a foreign prince as her husband, and just as inevitable that she should look first to the Habsburgs, whose heir apparent, Philip of Spain, was the most eligible man in Europe. The wisdom of this decision divided even Mary's supporters. The Bishop of Winchester, in one of those unaccountable errors of judgement that flawed his otherwise brilliant career, preferred the idea of a marriage to Edward Courtenay, the young and unstable Earl of Devon whom Mary's accession had released from the Tower. William Paget, Gardiner's former pupil, now vying with his old master for dominance of the Privy Council, threw his weight into the Habsburg camp.

Die-hard Protestants were even less enamoured of a marriage alliance with Europe's premier Catholic power, and began plotting against the queen, playing upon English xeno-phobia to broaden their base of support. In the event, the rising went off at half-cock. What should have been a series of co-ordinated risings across southern England became, in January 1554, a march upon London from the traditionally volatile county of Kent, led by Sir Thomas Wyatt. Showing characteristic Tudor spirit, Mary spurned the advice of her Council that she should flee London, and rallied the citizens with a speech at the Guildhall reminis-cent of Elizabeth's later and better-known speech at Tilbury in 1588. Wyatt was soon captured and his forces dispersed. This victory consolidated Mary's control of her kingdom, which never again came under serious threat.

The marriage with Philip went ahead. English fears were assuaged by a marriage treaty which, though recognizing Philip as King of England, severely restricted his powers. The wedding took place on 25 July 1554 at Winchester. But the marriage was never a success. Philip did not find Mary attractive, although he did his duty: by the end of the year it was widely believed, especially by Mary, that she was pregnant. However, by the summer of 1555 it was obvious that her pregnancy had been illusory, and perhaps also that her chances of childbearing were fading: she was now thirty-nine, and her health was not of the best. In September 1555 Philip left for the Netherlands. He returned to England only once more, from March to July 1557.

Philip's second visit to England was made in pursuit of his own political agenda. He was preparing for war with France, and hoped to throw the military and naval resources of England into the scale. Some of Mary's councillors had doubts about the war, but French involvement in a minor plot against her helped forge the necessary consensus behind the policy. The war was initially a success, as English troops helped Habsburg forces take the town of Saint-Quentin. But the euphoria of victory was dispelled by the counter-stroke of the French marshal, the Duke of Guise, who took Calais in January 1558, finally expelling the English from France after more than two hundred years. In the meantime, an unex-pected consequence of Philip's second visit was that Mary once more imagined herself pregnant. Her second false pregnancy turned imperceptibly into her final illness, perhaps as much mental as physical.

Mary's reign ended in a disarray that has coloured subsequent perceptions of her whole regime. War with France had brought England into conflict with the pope, Paul IV, an ally of the French and an old enemy of Reginald Pole, whom he wished to summon to Rome on charges of heresy. Ironically, Mary had recourse to some of her father's antipapal arguments in refusing to hand him over! In response, Paul IV refused to appoint any new bishops to English dioceses, which impeded the Catholic restoration and undermined resistance to religious change in the next reign. Taxes to pay for the war were unpopular, especially in years that saw both dearth and epidemic disease. As much as a fifth of the population of England died in the years around 1558 in what was probably the first outbreak of influenza ever to sweep this country. Over all this loomed the national humil-iation of Calais. The concatenation of crises was all too easily portrayed by Mary's enemies as providential chastisement from God.

Mary's own death came as both culmination of the agony and deliverance from it. She may herself have been finished off by the flu, although she was probably dying anyway. It certainly took off Reginald Pole, who died on the same day as his sovereign, 17 November 1558. This double blow settled the fate of Catholic England. The Cardinal who had stood up to Henry VIII (albeit from a safe distance) would surely have excommunicated Elizabeth rather than allow England to lapse once more into heresy and schism. As it was, joy at Elizabeth's accession outweighed grief at Mary's death, as it brought new hope to a troubled realm.

ELIZABETH I (1558-1603)

Born on 7 September 1533, Elizabeth Tudor was the first child of the English Reformation. Henry VIII had defied the papacy (and would go on to abolish papal jurisdiction in England) by putting away his first wife, Catherine of Aragon, in order to marry Anne Boleyn. After all that, the birth of a daughter rather than the expected son was something of a setback; but Elizabeth was nevertheless formally recognized as heiress presumptive to the crown in the Act of Succession of 1534.

Elizabeth lost her mother very early. Anne, having failed to bear a son, was executed on preposterous charges of treasonable adultery in 1536. Elizabeth probably remembered nothing of her, and was too young to be hurt as deeply as Mary had been by her mother's fate and her own exclusion from the succession. But her father made an indelible impression upon her, even though she was not often in his company. Awesome and charismatic, Henry VIII was Elizabeth's model of kingship. She frequently invoked his example and lamented her inability to command the same degree of obedience that he had. Her fiery hair and temper marked her as his daughter, but although she later boasted of having the 'heart and stomach of a king', she realized that having the body of 'a weak woman' doomed her to fall short of his ideal.

Elizabeth's childhood was divided between the relatively modest environs of her own household, usually at Hatfield in Hertfordshire, and the splendour of the royal court, to which she was an occasional visitor. She received her education at various hands, but her most important teachers were William Grindal and Roger Ascham, Cambridge graduates who in the mid-1540s initiated her into Latin and Greek and perhaps also shared with her their taste in divinity, which was inclined to moderate evangelical reform. Another crucial figure in her upbringing was her father's sixth and final wife, Catherine Parr, who introduced her to the French literature of Reformation in which her mother had also dabbled.

After Henry's death, Elizabeth was transferred to the household of Catherine Parr, who soon found a second husband in Edward VI's younger uncle, Sir Thomas Seymour. Seymour's indiscreet behaviour towards Elizabeth even during his wife's lifetime, and his plan to marry her after Catherine had died in childbirth in September 1548, not only brought him to the scaffold but also brought down troubles upon Elizabeth herself. She was interrogated at length on somewhat vague and unformulated suspicions, but came through the experience, and the reign, unscathed. The plan to put Jane Grey on the English throne was as much a threat to Elizabeth as it was to Mary Tudor, but Elizabeth's conduct during the dangerous days after her half-brother's death in July 1553 was characteristically circumspect. She gathered her own followers at Hatfield, assembling a powerful little force which she led to London in support of Mary – once, that is, it became apparent that Mary's cause had triumphed.

Elizabeth learned a lot from the reign of Mary: mostly from her sister's mistakes, but also from her own position. As heiress presumptive once again, she was the focus of whatever oppo-

Clockwise from top 134. The Spanish Armada. This dramatic engraving by Elizabethan cartographer Robert Adams shows an engagement between the Spanish and English fleets.
135. Coins of Elizabeth's reign.
136. Mary Queen of Scots: the 'Brocas' picture.

sition is possible in a monarchy. She realized the significance of her position in the aftermath of Thomas Wyatt's rebellion in 1554. Although the rising's avowed aim was merely to prevent Mary's marriage to Philip of Spain, Protestant sympathies motivated many of the rebels, and the government suspected that their objectives included setting Elizabeth on the throne. Certainly some of the rebels had contacted her, and so after the revolt Elizabeth was brought to the Tower of London for interrogation. It is unlikely that she had engaged in treason, and certain that not even the slender burden of proof required in Tudor treason trials was forthcoming. She was released from the Tower in due course, but was still kept for a year under house arrest. The remainder of the reign she divided between her own household and occasional visits to Mary's court. Her name continued to attract conspirators, but she herself was careful to have none of their plotting. And while she left no doubt about her religious sympathies, she conformed to Roman Catholicism so far as the law required.

Mary's final illness gave everyone time to prepare for the imminent change of regime, and Elizabeth's accession was the least troubled in the Tudor era. Representatives of Mary's Council brought official news to Elizabeth in person, and she set about forming her own Council with the advice of her secretary, William Cecil. While long-serving Tudor administrators such as William Paulet and William Petre were retained, Mary's East Anglian loyalists and zealous Catholic bishops were replaced mostly by men variously related to Elizabeth through her Boleyn family ties in a leaner Council with no clerical members. In the meantime, Elizabeth made a ceremonial entry into London amidst popular rejoicing on 28 November 1558. This largely unscripted event was surpassed by the carefully stage-managed ceremonies surrounding her coronation on 15 January 1559.

The first priority of the new government was the restoration of its own brand of true religion: Protestantism. Elizabeth herself signalled impending changes when she baulked at various aspects of Catholic liturgy at services around Christmas 1558, for example by walking out of Mass when the consecrated host was elevated for veneration. When her first Parliament convened in January 1559, the resettlement of religion was its first business. Yet Elizabeth's Reformation had a rougher ride than those of her predecessors. Mary's bishops were men of a new generation, polarized by the deepening religious divisions of Europe, and they led stiff resistance in the House of Lords. After several months, some sharp practice and some tight votes, Elizabeth got what she wanted: Acts of Supremacy and Uniformity restoring both royal control over the Church (now under the title of 'Supreme Governor' rather than Henry's 'Supreme Head', which had come to seem almost blasphemous) and the second Book of Common Prayer of 1552 (with some minor changes of wording to mollify conservative sensibilities). Now it was simply a matter of enforcement – though this was hardly a simple matter. After a generation of to-ing and fro-ing, it would take at least another generation to bed down the new religion firmly.

The most remarkable thing about the 'Elizabethan Settlement' of 1559 was that it proved to be just that: a settlement. Catholics hoped that Elizabeth's death, or some other providential intervention, would turn fortune's wheel once more in their favour. Serious Protestants in tune with the latest theology from Geneva could hardly believe that Reformation would go thus far and no further. Even the queen's own bishops initially expected further reform. It was only gradually that people began to appreciate Elizabeth's inflexible stance on religion, which set a high value on stability, and her suspicion of Catholics and the 'hotter sort of Protestants' (soon to be known as 'Puritans') whom she regarded alike as at least potential traitors. Committed

Opposite   137. Portrait of Queen Elizabeth I.

QVI MALY PENSE

POSVI TOREM
DEVM MEVM
ADIV

ELIZABETA D. G. ANGLIÆ. FRANCIÆ. HIBERNIÆ. ET VERGINIÆ
REGINA CHRISTIANAE FIDEI VNICVM PROPVGNACVLVM.

Immortalis honos Regum, cui non tulit ætas   *Queis ipsæ tantum superant reliqua omnia regna,*
  Ulla prior, veniens nec feret ulla parem,   *Quantum tu maior Regibus es reliquis,*
Sospite quo nunquam terras habitare Britannas   *Viue precor felix tanti in moderamine regni,*
  Desinet alma Quies, Iustitia atque Fides,   *Dum tibi Rex Regum cælica regna paret.*

In honorem serenissimæ Suæ Maiestatis hanc effigiem fieri curabat Ioannes Winutnelius belga.   Anno 1606.

Catholics dwindled within a generation to a small minority, as custom sanctified the new faith, and the machinations of European politics cast international Catholicism as a foreign force dedicated to the overthrow of the English State. When northern Catholics rose in defence of their faith in autumn 1569, and the pope excommunicated Elizabeth in 1570, the equation of Catholicism with sedition was established in many people's eyes. The succession of Catholic plots which the government uncovered in the 1580s and 1590s completed the demonization of Catholicism that was enshrined in John Foxe's *Book of Martyrs* – a text that treated Elizabeth herself as an honorary martyr on account of her tribulations under Mary.

Those who sought further Reformation were mostly inspired by the theology of John Calvin, which was so fashionable among English bishops and clergy that some scholars talk of a 'Calvinist consensus' in the Elizabethan Church. However, Elizabeth (who did not share her father's fascination with theology) found Calvinism repugnant. Calvin himself had renounced his allegiance to his sovereign, the King of France, in becoming a citizen of Geneva, and there was always a whiff of republicanism about his theology. Moreover, it was at Geneva that John Knox, enraged by Mary Tudor's burnings of Protestants, had published his notorious *First Blast of the Trumpet against the Monstrous Regiment of Women*, an untimely tract against government by women. Elizabeth blamed Calvin for allowing it to be printed, and could see only sedition in those who wanted to introduce his principles of ecclesiastical government to England. When, despairing of changing her mind or the law, Puritans sought to implement aspects of the 'discipline' (as they called it) through private associations and direct action, Elizabeth felt that her worst fears were being fulfilled. She found a clergyman after her own heart in John Whitgift, an unmarried Cambridge theologian. Appointed Archbishop of Canterbury in 1583, Whitgift embarked on a twenty-year campaign to repress Puritanism. Its success can to some extent be measured by the campaign of vilification against him in the so-called 'Marprelate Tracts' published around 1590. Yet if Whitgift repressed the public expression of Puritanism, he could not stamp out the Puritan mentality. Puritans kept their heads down, spread their word, and prayed for better days ahead.

Along with religion, it was the question of the succession that dominated the reign. From the start, the solution was obvious to everyone: Elizabeth should marry and bear children. The problem was that, from the start, she showed a marked disinclination to do anything of the kind. Her very first Parliament petitioned her to find a suitable husband soon, and she responded with gracious words that temporarily satisfied her hearers. However, even in this speech her stated preference for the single life (which was no doubt put down at the time to a becoming virginal modesty) was a foretaste of things to come. Future Parliamentary petitions, growing more urgent with the passing years, were rebuffed with brusque reminders that the royal marriage was a prerogative matter, not for debate in the House of Commons. And the queen's preference for the single life began to sound more like determination than modesty. Indeed, rumours spread that she was incapable of childbearing – although there is no pressing reason to credit them.

It has been suggested more recently that Elizabeth might have had psychological problems with sex and marriage. Admittedly, she responded so badly to the marriages of friends and relatives that great efforts were often taken by those involved to conceal the truth from her – the inevitable revelations predictably provoking even fiercer rages. And it is remarkable that Elizabeth never restored the laws permitting clerical marriage, and never allowed her bishops to bring their wives when they came to court. However, it cannot seriously be thought that, whether as a result of sexual orientation or of her early experiences with Thomas Seymour, she was averse to the company of men. On the contrary, her liking for Seymour was noted at the time, and her relationship with Robert Dudley, Earl of Leicester, in the early years of her reign can hardly be seen as anything other than courting. Rumour in this case not only put them in bed together but even reported an illegitimate child. Her closest advisers and most intimate confidantes thought the affair deadly serious. Nothing came of it, but Leicester was the first in a string of attractive young men with whom Elizabeth flirted over the years. In time, flirtation and mock courtship became political tools in her hands. The language and conventions of courtly love became part of the machinery of Elizabethan politics, helping to make sense of the unaccustomed dependence of men upon the favour of a woman in a society whose values were deeply patriarchal. But however formal and almost asexual such behaviour became, it clearly rested on a basis of relatively uncomplicated heterosexual attraction.

As for Elizabeth's reluctance to marry or settle the succession, this should be seen as a rational decision. Not only had marriage proved a personal or political disaster for many women close to her (such as her mother, her stepmother and her sister), but her sister Mary in particular had shown the dangers of marrying abroad, while her own affair with Leicester, which provoked great bitterness, showed how divisive it would be for a queen to marry a subject. Given that most of the genuinely eligible foreign princes were Catholics, and that Elizabeth was averse to surrendering any of her authority, her decision not to marry looks perfectly reasonable. And her own position under Mary Tudor had shown her the danger posed by the existence of a recognized successor. Ambitious men would always, to use her own words, look rather to the rising than to the setting sun.

For more than half the reign, the problem of the succession was complicated by the existence of an obvious successor: Mary Queen of Scots. The reason why Mary was a problem rather than a solution was that she was a Catholic of unquestionably legitimate birth. This made her more of a rival than a mere successor. Returning from France to Scotland in 1561, Mary concentrated on securing recognition as Elizabeth's heiress. Her chances were poor, as the entire Stuart line was excluded from the succession by Henry VIII's statute of 1544. In itself, this might not have mattered much: after all, it did not stop her son, James VI of Scotland, becoming King of England in 1603. But Elizabeth's advisers would never accept a Catholic succession that would certainly drive them into the political wilderness.

Fortunately for Elizabeth, Mary played into her hands. Having shown a far from sure touch in governing Scotland, Mary fled to England at a moment of crisis in 1568, seeking her cousin's help. The refugee soon became a captive, as her rebellious nobles convinced the English Council that she was guilty of countless crimes and that they should rule Scotland in the name of her infant son, James VI. From the moment she crossed the border, Mary was trouble. Her arrival encouraged the Duke of Norfolk, England's premier nobleman, to entertain hopes of making a royal marriage. The ensuing negotiations and conspiracies sparked off the Catholic rising of 1569, and so entangled the duke that he was executed for treason in 1572. The Catholic conspiracies of the next fifteen years invariably focussed on the person of the Queen of Scots, and in their fears for Elizabeth's safety her Parliaments clamoured for Mary's execution. Elizabeth resisted for years, and, when the pressure became intolerable, hesitated for months. She was well aware that, however irresistible the political logic of killing her cousin, she would never be able to escape the imputation of cruelty and injustice that her enemies would put upon the deed. But in 1587, after Mary had been found guilty of treason in court proceedings of at best dubious legality, Elizabeth signed her death warrant – though later she sought to cast the blame onto others.

Foreign policy (primarily the waging of war) was one of the main occupations of kings, but was always going to be a lower priority for a female ruler. Unable to lead troops in battle, a queen

138. Sixteenth-century drawing of Elizabeth I by a Flemish or French artist.
139. Seal of Elizabeth I.

could never reap the harvest of glory which success in war could confer upon a king. Elizabeth's foreign policy was therefore generally defensive and minimalist, although in her early years Elizabeth harboured some hopes of wiping out the stain upon England's honour by recapturing Calais. English intervention in France, which was made possible by the Wars of Religion then breaking out there, was in fact fruitless. But it testified to the most important fact about Elizabethan foreign policy: its domination by religion. England's now traditional foreign policy posture, alliance with Spain and the Netherlands against France, had been shattered by Henry VIII's divorce and break with Rome. The protection of Elizabeth's Protestant settlement, and indeed of her kingdom, thrust upon England (the leading Protestant power in Europe) the burden of supporting the Protestant interest abroad, chiefly in France and the Netherlands.

Elizabeth's policy towards Scotland and Ireland was likewise determined by religious considerations. The first problem her government faced abroad was in Scotland, where a Protestant Reformation driven by a noble faction offered the prospect of ending French influence and bringing the country into England's orbit. Despite her reluctance to commit money or troops to a cause that entailed rebellion against a lawful sovereign, Elizabeth was persuaded to do so, and English support was crucial in the Scottish Protestant triumph of 1560. The English attitude to Ireland was marked from the start by religious fears. At the start of her reign, the queen's advisers reckoned the 'addiction' of the Irish to the papacy an obstacle to her religious settlement. But Ireland, unlike Scotland, was Elizabeth's own kingdom. A Protestant Reformation was introduced through legislation in the Dublin Parliament of 1560, and the deep-rooted resistance it subsequently faced could at least be categorized as disobedience and treated accordingly. From Elizabeth's point of view, then, the history of Ireland was one of rebellion and repression, with several major revolts (1560-2, 1566-7, 1569 and 1593-1601) besides numerous lesser outbreaks of violence and disorder.

The greatest overseas involvement of Elizabeth's reign was the war with Spain: in the 1570s a cold war fought mostly by English privateers preying upon Spanish convoys from America, this turned during the 1580s and 1590s into a white-hot war on several fronts – the Netherlands, the Atlantic, the English Channel, Ireland, France and the coasts of Spain and Portugal. Elizabeth's advisers felt that there was a very real threat of Spanish Catholic hegemony in western Europe. The Netherlands, where a Calvinist minority led a protracted revolt against Spanish rule, became the cockpit of the struggle. Although Elizabeth was, as ever, reluctant to sanction rebellion, diplomatic support turned into direct military aid in the 1580s when English troops, led by Leicester, fought with the Dutch against the Spanish.

English aid may have saved the Dutch, but only at the cost of precipitating the greatest crisis of the reign. Philip II of Spain planned a great Armada to knock England out of his war. It set sail in 1588, but poor Spanish strategy and superior English naval tactics impeded its planned rendezvous with an invasion force at Gravelines. Fierce storms then broke up the Spanish fleet and scattered it into the North Sea, with massive losses. In the meantime, Elizabeth herself donned armour and appeared before her massed troops at Tilbury to inspire them with patriotic rhetoric. It was her finest hour, though she was lucky that her men never had to face the might of the Spanish infantry, who were probably the best troops in Europe. Celebrated in verse and prayer, in music and art, the defeat of the Armada became part not only of the national history but also of the national myth.

Despite the mood of triumph and thanksgiving that swept the nation after the dispersal of the Armada, things got worse rather than better for Elizabeth. The war with Spain raged on. Two other armadas set out but failed even to get within sight of England's shores, while English fleets in turn struck at the Iberian peninsula in 1589 and, more successfully, in 1596, when the Earl of Essex landed at Cadiz and looted it. In 1597 Essex led another raid against the Azores. As if that was not enough, the greatest of the Irish revolts broke out in 1593, under the leadership of the Gaelic chieftain Hugh O'Neill, Earl of Tyrone, who transformed an essentially local conflict into yet another arena for the Anglo-Spanish war. All this cost money (Ireland most of all), and unfortunately the English were already showing a distinct reluctance to meet the huge costs of the military operations which they were all too noisy in demanding. The greatest failure of Elizabeth's regime was its failure to create adequate and equitable forms of taxation with which to fund its public enterprises. The government had no other option than to squeeze whatever it could out of the royal prerogative; but even here Elizabeth lacked the grip that had enabled her grandfather, Henry VII, to do so well out of 'fiscal feudalism'. Her main expedient, the granting of trade monopolies, seriously damaged her relationship with the House of Commons in the 1590s.

The political driving force of the 1590s was the queen's last favourite, Robert Devereux, Earl of Essex. Following the death of Leicester in 1588, Essex emerged as the leader of militant Protestantism in England, and was the natural choice for command of major military enterprises in the 1590s. His downfall began in 1599, when Elizabeth commissioned him to suppress the rebellion in Ireland. In breach of his instructions, he made terms with Tyrone, and then bolted back to London to justify himself. But he had overstepped the mark, and spent 1600 in disgrace, mostly under house arrest, having been stripped of his offices. Foolishly backing his own considerable popularity against the queen's immeasurable charisma, Essex hoped to regain his position by a kind of palace coup, forcing a government of his own choosing upon her. Inevitably, his plans leaked, and were picked up by the government's network of spies and informers. In desperation, Essex led a few hundred men into the streets in February 1601, expecting an upsurge of popular support. He was in short order arrested, tried, and executed.

Elizabeth died early in the morning of 24 January 1603. She left her successor a relatively stable monarchy. The religion of the new national Church had triumphed over Catholicism to become the focus of a new 'traditional religion', based like the old on the parish church, but cheaper to run and far less garish. The Puritan demand for a purer Reformation, on the other hand, might have been muzzled but had not yet had its teeth drawn. Essex's successor in Ireland, Lord Mountjoy, had pacified the island in the most brutal sense of that term, and at the cost of digging an unbridgeable gulf of hatred between her two kingdoms. The triumph of Henry IV in France and the Twelve Year Truce signed in the Netherlands had all but disentangled England from continental commitments, so at least the huge military expenses of the 1590s were at an end. But the decay of crown finances over which Elizabeth had presided would cripple English foreign policy for half a century, and would be remedied only at the price of civil war.

Elizabeth's policy was one of survival and stability. She had lasted nearly forty-five years on the throne and had withstood every challenge to her State and her Church, at home and abroad. She had also won the genuine affection of most of her English subjects. But she was the ultimate short-termist, and traded too much on the fear struck into their hearts by her father. Her own successors would have preferred her to pay a little more attention to the longer term.

7

The House of Stuart
1603-1714

John Morrill

The death, without direct heir, of Elizabeth I in 1603 meant that dynastic accident finally brought about what her ancestor, Edward I, had attempted – and failed – to do by diplomacy and force: the dynastic union of England and Scotland. Although the administrative, legal and political institutions of the two realms remained separate, from 1604 to 1801 monarchs were styled King (or Queen) of Great Britain – along with France (a residual claim) and Ireland (a continuing issue). Of the seven Stuart rulers of Britain, four (James I, Charles II, William and Mary) came to the throne in contested circumstances. Two more (Charles I and James II) were driven from the throne. And when the seventh, Anne, died in 1714, few could be sure that there would not be a collapse into civil war that might draw in much of Europe and inaugurate a War of the British Succession. This was, then, a troubled dynasty. At the heart of much of its trouble lay religious passion and the search for a confessional identity for a composite monarchy of three separate kingdoms: England, Scotland and Ireland. In 1649 not only did Charles I lose his throne, but the monarchy itself was lost. The abject failure of kingless government in the 1650s forced the restoration of Charles II in 1660 and ruled out the more extreme forms of republicanism for centuries to come. But the recklessness of James II, and the ruthless willingness of William III to trade off the Crown's long-term independence for short-term gains in the waging of war, altered the nature of the monarchy. As the power of Britain grew – and the Treaty of Utrecht in 1713 completed the transformation of Britain as a European and colonial power – the power of the monarchy itself shrank. In 1714, the Hanoverians inherited little discretionary power, but a sophisticated state: and it was this that would form the starting point for world domination in the two centuries that followed.

James I (1603-1625) & VI of Scotland (1567-1603)

James VI of Scotland was the ninth member of the Stewart dynasty to rule in Scotland. (The spelling is only changed to Stuart, by convention, in relation to the family's rule in England.)

Clockwise from top left   141. James VI and his queen from a Scottish armorial, illuminated for Robert, Lord Seton towards the end of the sixteenth century.

142. The coat of arms of Anne of Denmark, James I's Queen.

143. James I, in the frontispiece to *The Workes of the Most High and Mighty Prince James* (1616).

144. Portrait miniature by Isaac Oliver (1551-1617) of Henry, Prince of Wales, the eldest son of James I & VI.

All of his Stewart predecessors had died violently, with the sole exception of James V, who famously 'turned his face to the wall and died' on hearing that half the Scottish nobility had been killed or captured at the Battle of Solway Moss in 1542. As the son of Mary, Scotland's first queen regnant, James could not help but become embroiled in faction and violence from his earliest childhood. His father, Lord Darnley, was assassinated in revenge for his role in the murder of Mary's alleged lover, and the queen herself was widely reputed (certainly among those who brought up James) to have been implicated. In the ensuing baronial and religious war, Mary was forced to flee to England, leaving her infant son behind to be brought up by the bitter enemies of herself and of her Catholic faith. Mary was eventually to be beheaded for plotting against her cousin Elizabeth I of England.

Effectively orphaned at eighteen months old, surrounded by a nobility at war with itself (all three of his regents met violent deaths, and James himself was twice forcibly taken hostage by extreme Protestant factions), the young king should have grown up a psychological cripple. That he emerged as the most academically gifted of British monarchs and as a prolific author is nothing short of astonishing. That he had such control over the paranoia that he did exhibit was also some achievement. It was Parliament, not James, that overreacted to the Gunpowder Plot in 1605. And although easily panicked by loud noises, James was to prove one of the most accessible of English kings.

James was educated my men who believed that – as one of them told him – he was 'God's silly vassal' ('silly' here means 'inoffensive' or 'frail' – perhaps 'utterly dependent'). They told him that he was the sword-arm in an alliance of Church and State to create a godly commonwealth and that he must take his orders from the Kirk that represented the head and brain of that commonwealth. It is not the least of James's achievements that he absorbed their Bible-centred Protestantism but rejected its austere theocratic political philosophy. He studied the ancient and the modern writers and came to articulate in print one of the lasting literary-philosophical achievements of the age. James's writings present a view of monarchy as standing above and mediating between the man-made institutions of Church and State. He portrayed himself as the enlightened philosopher-king who would preside over and harmonize the work of godly preachers, studious lawyers, and of an educated, responsible and paternalistic nobility. He understood early that the conditions were more favourable to the realization of such a vision in England; and he set his heart on making good his claim to the English throne as the direct descendant of Henry VII through his elder daughter, a claim better by law of inheritance than that of anyone else. He was Elizabeth's obedient and discrete northern neighbour, earning credit with her by refusing to take advantage of the acute instability created by the Spanish war and invasion threats. His problem was that Acts of Parliament, and the will of Henry VIII, barred him as ruler of Scotland from the English throne. It was central to his repeated emphasis on his divine right to rule that he had a 'natural right' by blood-line that no human law could set aside.

There was nothing inevitable about James's inheritance of the English (and Irish) Crown. For most of Elizabeth's reign, the bitter factionalism of her Council, deep divisions over religion, and the calculation of foreign princes well-used to interfering in other peoples' succession disputes, made it quite likely that there would be major international struggle for the English succession. It was only really with the fumbled rebellion and death of the unstable Earl of Essex that power around Elizabeth fell into the hands of a single group ready and willing to hand the throne over to James. His unwavering Protestantism, his proven ability to govern, and – after a half a century of dynastic infertility – his stock of sons and

145. Portrait of James I & VI and Anne of Denmark.

daughters (four alive at the time of his accession) secured him the throne. In the event, James's succession was far more peaceful and uncontested than anyone had dared to hope.

Although he ruled securely for twenty-two years after taking the English throne, James was never a king who inspired the love and affection of his subjects. For many Anglocentrically-minded memorialists of his generation, his reign was a period of drift and of missed opportunities. They portrayed him as an abstracted intellectual out of tune with English realities, a mismanager of Parliaments, a failed reformer of the Church of England, a poor judge of character (too much governed by homoerotic fancy), and a man who had good ideas but no stamina to see them through. But this influential contemporary interpretation seriously underestimates his aims and achievement.

His reign falls naturally into three parts. The first, which ran from 1603 to 1612, was the period during which he struggled and failed to develop the union of the Crowns into a much broader union of the kingdoms, during which he strove to be the Peacemaker of Europe, and during which he had, in the diminutive Robert Cecil, Earl of Salisbury, and the hugely corpulent George Home, Earl of Dunbar, two wily politicians who advised him wisely and served him well in England and Scotland respectively. Salisbury and Dunbar died in quick succession in 1611-12, and James was never again able to find their like. 1612 was also a turning point because it saw the death of James's beloved and multi-talented elder son, Henry. He never recovered from this blow. When Henry looked into James's eyes, he had seen pride and hope. When, after 1612, Charles, with his bandy legs, slow wits and stammer, looked into James's eyes, he saw only regret and disappointment. Nonetheless, if it had been James and not Henry who was carried off by disease in 1612, there is every reason to believe that the former's reign would be adjudged a triumph: a difficult succession achieved without violence, the Catholic threat quietly contained, the Churches of England and Scotland more closely aligned, the Anglo-Scottish border pacified, Ireland granted its first decade of uninterrupted peace for a century, and peace secured with James's considerable help across the whole of Europe. As it was, little was added, and some things lost, as the king grieved his way through another twelve years.

James sought to create a superior kingdom of Great Britain. Initially he hoped to create a single British Parliament, a single body of British law, a single British Council, and perhaps a single British Church. All his subjects would be British and they would have one coinage, one flag, one destiny. In 1604 he called on the Parliaments north and south to establish a commission to work out the detail. The Gunpowder Plot of 1605 and its aftermath – the torture and grim judicial killing of those responsible, the passing of new legislation to isolate and ostracize the Catholic minority – delayed the report of the Union Commission until 1606-7. James was content to follow its proposals for a gradualist approach, a process that needed to be rooted in 'a union of hearts and minds'. A united Britain would be an example to a world full of division, and it would be stronger of itself to bring peace and religious harmony to that troubled world. But that is not how the xenophobes and barrack-room lawyers saw it. They claimed that James was seeking to replace their ancient laws and liberties with a new constitution resting on his goodwill and prerogative. They said they did not object to Scotland being incorporated into a greater England (Scottish MPs joining an English Parliament, for example), but they would not surrender one iota of their ancient rights. This inability to grasp the possibility of a brave new world stymied James and brought him out of love with Parliaments. If he never again took their advice seriously, it is because he saw them as conservative, blinkered little-Englanders. And he was right. Parliament was also proving unrealistic about the true costs of running England, and although James was a slack manager of his household accounts, prudence there would not balance the budget. The attempt to have better and wider government services at lower cost (not for the only time in British history) showed a lack of realism in the parliamentary classes. James's answer – to use quite ruthlessly his prerogative power to regulate the level of customs duties so as permanently to double his revenues – caused political protests that grew feebler with every session. By 1625 it was clear he had won the argument.

James was able to get some limited legislative action to promote his union project. In the 'middle shires' (those on either side of the Anglo-Scottish border) he set up a commission of English and Scots nobles and gentry who gradually brought a level of law-abidingness that had not been known for centuries; and he was able to promote a common coinage and common symbols of his authority – the Union flag was one such initiative. He encouraged and rewarded intermarriage between the nobilities of the kingdoms, he brought Scottish preachers south to establish a higher standard of preaching in the English cathedrals, and he restored bishops with limited powers throughout Scotland. Progress was slow, but it was real. James broke his promise to return to Scotland every third year; but he ensured that most of his Scottish councillors spent part of every year in London, so that he could keep in touch with affairs there and, as he boasted, govern Scotland by pen.

James was a true ecumenist who believed it was possible to promote a much greater union of Christians. He proposed that a General Council of all Christians be called under his presidency, and he persuaded liberal Catholics and liberal Protestants in the Lutheran and even the Calvinist Churches to take him seriously. Wherever Protestants were in serious dispute with one another he offered to mediate, and the seriousness of this aim is demonstrated by the fact that both the French and the Dutch Calvinist Churches asked him to send delegations of theologians to resolve their internal differences. In earnest of this intention, James also set out to end the bitter divisions with the Church of England, and his policy of tolerance – allowing, even encouraging, a range of views on contended matters of doctrine, liturgical practice, and Church governance – certainly lowered the temperature. He himself presided at the Hampton Court Conference in 1604 in which he reproved both the bishops and their Puritan critics. If the Puritans were the more firmly rebuked, he left both sides in no doubt that he understood himself to be Supreme Governor of the Church, with a personal authority to resolve disputes. In 1604, he asked Convocation to bring together into a single body all the canon law of the reformed Church, he reissued a tidied-up version of the Book of Common Prayer, and he ordered English and Scottish theologians to prepare a definitive translation of the Bible into English. He also ignored demands that all such changes be approved by Parliament, and those demands, in turn, faded away.

James's attempts to bring peace among Christian Princes also bore fruit in this period. He made peace with Spain as soon as he came to the throne; he mediated in a number of disputes that could have flared up into wider conflicts (in particular a Catholic-Protestant disputed inheritance of the Duchy of Julich and Cleves in 1609-11); he identified in the Calvinist Elector Palatine and the Catholic King of Spain the two greatest threats to a general peace, and he determined to bring pressure to bear on them by marrying his daughter to the first and his son to the daughter of the second.

The second phase of James's rule began with a rash of deaths (Prince Henry, Dunbar and Salisbury) and extended over years of drift down to 1620. This was James's 'personal rule' in two senses: there was no chief minister, and no Parliament (except for the brief 'Addled'

Parliament of 1614, dissolved before it could pass a single act). The dubious morality of the court caused dissatisfaction. James lusted after and indulged Robert Carr, Earl of Somerset. Somerset in turn lusted after the Countess of Essex, and with James's indulgence and the help of perjured testimony, the lovers connived at the annulment of the countess's marriage on the grounds of her husband's alleged impotence. One of those who helped to procure this annulment, Sir Robert Overbury, was subsequently poisoned with powdered glass, but those involved in that plot leaked the detail and every aspect of the whole sordid affair came into the public domain and was widely publicized. James's pardon of the Somersets did nothing to encourage a return to a higher standard of public morality and by 1620 three former privy councillors and a former captain in James's personal bodyguard were awaiting trial on charges of sexual or financial corruption.

Meanwhile, the 'British' project continued to advance slowly. James brought a new ruthlessness to Ireland, by adapting methods he had deployed successfully in the Gaels of the West Highlands. His 'Plantation' of Ulster in the 1610s, in the course of which he planted thousands of English and Scottish Protestant settlers in the north of the island, was to have permanent consequences, although the most malign of them were not part of his plan.

The second phase of the reign is separated from the third also by a death, this time of James's wife, Anne of Denmark, his match in intellect, his superior in taste, and a soul-mate if not (once constitutional duty was complete) his bed-mate. Anne had brought a calm dignity to the court, and her patronage of a less insular, more cosmopolitan (and Catholic) style of court painting and architecture and her introduction of the masque were to have lasting consequence. Her own discrete Catholicism was little handicap to James: publicly, she kept her own Protestant chapel with its body of clever preachers, headed by John Donne. This was in strong contrast to the strident Catholicism of the French wife of her son, Charles. Anne's broad-mindedness had thus been a major asset. Her death caused James to give his head as well as his heart to a flighty lover, and arguably led to his reign ending in undeserved disarray.

The final phase of the reign was heralded by an increasing clamour for war. James's son-in-law, Frederick, had been elected King of Bohemia in 1618. The Habsburgs, who had long ruled that kingdom and treated the election of their family to that Crown as a matter of course, launched an assault aimed at driving Frederick from Bohemia and depriving him of his own territories in the Palatinate. Soon, all Europe would be sucked into what has become known as the Thirty Years War. English Protestant opinion was inflamed, especially when Spanish troops took a leading part in the occupation of the Palatinate. James wanted to resolve the crisis by a marriage treaty between Prince Charles and the Infanta of Spain, a treaty under which the Spaniards would promise to assist in the restoration of the Palatinate. He was willing to summon Parliament, and to ask it to make bellicose noises in order to put pressure on the Spanish. But he did not want war. Parliament tried to put pressure on Spain by a naval and privateering war, and wanted nothing to do with an Anglo-Spanish marriage. In 1621 and 1624 this caused king and Parliament to be at cross-purposes. But between the Parliaments, the Prince of Wales and George Villiers, Duke of Buckingham (who had made a reckless and futile secret journey to Spain in an attempt to bounce the Spanish into the marriage) had changed sides and had become committed to war. A poisonous atmosphere was heightened by the way feuds at court spilled over into a disaffected House of Commons: irresponsible councillors initiated the impeachment of a Lord Chancellor (Bacon) in 1621 and Lord Treasurer (Cranfield) in 1624.

146. Letter of Charles I to his eldest son, dated 5 August 1645, urging him to flee to France and put himself under the care of his mother.

147. In 1641 Charles I ordered five members of Parliament and one member of the House of Lords to be arrested and tried for treason. These are his instructions to the attorney-general for the proceedings.

As the court bickered and as Parliament snapped at its heels, the Duke of Buckingham came to engross much power and patronage in himself. Perhaps modelling himself on the Spanish *privado,* a chief minister who took all the more sordid aspects of government away from Philip III and Philip IV, Buckingham exercised a degree of power unparalleled since the days of Wolsey. The king's own physical and mental deterioration, and his refusal to endorse the war that everyone else wanted but was not willing to pay for, brought the reign to a messy end. At the time of James's death in 1625, there was widespread political disaffection in the country that coloured his memory and obscured his earlier achievements for many generations to come.

CHARLES I (1625-1649)

Charles I was not born to rule. He was a younger son of James I and Anne of Denmark, and until his thirteenth year he was very much in the wake of his elder brother, Prince Henry. Henry was all that a king could want in a son and heir: he was intellectually able; he was athletic, showing natural prowess at the martial arts as tamed for courtly display; he was passionately Protestant and committed to the international Protestant cause; and he was articulate. He was the veritable apple of his parents' eye. As a birth-gift, James wrote for him the *Basilikon Doron*, a public manual of the arts (and moral basis) of royal government. But in 1612, at the age of eighteen, Henry wilted and died; and Charles became the heir to the throne. He received little love or attention, let alone affirmation, from either parent. When he came to the throne in 1625, Charles tried desperately hard to follow to the letter the manual of government that James had written for Henry. It was holy writ to him. It made him unbending, unlistening, and it cost him his thrones and his life.

Charles inherited his father's lover, George Villiers, Duke of Buckingham, as his own chief minister. The psychopathology of this transferral has never been adequately explained. There is no suggestion of homoerotic feelings between Charles and George; but there is a strong sense of deep need for the approval of a surrogate parent. Buckingham supervised foreign policy, with disastrous results. A wise king would have let the high-profile minister responsible for such failures carry the can. But Charles refused to offer up Buckingham to Parliament's anger. In 1626 Parliament offered Charles money to carry on with his support for the international Protestant cause so long as Buckingham was dismissed. Charles refused, and used prerogative powers to raise the money that Parliament had offered with unacceptable strings. He imprisoned 200 leading gentry who refused to pay up, and refused to show the cause of their imprisonment when they sought to have the judges adjudicate his right to collect emergency taxation in those circumstances. In 1628 he was forced to accept a tighter definition of his power to raise emergency taxation and forced loans and of his right to imprison 'by special commandment' for reasons of state security (The Petition of Right). But Charles's assent was grudging and his subsequent attempts to change it were deceitful and reinforced distrust. Only with Buckingham's assassination by a deranged war veteran in August 1628 was the umbilical cord cut.

Charles was now free to fall in love with his wife, Henrietta Maria of France, in a relationship that proved strong, faithful and fateful. She was as reserved as her husband, with a deep, evangelistic Catholic piety and a conviction that everything (including the absolutist nature of monarchical authority) was better in France. Charles was also free to bring into office many men essentially loyal to him but alienated by Buckingham: Sir Thomas

Wentworth (who was sent to deal with the unruly North of England and then an unmanageable Ireland); Sir Dudley Digges, who had called Buckingham 'the grievance of grievances'; and William Noy who, as Attorney General, was the architect of the 'fiscal feudalism' or reliance on prerogative and feudal revenues that transformed Charles's peacetime revenues in the 1630s. It is striking that these men, although severe critics of royal policies in the 1620s, had not been prominent critics of Charles's religious policies. These 'Puritan' critics were pointedly left out in the cold. And Charles neither forgave nor fell in love with Parliament, which was dissolved indefinitely in 1629.

The word that had run through all James I's speeches as a key to his policy was 'union': he wanted a loose union of hearts of minds between his kingdoms and peoples, within his Churches, and among Christian princes. Charles I's mission statement, by contrast, was built on the theme of uniformity. He was a fastidious man, in his personal habits, in personal relations, and in his love of order and of dignity in worship and court protocol. He was incapable of the spontaneous, the exuberant, or the improvised. His was a repressed personality, outwardly dignified and inwardly raging. Charles was taught by the Archbishop of Canterbury, William Laud, that inner harmony came from the habit of external obedience and decorum. His deep yearning for external uniformity was therefore a product of his own inner insecurities.

Charles must have believed for most of the 1630s that his attempt to treat his subjects as players in a vast political masque was working. Peace was restored; the budget was balanced; the burden of debt was reduced; a programme of social paternalism was promoted by his Council; and the court was cleaned up. Charles planned a magnificent Renaissance palace to replace the straggling buildings of Whitehall. A nationwide collection was organized to make St Paul's Cathedral in London a model of what – drawing on Psalm 102 – was known as 'the beauty of holiness'. James I had always thought it best to get statutes passed, especially statutes regulating economic activity and social norms, and then to enforce them prudently and selectively. Charles, however, wanted to have the letter of the law enforced; and initiatives such as the 'Book of Orders' now required justices of the peace to report regularly on their implementation of the 'stack of statutes' that had resulted from Tudor social and ecomomic policy (the poor laws, the laws regulating employment, the grain trade and alehouses, and so on). Similarly, bishops were required to inspect their dioceses more thoroughly and to report annually to Archbishop Laud and to the king. Order, conformity, uniformity: these were the new hallmarks of royal policy.

The biggest and most important issue in this programme was religion. Laudianism – the particular brand of religious observation promoted by Charles's archbishop – certainly had its supporters and admirers. But, because of its Catholic overtones, it alienated many more. Those who wanted to experience worship exclusively as an encounter with the Word of God, and who were suspicious of clerical power and pretension, found its tenets intolerable. Laundianism placed particular emphasis, not surprisingly, on centralized ecclesiastical power, and thus offended those who preferred the maintenance of church fabric and the details of worship to be settled at a parish level and who were enraged at being told what to do by archdeacons and bishops. In so far as every aspect of the Laudian programme was approved and endorsed by Charles I, it inevitably brought the king himself into disrepute. By 1638 and 1639, even Laud was growing concerned at the scale of the backlash. It was not that he disagreed with the king's objectives, just that he thought that Charles was going too far, too fast.

Clockwise from top 148. Portrait of Charles I and Henrietta Maria.
149. Cast from a bust made from Cromwell's death mask.
150. Cast from Oliver Cromwell's death mask.

By 1640, Charles was in a dangerously isolated position. Everything he had done was, as he saw it, for his people's good. His conscience was clear, and he felt no need to justify his policies. It was for him to discern and to act, for his people to obey and feel the benefit. And for all the alarm and the grumbling, there was no thought of rebellion. Charles appeared mildly tyrannical, but a mild tyranny was better than the anarchy that civil war would unleash.

Charles, however, was king of three kingdoms; and his government of Scotland and Ireland was clumsier still. He had little experience, knowledge or understanding of the serious limits to his power as ruler in Scotland and Ireland. In Scotland, he sought to cancel all the land grants made by his predecessors since 1542 (and perhaps earlier) and to regrant those lands on terms that protected the interests of the Crown and the Kirk more fully. He imposed a series of changes on the Church of Scotland – new canons, a new ordinal, a new prayer book – without proper consultation. Most offensively, he introduced a new prayer book into Scotland without consulting the General Assembly, Parliament, or the Privy Council. He consulted with Laud's close allies in Scotland and then simply promulgated the book and made its use mandatory. It was a breathtaking act of constitutional impropriety and political folly. The Scots covenanted amongst themselves passively to disobey Charles's commands against the laws of God and Scotland. They needed to feel that decisions relating to property and the exercise of conscience were not made in England and imposed on them from without. Twice – in the summers of 1639 and 1640 – the king tried to use English, Irish and Highland (Catholic) troops to impose his will. But on both occasions the Scots armed more quickly and effectively and crossed over into England. On the second occasion they demanded that a settlement, on their own terms, be guaranteed by an English Parliament and that meanwhile they would remain – at English expense – in occupation of northeastern England. This required the calling of an English Parliament that the king would not be able to dissolve, in effect, without Scottish consent.

In 1633, Charles franchised an abrasive, self-confident, energetic Yorkshireman, Thomas Wentworth, to govern Ireland in his name. The king's fundamental goal was to make Ireland pay for itself and thus cease to be a drain on the English Exchequer. This was difficult because to mulct the population required increased garrisons that cost more than the money raised. So Wentworth's short-term goal was to exploit the recent settlers, to uncover all local corruption and misappropriation, and to bully and intimidate the New English into personal settlements that balanced the Irish budget. It was equally important to Wentworth to increase the effectiveness of the Church of Ireland, by bringing it into close alignment with the Church of England, by restoring the endowment and jurisdictions even more ruthlessly appropriated by the laity in Ireland than in England, and thus to render it capable of an effective evangelism, in due course, amongst the Catholic population. That Catholic population was in the meantime to be humoured, and there was a relaxation of persecution. Few Catholics had little doubt that, once he had brought the Protestant communities to heel, Wentworth would round on them, and indeed plans were being laid for a series of ruthless plantations in Connacht and Munster. In all this, Charles was the willing and fully-briefed sleeping partner.

The year 1640 was the turning-point of Charles's reign, in which his miscalculations set him on the course to deposition and death. Faced by the 'Long' Parliament (1640-53), Charles had first to surrender more than half his councillors to execution, to prison, or to exile. In the spring of 1641, he showed some willingness to bring his leading critics into his

Council, but he was more interested in giving them high-prestige posts than access to his inner counsels, and this attempt at accommodation was wrecked by two things: the unexpected death of the lynch-pin Earl of Bedford, Charles's intended Lord Treasurer; and Charles's attempt to use sections of his defeated 1640 army to stage a coup in order to save Strafford from execution. Up to that point, the two Houses had focused on the guilty men of the 1630s, and on securing guarantees both that Charles would not dissolve the Long Parliament without its own consent (even when the Scots returned home) and that thereafter elections would be held every three years whether or not the king authorized them. In the summer months of 1641, however, the king found himself having to agree to the dismantling of all those instruments of government, financial and administrative, that had made his period of personal rule possible. The Houses were unflinching, and Charles I assented to everything, albeit frostily.

When it came to ecclesiastical reform, however, Charles found that he had some room for manoeuvre. If Laud and the bishops identified with him had friends in Parliament, these men did not identify themselves, and the denunciation of the policies of the past decade was unequivocal. But when it came to debates on whether simply to go back to 'the pure religion of Queen Elizabeth and King James' or to replace the 1559 settlement with one based 'on the example of the best reformed Churches' (some meaning by that Scotland, some the Netherlands, and others New England), there was ever-growing dissension within and between the Houses. This gave Charles his first real chance to create a following. With notable good grace, he elevated anti-Laudian Calvinist heads of colleges in Oxford and Cambridge to episcopal sees, threw himself into a defence of the Prayer Book, and used every occasion to proclaim his commitment to 'the true reformed Protestant religion by law established, without any connivance of popery or innovation', thus in effect announcing his abandonment of Laudianism.

In the high summer of 1641 the king set off for Scotland to sign the treaty that turned Scotland into a self-governing Presbyterian theocracy, his own power reduced to that of a cypher. A wise king would have smiled sweetly, taken his medicine and bided his time until rivalries among the Scottish factions had caused one of them to offer him his power back in return for a monopoly of office. Instead, Charles colluded in a fumbled coup by disaffected Covenanters. If Charles had kept his cool in Scotland, and used the recurrence of plague or the need to be in the North to normalize things after the Scottish occupation to call a reconvened Parliament to York (which the great majority would have heeded), he could have reestablished control. Instead as he travelled south, news arrived that a series of rebellions had broken out in Ireland. Unhappily for Charles, some of the rebels produced forged commissions claiming that they were repossessing their land on his explicit authority. Although this was pure fabrication, there was no way Charles could prove his innocence, and the mud stuck. At the very moment when his religious moderation, the scale of the reforms he had countenanced, and growing social protest and increasingly violent iconoclasm were giving him a natural majority in both Houses of Parliament and thus the prospect of regaining the initiative, the Irish rebellion cost him many waverers.

Charles was a hard man to believe in, because of his manifest insincerity in making concessions, his constant willingness to use Catholics to impose his will on his Protestant subjects, the clearly malign advice of his wife, and his ineffectual attempts to use force to get his way. His infamous armed entrance into the House of Commons brandishing a warrant for the arrest of five members of the Lower House and one of the Upper House, only to find that his 'birds had flown', created enormous resentment. But the reckless use of mass picketing, the indulgence of radical and separatist religious activity, and the determination to pluck 'the flowers of the prerogative' (the king's right to choose his own ministers and to control the armed forces) also made the 'popular' leaders in Parliament increasingly unpopular. Once Charles had fled London and begun a long eight-month peregrination of England, politics inevitably became polarized. Most people desperately wanted some kind of accommodation and almost any settlement that avoided civil war. But the dread in one minority of royal tyranny if the king retained control of the executive and armed forces, and the dread in another of anarchy in Church and State if he was not restored on the basis of his grudging 1641 concessions, gradually led to a taking up of arms, and to the king's raising his standard at Nottingham on 20 August 1642.

By this act, Charles launched what turned into a four-year civil war. Throughout those years he showed great personal courage and resolve on the battlefield. There was nothing craven or undignified about Charles as a soldier, and although he frequently intervened in councils of war to end in-fighting by disastrous compromise settlements (the division of his army in the days before the fateful Battle of Naseby being the greatest mistake), he continued to lead from the front. In the course of the war, he visited at least twenty-six of the forty English counties, and he led his men in five of the ten greatest battles. He also tried to wage a just war. He delayed the introduction of war taxation, impressment, martial law and free quarter until after Parliament had introduced them, and he tried hard to sustain the rule of law. Parliament suspended much of the machinery of common law and ruled by committee diktat, but Charles sought the approval of grand juries for all his war taxation; and whereas Parliament confiscated the estates of thousands of 'delinquent' royalists by administrative decree, Charles sought to do so through formal indictment by jury at common law. This was admirable but inefficient, and as the war turned against him, he was forced into more and more desperate reliance on military requisition and plunder. His early reliance on English Catholic officers cost him much Protestant support; and his truce with the Catholic Confederate rebels in the autumn of 1643, which allowed him to recall the English army from Ireland, and his subsequent offers to establish a Catholic hegemony in Ireland in return for an Irish Catholic army in England, were highly counter-productive and lingered in the memory of those trying to create a post-war settlement. There were times during the wars when a simple majority of MPs were willing to make peace on terms that many of Charles's loyal advisors thought reasonable. But, hamstrung by the ghost of his father, the words of his coronation oath, and the prospect of answering on the Day of Judgement for the surrender of powers with which he believed God had invested him, the king overruled both his counsellors and common sense.

By May 1646, Charles faced total military defeat. In a dramatic cross-country dash of some 150 miles (from Oxford to Southwell, near Newark, via North London) he surrendered to Parliament's Scottish allies, hoping to sow dissension among his enemies. This was to be his stratagem for the next thirty months. And there was enough evidence that it was working to keep him at it. The Scots had one set of priorities; two increasingly bitterly opposed groups in Parliament (one supported by the Army generals) had two more sets of proposals; many regimental officers and politicized troopers in alliance with London radicals had yet another. The king blew hot and cold in respect of each group, and he was unfased by being passed around from group to group. In late 1647 he fled to the Isle of Wight, and from there he negotiated with a Scottish faction that was willing to use force against the English Parliament

151. Coin minted in Shrewsbury in 1642, the first of the 'Declaration' type. The translated
declaration reads 'The religion of the Protestants, the laws of England, the liberty of the Parliament'.
152 A siege piece struck during Charles I's reign. Colchester was besieged by Fairfax and
surrendered after eleven weeks in August 1648.
153. Coin of the Commonwealth period, depicting Oliver Cromwell, 1658.

in return for very reasonable terms. This is turn triggered a wave of rebellions across England by his long-term supporters and by disaffected Parliamentarians weary of parliamentary tyranny and indulgence of religious separatists. Gradually the New Model Army put down these rebellions and dealt efficiently with the Scottish invasion.

Ever since the king's duplicity in his dealings with them in the autumn of 1647, many in the army had sought his downfall. At the Army Council meetings at Putney in October and November, two officers had called him a 'Man of Blood', one against whom God would have judgment to atone for his shedding of innocent blood; and there were demands that he be put on trial. The Generals conceded that this might become necessary, but that the time was not yet right. From April 1648, the army was formally committed to Charles's trial, but throughout the year Oliver Cromwell and others were working for an alternative solution. They hoped to persuade or to bully Charles into abdication in favour of one is his sons.

The crisis of the Revolution occurred in December 1648. Since most MPs preferred a settlement at any price to putting Charles on trial, the Army was forced into staging a coup, surrounding the Palace of Westminster and permitting only those willing to work with them to take their seats. For three weeks the king was subjected to intense pressure to abdicate. But his obduracy, and his sense of vocation, strained against it. And so he was put on trial for treasons against his people. It was his finest hour. At last completely at peace with himself, steadfast in his willingness to embrace martyrdom, he won a huge moral victory over his enemies. He refused to acknowledge the authority of the High Court of Justice. He refused to enter a plea. He represented himself as standing up for the rule of law against an instrument of tyranny. Most of those appointed to judge him stayed away, but when the time came, he was condemned to death. The execution took place on a rostrum set out in front of the Banqueting House in Whitehall, on 30 January 1649. In his dying words, Charles gave equal prominence to his final defence of the Church and of his divine mandate to govern. He was killed with a single blow of the axe.

The king's enemies immediately had him sewn together again and moved discreetly for burial in St George's Chapel at Windsor, where some of Charles's happiest days had been spent in presiding over the annual services of dedication for Knights of the Garter. Charles's enemies were more enemies to him than to monarchy, and they havered over whether to impose the king's third son, Henry, as their stooge monarch. When it was clear this would not broaden their desperately narrow band of support, they finally determined to go it alone, and to declare England a Commonwealth. For eleven years, Charles I's obduracy and commitment to the dignity of his office rendered England a republic – and one committed to the most complete and ruthless incorporation of Ireland and Scotland into an enhanced English State that there has ever been.

CHARLES II (1649/60-1685)

In his own eyes, and in the eyes of a great majority of the inhabitants of the islands of Britain and Ireland, Charles II became king at the moment of his father's death; and a unanimous declaration of the Lords and Commons issued on 8 May 1660 declared it to have been so. Henceforth, all his instruments of government dated his reign as beginning on 30 January 1649. In a strict constitutional sense, Charles reigned for thirty-six years.

Opposite   154. Charles II by Samuel Cooper (1609-72).

Yet he spent the first third of that reign in exile. Most of the courts of Europe – whatever their private sympathy with his plight – proved unwilling formally to recognize him out of fear of alienating the mighty British Commonwealth, and he was frequently asked to move on to spare his hosts political embarrassment. He spent a miserable year in Scotland in 1649-50, the low point being his coronation at Scone on 1 January 1650 during which he had to endure an interminable sermon from Robert Douglas that enumerated the public and private sins of each of his predecessors. This Scottish escapade ended with a few days in England culminating in a crushing defeat at Worcester and with a desperate period on the run. Every attempt to regain his thrones – in alliance with Presbyterian Scots, Catholic Irish, English lovers of the proscribed Anglican order, Dutch sailors, French adventurers, Spanish tercios – crumbled into dust. Each new alliance meant the betrayal of former allies. And every year brought new humiliations, as grinding poverty, the surliness of creditors, and the condescension of grudging benefactors combined to remind Charles how little control he had over his own destiny.

All this was deeply embittering; but worst of all was the memory of his inability to prevent the execution of his father. Charles, born in 1630, had stayed close to his father's side throughout the years 1642, 1643 and 1644 but was then sent off, as a fifteen-year-old, to lead the royalist movement in the West. In the spring of 1646 he fled the country, first to Scilly, then to Jersey, and then to France. From those events and from the impotence of exile, he watched his father surrender his life rather than his principles. And in the years that followed, Charles II showed a willingness to surrender every principle, even the principle of princely loyalty to those risking everything in his name, as the price of the next expedient alliance.

By 1660, Charles had one obsession: restoration. Once back on the throne, his ambition was spent. He had no vision of what he wanted to achieve as king, no vision of unity or uniformity, no vision (as his brother was to have) of restoring Catholicism as the natural religion of his subjects. His sole desire was to be king. Unlike his brother James, who believed that their father had died by being weak and not pursuing his beliefs ruthlessly enough, Charles II was convinced that the old king had died by being too wedded to his friends, to the legitimacy of his actions, and to his Church, and was determined to avoid repeating these mistakes. All this is demonstrated by Charles's political claustrophobia, a great fear of being trapped and of being carried helplessly along by the surge of events, a prisoner of faction. He deeply resented attempts by ministers to smother him and to protect him from himself. He would not be told what to do or whom to employ. In particular, he feared being held to ransom by Parliament and was always looking for ways of raising money to ensure financial independence. Subsidies from foreign rulers, especially from Louis XIV, were a favoured option.

Charles was also profoundly cynical. Nurture rather than nature made him naturally dissimulating and quietly vindictive. He was, for example, one of the few English monarchs willing to authorize the assassination of political opponents as an instrument of policy. Unlike his father, he was quick to let his ministers take the blame for failed or unpopular policies. Thus the Earl of Clarendon took the blame in 1667 for the failure of the Second Dutch War, and the Earl of Danby was the scapegoat for the collapse of Charles's foreign and financial policies in 1679. The king liked to play ministers off against one another, allowing deep personal antipathies to mature in the fetid atmosphere of the court. Policy was made not in open Council, but in ad hoc groups summoned at dead of night to his presence chamber. His most remarkable characteristic was his ability to be affable and good-natured towards those whom he despised. He was approachable, egregious and witty. His open dalliance with his mistresses, his indulgence of foul-mouthed aristocratic *roués* such as the second Duke of Buckingham and the first Earl of Rochester, kept the prudish and the puritanical at bay.

But Charles also determined early on that he would give more power to his father's opponents than to his friends. His Privy Council and the judicial Bench in 1660 contained a simple majority of former Parliamentarians, and sixty per cent of the justices of the peace had similar sympathies. Charles's Lord Chancellor, the Earl of Clarendon, and the head of his household, the Duke of Ormonde, were amongst the few who had shared exile with him to get high office. He attempted a similarly broad approach to the reconstitution of the episcopal bench, and those closest to his father's archbishop, William Laud – men such as Peter Heylyn – were denied advancement. Although most of those who had served in the Cromwellian Church, such as Richard Baxter and Edmund Calamy, declined the offer of advancement, others, including Cromwell's brother-in-law John Wilkins and Edward Reynolds, accepted, and a majority of the new bishops were men who had kept a low profile in the previous decade and were ecclesiastical pragmatists.

As the reign progressed, old Royalist and Parliamentarian ideologies transmuted themselves into what came to be known as Tory and Whig ideologies. The first was rooted in the God-given (divine) right of the monarchy to govern, of the Church of England (an alliance of pious squire and parson) to monopolize religious practice, and of the gentry to rule paternalistically under the wing of king and Parliament. The second was rooted in distrust of executive power, a residual preference for contractual views of royal power, a dislike of religious intolerance, and a preference for either looser terms of Church membership or a measure of freedom for those with tender consciences – those who would not subscribe to the terms and conditions of Anglican Church membership – to worship discreetly in the light of those consciences. Charles might seem to have had everything to gain by backing the Tories; but he was temperamentally unhappy with the idea of a confessional State and the preciosities of Anglican clericism. His political instinct was to avoid persecution. Whereas most Tories believed that to indulge religious dissenters would be to indulge their penchant for subversion, Charles believed that his indulgence of their position would make them indulgent of his.

Charles's own religion has baffled all who have studied it. Perhaps he simply had no strong views, no personal encounters with God. His amorality and immorality, his amused indulgence of the frankly depraved in his court, and his careless religious practice suggest as much. But it is more likely that he long felt a strong pull towards the Catholic faith of his mother, his wife, his sisters, his surviving brother, all the mistresses whose views on public affairs he took seriously, and of all the kings of Europe he knew at first hand. He twice – in secret negotiations in 1663 which have been little studied, and in 1670 in the secret Treaty of Dover – committed to paper a personal confession of Catholic faith and a desire to announce his conversion if the political conditions in England made it possible. He was received into the Catholic Church on his deathbed. He strove much harder to procure liberty for strained Catholic consciences than for Puritan ones. When the political temperature rose, he was willing to permit new and vindictive anti-Catholic legislation, but he then worked to mitigate its implementation once the temperature fell. It was characteristic of his determined opportunism that between 1679 and 1681 he allowed thirty-five men to be executed for their part in an alleged Popish Plot to assassinate him that he knew to have been fabricated by a bunch of congenital liars.

Clockwise from top left   155. Charles II by David Logan (1630-93).
156. The original crown made for King Charles II at the restoration.
157. Coat of arms of Catherine of Braganza.
158. Catherine of Braganza, Queen of Charles II, painted by Dirk Stoop in the Portuguese dress
which she wore on her arrival in England, May 1662.

Although Charles II's return in 1660 owed little to his own efforts, the success of that return owed much to him. His willingness to refer all the knottiest issues to Parliament was crucial. He worked to limit the punishment of those who had overthrown his father and sustained the 'illegal' regimes of the 1650s. He worked to compensate those who had acquired the vast amount of land confiscated from the Crown, the bishops, the cathedrals and the more militant Royalists. He sought a religious settlement that was acceptable as possible to 'all species of Protestant' and to grant liberty within state-monitored limits to all those whose 'tender consciences' made it impossible for them to remain members of the State Church. He had a liberalizing influence in regard to indemnity and land; but he failed in his attempts to persuade the Parliament elected in 1661 to provide for a broad, comprehensive national Church; and he failed to gain freedom for Protestant and Catholic dissenters. He also ensured an easy Restoration by his gracious endorsement of the constitutional limitations his father had so begrudgingly conceded in 1640-2, and by drawing his ministers and officers, nationally and in the localities, from across the political spectrum.

This honeymoon period ended in 1664. The Commonwealth had fought a successful naval war over world trade issues between 1651 and 1654; Charles renewed it in 1664, but suffered a series of humiliating reverses. The Great Plague (1665) and the Great Fire (1666) were treated by some as signs of divine displeasure and generally made the capital a spoiled place. Charles was at odds with his prudish and self-righteous Lord Chancellor, Clarendon. The gilt was peeling.

A new phase of the reign was opened by Charles's determination to be free from financial dependence on Parliament and the need always to barter redress of grievance for cash-in-hand. From 1667 to 1674, Charles deliberately divided power between men with incompatible views on all the central issues. He made secret treaties with the French to fight the Dutch, secure subsidies, and disclose his secret Catholic yearning. Parliament frustrated his policies of religious liberalization, but it represented no deeper threat – although jealousies between the Lords and Commons over the nature of the judicial powers of the Lords deadlocked four sessions, preventing the progress of legislation. Eventually Charles got fed up of the politics of drift, sacked the ill-assorted 'Cabal' ministry and installed a man of impeccable Cavalier-Anglican background – Thomas Osborne, Earl of Danby – with a brief to give him greater freedom from the political wrangling. This Danby did by pursuing a pro-Dutch foreign policy (persuading Charles to allow the marriage of Mary, his elder niece and second in line to the throne to the Prince of Orange), by enforcing the Anglican monopoly on office and proclaiming the virtues of the confessional State, and by using government patronage in cash and office to secure the attendance at Parliament of the naturally-loyal Tory squires. Their presence was sufficient to keep the political temperature low for a while. But this attempt to buy the attendance of MPs could be made to look like the bribery of MPs to be poodles of the executive, and a clamour arose for the dissolution of Parliament and the first elections since 1661.

Charles privately hankered after a more pro-French policy and, while Danby got Parliament to fund a war against France, Charles told Louis XIV that he would abandon it in return for a very large annual subsidy. This could be made to look like an attempt to create a standing army. And so, out of a relatively clear sky, there came a torrent of anxious complaint that England was in danger of succumbing to 'popery and arbitrary government.' Charles's refusal to take the threat of popery seriously, his indulgence of his brother and heir James (now an openly confessed papist), his pursuit of policies identified in the popular mind with

Catholic princes (the promotion of standing armies, the subversion of representative institutions, the pursuit of deceitful and machiavellian policies), were blown out of all proportion. And the claim of some desperadoes that they were privy to a plot by papists hired by the pope and the King of France to assassinate Charles and put James on the throne fanned these anxieties into hysteria.

Between 1678 and 1681, Charles had to weather this storm. Danby was sacked and incarcerated. Thirty-five innocent men were executed after show trials based on perjured evidence. Three successive Parliaments demanded that James be excluded from the succession. Charles sailed with the wind. He sacrificed the innocent, he offered concessions short of conceding Exclusion. He let the storm blow itself out. He relied on a natural majority in the House of Lords to throw out the Exclusion Bills. And he skilfully exploited divisions amongst his opponents (for example between those who would have preferred the throne to pass to James's Protestant daughter Mary, those who sought the legitimising of the oldest of Charles's fourteen acknowledged bastard sons, the Duke of Monmouth, and those who would settle for Charles's divorce from his childless Portuguese wife and remarriage to anyone capable of bearing him a child). He waited for the benefits of the European peace of 1679 to swell English trade and thus his revenues. This, together with a substantial new subsidy from Louis XIV, gave him the chance to begin his own personal rule.

The final years of the reign (1681-5) are generally know as the Tory Reaction. Certainly, they were years when Charles II really let the heirs of the Cavalier-Anglicans have their own way: a near monopoly on national and local office; indulgence to harass Dissenters, especially the Quakers; freedom from direct taxation in exchange for a freedom from foreign adventures and from the meeting of Parliaments. Charles, for the first time allowed the gentry to remodel the government of provincial towns, and with that came the prospect of a strengthened loyalist return from the parliamentary boroughs. When he was struck down by a rapid terminal illness in February 1685, Charles was in complete control. He had one last trick up his sleeve. He was received into the Catholic Church on his deathbed. This time there was no Parliament to protest. When it comes to the arts of the expedient, Charles II brooks no rival amongst the rulers of Britain.

JAMES II & VII OF SCOTLAND (1685-1688)

Whereas Charles II thought that his father had conceded too little, too grudgingly, and was determined not to make the same mistake himself, James II and VII thought that his father's mistake had been to make any concessions at all. James had learnt the arts of war in the 1650s as a senior officer in both the French and Spanish armies, and he developed extensive experience of naval warfare. He belonged to a tradition that saw any concession as a sign of weakness that would encourage an enemy.

James became king at the age of fifty-one and he ruled for less than four years before being effectively expelled from his kingdoms to live out the final decade of his life in what one historian has called 'a state of religious dementia'. The most obvious thing about him was his blinkered Catholicism: he was determined to use his reign to promote the Catholic religion and to secure a full and irreversible civil and religious equality for those who shared his Faith. Just as obvious, but far less fully understood, are the circumstances of his life as Charles I's second son. He was the first prince of the blood royal for almost two hundred years – since the Richard, Duke of Gloucester in the reign of Edward IV – to succeed a brother as king.

He would always carry with him the knowledge that, in 1648, New Model Generals and their parliamentary allies wanted to put him on the throne in place of his father, and that he had refused their offer. He would carry with him, between 1650 and 1685, the conviction that his brother Charles was lacking in principle and backbone. He spent nearly fifty sentient years knowing that he was one heartbeat from supreme power, but also conscious that if his fecund brother ever divorced his childless wife – or if she predeceased him and he re-married – the prize would be snatched from him. By the time he secured the throne, he was a late middle-aged man in a hurry.

James – Duke of York in the English peerage and Duke of Albany in the Scottish – was born on 14 October 1633. For ten years he was brought up away from his parents. But much more than his elder brother, he spent significant periods of time with his father in the years 1642-6 and 1647. He spent the Civil War years in Oxford, and witnessed his father's despair as the royalists spiralled to defeat. Left behind when Charles I surrendered to the Scots, James was placed under house arrest, but once his father was brought up to Hampton Court in the summer of 1647, James was allowed to see him two or three times a week. Charles poured out his deepest feelings to his son, and he impressed three important things upon him. The first was that God was judging him not for his misgovernment in the 1630s, but for his surrender of his God-given powers in 1640-2. The second was that James must never allow personal ambition to lead him to the throne in place of his father or ahead of his brother. The third was the crucial importance of a king's conscience and the absolute duty to serve the Church that he loved. James made the first two the lodestars of his life; and while he abandoned the Church his father loved, he adhered to the principle of using kingly power to advance true religion as he saw it.

James spent the 1650s in exile, embroiled in feuds between his mother and his brother and learning the arts of war as a general in the French (1652-6) Spanish (1657-9) armies. In war James was brave, unflinching and inflexible. He may well have been in more bloody engagements than any other member of the blood royal. This gave him a belief in military rather than political solutions and heightened his impatience with Charles's endless attempts to wheedle his way back to his thrones by offering the moon to Irish Catholics, Scottish Presbyterians, English Levellers, and the courts of Spain and France. His relations with his brother veered between irritation and exasperation.

When Charles II was invited back in 1660, James was the first to spoil the party by the embarrassing revelation that he had impregnated the daughter of the prudish Lord Chancellor and intended to marry her. By Anne Hyde he had eight children in eleven years, and although only two survived, his daughters Mary and Anne, both were to play a decisive part in his downfall. And it may have been through the conversion to Catholicism of his wife that James made his own slow, painful and inexorable journey of faith.

For most of Charles's reign, James remained in irritated loyalty to his brother. He had a grudge that his brother kept him strapped for cash and that, the more important the issue, the less Charles took his advice. He was allowed great freedom to develop interests in overseas trade and colonial settlement as a governor of the Hudson's Bay, Royal Fisheries, and Royal Africa Companies. He used his position in the last to create a cold war with Dutch shipping and to provoke Charles into a war he did not want. He then organized and triumphantly oversaw the capture of the New Netherlands, renamed New York in his honour. He was given authority over the new colony and he ran it autocratically. He was less personally involved in the total reorganization of the royal navy, and he was unable to repeat

159. James II.
160. The coat of arms of Mary of Modena, Queen of James II.

the triumphs of Blake over the Dutch in the 1650s. This left him with an enduring dislike of the Dutch. It was more salt in the eczema of sibling rivalry that – against his wishes – Charles married off James's elder daughter Mary to William of Orange, the son of their own sister Mary. William, nephew and now son-in-law to James, was to be his nemesis.

James's conversion to Catholicism followed years of reflection and vacillation. James was as slow-witted, relentless and deliberate as Charles II was intellectually alert, lazy and supple. He consulted the best Anglicans and the wiliest Jesuits, and the latter hammered away on questions of authority and religious certainty. James was effectively convinced by 1669, but it took another three years for him to make the final break and to 'out' himself as a Catholic. From that moment forth, he was utterly convinced not only of all the claims of the Catholic Faith, but of the fact that anyone who came to the evidence with an open mind would be similarly converted. This was the key to the religious policies of his reign.

But first he had to survive the traumas of the Exclusion Crisis and the relentless attempts of three successive Parliaments to bar him from the throne. Charles's indulgence of James's enemies – his willingness to let James's innocent servants suffer the horrific death of traitors, his willingness to send James into exile, his running before the wind of popular opinion – embittered the prince. He used his time in Scotland in the early 1680s in a campaign of vengeance – the 'Killing Times' – against Protestant Dissenters. This did nothing to smooth the anxieties of those who had tried so hard, but in vain, to keep him out when Charles succumbed to a stroke in March 1685 and James became king.

There can be no doubt that James was determined to secure the religious liberties of his co-religionists in all three kingdoms, but that he had no intention of seeking to create a confessional State. In Ireland, he made rapid strides not only to suspend all the penal laws that prohibited Catholic worship, but also to remove all civil disabilities on Catholics. Midway through his reign he gave control of the Irish government and of the Irish Army to Catholics, as representing a natural majority (in fact more than three quarters) of his subjects there. But he was adamant that there would be no questioning of the Land Settlement of the 1650s and 1660s that had resulted in eighty per cent of the land being owned by resident or non-resident Protestants. In England and Scotland he sought first the suspension and then (mindful that his heir was his Protestant daughter Mary, married to the Dutch Calvinist William of Orange) the repeal of all laws against Catholics. Initially he expected to be able to work with the Tories, the Anglican traditionalists who had stood by him so loyally during the exclusion crisis. He failed to appreciate that they were loyal to the divine right of kings because it upheld the divinely ordained religious and social order: episcopacy, Prayer Book, semi-autonomous shires, and corporations under their direct control. When they had to choose between the rights of the Church and the rights of the Crown, to his bemusement and confusion, they unwaveringly chose the Church.

For the first eighteen months of his reign, James sought to build a coalition with the Tory-Anglicans, headed by his brothers-in-law, Henry Hyde, second Earl of Clarendon, and Lawrence Hyde, first Earl of Rochester, and by great loyalist dynasties such as the North and the Finch families. In the wake of the rebellions of the Earl of Argyll in Scotland and of Charles II's senior bastard, the Duke of Monmouth, in England, James expected these men to support his call for a larger army manned by (amongst others) Catholic officers with veteran service in foreign armies. The most loyalist Parliament of the century refused point-blank. Within months it was clear that this Parliament would not repeal the Test Acts or the Penal Laws. James called in every MP one by one and demanded that they agree to support such repeal, and one by one they refused to commit themselves. James bullied the judges (sacking five of the twelve of them in the process) into agreeing that he had the right to dispense Catholics from the anti-Catholic oaths so as to be able to hold office in national, local and military offices. He proceeded to appoint as many Catholics as he could conscientiously believe were capable of discharging public offices. In no sector did this represent more than a quarter of all posts, but it was already far beyond their proportion of the population. There was no let-up in the low-level persecution of Protestant dissenters in this first phase.

James wanted a strict equality for Catholics and Protestants. This meant that Catholics would not be subject to Protestant jurisdictions, would not have to pay tithes for the main-tenance of Protestant clergy, or rates for the maintenance of Protestant churches. It meant the restoration of some Oxford and Cambridge colleges for the training of young men in the Catholic professions and, in towns with too many medieval churches, the licensing of some for Catholic use. This was a search for equality, not supremacy. But it enraged the Anglican establishment. Believing that the Protestants had had a monopoly on print culture for more than a century, James issued proclamations against anti-Catholic publications (and suspended the Bishop of London for refusing to discipline one of his clergy for one such polemic), but he encouraged and financially supported Catholic evangelism. James was, in other words, a proponent of affirmative action on a massive scale.

At the beginning of 1687, James decided to abandon the Tory-Anglicans, who were sulking and obstructive, and to seek to build an alliance with the Protestant Dissenters. He now began an extraordinary campaign against the Tories. All local appointees were asked in writing whether they would support the repeal of the Test Acts and Penal Laws (or support parliamentary candidates who would do so). As a result of the negative and prevaricating replies, more than half of all Lord Lieutenants, Deputy Lieutenants and justice of the peace were sacked. James also called in the charters of most boroughs and remodelled them, restricting the parliamentary franchise to town councillors whom he named within the new charters. This was by far the most blatant and deliberate attempt yet to secure Crown control of the House of Commons; and it might just have succeeded. James was not willing to pack the House of Lords with men lacking the substance of a landed peerage, and the massive Tory majority in the Lords could still have frustrated his plans. But in any case, alarm bells were ringing throughout the manor houses of England.

James compounded his errors by a head-on clash with the bishops. He ordered them to instruct their clergy to read out a declaration granting a general toleration to non-Anglicans. Seven of them – including Archbishop Sancroft – publicly declined to do so, and petitioned James, saying that the content of his declaration was illegal. James had them arrested and tried for seditious libel before three senior judges and a hand-picked jury (including in its ranks the purveyor of meat to the royal kitchens, whose contract was up for renewal). Even so, only one of the judges and none of the jurors was willing to convict the bishops and, to general rejoicing, they were acquitted. For James – who had intended to pardon them as a great gesture of reconciliation once they were convicted – this was a catastrophe.

By now, James had few friends amongst the ninety percent of the population who were Anglican. Catholics were divided as to whether he was going too far for their long-term good, and Protestant Dissenters were divided over whether the offer of religious freedom and political power would simply cause them more problems. A key group of aristocrats was secretly negotiating with William of Orange to see if he would bring over an army to put an end to the Catholic project. William was tempted, because he wanted to compel England into the war looming between himself, the Emperor and others, and Louis XIV of France.

In 1673 James had married, as his second wife, Mary of Modena. The birth of a son to Mary in late June 1688 was the true trigger to the Revolution that followed. This made everyone – and, above all, William of Orange – aware that James might found a Catholic dynasty. Many Protestants who had decided to weather the storm and to await a Protestant succession now had to think darker thoughts. And William had to consider whether to gamble on a seizure of the throne. It is surprising that he risked so much on so uncertain an outcome. But it worked. James found that, while William got less popular support than he had expected, he, James, got no support at all. The Tories did not believe in active resistance to a divinely ordained king. But they did not believe they had any duty to lift a little finger to help a king like James. He was dependent on his standing army, and – by all appearances overwrought and suffering some kind of mental breakdown – James so alarmed his senior commanders when he appeared at army headquarters in Salisbury that several of them deserted him, and he himself then fled back to London and (at a second attempt) to the Continent. The reign was held to have ended at James's departure on 11 December 1688.

In England, all the political in-fighting of the next few months was over how to replace the king. James's supporters were disoriented and scattered. In Scotland, James had much more support, but he gave his party confused and contradictory instructions. They, meanwhile, speedily lost the battle for control of the Scottish Parliament, and then, more slowly, a military struggle for the Highlands. In Ireland, James had majority support. Initially, his men ran the country and William found that vital military, naval and fiscal resources he desperately wanted to deploy against Louis XIV were needed to overthrow James. William himself began the 'liberation' of Ireland by relieving Londonderry and a crushing victory over James himself at the Battle of the Boyne, driving the latter into permanent exile. But six more years of attrition were necessary before Ireland was fully secured for an even firmer and nastier Protestant ascendancy.

James lived out his remaining years in French exile: convinced that his defeat was God's judgment on him for his unrestrained libido in previous years, he spent much of the time on his knees in penitential prayer. Most of those disillusioned with William who sought him out and offered to help him back were left in no doubt that he was unrepentant for his policies and would redouble them if he were restored. Only resolute Catholics found it possible to stay around. Even Louis despaired of him and found his inflexibility and religious dementia exasperating. He died and was buried in France, leaving his son to lead a lost cause for another half-century.

WILLIAM III (1689-1701) AND MARY II (1689-1695)

The English Parliament deemed that James II had abdicated his thrones of England and Ireland by deserting those realms in December 1688. But the English Parliament did not seek to declare that James no longer occupied the throne of Scotland. That was decided by the Scottish Parliament, and on different grounds. James was deemed to have forfeited the throne of Scotland by his despotic actions. The English Parliament declared that James had abdicated; the Scottish Parliament deposed him. In deciding how to replace him, both passed over the infant Prince of Wales in constitutional silence. (In any case, many publicly asserted the child was suppositious, a miller's son smuggled into the queen's bed in a warming pan;

and many more said that there were too many doubts about the child's legitimacy for him to be considered as a future king.) After a period of interregnum, early in 1689, first the English Parliament and then the Scottish Parliament created a constitutional anomaly: the joint occupation of the thrones by James's elder daughter Mary and her husband and cousin, William of Orange. In a single coronation ceremony, they were both anointed and crowned side by side. But all the authority and all the prerogatives of the Crown were concentrated in the hands of William. Mary was strictly powerless, and when she acted as head of State in William's absence on military campaign in the summers of 1692-5, she acted as his regent, not in her own right.

For the English Whigs and for the 'Presbyterian' party that dominated the Scottish Parliament, what had happened was a vindication of the principle that monarchs were elected to serve their people. For many Tories, what had happened was that James, the rightful and lawful ruler, had been suspended indefinitely as a result of his wilful desertion of his subjects, and William and Mary were caretaker rulers, necessary for the preservation of order and the prevention of anarchy, but not 'rightful and lawful' monarchs. Throughout the reign, the Tories – representing a clear majority of the landowning and governing elite – refused to take any oath that acknowledged William and Mary's status as such 'rightful and lawful' rulers. And the Tories won a significant skirmish during the constitutional crisis of 1688-9. They got the English Parliament to declare that the order of succession would be: first, the heirs of Mary's body by William, or by any subsequent husband should William predecease her; secondly, Mary's younger sister Anne and then her legitimate children; and thirdly, the children of William by any marriage he contracted after Mary's death. Had William remarried between 1695 and 1701 and had children, those children would not have succeeded him: Anne would. The Tories had succeeded in treating the 1689 settlement as a temporary and necessary aberration. The hereditary succession would reassert itself.

The monarchy of William and Mary is thus steeped in ambiguity. It was indeed essential to its success that the contradictions and silences of the constitutional declarations allowed all kinds of different interpretations. And, of course, there were many in all three kingdoms who never accepted their legitimacy. A Parliament elected in Ireland in 1689 declared unequivocal loyalty to James II, who later in the year brought an army of English exiles and French troops to Ireland intending to secure that island as a preliminary to reclaiming his British Crowns. Irish Catholics flocked to him and William had to send the cream of his Anglo-Dutch armies to Ireland to subdue the threat. The flight of James after the Battle of the Boyne and his abandonment of the loyal Irish to the Protestant vengeance set back Irish Jacobitism by half a generation – Seamus the Shite was no hero in Ireland, although his son was to be one. In Scotland, there was a more consistent Jacobite loyalty in the Highlands, and spasmodic Jacobite violence there was to destabilize British politics for many decades. In England, there was much passive refusal to acknowledge William: a third of the bishops, a tenth of the clergy, and a swathe of unbending Tory families (such as the second Earl of Clarendon, and the North family, who had served as law officers to successive monarchs) cut themselves off from public life. There was much dry tinder, and sparks from elsewhere in Britain and Ireland or from the Continent constantly threatened to turn it into a bush fire. The one thing the Glorious Revolution was not was bloodless. In a British and Irish context, it launched a 'war of the two dynasties' that was to last, declared and undeclared, until at least 1746, and perhaps until 1760.

It is an abiding mystery why Dutch William gambled so much on this troubled inheritance. One of the insoluble mysteries of British history is what exactly he intended when he landed at the head of his Dutch army in Torbay on 5 November 1688. He wanted control of England, and he wanted a guarantee that English cash would bankroll and English armies and navies broaden the ramshackle coalition that William had assembled to break the arrogance of Europe's only superpower, France. If that meant removing James, or breaking his personal power, so be it. But it is hard to believe that he wanted the Crown. He wanted power. His complete indifference to keeping the succession in his family is perhaps the key. He wanted English partnership in the war with Louis, not the rulership of England or Britain. We should never forget that he was not king of the Netherlands but *stadtholder*, chief executive and head of the army. He simply wanted to be *stadtholder* of England (and, if necessary, of Scotland and Ireland); if it had not been necessary to take the royal title, he would have settled for less.

William was intense, brooding and single-minded. He formed few friendships, but was deeply loyal to those he favoured. His was a repressed personality, probably homosexual, and his early experience took its toll: his father died almost at the moment of his birth, and his lonely childhood had been spent in internal exile as his enemies suspended the office of *stadtholder*. It was Louis XIV's declared intent to destroy the Dutch Republic and asset-strip it that gave William the chance in 1672 to restore his family's position and its Protestant crusade against the malevolent claims of Catholic kings. Taking control of England was unequivocally a means to that end, and meant nothing in itself.

Mary was the eldest surviving child of James, Duke of York, a product of his shotgun marriage to Anne Hyde, daughter of the Lord Chancellor. In due course, Mary was given little choice but to marry her cousin William. At the time of the match in 1677, he was thirty and she was seventeen. Theirs was a loveless and childless match, rooted in his indifference and her pointless devotion. She had no real power, and her importance was to be a Protestant Stuart. It is indeed a great irony that, while almost all the children of Charles I (who died for the Church of England) became Catholics, and while both Mary's parents became Catholics, Mary herself was a rock-solid Protestant. It was devotion to the Church, not to her husband, that made her a reluctant conspirator against her father. She died in December 1694, after which William, who never re-married, ruled alone under the terms of the 1689 settlement.

William's reign was dominated by war: he held together the great coalition of the Emperor, the Princes of Germany, the Dutch and the British to fight on land and sea against Louis XIV. The Treaty of Ryswick of 1697 was a winning draw for the allies, but it had cost many thousands of lives, not least British ones, and it had cost the English people more in taxation than the comparable period of the Civil War. To fund it, the English Parliament had created the National Debt and set up the Bank of England to service it. War had transformed (as the Revolution Settlement had not done) the role of the English Parliament, which ever afterwards had to be called every single year to raise money to meet the interest charges on the National Debt – more evidence of William's priorities.

William worked with anyone who would support his obsession with cutting Louis down to size. He was utterly pragmatic in his relations with ministers and ministries, and replaced them as soon as they failed to deliver the military budgets he wanted. After 1697, the national mood was for the disbanding of armies and navies and cutting taxes; but William (wisely as it turned out) could see another war coming. Carlos II of Spain, the childless epitome of decrepitude, could not live much longer, and with his death the whole Spanish empire was up for grabs. Louis XIV's grandson, the Emperor's son and the Elector of Bavaria all had strong claims.

161. William III with a view of the Battle of the Boyne in the background, probably
painted by Jan Wyck.
162. Coin of Queen Anne, 1713.

William worked hard to broker two Partition Treaties that would divide up the Empire so as to keep the French out of Spain and its American lands, but, as he feared, when Carlos finally died, he left everything to the French and Louis could not resist accepting Carlos's will rather than the treaty he had signed. Fortunately for William, Louis decided not to buy off the English but to bully them into accepting the fait accompli, and thus overplayed his hand. William's last political triumph was to commit the British to the biggest of all its early modern wars.

The last twenty months of William's life was dominated by death. On 30 July 1700, Princess Anne's last child died, creating a medium-term problem for the succession and provoking the English Parliament into passing an act that – passing over the claims of at least forty-eight Catholic descendants of James I – offered the Crown to the Lutheran Electress of Hanover and her heirs. The Scottish Parliament, however, failed to follow suit. William stood mute in the face of this problem. On 21 October 1700 Carlos of Spain died and left his dominions to Philip, grandson and heir of Louis XIV. William, with difficulty, got Parliament to put the country on standby for the war that was to span almost the whole of Anne's reign. Then, on 6 September 1701, James II died. Again Louis provoked a crisis by recognizing his son, the putative warming-pan baby, as King James III. Finally, on 8 March 1702, William himself died of pneumonia following a bad fall from his horse in Hyde Park that had fractured his collar-bone. The mourning of the English people was perfunctory.

William had been a very good *stadtholder* of Britain, but a very irresponsible king. To maximize Britain's contribution to his international cause, he had improvised cabinet government (a committee of ministers to ensure the management of Parliament), created the National Debt and set up the Bank of England. Debt guaranteed annual sessions of Parliament and the circumstances of his accession helped to crystallize two political philosophies – Tory and Whig – that was to yield a two-party system that lasted two hundred years. William's reign, more than any other, demonstrates the law of unintended consequences.

ANNE (1702-1714)

Queen Anne's reign was profoundly conditioned by chronic ill-health and the crippling memory that, in November 1688, she had betrayed her own father and broken his heart. It is too easy to see her as stupid and stubborn. Constant physical agony made her difficult to budge and fiercely resistant to those who tried to prod her guilt or open emotional sores; and her growing dependency on laudanum did not help.

Anne was the fourth of the eight children born to James, Duke of York, and Anne Hyde, and one of only two to survive infancy. In due course she was herself to become pregnant eighteen times. She endured twelve miscarriages, three neo-natal births, and bore three children who lived for seven and nineteen months and, in the case of William, Duke of Gloucester, eleven years. By her thirtieth birthday, rheumatism and gout made walking difficult and climbing stairs impossible, so that she had to be carried to the throne for her coronation. Thereafter she suffered from a dropsy that made her grossly overweight and subject to abscesses in the lymph glands of the groin. It is a miracle that she lived to the age of almost fifty. Anne was sustained by a deep, unquestioning Protestant faith and – until his death in 1709 – by a deep, unquestioning love for her husband George of Denmark. Together they grew prematurely old, fat and emotionally interdependent, he as disabled by chronic asthma as she by gout and dropsy. His death condemned to her five years of profound loneliness, bullied and hectored by chauvinist ministers.

Anne's faith led her to the most desperate decision of her life, to abandon and betray her father. He made no secret of his hope that she would see the light and convert to Catholicism, but he did not harry her. But some of his more extreme advisers did, and she resented his not calling them off. In the spring of 1688 she wilfully refused to believe in Mary of Modena's pregnancy and sowed the seeds of doubt in her sister Mary's mind. She went to Bath to avoid being at Whitehall for the birth. She feigned pregnancy (doubly ironically) so as not to be present at the Privy Council on 22 October when all those present at the queen's delivery swore to the true birth of Prince James Edward Francis. When her father pleaded with her publicly to endorse the Prince, Anne refused. This was neurosis of a high order. She colluded secretly with Mary and William to assist them in their invasion, and she leaked to them that George of Denmark would come over from James's army to William's, which he did on 23 November – two days before Anne left London with Bishop Compton to join the rebels in the North. While this act of treachery was rooted principally in a desire to safeguard English Protestantism and the Protestant succession, it was also driven by a desire to protect her own rights to the throne in succession to Mary.

After the Revolution, indeed, Anne was just as determined to protect that right, and she persuaded a group of peers and bishops to campaign for Mary to govern by herself, with Anne as her heir, cutting out William. William's total rejection of this plan, and his declaration that he would return to the Continent unless he was made king, was the principal source of the mutual hatred between him and Anne over the next thirteen years. She resented his contemptuous treatment of her husband, his failure to give her due respect as heir presumptive, his refusal to spare money to sustain her household. She called him 'Mr Caliban'. Throughout his reign, he heaped insults on injury. When James II died, sending her testimony of his unconditional forgiveness of her betrayal of him, William absolutely forbade her to go into mourning dress for her father. She hated him all the more. The first thing she did upon William's death was to don black for her father, and flashes of purple in mourning for her predecessor.

Throughout the 1680s and 1690s, Anne was emotionally and intellectually dependent upon Sarah Churchill and her husband John, from 1689 Earl, and from 1702 Duke, of Marlborough. Sarah Churchill was her constant companion. She and George took their political cues from John, up to and including deserting James's camp for William's in November 1688. They all shared disillusionment with William and his actions as king. Marlborough entered into correspondence with the exiled court, and William got wind of it. He was imprisoned and charged with treason. Mary ordered Anne to dismiss Sarah from her service. She refused. William banned Sarah from entering the royal palace. Anne rented the Duke of Somerset's London home on the river and moved, with Sarah, into it. Anne and Mary never spoke again, and Mary wrote that 'in all this I see the hand of God and look on our disagreeing as a punishment upon us for the irregularity by us committed upon the Revolution'. On this at least, the sisters agreed; and certainly Anne looked upon Mary's death from smallpox at the age of only thirty-two as a divine judgment.

Her own sufferings were more lingering ones. To physical pain, and the loathing of Mr Caliban, came the excruciating death of her beloved son William, Duke of Gloucester, in 1700. Hydrocephalic, clumsy and slow-witted though he was, he was the last hope of the dynasty. Smallpox claimed him too. It is almost certain that Anne responded by writing to St Germain, telling James Edward Francis, her half-brother (as she now tacitly recognized him to be) that, if he left her at peace and on the throne, she would make him her heir. Parliament

163. Queen Anne giving assent to the Treaty of Union between England and Scotland, 1707.
Mezzotint by Valentine Green.
164. Coats of arms of Queen Anne.

might decree the succession after Anne to the House of Hanover; but Anne as queen could plan to subvert their intention. Guilt and the testimony of providence suggested that she should atone for the sins of 1688. The memory that she had been jilted in 1680 by a Hanoverian prince confirmed the need.

In March 1702, William III fell off his horse and died. Dropsical Anne was finally queen. Over the whole of her reign lay the dilemma of the succession: establishing mechanisms for ensuring that the country did not dissolve into civil war (the Regency Act of 1706); establishing a true union of the kingdoms of England and Scotland so that the northern kingdom could not secede (the Treaty and Acts of Union, 1707); perfecting the Anglo-Irish ascendancy in Ireland by a succession of brutal penal laws. And, for nearly a decade, Anne followed the advice of John and Sarah Churchill, helping to ensure that British lives and British money were poured into the war to prevent Louis XIV from gaining control of Spain and its dominions in Europe and America. In all this, Anne was no passenger and no pushover. She had more doubts now than in 1688 about her right to rule; but she also touched for the King's Evil more than most monarchs, suggesting a certain confidence in her divinely-appointed role (she was, in fact, the last British monarch ever to observe this medieval practice). Hers was a necessarily sedentary reign. Illness confined her to a triangle based on London, Hampton Court and Windsor. But that did not make her politically inactive. A Tory in all matters of religion, she was a Whig in foreign policy, and a Protestant Jacobite in the all-important question of the succession, constantly beseeching James Edward Francis to recognize that London was worth a holy communion (a theme preached by the prince's Jesuit confessor to equally little effect). She hated those who rejoiced in the 'Glorious Revolution'; she loved those who loved the forms and witness of the Church of England.

Gradually the queen lost confidence in Sarah Churchill, who had become more and more possessive, more and more jealous of all others, and less and less empathetic as her own children wilted and died. A fatal and irrevocable rift occurred in 1708-9, exactly when Anne's truest companion and soul-mate, George, succumbed to obesity and asthma. Those who were her constant companions in her final years were more shrilly the creatures of faction. As her own life ebbed away, the dynastic question became ever more insistent and ever more divisive. Most of the country would have rallied to a James III who dissimulated over religion. But he would not dissimulate. And so the country polarized between those who would grit their teeth and risk another Catholic Stuart, and those who – with varying degrees of enthusiasm – would take on the House of Hanover with the prospect of returning Britain to the status of milch-cow for the continental ambitions of a foreign ruler. In the throes of death, faced by that ultimate and unwelcome choice, when the hope against hope for a Protestant-Jacobite succession was broken, Anne resisted the clamour of the Tory ultras around her, and acted to secure the Protestant succession. It was the act that finally broke her heart.

8

THE HOUSE OF HANOVER 1714-1837

JEREMY BLACK

The accession of a new dynasty – the House of Hanover – to the English throne in 1714 was the product of two failures. First, there was a failure of politics. In 1688-9, James II had lost kingdom and crown to his nephew and son-in-law, William III of Orange. The second failure was dynastic. William and his wife and co-ruler, Mary II, had no children; and while their successor, James's younger daughter Anne, had many, none survived to adulthood. As a result, the issue of the succession, which had been pushed to the fore when James II was excluded from the throne, was revived. To keep James's son, another Catholic, from the throne, the title of king was given instead to the descendants of James I's daughter Elizabeth through her marriage to Frederick, Elector Palatine, one of the leading Protestant rulers in Germany.

The rulers of the duchy of Hanover, which had become one of the electorates of the Holy Roman Empire under George I's father, did not know much about Britain. Nor, for that matter, did many of their British subjects care much for them. The indifference is reflected in modern scholarship: there have been few systematic biographical studies of the Hanoverian rulers. This neglect reflects in part a sense that these kings did not dominate their age as their predecessors had done. Yet they certainly had their successes. The succession was maintained in the Hanoverian line, and there was no repetition in Britain either of the republican episode of 1649-60 or of the monarchical coup of 1688-9: republicanism was only to be successful in North America. This was a particularly important achievement because the Glorious Revolution of 1688-9 created a fundamental schism of loyalty in Britain, between those loyal to the Protestant establishment and those who formed the Jacobite movement, the supporters of the Catholic descendants of James II. The extent of Jacobite support is a controversial topic among historians, but there is certainly an argument for including 'James III and VIII' and his sons, Charles Edward Stuart ('Bonnie Prince Charlie') and Cardinal Henry Stuart ('Henry IX'), in any treatment of British monarchy in this period. Correspondingly, the decisive defeat of their threat at Culloden in 1746 marked the full and final establishment of the Hanoverian dynasty.

This new-found dynastic stability also helped to bring an inherent stability to British politics. The 'limited' or 'parliamentary' monarchy that was a product of the Glorious Revolution was successful because it was flexible: it could respond to the differing interests and abilities of individual monarchs, to changes in their responses to the political world, and to alterations in their own position – for no monarch should be seen as an unvarying feature of the political landscape, particularly not those who reigned as long as George II and George III. While much of the credit for Britain's constitutional monarchy rests with those who re-defined the royal position between 1689 and 1707, it remained (and remains) true that much also rested on the attitude and role of individual kings. The competence, character, and interests of the monarchs were therefore central to the workings of parliamentary monarchy.

GEORGE I (1714-1727)

To contemporaries, the Hanoverian George seemed a distant figure. Unlike William III, who had seized power in 1688-9 and who was familiar with English politics and politicians from earlier visits, marriage into the English royal family, and extensive intervention in English domestic politics, George knew relatively little of England. He was also a relatively old man when he came to her shores: born in 1660, he was already fifty-four when he became king.

George's failure to learn English and his obvious preference for Hanover further contributed to this sense of alien rule. It caused considerable complaint, among Whigs as well as Tories. Lady Anne Paulet was ready to believe a report that George would not return to Britain from Hanover for the winter of 1716-17 'for I fancy he is so much easier where he is that he will like to be from us as long as he can'. This concern was exacerbated by a sense that the preference for Hanover entailed an abandonment of British national interests, as resources were expended for the aggrandizement of Hanover, and as the entire direction of British foreign policy was set accordingly. A reasonable critique of foreign policy was advanced on this basis. Within five years of his accession, George was at war with Spain, close to war with Russia, and, having divided the Whigs and proscribed the Tories, was seeking to implement a controversial legislative programme. William III and Anne's continental interventionism, though costly, lengthy and of mixed success, was directed against an unpopular power, France, that many found threatening. In contrast, allied with France from 1716, George pursued a foreign policy that struck little resonance with the political experiences and xenophobic traditions of his British subjects.

On the other hand, George's reign was not so much the wholesale Hanoverian takeover that some feared as an implicit agreement, but more like the dual monarchy of nineteenth-century Austria-Hungary. Despite periodic rows about Hanoverian interests, George I did not swamp Britain with German ministers or systems. Instead, he adapted to British institutions, conforming to the Church of England despite his strong Lutheranism. Even his dispute with his son fitted into a parliamentary framework with Court and Leicester House parties at Westminster. And the failure of the Jacobite rising of the 'Old Pretender', James Edward Francis Stuart, in 1715 indicated early in the reign that the establishment on which George depended was determined, in turn, to maintain his rule.

George's place in politics was not of his choosing but a consequence of the limitations in royal authority and power that stemmed from the Glorious Revolution of 1688-9 and subsequent changes. George was sensible enough to adapt and survive: unlike James II, he was a pragmatist who did not have an agenda for Britain, other than helping Hanover. In part this was a sensible response to circumstances, and in part a complacency that arose from diffidence, honesty and dullness: George simply lacked the decisiveness, charisma and wiliness of Louis XIV of France and Peter the Great of Russia. George did not have pretensions to mimic the lifestyle of Louis XIV, and appeared to do so in a relatively modest way. He was also accommodating and quite prepared to be prodded into levées, ceremonies and public appearances.

The major domestic issue of the reign was George's antipathy towards the Tories. In July 1721, the Duke of Newcastle wrote that 'the report of the Tories coming in having reached the king's ears, he has been so good as to declare to me and many other of his servants the concern he has at the report, and has assured us that he neither has or ever had any such thoughts, and is determined to stand by the Whigs, and not take in any one single Tory. He is very sensible the Whig party is the only security he has to depend on, in which he is most certainly right.' Individual Tories were accommodated, but only at the price of abandoning their colleagues and principles. This was not a coalition government. In 1723, Newcastle noted that Carteret, the Secretary of State for the Southern Department, who was seeking to supplant Sir Robert Walpole, had broken off with the Tories, 'thinking to carry his point with the Whigs, which he knows agreeable to the king'. The dislike of Tories extended into the country, where they were dismissed from a range of posts – a course of action that pressed hard on a landed society that had been suffering from the dangerous combination of high wartime taxation and an agrarian depression. Commissions of the peace were brought under Whig control, Tories were dismissed from the armed forces, and Whig clerics found promotion open to them. The Tories were treated far more harshly than under William III.

The reliance on the Whigs, however, ultimately weakened George I's regime. Concern about Hanover contributed powerfully to the 'Whig Split', a deep division among the Whigs in 1717-20 that led a section under Robert Walpole to seek co-operation with the Tories in order to achieve the overthrow of the Whig government. This can be seen as a serious defeat for George, provoked by his foreign policy and his handling of the struggle for influence between the leading Whigs.

George's greatest vulnerability flowed from family disputes. His choleric quarrel with his son and heir, the future George II, which interacted with and seriously worsened the political disputes, was a classic feature of dynastic politics: the tension between ruler and heir, and between those who looked to one or the other. Such disputes may look modest in comparison with what happened elsewhere at this time: George I's contemporary, Peter the Great of Russia, had his son and heir, Alexis, killed; another, Victor Amadeus II of Sardinia, was imprisoned by his heir, Charles Emmanuel III, when he tried to retract his abdication. And yet, these family disputes had the capacity seriously to disrupt British politics and thus to affect the stability of the Crown.

To note problems shared with other dynasties is not the same as to deny responsibility or blame. If the Hanoverians faced tensions in their family and divisions among their ministers, then part of the art of royal politics was the ability to tackle such problems. The assertion of royal will, without the creation or worsening of serious political divisions, was crucial, whatever the formal constitutional powers of the sovereign. In 1717, George I proved unable to assert himself in this manner, and thus helped to precipitate a crisis. Father and son were reconciled in 1720, but only to the extent of a mutual coldness. Although there is little sign of any difference of opinion between father and son over policy in the 1720s, there was a continued tension over the prince's position. George refused to have his son as regent in England during his absences in Hanover, and he turned down the younger George's request for a military post in any European conflict that might involve Britain.

Ministers found it essential to win the public support of the monarch in order to underline their own influence and hold on power, but the degree to which the king would allow a minister or group of ministers in effect to deploy royal power or influence itself posed problems. In the Whig split of 1717, George I lost the support of Robert Walpole and Charles Townshend because he was too closely associated with their rivals, the Earls of Stanhope and Sunderland. The last wrote in 1717, 'upon the whole, I don't doubt, the king's steadiness will carry it.' Once the king was thus associated, it was difficult to avoid the consequences of criticism and opposition from those opposed to such ministers, and, more particularly, to escape damage if those ministers were weakened: 'The king is resolved that Walpole shall not govern, but it is hard to be prevented.' George, however, had eventually to accommodate himself to Walpole, and to accept the latter's position as chief minister. The maverick Tory Lord Bolingbroke was foolish to believe in 1727 that George was going to dismiss Walpole.

The Swiss visitor, Cesar de Saussure, recorded that the London mob cheered George I in 1725 and subsequently mourned him in 1727, while also celebrating George II's accession. It is unclear whether this was simply the fickle mob using any opportunity for an 'event', or a phenomenon particular to London, or evidence that the general unpopularity of George I and II has been overstated. They were the Whigs' monarchs, although it is unclear how much personal popularity this brought them. As an individual, George I was a figure of suspicion because of the incarceration of his adulterous wife, Sophia Dorothea, and the disappearance in 1694 of her lover, Philipp Christoph von Königsmarck, and because of rumours about his own personal life. Scurrilous ballads made much of the theme of the royal cuckold. *Sir James King's Key to Sir George Horn's Padlock* dwelled on the theme, while an *Address to Britannia* included, 'Pray let no cuckold be still ruler over thee/ Nor any German bastard begot in privity'. Another manuscript verse that circulated satirized George and his alleged mistresses, condemning their influence on him and their competition for his attention by contrasting them with the goddesses vying for the attention of Paris. Certainly, the estrangement from Sophia Dorothea, the extra-marital relationships, and the illegitimate children were an established feature of George's lifestyle when he became king, and the reputation thus arising was an enduring stick with which his British subjects could beat their ruler.

As later with radical pornography in the 1790s and 1800s, however, humiliation was a powerful political weapon. To demystify the monarch and subject him to ridicule and abuse was part of a determined attempt to weaken his position. It could also be argued that the scurrilous ballads and verse that circulated provided an opportunity for popular expression about George I that helped to secure his position. Such expression was tolerated, in marked contrast to the more repressive position in continental Europe. The satire also provided George with an identity that was not Hanoverian. It was far better for him to be lampooned for human weaknesses than to be perceived as alien – although the latter critique was also advanced. Governmental sensitivity over George's life continued after his death. In 1732, the diplomatic service was used in an attempt to suppress the sale of the anonymous *Histoire secrette de la Duchesse d'Hanover* (in fact the work of Karl Ludwig von Pöllnitz).

Assessments of George I as king have focused on the period 1714-21. This is understandable given that these were the years in which George worked through the consequences of gaining the throne, that international relations were particularly complex and important in this period, and that the years 1722-7 are (relatively speaking) more obscure both in domestic politics and in foreign policy. However, this chronological emphasis on the first half of the reign is unfortunate, since the way in which George I worked with the Walpole-Townsend group is also of considerable interest. The king had to accommodate himself to Walpole, but it is also clear that Walpole had to adapt to George, and the king showed both political skills and a sense of responsibility.

An incompetent and unyielding monarch might well have led to the end of Hanoverian rule in Britain, just as James II had brought about the end of the male line of the Stuarts.

The way in which Walpole had to respond to George also throws light on royal preferences. Support for Hanover included a subsidy treaty with Hessen-Kassel, by which Hessian troops destined for the defence of Hanover were paid by Britain and not by Hanover. Walpole was expected to find money for George I's female German connections. He also had to spend time as a courtier, attending on the royal family: as, for example, on 3 July 1724, when he was present at George I's review of the Foot Guards in Hyde Park.

George honored Walpole publicly, with the newly created Order of the Bath in 1725, and the much older and higher-ranking Order of the Garter the following year. Walpole, the sole commoner with that latter honour, and the first to be promoted to it since 1660, found his Garter a cause of anger and criticism. The award also showed George's careful adaptation to the nature of power, a parallel to his conforming to Anglican liturgy in his Chapel Royal. James II and his son were not willing to make such an adaptation. It is easy to see why George I was unpopular, especially as a result of his multifaceted 'Hanoverianism'; but it is also clear that, eventually, after having initially pursued very divisive policies, he helped to make the political system work, and thus, by the last years of his reign, to bring a valuable measure of political stability to the realm. At his death, on 11 June 1727, there was no question that the succession would pass anywhere other than to his son and rightful heir.

GEORGE II (1727-1760)

It is not easy to evaluate George II. Born at the Hanoverian Palace of Herrenhausen on 10 November (new style) 1683, the only son of George I and Sophia Dorothea, he left relatively few sources. Whereas George III's correspondence takes up twelve substantial volumes in modern editions, there is little such evidence surviving for George II (or, indeed, for George I). Furthermore, George II tends to be overshadowed by his more vivacious wife, Caroline of Ansbach (1683-1737), whom he married in 1705. It was generally believed that George was heavily influenced by his wife. In November 1727, Sir Robert Walpole, telling Lord King, the Lord Chancellor, 'of the great credit he had with the king', attributed it to 'the means of the queen, who was the most able woman to govern in the world'. The contrast between the queen's bright, sparkling, witty nature, and George's more dour, boorish demeanour greatly influenced contemporary commentators such as Lord Hervey. Writing later in the century, William Coxe regarded George as a puppet manipulated by his wife: 'Caroline … almost entirely governed the king … [and] contrived that her opinion should appear as if it had been his own.'

It is possible, however, that Caroline's influence has been exaggerated. The picture of George as a headstrong, blinkered boor, manipulated by his wife and by Walpole, is one that has enjoyed much support, but is largely based on the malicious views of a few contemporaries such as Hervey. In two spheres, the army and foreign affairs, George displayed particular and consistent interest. There was no doubt of his great interest in and affection for the army. He relished attending military reviews and drilling troops – both his own, whether British or Hanoverian, and those of his Hessian allies, which he usually reviewed on each of his frequent trips to Hanover. George was keen to discuss military matters, and he enjoyed the company of military men such as Charles Hotham, William Stanhope and Richard Sutton. He also showed favour to foreign envoys with a military background. George kept a close eye on military developments in other countries, and followed European campaigns with great interest. He was determined to

166. George I by Sir George Neller.
167. George II by Thomas Hudson.
168. Caricature of the Battle of Culloden.

control military patronage within Britain and he refused to accept ministerial suggestions in this sphere. George had the Guards' regimental reports and returns sent to him personally every week, and when he reviewed his troops he did so with great attention to detail.

Described in the House of Lords' Address of 7 February 1728 as 'formed by Nature for the greatest military achievements', George associated the army with his 'gloire', and believed that the military reviews he conducted were the most obvious and impressive display of his power and importance. Possibly the fondest memory from his youth was of his campaigning in the Spanish Netherlands against the French in the War of the Spanish Succession. He had displayed great personal bravery when, in 1708 at the Battle of Oudenaarde, he had charged the French at the head of the Hanoverian dragoons, and had his horse shot from under him. George bored people with his reminiscences of this period for many years.

In this he was not alone. George's brother-in-law, Frederick William I of Prussia, had fought against the French at Malplaquet in 1709, and held annual celebrations on the anniversary. For these German princes, the campaigns of the 1700s represented a time of youthful freedom and excitement that they later hankered for and sought to rediscover. George II did so in Dettingen in 1743 when he commanded an Anglo-German army against the French and defeated them, becoming the last British monarch to lead an army into battle. His victory was celebrated by Handel with the Dettingen Te Deum.

George's personal interest in the army (but not the navy) could be a major nuisance for his British ministers since, as a result, they had less room for concession and parliamentary manoeu-vring over such issues as the size of the armed forces and the policy of subsidies paid to secure the use of Hessian troops. The impact of George's martial temperament upon his conduct of foreign policy also concerned the government. Yet the king could also prove susceptible to manipulation. In 1732, Viscount Perceval recorded a visit from his cousin Mary Dering, Dresser Extraordinary to the king's daughters:

> She gave an instance how princes are imposed upon by their ministers. She said that when the king came to the Crown his resolution was to continue in his service as chaplains all those who had been so while he was prince, and to fill up the number belonging to him as king with as many of his father's chaplains as could be admitted, but one of his chaplains he particularly named to be continued on account of some extraordinary services he had done him when prince. But when the then Lord Chamberlain… brought him the lists to sign, he did it without further examination than observing the chaplain's name was there, yet afterwards it proved that the man was removed, and neither all his old chaplains, nor many of his father's continued, but a good many new persons placed.

There was simply not enough time for George to supervise all that he wished to control and for him to see that his orders were carried out. Some of the bold claims he made soon after his accession about what he would do as monarch can be attributed to inexperience and nervous excitement. In some spheres, such as the Church and the law, George's interventions were episodic, though he could be extremely determined in the defence of his prerogatives. The Walpole ministry, for example, was to find it difficult to persuade George to offer preferment to clerics whom he disliked.

George II's amiable, but occasionally choleric, lack of imagination produced a comfortable complacency, though one that at times could be difficult. Fortunately for the ministers, his personal life did not cause them too many difficulties. Before his accession, a confidant of the prince who was believed to enjoy great influence was his mistress Henrietta Howard, Countess of Suffolk. She had links with the parliamentary opposition and was in touch with other critics of Walpole. George's favour for her had been seen as a sign that Walpole would not survive the change of monarch, but in fact after George came to the throne she enjoyed little power.

Amalia Sophie Marianne von Walmoden was to be more effective and was certainly a spur to George's visits to Hanover in the 1730s. George made her Countess of Yarmouth and she became an influential political figure because of her access to the king. She was alleged to have recommended at least three peerage creations in return for bribes. George's favours to her were not ignored by the populace. In 1736, William Pulteney reported:

> One Mrs Mopp, a famous bone-setter and mountebank, coming to town in a coach with six horses on the Kentish Road, was met by a rabble of people, who seeing her very oddly and tawdrily dressed, took her for a foreigner, and concluded she must be a certain great person's mistress. Upon this they followed the coach, bawling out, 'No Hanover Whore, No Hanover Whore.' The lady within the coach was much offended, let down the glass, and screamed louder than any of them, that she was no Hanover whore, she was an English one, upon which they all cried out, 'God bless your Ladyship', quitted the pursuit and wished her a good journey.

After the queen died in 1737, George settled down into a domestic relationship with Madame Walmoden. Her second son, John, born in 1736, was reputed to be the king's child, and rose to be a Field Marshal in the Hanoverian army. By Caroline, George II had had eight children, three boys and five girls. His relations with his eldest son, Frederick, Prince of Wales (1707-51) were particularly difficult, mirroring those of George II with *his* father. The prince's opposition was crucial to the fall of Sir Robert Walpole in 1742, after the latter's poor electoral showing in 1741 – a fall that George II himself bitterly regretted.

In 1744, George was again forced to part with a leading minister – John, Lord Carteret – in whom he had confidence. This led to a crisis in 1746 when George attempted to put Carteret back into power against the wishes of the Duke of Newcastle and his brother Henry Pelham, the ministers who dominated Parliament. They, in turn, provoked a political crisis that forced his hand by resigning their posts in the government. By withholding his confidence from his ministers, George II had undermined their position in Parliament. But this also provoked their desperate resignation at a time of war and rebellion, and left George little room for manoeuvre. The king's self-imposed political rules also created limitations upon his effective action. He did not want to turn to the Tories to support the ministry, and wanted to employ favourites such as Carteret, now Earl Granville; yet he also regarded as essential the Old Corps Whigs, who were implacably opposed to those same favourites. With a parliamentary majority, George II possibly could have cleared out the Old Corps, as George III was to do in the 1760s; as it was, he remained dependent on the Old Corps in Parliament.

In 1745-6, the stability of the monarchy, if not of the realm, was briefly jeopardized when the Jacobite movement, which had apparently been defeated decisively in 1715, erupted again in support of 'Bonnie Prince Charlie', Charles Edward Stuart, the son of the Old Pretender and grandson of James II. The 'Young Pretender' was a glamorous twenty-five-year-old whose romantic reputation was seen by some to compensate for his own lack of political agenda and the Hanoverians' consistent absence of charisma. Without an effective standing army, and with many members of the gentry unwilling to commit themselves to fighting the invaders, George II looked on as the accumulating forces of the Catholic enemy excited support in Scotland and drove deep into the heart of the English Midlands. In the event, the rebellion failed. Two rival princes competed at Culloden in 1746: Bonnie Prince Charlie and George II's second and favourite son, William, Duke of Cumberland. Here, at perhaps the greatest moment of crisis for the Hanoverian State, the royal family therefore played a vital role. After Culloden, not only was the Protestant establishment affirmed, but the Hanoverian dynasty was also finally and explicitly accepted as representing the aspirations and security of the realm.

The political agenda of George II's last years was dominated by war. Between 1739 and 1748, the War of Captain Jenkins' Ear and then the War of Austrian Succession set Britain against both Spain and, eventually, France and created the framework for a further, and wider, bout of hostilities during the Seven Years War (1756-63). This latter confrontation was played out on a global stage, in India, in North America, and in the West Indies, and demonstrated both the degree to which Britain had become an imperial power and the remarkable impact that disputes between European powers could now have on world affairs. At home, the early stages of the war left the Old Corps Whigs discredited and allowed for the ascendancy of William Pitt the Elder, the greatest war minister of the day – perhaps, indeed, of any time. The achievements of Clive in India and Wolfe in North America redounded – sometimes in exaggerated form – to the credit of Pitt, who was seen as the great architect of the *annus mirabilis* of 1759. It was at the height of the resulting euphoria that George II died, on 25 October 1760. Time would tell whether the war abroad, and the new political dispensation that it had created at home, would bring further benefits to the regime of the new king.

GEORGE III (1760-1820)

George II's son, Frederick, died in 1751, leaving a son, George, to succeed him as Prince of Wales and, in due course, to succeed as King George III in 1760. Born in 1738, George early developed a sense of antagonism towards the prevailing political system, which he thought oligarchical and factional. The young prince and his confidant, John Stuart, third Earl of Bute, favoured the idea of politics without party and a king above faction. In 1763, George was to complain to the French ambassador about 'the spirit of fermentation and the excessive licence which prevails in England. It was essential to neglect nothing that could check that spirit and to employ firmness as much as moderation. He was very determined not to be the toy of factions… and his fixed plan was to establish his authority without breaking the law.'

As much as any continental ruler who did not have to face a powerful representative institution, George III was determined to reject what he saw as the politics of faction, and, in particular, to thwart the efforts of unacceptable politicians to force their way into office. He thought that much about the political system was corrupt, and, in part, ascribed this to the size of the National Debt. As a consequence, George's moral reformism was specifically aimed against faction and luxury. In addition, like other rulers, George found it most difficult to create acceptable relationships with senior politicians at his accession, when he had to persuade both those who had had a good working relationship with his predecessor, and those who had looked for a dramatic change, to adjust to his wishes. George broke with Pitt the Elder in 1761 and with Pitt's ally, the Duke of Newcastle, in 1762, when the king's favourite, Bute, became First Lord of the Treasury. This was not simply a matter of the politics of office. Issues were at stake. Pitt was a determined advocate of continued war with France, and was unwilling to heed financial arguments for peace. In May 1762, he told the Commons:

Clockwise from top   169. Irish coin of George II.
170. The coat of arms of George III.
171. Queen Charlotte, consort of George III.

When I give my advice in the House I consider myself as giving my advice to the Crown … I am convinced this country can raise 12, 13, 14 or even 15 million the next year: I know it without seeking information from bundles of papers and accounts. The only question is whether, grievous and permanent as that tax must be, it is not to be preferred to the perpetual dishonour of the nation, the aggrandizement of the enemy, and the desertion of your allies, all which tend to an inglorious and precarious peace.

In the event, the general desire for peace, the initial popularity of the new king, and the government's success in both war and peace blunted the force of parliamentary and political criticism. The Peace of Paris (1763) encountered more parliamentary attacks than that of Aix-la-Chapelle (1748) had done, a measure of the stronger sense that Britain had had a bad deal. But the ministry carried the Address of Thanks on 9 December 1762 by 319 to 65, and there was no division in the Lords. As so often in Hanoverian Britain, it was the parliamentary strength of the government, rather than the vigour of its critics, that was most strikingly apparent to observers, both domestic and foreign, and their view of ministerial power owed much to this strength.

Nevertheless, ministerial stability proved elusive. The ambiguity of a number of constitutional points, such as the collective responsibility of the Cabinet and the degree to which the monarch had to choose his ministers from those who had the confidence of Parliament, exacerbated the situation. Not until 1770 did George III find a satisfactory minister who could control Parliament, lead a ministry and run the government: this was Frederick, Lord North. What Bute called 'the violence of party' owed much to the king's conscious abandonment of party government. The ending of Old Corps Whig cohesion was an important aspect of the instability of the 1760s: it is difficult to imagine the likes of Walpole losing power as his successors in the 1760s were to do. The dearth of leaders appointed from the Commons was also important: before the premiership of Lord Liverpool (1812-27), there was not to be a single ministry led from the Lords that endured for any significant time, whereas the sole ministry led by someone sitting in the Commons *not* to have a substantial period in office was that of George Grenville (1763-5). Circumstances varied, but it seems clear that dividing the key functions of the First Lord of the Treasury (in effect, the prime minister) and the leadership of the Commons made for weak and unstable government.

The volatile political atmosphere in London also contributed to a sense of crisis in the 1760s. Dissatisfaction in the city was exploited by a squinting anti-hero, John Wilkes, an entrepreneur of faction and libertine MP who fell foul of George III as a result of bitter attacks on the government in his newspaper the *North Briton*. Wilkes's denunciation of the Peace of Paris in Number 45 (issued on 23 April 1763), with its implication that George had lied in his speech from the throne, led to a charge of seditious libel. The government took a number of contentious steps, issuing a general warrant for the arrest of all those involved in the publication of the offending issue and seeking to arrest Wilkes, in spite of his parliamentary privilege. Though released, Wilkes was accused of blasphemy later in 1763 because he attributed his indecent *Essay on Woman* to a cleric. The Commons resolved that seditious libel was not covered by parliamentary privilege and in 1764 Wilkes was expelled from Parliament and eventually outlawed. His expulsion was exploited by opposition politicians keen to throw doubts on the legality of ministerial actions. In 1768, he returned to England and was elected for the populous and populist constituency of Middlesex. However, he was imprisoned for blasphemy and libel and was once more expelled from the Commons. Three times re-elected for Middlesex in 1769, Wilkes was declared incapable of being returned to Parliament and his opponent was declared elected, a thwarting of the views of the electors that aroused considerable anger.

Wilkes became the focus of more widespread popular opposition to the government, of fears of royal tyranny and of aristocratic oligarchy. There was some resistance to the burning of Number 45 of the *North Briton*: 'Mr. Harley, the Sheriff, no sooner appeared with the paper to give it up to the all devouring flames, than the mob arming themselves immediately with the faggots already laid for the conflagration, drove Mr. Harley back into his chariot with the loss of some blood on his part.' Economic problems also contributed to a growing strain of radicalism, and would provoke a series of riots in London in 1768. Meanwhile, public discontents interacted with ministerial divisions. Although his ministry enjoyed solid majorities in both Houses of Parliament, Bute found the stress of politics unbearable and he was replaced as First Lord of the Treasury in 1763 by George Grenville, whom George III soon found arrogant and overbearing. The king himself was acutely irritable, possibly as a result of poor health.

In 1765, George III was able to dispense with Grenville, though his replacement, Charles Watson-Wentworth, Marquis of Rockingham, a former protégé of the Duke of Newcastle, was not much to his liking. The new government inherited a difficult political situation. Britain after 1763 was a much wealthier and more self-confident nation than hitherto, but faced serious problems in imperial government and finance. The role of the British State in the affairs of the East India Company and the protection of British India increased appreciably, and this proved a source of considerable controversy. American affairs were increasingly politically charged, not least because of the large number of British emigrants in North America, the close links with the British economy, and the controversial issues raised by the determination to make colonies that were un-represented in Parliament pay a portion of the burden of their defence.

The strains of paying for the Seven Years War, never appreciated sufficiently by the bellicose Pitt and his supporters, had forced the ministers of the early 1760s to think of retrenchment and new taxation. The unpopular cider tax of 1763, repealed in 1766, created a furore, but nothing to compare with Grenville's Stamp Act of 1765, which imposed a series of duties in the North American colonies and raised the issue of parliamentary authority there. The Rockingham ministry sought to defuse the crisis. Concerned about the violent response in America and influenced by pressure from British merchants who were worried about an American commercial blockade, the Rockinghamites repealed the Stamp Act in 1766, despite the reluctance of George III. Nevertheless, when the act was repealed, a Declaratory Act was passed, stating that Parliament 'had, hath and of right ought to have full power and authority to make laws and statutes of sufficient form and validity to bind the colonies and people of America in all cases whatsoever'.

The Rockingham ministry suffered not only from royal disfavour but also from division. Hoping 'to extricate this country out of faction', in July 1766 George III sent for William Pitt the Elder. The latter's ministry was not a success, in part because his acceptance of a peerage as Earl of Chatham weakened his control of the Commons. The sickly Pitt became an invalid in the spring of 1767, probably as a consequence of stress and depression. The succeeding ministry, that of Augustus Fitzroy, Duke of Grafton, was also weak and divided. Nevertheless, there was no fundamental political crisis. Indeed, the re-integration of the Tories into the political mainstream helped heal a long-standing divide dating from the mid-seventeenth century. Once George III found an effective parliamentary manager in Lord North in 1770, the political situation within Britain, and Parliament's role within it, became far more quiescent. North was also able to manage government business and maintain a united government. He was helped by the disunited nature of the opposition, especially the rivalry between Chatham and the Rockinghamites, and by a rallying of support to the Crown, the natural focus of most politicians'

Clockwise from top left   172. George III by Alan Ramsay.
173. Queen Charlotte by Ozias Humphrey.
174. The map on which the British negotiators for peace with the Americans marked out their
interpretation of the new boundary between the United States and the province that later
became Canada at the end of the War of Independence. It was presented to George III to show
him how the settlement worked on the ground.

loyalty, in response to the extremism of some of the Wilkesites. North had little difficulty in winning the general elections of 1774 and 1780 or in keeping the Rockinghamite opposition at bay. The latter was convinced that there was a royal conspiracy against liberty, and provided a paranoid tone to politics. Few in, or outside, the political nation believed that they were suffering under executive tyranny.

The mood was to change as a result of the war with the American colonies that broke out in 1775, and which created strains and divisions as well as problems of political management. For example, opposition to the war impeded recruitment, and the latter fuelled protests against the war. North's reliance on Highland Scots and Irish Catholic regiments added to parliamentary disquiet. The situation reached crisis-point when Cornwallis's surrender at Yorktown in October 1781 led to a collapse of confidence both in the war in America and in the North ministry. On 27 February 1782 the government lost a Commons' motion relating to the further prosecution of the war in America, and on 20 March North announced his resignation. George III was forced to turn to the Rockinghamites, a group he distrusted, who were pledged to independence for America. After Rockingham died, the Earl of Shelburne was appointed to head the ministry in July 1782. A protégé of Pitt the Elder and a former Secretary of State, Shelburne was an opponent of party – or, in his terms, 'faction' – a view he took from Pitt. Shelburne's views on this important theme in eighteenth-century political culture helped to ensure that, although his interest in parliamentary reform and his somewhat radical views were unwelcome to George, he was in fact acceptable as a first minister, certainly more so than any Rockinghamite.

George's failure to choose the new leader of the Rockinghamites, the Duke of Portland, led to a resignation of prominent Rockinghamites, especially Charles James Fox, but the king's determination to defend his prerogative of choosing his own ministers was generally accepted. Shelburne also defended the king's right to choose his ministers and his rejection of Foxite ideas regarding the choice of prime ministers and collective responsibility within the Cabinet. Widely distrusted, and disliked for arrogance, Shelburne's brief period of office revealed how a personally unpopular prime minister who lacked the support of a party and had to win parliamentary support for contentious measures could not prevail. In February 1783, Shelburne had to persuade Parliament to accept peace preliminaries with the American separatists. These were genuinely unpopular, especially because they lacked any guarantees for the loyalists in the former colonies or for the debts that Britain had incurred in fighting the war. Defeated twice, Shelburne resigned.

The largest groupings in the Commons, led by Fox and North, were now clearly aiming to secure office, and were prepared to do so regardless of any claim by the king to choose his ministers. Former enemies, the two men formed a coalition ministry, headed by the Duke of Portland, in April 1783, despite the bitter disapproval of George III. Interestingly, the formation of the Fox-North ministry helped to contribute to a sense of political failure, even collapse. This suggests that contemporary expectations of the political system were not of frequent changes of government in response to shifts in parliamentary and electoral opinion but rather of a stable ministry responsive to (and thus, if necessary, limited by) responsible parliamentary and popular opinion. The assumption was shared abroad: rulers such as Catherine II (the Great) of Russia, Frederick II (the Great) of Prussia and Joseph II of Austria argued in the early 1780s that Britain was weak, that this was the result of the inherent characteristics of its political system (which would probably lead to the dissolution of its empire), and that its weakness made it an undesirable ally.

The resolution of the crisis, in the shape of a stable ministry under William Pitt the Younger, was far from inevitable. It was not certain that Pitt would secure a Commons majority simply because George III had appointed him to office in December 1783, after helping defeat the East India Bill, a crucial item of government business, in the Lords. George's action brought out the lack of agreement about the constitution and the fluidity of constitutional conventions that tend often to be forgotten by historians. George's actions, which were regarded by some as unconstitutional, were countered by a collective resignation of office holders. George saw himself as 'on the edge of a precipice'. Commons' defeats in January 1784 led Pitt to think of resigning and George III to reiterate his willingness to abdicate.

An unsuccessful attempt by independent MPs to create a broad-based government of national unity, a frequently-expressed aspiration during the century that reflected widespread suspicion of what was seen as the factious nature of party politics, gave Pitt breathing space. His position was improved further by a swelling tide of favourable public opinion, shown in a large number of addresses from counties and boroughs, with over 50,000 signatures in total, in favour of the free exercise of the royal prerogative in choosing ministers. The formation of the Pitt government had not needed the crisis created by the poor relations between George III and the Fox-North ministry, but it had changed its nature, and brought monarch and government on to the same side. The more public nature of the transformed crisis led to an upsurge in popular interest that focused on support for George (itself a testimony to the potential popularity of the monarchy), and thus for his new ministers. Parliament was dissolved when Pitt felt able to face a general election; and the elections, many of which were contested on national political grounds, were very favourable for the ministry.

Pitt the Younger dominated politics for over two decades: he served as First Lord of the Treasury from 1783 until 1801, and then again in 1804-6. George was unhappy with some aspects of Pitt's policies, especially his support for parliamentary reform in 1785 and for Catholic Emancipation. In the 1790s, George opposed the extension of rights to Catholics in Ireland or Britain. Arguing that such moves would breach his coronation oath, George stated that he would not give royal assent to such legislation. This helped to precipitate Pitt's resignation in 1801 and the fall of the Grenville ministry in 1807. However, Pitt was very much George's own minister and there was an essential stability at the centre of politics. As a consequence, the king tended to remove into the political background.

It was this very distancing of the king from the daily processes of government that also contributed to his growing popularity. In the 1760s George had been a controversial figure. The early 1770s had brought an improvement in his reputation, although the American crisis inevitably took its toll. In July 1773, Sir Joshua Reynolds wrote after George's return from the review of the fleet:

The king is exceedingly delighted with his reception at Portsmouth. He said to a person about that he was convinced he was not so unpopular as the newspapers would represent him to be. The acclamations of the people were indeed prodigious. On his return all the country assembled in the towns where he changed horses. At Godalming every man had a branch of a tree in his hand and every woman a nosegay which they presented to the king (the horses moving as slow as possible, till he was up to his knees in flowers, and they all singing in a tumultuous manner, 'God save the King'. The king was so affected that he could not refrain shedding abundance of tears, and even joined in the chorus.

Arguably, Portsmouth was a special case. Huge numbers of its population were directly dependent on the Crown, and any association with the Royal Navy was popular. But in the 1780s, George felt that the monarch could reach out, beyond antipathy and factional self-interest on the part of politicians, to a wider, responsible, and responsive royalist public opinion. After the attempt by Margaret Nicolson to assassinate him in 1786, George wrote about 'the interposition of Providence on the late attempt on my life by a poor insane woman … I have every reason to be satisfied with the impression it has awakened in this country.'

George was to become even more central to public ideology as the challenge of the French Revolution of 1789 helped to produce a rallying of the social elite (and of more general public opinion) around the themes of Country, Crown and Church. The monarchy served as a potent symbol of national identity and continuity, especially after the execution of Louis XVI in January 1793. This led to a powerful reiteration of monarchical ideology in Britain: indeed, monarchy now became seen as one of the fundamental features by which the British were differentiated from the French. On 30 January 1793, Samuel Horsley, Bishop of St Davids and a supporter of Pitt, gave the annual Martyrdom Day sermon in Westminster Abbey before the House of Lords. This marked the anniversary of the execution of Charles I, the individual elevated most closely to sainthood by the Church of England. In the first half of the eighteenth century, 30 January had often been a focus for discontent, riots and other signs of the Jacobite challenge to the dynasty. Now it served to affirm not the House of Stuart but the institution of monarchy itself. Horsley delivered a powerful attack on political speculation and revolutionary theory. He presented the constitution as the product and safeguard of a 'legal contract' between Crown and people, while the obedience of the latter was a religious duty.

The throne therefore played a much greater role in the political ideology of the nation during the 1790s than it had done between 1689 and 1746. In the earlier period, an emphasis on monarchy had been compromised by serious differences over the legitimacy of the dynasty and by the contentious nature of constitutional arrangements arising from the Glorious Revolution. No such problems hindered an emphasis on monarchy by the powerful forces of conservatism after the 1790s: however much the personal and political failings of individual members of the royal family, and however much George's own ill health would compromise his activity, the role of the monarchy was one that conservatives could support. In 1809, George III celebrated his jubilee (which was timed to coincide with the inception, rather than the completion, of his fiftieth year as king): the public event not only symbolized the stability that he had provided in an age of volatile politics, but also expressed the genuine affection and admiration that his subjects now had for their monarch.

In 1765 George had been seriously ill. Although he had apparently been restored to good health, in 1788 he was incapacitated by an attack of porphyria, which, to contemporaries, appeared to betoken the onset of insanity. This generated a crisis over the regency that ended only when the king recovered in February 1789. This recovery seems to have been only partial, and in the 1800s the king was once again seriously incapacitated. His sight went, he lived in seclusion, and in 1811 the Crown had to be put into commission with the passing of the Regency Act and the appointment of the Prince of Wales as the king's lieutenant. The situation remained unchanged for the last nine years of George III's life, and he died in a state of apparent oblivion on 29 January 1820.

'Farmer George' as the king became known affectionately for his love of the country and the simple life, may in some respects be seen as the originator of the emphasis on domesticity in the British royal family. His wife, Charlotte of Mecklenburg-Strelitz, whom he married in 1761, struck up a genuinely close relationship with him. In his letter of 1773, Sir Joshua Reynolds commented on George's public expressions of affection for his wife:

When he came to Kew, [the king] was so impatient to see the queen that he opened the chaise himself and jumped out before any of his attendants could come to his assistance. He seized the queen, whom he met at the door, round the waist and carried her in his arms into the room.

The sense of an idyllic domesticity was easy to maintain when the royal couple's children were young, but as their numerous children grew to adulthood (the queen bore a total of nine sons and six daughters), there arose a conflict between George's own sense of propriety and the dissolute lifestyle adopted by most of his brood of boys. The members of the younger generation were especially loath to accept the king and queen's choices of marriage partners and entered into liaisons which, while often stable and personally fulfilling, hardly redounded to the increasingly prudish image that George III himself wished to promote. The alienation between the generations was represented most strikingly in the endless disputes between the king and the Prince of Wales and in the very public sense of glee that 'Prinny' demonstrated when his father became too ill to rule.

George III was the last ruler of Britain ever to exercise the title of 'King of France'. The claim, first advanced by Edward III in 1340, was finally dropped from the royal style in 1801, after which George's title was formally expressed as ruler of 'the United Kingdom of Great Britain and Ireland'. Hanover (which title was never included in the royal style as exercised in the British Isles) was raised to the status of a kingdom in 1814. In spite of the regency of 1811, George III held his titles until the very end of his life, and by the time of his death had ruled longer than any previous British sovereign, exceeding Henry III's record by reigning for fifty-nine years. The monarchy, or perhaps the *image* of the monarchy, had been reconstructed in important ways during the later years of George's reign. The strong patriotism of the war with France, and the king's virtual disengagement from day-to-day politics, combined fruitfully to facilitate the celebration less of the reality and more of the symbol of monarchy. In this sense, the precondition of the creation of a popular monarchy was (ironically but significantly) the perceived decline in the Crown's political authority.

GEORGE IV (1820-1830)

Born in 1762, George IV was the first of the many children of George III and Queen Charlotte. Born in the purple, he was given the title of Prince of Wales while still a baby and was brought up in the framework of political and personal morality created by his narrow-minded parents: George III set standards of prudence and austerity that have been characterized (disparagingly) by modern historians as 'middle-class'. The future George IV waited longer than virtually any previous heir to become king, and his increasing alienation from his father simply added to the sense of exasperation and urgency with which he pursued power. He was not, however, a man able effectively to resist the trend towards a lesser political role for the monarch, however much he might spasmodically insist on his views of his own importance. He lacked his father's strong sense of duty, as well as his moral concern, and the absence of both was reflected in his failure to follow George III's pattern of royal diligence. George IV could scarcely have issued a proclamation against vice and immorality as the pious George III did in 1787! Cartoonists may have lampooned George III and Queen Charlotte for austerity and boring parsimony, but they also excoriated their sons for extravagance and lust. George IV displayed little concern for this bad press, or the political ability to manage scandal in any effective way. His stamina was weakened by laziness, self-indulgence and poor health.

George became Prince Regent in 1811 after the insanity of his father required the creation of a formal lieutenancy. He therefore led Britain at the time when the great spate of wars with France came to a resounding culmination in the defeat of Napoleon. The prince himself, though earlier included in the massive *George III, Reviewing the Troops*, painted by Sir William Beechey in 1793, was no military figure. He was not like his brother, Frederick, Duke of York, now best remembered in the nursery rhyme for marching troops up and down hills – a reference to his unsuccessful invasion of Holland in 1799. Another brother, Ernest, who served against the French with Hanoverian forces in 1793-4, 1806 and 1813-14, did so without particular success, but acquired a justified reputation for bravery. George IV was very keen to associate himself with military success, but his pretensions verged on the ridiculous: later in life, he used to tell people that he had been at Waterloo and would seek confirmation from the Duke of Wellington, winning the tactful reply, 'So you have told me, Sir'.

George III died in 1820, and the prince at last achieved the status of king at the age of fifty-seven. He immediately set about rectifying what he regarded as an intolerable anomaly in his family life. In 1795 he had married Caroline of Brunswick-Wolfenbüttel, but they had rapidly separated after the birth of their only child, Princess Charlotte, in 1796. Charlotte herself had died in 1817 and it was clear that the succession would pass, after George's day, to one of his brothers. The new king therefore saw no reason why the (allegedly) disreputable Caroline should have the satisfaction of being crowned queen. In 1820, divorce proceedings began in the House of Lords. The press lapped up the sexual details and engaged in a vicious and personal debate about whether Caroline was a wronged woman or a disgrace to her sex. Her cause was taken up by the public, and the debate lent focus and interest to political controversy. The government felt obliged to abandon its campaign against her, although she was successfully denied coronation. There was much that was ridiculous and degrading about the controversy. Fortunately for George, Caroline died in 1821.

George's coronation, a ceremony of great pomp and expense, was followed in 1821-2 by popular visits to Ireland, Hanover, and Scotland, the first to Ireland and Scotland by the monarch for over a century. George's wearing of Highland dress was particularly successful in courting popularity in Scotland. Thereafter, however, he retreated from the public face of monarchy and, after 1823, made no public appearances in London except for the ceremonial opening and proroguing of Parliament. Instead, he spent most of his time at his favourite haunts of Brighton and Windsor, much of it in the company of his mistress, Lady Conyngham. One of the reasons why George showed himself so rarely in London was that he was very unpopular there. But he also felt ridiculous as a result of his girth, and was affected by poor health. His reign was therefore a rather sad, as well as at time ludicrous, postlude to the great days of his career when, as the leader of fashionable society, he had created a new, alternative image of royalty and a new standard of English and international elegance: the Brighton Pavilion stands today as testimony to his idiosyncratically high sense of taste. By the 1820s, it was the restoration French court of Louis XVIII (1814-24) and Charles X (1824-30), not that of George IV, that set the tone and fashion for court life throughout Europe, whether in female dress in England, mourning in Naples, or receptions in Turin.

Politically, George IV benefited from the stability of the ministry of Lord Liverpool (1812-27), in much the same way that George III had benefited from that of Pitt the Younger. However, after Liverpool had a stroke and retired, George IV found politics troubling. The crisis of Liverpool's succession was eventually resolved by making George Canning head of the government, against the initial wishes of the king, but Canning's death in August 1827 reopened the

175. George IV when Prince of Wales, by John Russell.
176. The coat of arms of George IV.

political situation. George helped to put in a weak government under Lord Goderich (1827-8), and, after that collapsed, a stronger ministry under Wellington. However, ministerial stability was challenged by the pressure for Catholic Emancipation, an issue that divided the conservative interest. The king was adamantly opposed, but Wellington applied unremitting pressure, and, under the threat of a government resignation, the Roman Catholic Emancipation Act was passed in April 1829.

George IV might have been earlier termed the 'first gentleman in Europe', but as monarch he lacked charisma, and was widely believed to have no sense of integrity. His reign indeed was a lost opportunity for assertive monarchy. In some respects, the history of the British monarchy has been often such, especially under the Hanoverians. But whereas Georges I, II and III were not without success, under George IV the British monarchy blatantly lacked flair, and George himself had a general and sustained unpopularity that was greater than that of his immediate predecessors. When the king died (on 26 June 1830), *The Times* remarked 'Never was there a human being less respected than this late king... what eye weeps for him?'

WILLIAM IV (1830-1837)

After the dismal story of the last years of George III and the purposeless regime of George IV, William IV's reign can be seen as beginning the process of revival that was to culminate in the development of imperial splendour under Victoria and Edward VII. Born in 1765, William was the third son of George III and Queen Charlotte. His father decided that he should enter the navy, and he did so in 1779, beginning as an able seaman and (in 1780) becoming a midshipman. In 1790, William, who had been created Earl of Munster and Duke of Clarence and St Andrews in 1789, became a rear-admiral, in 1794 a vice-admiral, in 1799 an admiral, and in 1811 admiral of the fleet and thus commander in chief. It was not until 1821, when George IV promoted the Earl of St Vincent, a distinguished veteran, that there was a second such commander. In 1827, William was made Lord High Admiral, a post created for him.

The late eighteenth and early nineteenth centuries was the period of British naval triumph and hegemony. The Duke of Clarence, however, was not responsible for such triumphs. He had seen active service during the War of American Independence and commanded ships in peacetime in 1786-90, but thereafter he did not serve afloat other than for brief ceremonial purposes. In 1814, Clarence commanded the escort of Louis XVIII when it was reviewed by the Prince Regent and the allied sovereigns at Spithead. In 1828, the duke put to sea in command of the Channel Fleet, despite the view of George IV, the Prime Minister (Wellington) and the head of the Admiralty Board that his position as Lord High Admiral did not give him the authority to exercise military command. Their complaints led to Clarence's resignation. This was scarcely a career to match that of Horatio Nelson, who served with William in the West Indies and was a friend. When Nelson was married, William gave away the bride, and Nelson praised his abilities as an officer; but there are no signs that he had the capability to be an effective admiral – and in any case, he was never given a chance.

William's time as king was dominated by the issue of political reform, and specifically by pressure to change the electoral franchise. This was opposed by the Tories, who dominated the House of Lords. The general election that followed William's accession produced a new Whig government under Lord Grey, replacing Wellington's Tories. Grey supported reform, thinking the situation 'too like what took place in France before the Revolution'. Rejected by the Commons in April 1831, the Reform Bill passed in June after another general election had returned Grey with a very large majority, but it was thrown out by the Tory-dominated Lords in October 1831. There was much popular agitation, including riots in Bristol, Merthyr and Nottingham. In June 1832, the Lords finally gave way when William reluctantly agreed that he would make sufficient new peers to create a Whig majority for change. He had made such an undertaking and then withdrawn it, provoking the resignation of the government and, in turn, forcing him to return to his undertaking. The king was encouraged to back Grey by the wide-spread support for reform, by the view that the choice was between reform and widespread disorder, by Grey's opposition to further changes, and thus by the sense that the Reform Bill would not be followed by a total transformation of British politics.

William himself was publicly reputed to be a zealous supporter of reform. In the cartoon *The Reformers' Attack on the Old Rotten Tree*, which advocated electoral reform, William was portrayed on 'Constitution Hill', applauding the process of reform and surrounded by respectful figures representing England, Scotland and Ireland. He was seen as wanting to be a 'constitutional' monarch – which, indeed, he sought to be. His (alleged) support for the Bill was used exten-sively, and to considerable effect, by supporters of Reform in the 1831 election. However, any lasting assessment of the political role of William is complicated by his dismissal of Melbourne's Whig ministry in 1834, the last time a British monarch dismissed his ministers and called on others to take their place. Certainly, contemporaries saw parallels between the controversial actions of William's father in 1783-4 and those of their king in 1834-5. Crucially, however, the sequel was different: Pitt had won the 1784 election, but the Tories under Sir Robert Peel lost the 1835 election, and Melbourne returned to office.

William was somewhat eccentric: his conversations went off at a tangent, leading him to be dubbed 'Silly Billy'. But he was popular and seen as having integrity. In particular, his personal life caused less offence than that of George IV. Between 1790 and 1811, William lived publicly but quietly with the actress Dorothy Jordan; they had ten children, and after his elevation to the throne William created the eldest of them Earl of Munster. But already, before the death of George IV, William had separated from Mrs Jordan in order to marry a wife appropriate to his station. Adelaide, daughter of the Duke of Saxe-Meiningen, whom he married in 1818, bore William two daughters, but both died in infancy; as a result, when William himself died in 1837, he was succeeded by Victoria, the daughter of his deceased younger brother the Duke of Kent.

William's ultimate flexibility over reform showed that his was not the cause of the reactionary ultras. Indeed, from William's reign on, the British monarchy was not conspicuously associated with the forces of political conservatism as it would have been (for example) if his brother Ernest, Duke of Cumberland, had been king. Whether Edward VIII's political sympathies would have led in that direction is unclear, but his abdication in 1936 represented another failure of the possibility of assertive monarchy. There was nothing predictable about political developments in 1827-32, and a different attitude on the part of the last two Hanoverian monarchs might well have proved crucial. As it was, the process of reform – which in due course opened the way for considerable further constitutional, political and social change in the nineteenth and early twentieth centuries – was carried through with the active support or passive consent of successive monarchs, and created a sense that the monarchy was on the side of progress. This enduring belief contributed in a very real sense to the survival and further prospering of monarchy in Britain.

By 1837, Britain's situation in the wider world was totally transformed. France and Spain had lost most of their empires. Britain had lost its Thirteen Colonies and the 'Old Northwest' beyond the Appalachians, and had failed in its expeditions to Argentina in 1806-7; but it was now the strongest state in the world, the leading power on the oceans, and had the soundest system of public finance. Australia and New Zealand were British colonies, the colony of South Australia being founded in 1836. Canada was under British control. The British dominated much of India, particularly Bengal and the South, and also ruled Ceylon (Sri Lanka) and parts of Burma. The Congress of Vienna of 1814-15, which drew up the peace treaties that ended the Napoleonic wars, recognized British gains including Cape Colony, Trinidad, Tobago, St Lucia, Malta, Guyana and the Ionian Islands. In the two decades after the Congress, British policy and power played a crucial role in securing Greek Independence and that of Latin America. The British Empire, which is popularly associated today with the Victorian age, was in large measure formed during the reigns of the Hanoverian kings.

9

FROM THE HOUSE OF HANOVER TO THE HOUSE OF WINDSOR 1837-PRESENT

A.W. PURDUE

In 1837 William IV was succeeded to the throne by his eighteen-year-old niece, Victoria. She became Queen of Great Britain and Ireland, but not of Hanover, where Salic Law determined the succession and where her uncle, Ernest Augustus, Duke of Cumberland, the fifth son of George III and the nearest male relative of William IV, accordingly became king. Victoria's accession therefore meant the end of the connection between the British monarchy and Hanover. There was, however, no formal change of dynasty, for Victoria came to the throne as a princess of the House of Hanover. With her marriage to Prince Albert of Saxe-Coburg, the queen took her husband's name in a personal capacity, but as a sovereign she, in accordance with British tradition, retained the name with which she had come to the throne. It was only on her death in 1901, then, that the dynasty formally changed, and Edward VII became the first monarch of the House of Saxe-Coburg. His son, George V, changed the family's name to Windsor in 1917. The shift was the result of a kind of crisis of identity in the country: the outbreak of the First World War left public opinion intolerant of the notion that the British monarchy might in fact be in the possession of a German family. While the dynasty's German connections remained strong, the decision of 1917 therefore marked the culmination of that process of symbolic disengagement from Germany begun by the division of the thrones of Britain and Hanover in 1837.

Along with these re-alignments went several changes in the formal royal style. Victoria inherited the title of 'Queen of the United Kingdom of Great Britain and Ireland'. In 1876, she assumed the style 'Empress of India', to which her son, in 1901, added 'and of the British Dominions beyond the Seas'. In 1947, George VI formally abandoned the title of Emperor of India; but the earlier secession of the Republic of Ireland from the British Crown did not immediately impact on the royal style. The accession of Elizabeth II in 1953 was marked be a number of changes: at home, she was styled 'Queen of the United Kingdom of Great Britain and Northern Ireland and of her other Realms and Territories', while in each of those countries of the Commonwealth that remained monarchies she was styled queen of that country 'and of her other Realms and Territories'. Behind these shifts in the formalities of title lie fundamental constitutional and political changes in the structure and style of governance of the huge territorial interests built up by the British monarchy in other parts of the world during the eighteenth and nineteenth centuries.

The period between 1837 and the present has also witnessed several remarkable re-definitions of monarchy within Britain itself, some of them generated from within the ruling dynasty and some of them forced upon it. The emphasis on Britishness and on the family, evident in the personal styles of George III and William IV, became the very hallmark of monarchy under Victoria, George V, George VI and Elizabeth II. Equally, the matriarchy created by two long-lived queens regnant (Victoria and Elizabeth II) and promoted by a number of equally enduring queens consort (Queen Mary, wife of George V, and Queen Elizabeth, wife of George VI) established within the royal family a remarkable tradition of strong – and sometimes charismatic – women unknown since the time of Gloriana. The accession of Elizabeth II in 1952 was thought to be the high moment of this gynocracy, a veritable new Elizabethan age. But there was still more to come: during the 1980s, the public life and image of Elizabeth's daughter-in-law, the ill-fated Diana, Princess of Wales, was to create the belief that a woman born outside the royal family was the harbinger of modernisation and, indeed, the only hope for the political survival of the monarchy into the twenty-first century. It is to Diana's son, William, that many therefore look for yet another of those transformations by which the modern royal family has so frequently re-invented itself.

THE HOUSE OF HANOVER: VICTORIA (1837-1901)

The view that the accession to the throne of Queen Victoria in 1837 marked a fresh start for the British monarchy is firmly fixed in the popular imagination, not least by visual images. Sir David Wilkie's portrayal of the young queen, dressed in a virginal white gown (she really wore black, being in mourning for William IV), as she presided over her first Privy Council meeting, was massively influential. Fifty years later, H.T. Wells depicted the princess, at once vulnerable and self-possessed, receiving the news of her accession, an image that was to be faithfully copied in one of the most successful films of the 1930s, *Victoria the Great,* in which Anna Neagle starred as Victoria. Much of the force of this image lay in the implicit physical and moral contrast between the dutiful and innocent woman of eighteen and her immediate predecessors, her 'wicked uncles', but posterity has often read more into the commencement of the new reign, seeing it as marking the beginning of the modern British monarchy. Whatever licence artists and writers may have used in depicting Victoria's first day as queen, there is a piquancy to the scene, which comes from the difference between the life the princess had led and the glamour and power of her new position. For the childhood of Victoria had not been happy.

Victoria's very existence was the result of the inheritance crisis caused by the death of the then Prince Regent's only child, Princess Charlotte, in 1817. The sons of George III were fecund enough, but their surviving offspring were illegitimate and Charlotte's death inspired the regent's younger brothers, the Dukes of Clarence, Kent and Cambridge, to marry in the hope of producing an heir to the throne. Edward, Duke of Kent, the fourth son of George III, ruthlessly put aside his mistress of twenty-seven years, Madame de St Laurent, and married the Dowager Princess of Leiningen, a widow of thirty with two children. She was, by birth, a princess of the House of Saxe-Coburg and was the elder sister of Leopold, widower of Princess Charlotte and later King of the Belgians. Victoria was born in May 1819 with a ticket in the inheritance stakes, but it seemed probable that the Kents might yet produce a son, while the

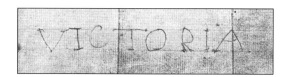

Clockwise from top left   178. Princess Victoria's signature at the age of four.
179. Princess Victoria at eleven from a picture by R. Westall.
180. A drawing of the Princess Victoria by R.J. Lane in 1837, the year she came to the throne.
181. Prince Albert at the time of his marriage.
182. The Coronation Chair in Westminster Abbey, used for Queen Victoria's coronation.

Duke of Clarence, already the father of a large illegitimate family, and his wife, Adelaide, were also preparing for a family. But the sudden death of the Duke of Kent only six months after Victoria's birth left his daughter the only outcome of the marriage, while, although the Clarences had two daughters, both died soon after birth.

The Duchess of Kent, widowed for the second time, in a foreign land whose tongue she could at first barely speak, gave her child a confined and closeted upbringing. Although the tone and atmosphere of the household was Germanic, she ensured that Victoria was brought up to speak English as her first language and that she was given a good education under the supervision of her governess, Baroness Lehzen. The duchess was, however, over-protective, even to the extent of insisting that her daughter sleep in the same room as her to the age of eighteen, while, prudish and censorious, she was estranged from the rest of the royal family and kept Victoria well away from the court and society. The baleful influence over the duchess of the household comptroller, Sir John Conroy, made him almost the wicked stepfather of the story. An unscrupulous and crudely ambitious man, Conroy seems to have seen in Victoria a means to power for himself, and he worked to inflame the animosity between William IV and the Duchess of Kent. Indeed, the sick king seems to have willed himself to stay alive until Victoria was eighteen in order to obviate the need for a regency. It says much for Victoria's strength of character that her first acts on becoming queen were to refuse to have anything to do with Conroy and to distance herself from her mother, taking only the faithful Baroness Lehzen and her dog, Dash, into her new life.

There can have been few such sudden transitions in a life as when Victoria became queen. After beleaguered days in a dull household, where she was allowed little freedom, she was, within hours, the font of authority with her own household, palaces and government. In her Whig Prime Minister, Lord Melbourne, she found a friend and adviser, very different to any man she had previously known. Still handsome in his late fifties, Melbourne was urbane, witty and cynical. The queen was entranced and half in love with him, to the extent that gossips and enemies began referring to her as 'Mrs Melbourne' or as 'Queen of the Whigs'. Thus began the gayest and most light-hearted period in Victoria's life. Never beautiful, she was attractive in her late teens and early twenties and she delighted in balls, dinners and visits to the theatre; the many candles in Buckingham Palace burned into the early hours of the morning.

A new reign and a young queen made a welcome change; but the notion of Victoria immedi-ately capturing the hearts of the nation is largely a romantic fancy. There was, as yet, no effective royal public relations machine, nor illustrated magazines, to help project her image, while the pageantry of monarchy had become rusty and ill-rehearsed. The coronation in June 1838 was little better organized than William IV's 'half-crownation' and provided no great spectacle. The carriages failed to keep in line and the foreign ambassadors provided the only splendour, while the choir was inadequate, a bishop lost his place in the order of service and the Archbishop of Canterbury forced the ring onto the wrong finger. This lack of magnificence may well have disappointed the crowds, which, although numerous, were quiet. Victoria had little taste for great public occasions and never appreciated how important it was for the Crown to project itself with pomp and ceremony. In order to appeal to the multitude, the monarchy had to glitter.

Nor did the queen have any plans for changing the essential nature of the monarchy. King Leopold sent to her the Saxe-Coburgs' *eminence grise,* Baron Stockmar, as secretary and constitu-tional adviser; Stockmar had applied his logical mind to the unwritten British constitution and come up with an interpretation that was rational, but bore little relation to practice. For the moment, however, it was Melbourne who was, in effect, her tutor, and his view of the constitu-tion was pragmatic and conservative. Neither in political terms (for she had no desire to rule over a 'democratic monarchy') nor in relation to its social and symbolic role did Victoria have a new vision of monarchy. She came to a throne that still exercised considerable political authority and she regarded Melbourne's government as *her* government. Such was her close relationship with Melbourne that she was very much a Whig partisan. Indeed, it was fortunate for her that it was the Tories, with their axiomatic loyalty to the Crown, who were in opposition: otherwise, her refusal to accept that some of her Whig Ladies of the Bedchamber would have to be exchanged for Tories when there was a proposed change of government in May 1839 might have led to a constitutional crisis. If the 1841 general election was the first that had the direct result of bringing about a change of government, this was not a development that amused the young Queen Victoria.

Victoria's reign was, nevertheless, to see significant developments in the making of the modern British monarchy. Central to the success of the monarchy, and firmly established by the early twentieth century, were its diminished political influence, a stress upon the Crown's symbolic position as representative of the nation and the centrepiece of national ceremonies and rituals, an enhanced role in the leadership of civil society, and an emphasis upon what the Victorian writer on the constitution, Walter Bagehot, called, 'a family on the throne'. Few of these changes were willed by Victoria; some were influenced by her husband Albert; and others were promoted by her son Edward VII. But much change also came about by accident or unconscious adaptation during a long reign.

The young Victoria was in no great hurry to marry, but it was in the interests of the monarchy and the nation that she should find a suitable husband and produce an heir to the throne. The prevailing practice of royalty marrying only royalty had the disadvantage that, almost inevitably, this meant marriage to a foreigner drawn from the limited pool of Protestant princes. Prince Leopold had long pressed the candidature of Victoria's cousin, Prince Albert of Saxe-Coburg, and the queen conveniently fell for him when he visited Britain in 1839. The marriage, which took place in 1840, was not universally popular. The British people were suspicious of foreigners and the aristocracy and the working classes particularly considered a prince from a minor German state no great catch. Florence Nightingale, an observer outside the Chapel Royal, where the marriage took place, commented that Albert's clothes (the uniform of a British Field Marshal) looked 'borrowed to be married in', while the wife of the American Minister found it amusing when Albert promised to endow the bride with all *his* worldly goods. Parliament voted Albert a lesser allowance than that proposed by Melbourne, while Victoria's wish that her husband be made King Consort was not granted.

Albert's influence upon Victoria, the monarchy, and influential sections of British society, was considerable. To a great degree it was Albert who turned Victoria into a 'Victorian', imparting that emphasis upon seriousness, morality and respectability that was to become typical of many (though by no means all) of her subjects. To some extent this simply represented a reinforcement of the Saxe-Coburg influence exercised by the queen's mother, King Leopold and Baron Stockmar; but, as Victoria was much in love with Albert, his influence was profound. Albert, in his own right and via his sway over Victoria, aligned the monarchy with the values of progressive middle-class Britain. This was to be seen in a change of emphasis in the approach to good works. While Victoria's charitable feelings were warm, personal and impulsive, Albert patronized societies for improvement and took a scientific approach to social problems. He also revived the royal role as patron of the arts and sciences and was an enthusiast for the reform and modernization of the universities. Such activities did much to bind the monarchy to important sections of civil society. Royal support for charities and for the arts and sciences was far from a new development, but Albert gave a new impetus to what was to become a central characteristic of the monarchy.

The social image of Albert and Victoria's lifestyle had much to recommend it to many of their subjects. Their life together was a combination of the formality and domesticity often found at German courts. There was an insistence on precedence and rules of behaviour along with unpretentious cosiness and contented family life; courtiers might be bidden to join in games or in singing around the piano. The example of private life set by Victoria and Albert was very much in tune with the concerns of a society that set much store by the virtues of home and family. Central to this atmosphere was the bearing and upbringing of children. Victoria resented her regular pregnancies and bewailed the lot of women in this respect. She had, however, a hearty sexual appetite and responded to her doctor's suggestion of abstinence as the only way to avoid frequent pregnancy with the memorable words, 'Am I to have no more fun in bed?' She bore Albert nine children between 1840 and 1858: Victoria; Albert Edward, Prince of Wales (later Edward VII); Alice; Alfred, Duke of Edinburgh (who became Duke of Saxe-Coburg in 1893); Helena; Louise; Arthur, Duke of Connaught; Leopold, Duke of Albany; and Beatrice. This large family seemed to many the model of the domestic idyll.

There had always been interest in the private lives of royal families, whether exemplary or scandalous, but, as more and more family magazines came on the market in the 1840s and 1850s, the details of the royal menage became common knowledge. The frenzied interest of the press in royal fashions, tastes, furniture and pets had begun. The royal family helped sell papers, while stories about royal tastes and habits sold products. The growth of the pictorial press, especially *The Illustrated London News*, which began publication in 1842, played a large part in conveying to the public an idealized version of the life of the royal family. When thrones trembled all over Europe in 1848, *The Illustrated London News* carried an illustration of Victoria, Albert and their children enjoying a blissful Christmas beside their Christmas tree, a German introduction to Britain which, within a decade, most British people considered part of the traditional Christmas. It was not only the press and magazines that brought the royal family to the people. Improved physical communications, especially the railways and steam yachts, also made the monarchy more mobile than ever before. Victoria and Albert were able to travel with increased ease, making the monarchy less London-based as visits to provincial towns became part of a regular routine. The magic of royal visits triumphed over the lack of pageantry and display, which accorded with the royal couple's tastes. No doubt the Scottish tourist industry would eventually have burgeoned even if Victoria and Albert had not acquired Balmoral and fallen in love with the Highlands, but details of tartan-clad royal holidays amidst the glens certainly helped.

Historians have made too little of just how German this mid-Victorian monarchy was. The powerful British nation, rejoicing in its pre-eminent economic position, was presided over by a family that had not been so essentially German since 1760. The Hanoverian monarchs had all found wives in the marriage market of the minor German States; but Victoria herself was much more completely German as the product of the upbringing of her Saxe-Coburg mother. Albert, in turn, made little effort to anglicize himself; indeed, his German manner, tastes, life-style and even dress did not endear him to the working classes or to the aristocracy. It did him less harm, however, with the middle orders of society, for there was much enthusiasm for things German amongst the middle classes and intelligentsia in the mid-nineteenth century, manifesting itself in such diverse fields as charitable endeavours, art and philosophy, furniture, and attitudes to nature. Nineteenth-century commentators were apt to refer to Britain's 'Teutonic roots'. Victoria and Albert spoke German when alone. The queen's attitude to Germany was somewhat quaint: she seems to have regarded German as a peculiarly 'royal'

Numb. 19795. **2411**

The London Gazette
EXTRAORDINARY.

Published by Authority.

SATURDAY, NOVEMBER 23, 1839.

HER Majesty being this day present in Council, was pleased to make the following Declaration, viz.

I HAVE caused you to be summoned at the present time, in order that I may acquaint you with my resolution in a matter which deeply concerns the welfare of My people, and the happiness of my future life.

It is My intention to ally Myself in Marriage with the Prince Albert of Saxe Cobourg and Gotha. Deeply impressed with the solemnity of the engagement which I am about to contract, I have not come to this decision without mature consideration, nor without feeling a strong assurance that, with the blessing of Almighty God, it will at once secure my domestic felicity and serve the interests of my country.

I have thought fit to make this resolution known to you at the earliest period, in order that you may be fully apprised of a matter so highly important to Me and to My kingdom, and which I persuade Myself will be most acceptable to all My loving subjects.

Whereupon all the Privy Councillors present, made it their humble request to Her Majesty, that Her Majesty's Most Gracious Declaration to them might be made public; which Her Majesty was pleased to order accordingly.

C. C. Greville.

Clockwise from top left 183. Extract from the *London Gazette* of Saturday 23 November 1839, announcing the Queen's engagement to Albert.
184. Queen Victoria was a prolific artist: this is an etching dated 1841.
185. An official painting of the Royal Family: Victoria, Albert and five of their nine children.

tongue, and once remarked on a visit to Germany that it was 'curious to find the ordinary people speaking German'. She clearly conceived that monarchy was the special business or duty of an extended German-speaking family.

The 'Albertine' monarchy, which from the 1840s increasingly replaced the early Victorian regime and reached its zenith in the years immediately before Albert's death in 1861, pointed British constitutional development in a different direction to that which it was eventually to take. Victoria's love and respect for her husband warred with her pride in her own pre-eminent position, but his greater capacity for hard work and the queen's many pregnancies meant that many decisions were left to Albert. Albert's conception of the role of the constitutional monarch was that of neutrality between political parties combined with intervention in government policy. Albert saw the Crown as providing providential leadership and a guiding hand, an encouragement to sensibly progressive forces and a bulwark against democratic excesses. It was the model followed by many continental monarchies (indeed, the present Belgian monarchy still resembles it), but it depended on the wisdom and tact of the monarch and a consensual political climate.

This interpretation of constitutional monarchy worked reasonably well in the 1840s and 1850s. Its possibilities were revealed by Albert's great success, his role in creating and organizing the Great Exhibition of 1851 and developing 'Albertopolis', the cluster of institutions devoted to the arts and sciences in South Kensington. Its limitations were also, however, evident. Though his cool head and considerable knowledge of European affairs were often a benign influence on foreign policy, Albert's quarrels with Lord Palmerston, and his great unpopularity when he sought to prevent war with Russia in 1854, demonstrated that it was unwise for the monarchy to stand against patriotic and popular opinion. Albert was in tune with the 'common sense' of informed progressive opinion in his time, but it is unlikely that he or his conception of monarchy would have thrived in the circumstances of mass democracy.

Albert's death in 1861 plunged Victoria into a period of mourning that endured for the remaining forty years of her reign. Her withdrawal from public life was accepted for a time by her subjects, but gradually began to make the monarchy unpopular. The queen was not prepared to allow her son, Albert Edward, Prince of Wales, to take over her public and ceremonial duties; nor, distrusting his judgement, did she share any matters of importance with him. Victoria did not neglect what she conceived of (rather narrowly) as her duty. She continued to work her way through her despatch boxes and insisted on being informed of state affairs – a great inconvenience to her ministers, who often had to travel to Balmoral to consult her. She was, however, adamant that, in her grief, she could not be expected to perform public duties. On only six occasions between 1861 and 1886 did she agree to open Parliament (occasions that tended to coincide with her need to request votes for annuities for members of the royal family), and even then she insisted that there be a minimum of ceremony, that she wear her widow's weeds, and that her speech be read for her. The 1860s and 1870s saw the nadir of royal grandeur.

The queen's self-indulgent retirement from her subjects resulted in criticism in the press, most of which concerned her seclusion at Windsor, Osborne or Balmoral, her avoidance of London, and her marked preference for her Scottish servants. Her closeness to John Brown, who was given the post of 'Queen's Highland Servant', gave rise to much gossip and the nickname for the queen of 'Mrs Brown'. In these circumstances, the monarchy grew unpopular, and there were expressions of republican feeling. In the end, however, such subversions came to little. If the widespread celebrations when the Prince of Wales recovered from typhoid fever in 1871 were more a demonstration of the monarchy's continued appeal than the cause of a royalist revival, they did seem to mark a turning of the tide of opinion. As the queen grew older, the nation became more prosperous and more powerful, and she became more respected and popular than any previous sovereign.

It may well have been the queen's seclusion that led Walter Bagehot (whose influential book, *The English Constitution,* was published in 1867) to exaggerate the extent of the decline of the sovereign's political influence and to write that 'a republic had insinuated itself beneath the folds of a monarchy'. Victoria was no cipher and insisted upon her prerogatives; without Albert's influence, she also returned to her old path of political partisanship. Decline there was, however, for Victoria did not initiate policy, even if she could obstruct policies and ministers of which she disapproved. The growth of well-organized political parties left little scope for direct royal inter-vention, save when no party had a clear majority in the Commons or it was the monarch's responsibility to choose a new prime minister. Where Bagehot was correct was in his perception that the monarchy's diminishing political power could be compensated for by its religious and mystical appeal as the symbol of the nation, by its social leadership, and by the idea of a 'family on the throne'. If Victoria herself, with her rather bureaucratic and political view of the monarchy's functions, did not appreciate these opportunities, the last decades of her reign were to see their development.

Reluctantly, the queen allowed herself to be the centrepiece of grand state theatre to celebrate her Golden Jubilee in 1887. The Diamond Jubilee of 1897 was an even more elaborate and glit-tering affair, able to call upon exotic representatives of the expanding British Empire to reinforce refurbished pageantry. That amidst all the pomp and glitter was a small, plump lady in black made the occasions no less effective. The jubilees themselves increased interest in the lives of the members of the large royal family, and royal births, marriages and funerals came to be treated as public, rather than private, events. If the monarchy was going to show itself to the people, patronize innumerable charities and societies, and make constant visits to provincial towns to open buildings, lay foundation stones and attend dinners given by the local 'great and good', then junior royals would have to be enlisted and accepted as part of the royal establishment. This process made the monarchy and royal family, as never before, the unchallenged leaders of society. Victoria had not willed it, had even disapproved of it, but her long reign had seen the emergence of a transformed monarchy in which power had, in effect, been replaced by influence. By the time of her death, on 22 January 1901, Victoria had not only reigned longer than any other British monarch (sixty-three years); she had also made the Crown an indispens-able element in a new, modern, British society.

The House of Saxe-Coburg: Edward VII (1901-1910)

The man who belatedly became king as Edward VII was born at Buckingham Palace on 9 November 1841. Created Prince of Wales when he was a month old, he was nearly sixty when he eventually came to the throne. A principal attraction of monarchy as an institution is that its rhythms are those of human lives and their rites of passage: kings and queens may come to thrones as children or as octogenarians. One problem is, however, that for heirs to a throne, born to young and healthy monarchs, much of a lifetime may be spent in preparation for a future role. The life of Edward VII is an illustration of this problem.

Albert Edward, as he was christened, was the second child and eldest son of Queen Victoria and Prince Albert. If great hopes were invested in him by his parents, there were also fears that, without a careful upbringing, he might follow the paths of previous Princes of Wales. The relations between the heirs apparent of the Hanoverian dynasty and their parents had not been cordial, and the figure of the most recent Prince of Wales, who had become George IV, loomed as a dreadful warning. It was therefore ironic that Victoria and Albert made the same mistakes as had George III in the upbringing of the heir apparent. Prince Albert Edward did not respond to his rigorous and carefully planned education to his parents' satisfaction. They must often have wished that it was his dutiful and serious elder sister, Victoria, the Princess Royal, who was the heir to the throne.

Albert Edward's potential as monarch of a democratic and mass society was in fact considerable, for the young prince was affable, possessed considerable social skills, and made an effective centrepiece of ceremonial occasions. These, however, were not accomplishments that his parents valued. He enjoyed great success when he visited Canada and the USA in 1860, but he had none of the seriousness, the intellectual interests, or the worthy dedication of his father. Worse still, he inherited the sensual appetites of many of his Hanoverian ancestors. Queen Victoria blamed him for the distress that his affair with an actress, Nellie Clifton, caused to Prince Albert in the months before the latter's death.

The prince was certainly not an apposite heir to the Albertine model of monarchy, which demanded a role as moral exemplar and a force for progress and reform. Yet Albert had not been popular outside the fairly narrow, though highly influential, sections of society that encompassed the professionals, the serious-minded, and the highly respectable. Much more at home in 'society' than either of his parents, the Prince of Wales also had an innate understanding of what the working classes demanded from the monarchy, and appreciated the need for royalty to show itself to the people. He repeatedly pointed out to the queen in the 1860s that her prolonged mourning and refusal to perform public duties were making her unpopular. Such advice was not welcome.

During the long period in which he was heir apparent, the Prince of Wales was not given any real share of royal duties or responsibilities. The queen saw her despatch boxes, her relations with her ministers, and domestic and foreign affairs, as no concern of her son's. Suggestions that the Prince of Wales be given special responsibilities, allowed a career in the army, or be made Viceroy of Ireland, were ignored. Not surprisingly, he therefore devoted himself to social life and pleasure. His home, Marlborough House, became the centre of fashionable society, perhaps a centre of social opposition, but never, as with past Princes of Wales, a centre of political opposition, to the reigning monarch.

The prince's marriage to Princess Alexandra of Denmark in 1863 provided a moment of restrained pageantry amongst the gloom of a monarchy dedicated to mourning. Alexandra was a great beauty whose hairstyles and dresses were avidly represented in illustrated magazines and widely copied. She became very popular but almost childishly sentimental. Increasingly deaf, she preferred to centre her social life on family and children, and presented obvious limitations as a partner for the out-going prince. The couple were fond of each other, and were united in their affection for the five children they produced: Albert Victor, Duke of Clarence (who died in his twenties); George (later George V); Louise; Victoria; and Maud. The Prince's sexual liaisons, which continued with his last mistress, Mrs George Keppel, into his reign, were, however, numerous, and his fondness for 'fast' society attracted criticism. He was involved in several scandals and was subpoenaed to appear in two court cases, the Mordaunt divorce case in 1870 and the Tranby Croft case in 1891, which centred on the accusation that one of the prince's fellow house guests had cheated at cards. His relations with his mother were often strained. She disapproved of his social life and his friends, while he disapproved of the privileged position she gave to her Scottish retainer, John Brown.

Although the prince's self-indulgent social life and his affairs resulted in criticism from the more censorious sections of society – which included most of the press – he was nevertheless a popular figure, and his recovery from typhoid fever in 1871 was the occasion of widespread rejoicing. His love of the racecourse, gambling, high-living and the music hall did him little harm with those (many) of his subjects who embraced a hedonistic popular culture. Walter Bagehot in his *British Constitution* had argued that it was the role of a Prince of Wales 'to taste all the world and the glory of it, whatever is most attractive, whatever is most seductive'. As Lord Glanville put it, 'The Prince of Wales is loved because he has all the faults of which the Englishman is accused.'

Edward's support for what has been called the 'welfare monarchy' has been underestimated. He was the patron or supporter of hospitals and charities in Britain and the Empire and he set up the Royal Commission on the Housing of the Working Classes. If he can hardly be described as an assiduous social worker, he adorned his charities, flattered the charitable, and usually said the right thing. It was, however, Alexandra, both as Princess of Wales and later as queen, who became especially identified with charitable activities. She developed a new style of royal philanthropy in which beauty and high fashion came together with a ready sympathy that did not flinch from comforting the worst cases – even to the extent of braving the countenance of the 'Elephant man'.

Albert Edward's social influence was, however unintentionally, beneficial. If he was, at heart, arrogantly royal, he was a 'man of the world' and recognized new money as well as old blood. British society saw an easier symbiosis of the aristocracy and the upper middle class than was found on the Continent, and this was a development that Albert Edward encouraged through his friendship with those who had made their fortunes in business. Such friendship was far from disinterested, for he enjoyed the extravagant hospitality of the rich; but they also eased the path to acceptance of important sections of society. That the most successful of British Jews were absorbed so quickly into the upper class owed much to the royal example.

The prince's one semi-political gesture of opposition to his mother was also positive. The queen detested her Prime Minister, Gladstone, and Albert Edward cultivated him, realizing how dangerous his mother's Tory partisanship was. Gladstone and the prince may have had little in common, but the 'people's William' valued the prince's support. At Gladstone's funeral, the Prince of Wales and his son, George, acted as pallbearers, at once a fitting tribute to a great prime minister and a shrewd piece of public relations.

When, as Edward VII, Albert Edward entered enthusiastically into his long-awaited inheritance, he made one outstanding contribution to the development of the modern monarchy. He set it amidst ceremony and theatre. As Prince of Wales he had ensured that the celebration of Victoria's jubilees should be magnificent and well-organized spectacles. As king, with the aid of his confidant and adviser, Lord Esher, he built upon the experience of the jubilees and state and royal occasions were mounted with great pomp and panache. He set a stamp upon the public and ceremonial side of the monarchy that has endured. His delight in showing himself to his subjects resulted in a great increase in the number of visits paid to provincial towns, which also set a model that his successors were to follow.

The political power of the Crown had decreased considerably during Queen Victoria's reign and Edward accepted this. He insisted, however, upon his prerogatives and, believing that he had the right to be consulted, tried to insist on seeing cabinet papers at the stage when policy was in the making. He lost this battle when the Prime Minister, A.J. Balfour, brushed aside his demand. The king felt strongly that in two areas, military affairs and foreign affairs, he had a special right to influence policy, and intervened several times on matters concerning the modernization of the armed forces. Despite his outdated support for red as opposed to khaki uniforms, he generally supported army reforms and this led to clashes with two Conservative Ministers for War, St John Broderick and H.O. Arnold Foster, though he enjoyed good relations with the reforming Liberal Minister, R.B. Haldane. He also gave consistent support to Admiral Sir John Fisher in the latter's struggle over naval strategy with Admiral Lord Charles Beresford.

There is considerable disagreement about the extent to which Edward VII influenced foreign policy. He was at home in Europe where, as Prince of Wales, he had travelled and sojourned regularly. His travels had had no lofty motive, for his purpose had been pleasure away from the eye of his mother. As king, the purpose was simply pleasure. He did, however, know Europe well, while as the 'uncle of Europe' he was related to most heads of state. Ironically, it is the improvement in relations with republican France that is seen as his great achievement and he has been credited with doing much to facilitate the Anglo-French *Entente Cordiale*. Many European statesmen thought that the king wielded enormous influence, Germans in particular feeling that he inclined government policy against their country; indeed, his detestation of his nephew, Kaiser Wilhelm II, may have influenced his views on European affairs. Certainly the British government utilized Edward as an instrument of policy and made use of his many personal contacts. In the end, however, it is difficult to evaluate the extent of his influence because his views on foreign affairs were largely in harmony with the weight of opinion at the Foreign Office and in the Cabinet.

Edward, though he exerted political influence, was a modern constitutional monarch, accepting governments that the electoral process and the party system determined should have a majority in the House of Commons. The boundaries of royal power were not yet as clear, however, as they would be in future reigns. In the last year of his life, it seemed that he would be called upon to give an undertaking to create sufficient Liberal peers to allow the Parliament Bill introduced by Asquith's government to pass through the House of Lords. The king, convinced of the impropriety of this demand, considered calling upon the Conservative leader, Balfour, to form a minority government rather than agree to it. Edward died before the decision had to be made.

The greatest achievement of Edward VII was not in the political field but in his refurbishing and re-packaging of the institution of monarchy as a national symbol at once magnificent and popular. Some might cavil that he vulgarized the monarchy in a rich and glittering Edwardian way; but this was also, perhaps, what monarchy in a democracy needed. Edward was a popular king and, at his death in 1910, was deeply mourned. As he lay in state at Westminster a queue 'six to eight abreast stretched seven miles to the entrance', while at his funeral it was estimated that some two million people lined the streets of London.

The House of Windsor: George V (1910-1936)

Prince George, who was born in 1865, was the younger son of the Prince and Princess of Wales, later Edward VII and Queen Alexandra. It was only on the death of his older brother, Albert Victor (Prince 'Eddy'), Duke of Clarence, in 1892 that he came into the direct line of succession to the throne. The Prince and Princess of Wales were devoted to their children and Alexandra lavished intensive affection upon them. When in 1877, George and his elder brother were sent to the training ship, HMS Britannia, the transition to a disciplined and tough life was sudden. After two years, they set forth on a three-year voyage round the World on HMS Bacchante

Clockwise from top   186. Edward VII at Balmoral.
187. A rare photograph of George V smiling at the wedding of Princess Maud to Lord Carnegie
in November 1923. The King is seen chatting to his son the Duke of York, later George VI.
188. George, Prince of Wales, *c.*1908.

accompanied by a tutor, the Revd J.N. Dalton. Thereafter, the brothers parted, Eddy to be prepared for eventual kingship, George to continue in the Navy.

The death of the Duke of Clarence was much mourned by his family, though given the prince's lack of energy, dissipation and limited ability, the event may in the longer term have been fortunate for the monarchy. For Prince George, who had spent some fifteen years in the Royal Navy, life changed completely. He had to give up his plans for a naval career and to take over the future that had been mapped out for his brother. That map included Eddy's fiancee, Princess Mary ('May') of Teck, a daughter of the queen's first cousin and a member of a junior and relatively impoverished branch of the royal family. Her engagement to Eddy and subsequent engagement and marriage to George were encouraged by Queen Victoria.

The Duke of York, as he now became, was a short, bearded and somewhat morose-looking man. Without the intellectual interests of his grandfather or his father's charm, he preferred, when not fulfilling public engagements, to live quietly at the rather cramped and gloomy York Cottage, Sandringham, enjoying his shooting and assembling a massive stamp album. His official biographer, Harold Nicolson, confided to his diary, while writing about George's period as Duke of York, that 'he did nothing at all but kill animals and stick in stamps'. He was typical of a certain type of naval officer, usually not promoted beyond middle rank, who fails to see that the need for 'good order and discipline', correct dress and time-keeping are means to an efficient service not ends in themselves. Such men often end up, after early retirement, barking orders at their unfortunate families. The navy had given the Duke of York an obsession with punctuality, a stiff social manner, a strong sense of patriotism, a conviction of British superiority and a deep devotion to duty.

Between 1894 and 1905, the Duchess of York bore her husband one daughter and five sons: Edward Albert, the future Edward VIII, born in 1894; Albert George, the future George VI, in 1895; Mary in 1897; Henry, Duke of Gloucester, in 1900; George, Duke of Kent, in 1902; and John in 1905. The duchess was much in awe of her husband and his position. She zealously supported him and subordinated herself, even in dress, to his wishes. A better wife than a mother, she had little time for babies and small children; and since the king, with his obsessions about punctuality and correct dress, was a cold and unsympathetic father, the couple's children grew up starved of affection from their parents. When the youngest son, John (1905-19), was diagnosed as suffering from epilepsy, he was gradually removed from the family circle and left to the care of retainers. Relations between parents and children were thus in contrast to the emotional bonds between George and his own mother and the easy and cordial relations he enjoyed (unusually for the royal family) with his father.

The death of Queen Victoria in 1901 brought King Edward VII to the throne and the Duke of York was made Prince of Wales. This meant a much more public role for George, while the king, conscious of how Queen Victoria had excluded him from state business, kept his son informed of government policy and encouraged him to prepare himself for his future role. Lacking the king's familiarity with Europe and its problems, the prince had in fact toured the Dominions and therefore had rather more knowledge of the Empire than his father. He was, however, considered to be inexperienced and to be something of a Conservative partisan. There was foreboding that, with a Liberal government in power after 1905, he would not be a successful constitutional monarch.

George V's succession to the throne on 6 May 1910 came at a difficult time. He found himself in the midst of the constitutional crisis caused by the determination of Asquith's government to pass a bill curbing the powers of the House of Lords. At the time of his death, Edward VII was considering resisting any demand by the government that he promise to make sufficient Liberal peers to allow the Parliament Act through the Lords. The new king gave way when Asquith made the demand in November 1910, but he did so reluctantly. He was angry when he later found out that Lord Knollys, one of his two private secretaries, had withheld from him the information that, had he refused, Balfour, the Conservative leader, might have been prepared to form a minority government.

George V was, however, to prove to be a successful constitutional monarch. Despite his somewhat grim appearance, he was unsure of himself and had to force himself to emulate the grand figure of his father in the midst of the theatre of kingship that Edward had created. If he continued with the public glitter of monarchy, George's court combined dullness with formality. He revived 'Balmorality' and heavy respectability, which, if something of a joke to fashionable society, appealed to a middle-class Britain that still clung to Victorian standards. His limitations were not necessarily disadvantages. He had strong prejudices but was too cautious to act upon them. He came to a throne with a diminished political role and his tutors had imbued him with Bagehot's view of monarchy; duty and innate conservatism disinclined him to question this. He bent to the political currents of that day and managed to be impartial between parties, while preserving, discretely, the royal prerogatives. When crises came, he exhibited an unexpected sure touch and an empathy with public opinion.

The First World War placed the royal family, with their German ancestry, in an awkward position. George V considered himself entirely British and worked hard at raising morale in support of the war. As Germanophobia mounted, however, the German connections of the monarchy came under attack. H.G. Wells went so far as to call for the end to 'an alien and uninspiring court', at which the king protested, 'I may be uninspiring but I'll be damned if I'm an alien.' His answer was to emphasize the Britishness of the monarchy by changing the name of the royal house in 1917. The name, Windsor, suggested by his secretary, Lord Stamfordham, was a brilliant choice, redolent of British royal tradition (even genealogical experts differed as to what the new name was replacing and whether it was Saxe-Coburg, Coburg, Guelph or Wettin). At the same time, junior members of the family had to change their names, Battenburgs becoming Mountbattens and Tecks becoming Cambridges, while German princes were relieved of their British titles. King George demonstrated that his concern for his throne was tenacious. He ignored the demands of kinship and monarchical solidarity when he argued against allowing the Tsar of Russia and his family to take asylum in Britain because this would be unpopular.

The effects of the First World War upon the British monarchy were profound. Henceforth, the monarchy had to be resolutely British. Even had the number of foreign monarchies not been so savagely diminished, it would have been unlikely that marriages between scions of the royal family and German dynasties would have continued to be acceptable. Three of George V's children married British spouses and only one, the Duke of Kent, married a member of a foreign dynasty. The Empire had become a dimension of British patriotism and of the monarchy from the late nineteenth century, but after the war it became more important than ever. King George associated the monarchy more closely with the Empire, having fond memories of his imperial tours as Duke of York and Prince of Wales and of his durbar at Delhi in 1911.

In the fluid political circumstances of post-war Britain, when, with the Liberals in decline and the Labour Party improving its position, three political parties contended for power, the remaining political functions of the monarchy became important and King George had to play an active role on three occasions. In 1923, on the resignation of the Prime Minister, Andrew Bonar Law, he was required to call upon a leading Conservative to form a government; he chose

Stanley Baldwin rather than Lord Curzon, largely on the grounds that it was desirable that the Prime Minister be a member of the House of Commons. The general election late in 1923 produced a hung parliament, with Labour as the second largest party, and the Conservatives and Liberals were not prepared to co-operate with each other. After some initial hesitation, the king took the constitutionally correct course and called upon Ramsay MacDonald to form a minority Labour government in January 1924. Strongly opposed to socialism though he was, the king got on well with MacDonald and several of his Cabinet in this short-lived administration. In 1931, George took a more controversial initiative when he persuaded MacDonald, who had come to tender his and his Labour government's resignation, to stay on and form a national government. In each instance, the king acted after seeking advice from leading politicians and with constitutional propriety.

A very conservative man, George did not welcome most of the social developments of his reign. He disliked lipstick, cocktails and new fashions in dress and this led to clashes with his son, the Prince of Wales, who was the very acme of modernity. The king also disliked high art, especially in its modernist manifestations. In the words of one of his biographers, Kenneth Rose, he, 'liked a book with a plot, a tune he could hum and a picture that told a story'; so, of course, did most of his subjects. He demonstrated, however, considerable ability with one very modern medium, radio. His Christmas broadcasts to the nation and Empire, the first of which was written for him by Rudyard Kipling, began in 1932. They were an enormous success and were to be continued, if not always with such panache, by his successors.

Most of the nation appears to have perceived George V as a steady, reliable, rather irascible but good-hearted figure. He made a considerable contribution to the stability of inter-war Britain. He himself did not seem to appreciate how popular he was with all classes. The Silver Jubilee of his reign was celebrated in 1935, the last year of his life, with a national outpouring of loyalty and affection. This surprised him. 'I never knew they felt like that about me', he said.

EDWARD VIII (JANUARY-DECEMBER 1936)

The reign of Edward VIII lasted from 20 January to 11 December 1936, when the king abdicated to marry Mrs Wallis Simpson. It was a great anti-climax. After an apprenticeship as Prince of Wales lasting nearly a quarter of a century, Edward was never crowned. His abdication came as a great shock to the nation, and for a while it was thought that he had seriously undermined the standing of the monarchy.

Prince Edward Albert Christian George Andrew Patrick David was born at White Lodge in Richmond Park on 23 June 1894, the son of the Duke and Duchess of Kent (later George V and Queen Mary). From this plenitude of names, paying respect to the family and to the United Kingdom's patron saints, it was (appositely for one who would be Prince of Wales for a quarter of a century) 'David' by which the prince was known to his family. The Duchess of York had little understanding or fondness for babies or young children, and David and his younger brother Bertie spent their early years in the nursery. This was the usual arrangement among upper class families, but in this case the nanny was a disastrous choice. She was not only incompetent but she abused the children. She treated David with a mixture of affection and sadism and totally neglected his younger brother to the extent of forgetting to feed him. It took three years before the parents discovered this pattern of mistreatment. The brothers may have been royal, but they were scarcely privileged. Their mother, in awe not only of her husband but of her own position, was as formal and unbending in private as she was in public

189. George, Prince of Wales, with his father Edward VII at a tea party in Corfu, *c*.1908.
190. The king who was never crowned. A commemoration flag made in preperation for the coronation of Edward VIII.

and had unrealistic expectations of children's behaviour. When queen, she justified her distant relationship with her children: 'I have always to remember that their father is also their king.' The children enjoyed the time their parents were away on a lengthy tour of the Empire in 1901, when they were indulged by their affectionate grandparents, King Edward and Queen Alexandra.

The education of the heir to the throne was, as usual, a disaster. After lessons at home with a tutor, Henry Hansell (a former schoolmaster and a muscular Christian but an unimaginative teacher), David entered the Royal Naval College, Osborne in 1907. In this school of hard knocks he survived, even though Hansell had not prepared him well for the narrow curriculum. Having transferred to the Royal Naval College at Dartmouth, the prince was beginning to look forward to going to sea when his father's succession to the throne in 1910 brought his career in the Navy to an end.

At the age of sixteen, David was heir to the throne and in the public eye. He was an immediate success. At the coronation the slight, golden-haired figure kneeling at his father's feet to say words of homage moved all hearts, as did his performance in the re-invented tradition of investiture as Prince of Wales at Caernarfon Castle a few weeks later. Already, though, he was ambivalent about his future role. He played the part of Prince Charming to perfection, while complaining about the ridiculous outfit of white satin breeches and a purple velvet surcoat he was compelled to wear for the investiture. His education continued with periods in France and Germany to improve his French and learn German, and a spell as an unenthusiastic undergraduate at Magdalen College, Oxford.

On the outbreak of the First World War, the Prince of Wales joined the Grenadier Guards, naively expecting that he would go with his regiment to fight in France, like any other junior officer. If this did his patriotism and courage credit, it said less for his appreciation of his role and position. The government could not allow a Prince of Wales to be killed in action. He was eventually allowed to go to France, but to a staff appointment rather than to the trenches. He spent most of his war trying to get as close to action as possible and bitterly resented being awarded a Military Cross that he felt he had not deserved. His very presence on the Western Front, however, earned him the respect of many servicemen; and this, together with his good looks and personal charm, made him an ideal representative after the war, when it was felt that the monarchy had an essential role to play in maintaining the loyalty of the Empire. His successful visits to the Dominions contributed to making him the most popular member of the royal family with the press and the public. His success was not confined to Britain and the Empire, for he was also given an enthusiastic welcome in New York.

During the 1920s the Prince of Wales became the first royal superstar, perhaps the first international superstar. He had a charisma that was almost entirely physical: although he could be charming enough in conversation, it was his physical magnetism that worked so well in photographs and news film, for the camera loved and flattered him. It was not just that he was handsome, that his movements and gestures were graceful, that he was fashionable and young in a post-war world that valued youth and fashion, or that he could (when he wished to) exude empathy and sympathy. His true appeal lay in the combination of poise and vulnerability, in hints of moodiness and a suggestion that there was sadness behind the ready smile. Similar qualities were to be found in stars of the future such as James Dean and Princess Diana.

Not for the last time, the monarchy rode high on an image that lacked substance. Behind the almost shy smile and the ready sympathy lay confusion and a strong streak of self-indulgence. Courtiers and equerries were soon aware that the Prince lacked responsibility.

191. Edward VIII when Prince of Wales, at the age of nine, with Sir Charles Cust.

Previous Princes of Wales had loved pleasure and taken mistresses, and David's taste for cocktails, jazz, night clubs and married women could be seen as merely contemporary expressions of his grandfather's tastes. His clashes with his father over his clothes, his friends and his disregard of certain royal duties and court procedures could also be excused as the most recent manifestation of the traditional clash between royal generations. More serious were indications of the prince's reluctance to accept that his fate and duty was to be king, and of his emotional instability. His incessant dieting (for he was convinced, absurdly, that he was getting fat) again foreshadowed Princess Diana, while he seemed to seek out risks in steeple-chasing, at which he was not very good. Tardiness in getting around to finding a wife was one thing but, as the prince moved into and through his thirties, seemingly content with a succession of married or divorced women at his side, his single status increasingly seemed like a defiance both of maturity and of duty.

The prince's closest companion from 1934 was the elegant American, Mrs Wallis Simpson. Born in Maryland in 1896, Wallis Warfield had already had one unsuccessful marriage before marrying, in 1928, Ernest Simpson, a British shipping broker. Elbowing aside her erstwhile friend, Thelma Furness, who had introduced her to him, Wallis soon had the prince entranced. Many imaginative explanations have been advanced for the hold that she exercised over him; at the least, there seems to have been a sado-masochistic element in the relationship, with the prince positively enjoying the minor humiliations that Wallis inflicted on him. For the rest of his life, he would be dependent on her.

Towards the end of his reign, George V said to Stanley Baldwin, 'After I am dead, the boy will ruin himself within twelve months.' It was an astonishingly accurate prophecy. On George's death on 10 January 1936, Edward emphasized that the new reign had a new style by flying from Sandringham to Hendon to attend his Accession Council at St James's Palace. He wanted to be a modern sovereign. He also wanted to be a 'people's king'. It is clear, however, that he lacked the emotional or intellectual commitment for any serious vision of monarchy. Within a few months of becoming king, it became clear that he was paying little attention to state papers, sometimes leaving his despatch boxes unopened for days or weeks. Mrs Simpson appears to have absorbed all his thoughts. From early in his brief reign, the king's relationship with Wallis was the cause of concern to court and government. Stanley Baldwin had no desire to interfere between the king and his mistress, though he found Edward's lack of discretion worrying. No doubt, with a little caution, the king could have continued to retain his mistress, but marriage to her was incompatible with staying on the throne: and on marriage he was now determined. An embarrassment therefore became a constitutional crisis.

In August 1936, Edward, accompanied by Mrs Simpson, went for a cruise along the Dalmatian coast, a progress that was fully covered by the American and European press. The British press, however, while reporting on the king's holiday, made no mention of his insepa-rable companion. In September, Wallis stayed with the king at Balmoral. By October, Baldwin was steeling himself to discuss the relationship with King Edward, when he learnt that Mrs Simpson had begun divorce proceedings against her husband, alleging adultery. Once divorced, there would be no legal obstacle to her marrying Edward. Baldwin asked the king to persuade her to withdraw the divorce petition. Edward refused. By the end of October she had received a decree *nisi* and would be free to marry again in April 1937. On 16 November, Baldwin informed the king that neither the British Government nor the Dominion Governments would accept the marriage. The king replied that he would marry Mrs Simpson and that if he could not do so as king, he was prepared to abdicate.

The end of the affair came quickly. There was talk of a 'king's party' led by Winston Churchill and Lord Beaverbrook, but Edward made no attempt to organize or accept political support. The idea of a morganatic marriage by which Mrs Simpson could have become the king's wife but not his queen was aired, but turned down by Baldwin and the Dominions. On 10 December 1936, Edward signed the Instrument of Abdication. The following day he broadcast to the nation, explaining that he was quitting the throne in order to marry the woman he loved, and that evening he crossed the Channel. He was beginning, though he did not know it, a life of exile.

What is most revealing of Edward's limitations, of his lack of understanding of the constitutional position of the monarchy, of his failure to comprehend the nature of British society, and even of his misreading of the reactions of his own family, is that he did not really grasp what he had done by abdicating the throne. He expected that, if no longer king, he would be continue as a central figure of the monarchy, live in Britain and be given important duties to fulfil. Instead, the rest of his life would be a long and undignified diminuendo spent in a melancholy and purposeless exile.

Edward married Wallis in a chateau near Tours on 3 June 1937. No member of the royal family was present. In March, His Royal Highness Prince Edward had been created Duke of Windsor but, although Wallis became Duchess of Windsor with her marriage to the duke, the title 'Her Royal Highness' was not extended to her. After complex negotiations, in which Edward was less than forthright about his position, a financial settlement was arrived at. There was a sting in the tail as the government persuaded the new king, George VI, to add to the payment of a generous allowance the condition that the duke was not to return to Britain without permission.

The Duke and Duchess of Windsor were to prove a considerable embarrassment to the new king and the British government. Much has been written about Edward VIII's pro-German opinions, and it has been alleged that in the early stages of the Second World War he was a potential, even an active, traitor. It is more likely that he was simply foolish and indiscreet and determined to find some stage on which he could feel important again and his wife be fully accepted. His visit to Germany in October 1937, where he and the duchess were much feted by the Nazi leadership, was, at the least, ill judged. When France was on the verge of defeat in May 1940, the duke, who had been given the post of Liaison Officer with British Military Mission in France, left, in somewhat dubious circumstances, with the duchess and a great amount of luggage, for Spain and then Portugal. Fearful that the duke might be captured or kidnapped by the Germans, the British Government persuaded him to leave Europe and take up the post of Governor of the Bahamas, a post he filled until 1945.

After the war, the duke and duchess lived in France. They had a beautiful house in the Bois de Boulogne and a country property within easy driving distance of Paris. By now aware that there would be no reconciliation with the royal family, the duke passed the time with gardening, golf and travel and in 1951 published his memoirs, *A King's Story*. The prince who had so despised the formality of monarchy, had become an exile duke who maintained a quasi-royal court with servants in royal livery. On his death in 1972, Edward VIII's body was flown to England and buried at Windsor with the necessary state for one who had been King-Emperor. The frosty reception offered by members of the royal family to his widow was testimony to the enormous tensions – personal, as well as political – that his abdication had caused in the British establishment thirty-six years earlier.

George VI (1936-1952)

George VI was born at Sandringham on 14 December 1895, the second son of the Duke and Duchess of York, later George V and Queen Mary. Like his older brother, 'Bertie' (for the prince was christened Albert Frederick Arthur George) had to endure a neglected and unhappy childhood. His digestion was impaired for life by his mentally disturbed nurse; his father insisted that his legs were encased in splints to straighten his knock-knees; naturally left handed, he was made to write with his right hand; and his mother was notably, if not deliberately, sparing in maternal warmth. At the age of eight, he developed a stammer that he was never to lose.

Second sons in royal families are inevitably conscious from an early age of their subordinate position to their older brother; but in Bertie's case particularly the good looks and charm of David emphasized the inferiority. As one of his tutors remarked, comparing Bertie with David 'was rather like comparing an ugly duckling with a cock pheasant'. As they grew up, it was David who received the attention. There is little evidence that Bertie resented this, for he admired his brother, had little desire for the limelight, and, more dutiful than his brother, strove to gain his parents' approval.

Bertie followed his brother to the Royal Naval College, Osborne, where, in his final examination he came bottom of the entrants. He was, nevertheless, destined for a naval career. At Dartmouth his performance improved slightly, and he became a competent, if reserved, midshipman on HMS Collingwood. The outbreak of war in 1914 saw the young Prince Albert eager to play his part in the conflict but, almost immediately, he became ill with the gastric problems that had dogged him since childhood. An operation for appendicitis failed to cure his persistent problems and for the next three years he spent most of the time in hospital or convalescing. He was, however, able to rejoin the Collingwood just before the ship went into action in the great naval engagement of the war, the Battle of Jutland. Leaving the sick bay, where he was confined with his perennial stomach problems, he took his place in his gun turret and fought throughout the action. In 1917, he was operated on for an inflamed duodenal ulcer and thereafter, though he was never robust, his health improved. Despite his weak constitution, he was a better sportsman and rider than his brother, and his physical dexterity stood him in good stead when he spent the last months of the war in the Royal Naval Air Service and then the newly formed Royal Air Service, becoming the only member of the royal family to be a qualified pilot.

After the war, Bertie and his younger brother Henry studied constitutional history at Cambridge for a year. Having been made Duke of York in 1920, he settled into the role of a prince who was second in line to the throne. He enjoyed some success at tennis, a game he played left-handed. He and his partner, Louis Greig, a naval doctor who had befriended him at Osborne, won the RAF doubles. Greig, Prince Albert's equerry for a time, was an important and supportive influence on his early life. He helped give him confidence and claimed to have 'put steel into him'. The partnership played in the men's doubles at Wimbledon in 1926; they were defeated in the first round; but very few tennis players are good enough even to get to play in such a tournament.

At a time of industrial unrest and worries about class animosity, Bertie found a role in travelling around the country visiting factories and mines and meeting industrial workers. His family began to refer to him as the 'foreman'. He was also a prominent patron of the Industrial Welfare Society and the Duke of York's camps, to which public schoolboys and boys from working-class homes were invited in the hope of promoting social harmony, were an annual feature of the

192. The future George VI and his wife Elizabeth, better known today as the
Queen Mother, meet Captain Sulivan aboard HMS Renown, 1927.
193. The royal party playing deck tennis aboard HMS Renown, 1927.

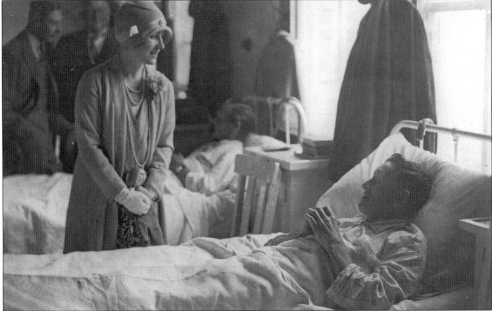

194. George VI and Queen Elizabeth crossing the equator on the way to Australia and New Zealand aboard HMS Renown, 1927.

195. Queen Elizabeth visiting Evelyn Firth Home, Auckland, as part of the royal tour of Australia and New Zealand, 1927.

inter-war years. Although from an early twenty-first century perspective, these camps – at which the duke led singing around camp fires – may seem awkward and artificial exercises, they were popular at the time with those who attended them and with a wider public.

The importance of the Duke of York's marriage to Lady Elizabeth Bowes-Lyon in 1923 in terms both of his own happiness and of the future of the monarchy can scarcely be exaggerated. The bride, pretty and vivacious, if rather more plump than was fashionable, shared the duke's love of country life and brought some of the sturdy virtues of the Scottish aristocracy into the royal house. The marriage gave large sections of the public what they wanted: romance; a royal marriage; and soon, with the births of the Princesses Elizabeth in 1926 and Margaret in 1930, a model family. Prince Albert, conscientious but nervous, was a man who needed support. He had found encouragement in Sir Louis Greig, and now he was to find it in his wife. The Duchess of York was, however, more than simply a good wife and mother: she had star quality. Furthermore there was, as a future suitor for her younger daughter's hand, Group Captain Peter Townsend, was to put it, 'steel within her velvet glove'.

The Yorks had been married for thirteen years when the abdication of Edward VII drastically altered their lives. They had lived contentedly. Their public duties were not over-arduous and, save for a six-month world tour in 1927, amounted to official engagements at home and more rarely abroad, leaving time for long holidays at Balmoral or Sandringham. It was, after all, the Prince of Wales who would inherit the throne, even if his tardiness in finding a wife pointed to the young Princess Elizabeth as a possible future successor. Then came the year of three kings in 1936.

King Edward's abdication came as a great blow. The Duke of York had turned himself into a useful ancillary member of the royal family, but he had not been prepared for kingship: indeed, his delicate constitution and his stammer seemed to make him unsuited to the role. The personal animosity between the duchess and Mrs Simpson, an animosity that would gradually be extended to the ex-king, added venom to consternation. Matriarchy in the shape of Queen Mary and the new Queen Elizabeth closed ranks in defence of the monarchy and against the man who had let it down and the woman who had led him astray. Without the influence of the queens, it seems likely that the Duchess of Windsor would have been allowed the title 'Her Royal Highness', the withholding of which did so much to sour relations, though King George's estrangement from the brother he had looked up to since childhood would almost certainly have developed in any case.

The agenda for court, government and the new king and queen was twofold: to restore the dignity and prestige of the monarchy; and to rub out the memory not just of the abdication crisis but of the man who had for so long been the nation's Prince Charming. The coronation was mounted with lavish expenditure and careful organization. It was attended by representatives of all the Dominions, and it was broadcast on radio. In the presentation of the new king to his people, emphasis was placed upon his position as a happily married man. The 'family on the throne' was the message consistently orchestrated by the media, and the queen and the princesses featured almost as much as the king himself. Visits to France and to Canada and the USA fulfilled the twin tasks of projecting the king and queen and cementing Britain's relationships with friendly powers as fears of war grew.

George's dedication to duty was manifest throughout the Second World War. The decision of the royal family to remain in London during the blitz and be seen visiting bombed areas in it and other towns and cities was important in maintaining morale. The king spent the war in uniform, and Princess Elizabeth joined the ATS when she became eighteen. It was important that the

196. George VI and Queen Elizabeth at Wellington, New Zealand during the royal tour of 1927.
197. George VI inspecting pilots at Antwerp, 13 October 1944.

royal family was seen to be enduring the discomforts and dangers of the rest of the population: something that was brought home by the death of the king's brother, the Duke of Kent, in an air crash. A royal initiative was the creation of the George Cross and George Medal; the king awarded the former to the besieged island of Malta when he visited it in 1943. As in the First World War, he yearned to be as close to action as possible and, like Winston Churchill, was persuaded only with difficulty not to be present at the Normandy landings. The king was, however, in Normandy encouraging the troops ten days later.

King George exercised political influence, though the political circumstances of his reign meant that he was not called upon to use the residual prerogatives of the Crown in terms of calling upon politicians to form governments or respond to requests for dissolutions of Parliament. He expected, however, that his rights to be consulted, to encourage, or to warn should be respected. His early attempts at more assertive initiatives were not welcomed: the Foreign Office vetoed his proposal to appeal personally to Hitler as 'one serviceman to another'; it also squashed his proposals to communicate directly with Mussolini and Emperor Hirohito. The king was a warm supporter of Neville Chamberlain at the time of the latter's return from Munich, and he was not pleased when Winston Churchill became Prime Minister in 1940. Churchill had, after all, been Edward VIII's champion in 1936, and the king would have preferred Lord Halifax. However, he soon developed a good relationship with Churchill, and was distraught when the wartime leader lost the 1945 election. When Clement Attlee, the new Labour Prime Minister, told him of his intention to place Ernest Bevin at the Treasury and Hugh Dalton at the Foreign Office, the king, who did not like Dalton, the son of Canon Dalton, George V's tutor, suggested that the appointments should be reversed. Attlee agreed.

In victorious, though weakened and shabby, post-war Britain, the monarchy was a source of stability and pride. The Labour Government was pushing through a vigorous programme of economic and social change. It had the mandate of a sweeping electoral victory but its great majority in the Commons did not reflect such a sweeping majority in terms of votes, and there might have been much greater tension had it not been for the emollient influence of the monarchy. The king did not welcome sweeping changes at home or the beginning of the dismantling of the Empire, but he performed his duties impartially and positively. He hated not being Emperor of India (a title he renounced in 1947), but he placed his hopes in the vision of the Commonwealth as a transformed, more democratic, empire.

Throughout his reign, George VI strove to ensure the prestige of the Crown he had so reluctantly worn. He insisted on the continuation of the ceremonial and mystical side of monarchy, believing glitter and formality were essential if the royal presence was to remain special. He was, almost certainly, right. At the end of his reign, when the Festival of Britain, a re-assertion of the character, identity and creativity of modern Britain, was planned, the event only began to capture the public imagination when the king and queen agreed to become patrons.

In one sense, there was not much about George VI save that he was a fundamentally decent man who did his duty when thrust upon a throne he did not covet. But his reign was also an achievement. He served his country well, and he left the monarchy secure and loved. While his widow believed that his life had been cut tragically short by the irresponsibility of his older brother (he died, at the age of fifty-six, in 1952), the collective amnesia encouraged by the royal family in relation to the unfortunate reign of Edward VIII had evidently been successful, and his people generally preferred to see George VI as having given up his health as an act of sacrifice for the benefit and safety of his war-torn realm.

ELIZABETH II (1952-PRESENT)

Princess Elizabeth Alexandra Mary was born on 21 April 1926 at 17 Bruton Street, the London home of her maternal grandparents, the Earl and Countess of Strathmore. Her father, Prince Albert, Duke of York, was second in line to the throne when he married Lady Elizabeth Bowes-Lyon in 1923, and it was not until Elizabeth was ten years old that Edward VIII's abdication brought her father to the throne. This event changed everything for the princess.

Her childhood, uniquely among those who have ascended to the British throne in the modern period, was entirely happy. The arrangements for her welfare and education were traditional: there was a nanny and a nursery maid, who were, in due course, joined by a governess. The Duke and Duchess of York were fond parents ever ready to play with and find time for the princess and her younger sister, Margaret Rose. Even though, by the early 1930s, there appeared a chance that she might inherit the throne one day, Elizabeth was not given an intensive or indeed a thorough education, but rather received the upbringing and training conventional for girls of aristocratic birth. This involved much time spent in the open air and the countryside with dogs and horses, and the acquisition of accomplishments. If this upbringing had disadvantages as a preparation for the throne, it did produce a confident, poised and well-balanced young woman.

George VI's accession brought to an end the serenity of his family life. From now on, his wife and daughters were constantly in the public eye, and attention focused particularly on Princess Elizabeth as the new heir presumptive to the throne. She appears to have been already dignified, mature and responsible beyond her years, and these characteristics became more evident with her growing awareness of her future responsibilities. She enjoyed a particularly close relationship with her father, and his influence on her understanding of the responsibilities of the monarchy was profound. Having had to master a role for which he had not been prepared, the king was concerned that Princess Elizabeth should be fully educated in her future duties as queen. Steps were taken to broaden her education; from Windsor Castle, where she spent most of the war, she crossed the river to Eton where she was tutored in constitutional history and French. At the age of eighteen, she was made a State Counsellor and was taken more and more into the king's confidence. If the monarchy was, in the king's words, a 'family firm', then Elizabeth was, from her late teens, understudy to the chairman.

Elizabeth's life from the late 1930s was intimately bound up with the mood, the hopes and the tribulations of the nation. She and her sister were the adored 'Little Princesses', at once royal and ordinary children whose progress was followed by the press and the cameras. When war came and the royal family sought to identify with their subjects' experiences and hardships, she spoke to the nation's children on the BBC's *Children's Hour*; towards the end of the war, she joined the ATS and was photographed servicing an army lorry. The rather austere atmosphere of post-war Britain was lightened by her wedding in 1947, while her coronation in 1953 seemed to mark a revival of British confidence. It was almost as though she lived on behalf of her people.

Princess Elizabeth's marriage in 1947 to Prince Philip of Greece had much to do with the machinations of Earl Mountbatten of Burma, the king's cousin and uncle to the groom. Mountbatten played the same part in encouraging this match that King Leopold had played in the marriage of Queen Victoria and Prince Albert. Elizabeth had first met her future husband when, with the king and queen, she visited Dartmouth, where Philip was a naval cadet, in 1939; she was immediately captivated by Philip's good looks and charm. The diarist 'Chips' Channon observed as early as 1941, 'He is to be our Prince Consort and that is why he is serving in our

Navy.' The king approved of Philip but was reluctant for his daughter to marry, though he eventually gave his consent. The match necessitated some re-labelling in the spirit of Britishness that the royal family had consistently promoted since George V's time: Philip abandoned his father's sonerous family name of Schleswig-Holstein-Sonderburg-Glucksburg, and it was announced that His Royal Highness Prince Philip of Greece had become Lieutenant Philip Mountbatten RN. The day before their wedding in November 1947, he was created Duke of Edinburgh, the style by which he has since usually been known, since he was not, on the Victorian precedent, granted the title of Prince Consort on the accession of his wife as queen.

The newly married couple hoped that Princess Elizabeth's succession to the throne would be long delayed, and that Prince Philip could in the meantime pursue his naval career. It was not to be. The birth of Prince Charles in November 1948 and of Princess Anne in August 1950 created family contentment, but also focused further attention on the new generation of royals. Meanwhile, the king's failing health meant that the princess had to take over many of her father's duties. King George's death, on 6 February 1952, came when the princess and her husband were in Kenya beginning a Commonwealth tour.

The coronation of Elizabeth II in 1953 was a great event both in itself and because of its wider significance. Thanks to television and film, the great majority of the population as well as millions overseas witnessed the ceremony. The image of the young queen dedicating herself to service to her nation and her Commonwealth melted even the most hardened of hearts. Contemporary observers were united in detecting a people re-affirming their faith and pride in themselves, their past and their future.

That, despite a new prosperity, the much heralded 'new Elizabethan age' did not seem to arrest national decline, nor the much acclaimed Commonwealth seem a substitute for the Empire, created something of a reaction against the monarchy in the later 1950s. A number of intellectuals began to argue that, rather than leading national regeneration, the monarchy was an obstacle to 'modernization', a key word in late twentieth-century Britain. The queen held firmly to the model of monarchy bequeathed by her father; but critics found this too formal, too much part of the 'establishment', and too grand. Despite the supposed attractions of northern European styles of monarchy, in which sovereigns, it was held, tended to ride around on bicycles, there was little evidence that the wider British public wished for a new type of royalty. There were, nevertheless, modernizers in the palace, among whom was the queen's husband, Prince Philip, Duke of Edinburgh, who felt that style and presentation had to adapt to social change. The problem was how to modernize an institution that gained so much from its traditional and historic nature without thereby also destroying it.

The solution was believed to be better presentation: to let the cameras in; to allow the public a more informal image of the royal family as 'ordinary' people; but also to show that the British throne was still capable of doing things with the appropriate pomp and display. The combination of the television programme *Royal Family* and the investiture of Prince Charles as Prince of Wales seemed to re-launch the monarchy. The tactic of using media interest in the lives of the members of the family rather than simply accommodating such interest was, however, dangerous because the nature of the British press and, perhaps, British society were changing.

Arguments about the image of the monarchy tended to be concerned with its 'dignified' role and its position as focal point of national cohesion. Queen Elizabeth had, however, to deal, far more than her father, with the monarch's remaining political duties and prerogatives within the 'efficient' part of the constitution. When Churchill resigned as Prime Minister, few doubted that the queen had much choice other than to send for Sir Anthony Eden and ask him to form a government; nor was her subsequent granting of his request for a dissolution of Parliament questioned. The then lack of formal procedure for electing the leader of the Conservative party while the party was in office led, however, to the queen having to decide which Conservative politician to ask to form a government on two occasions when the choice was controversial. In 1957 it was Harold Macmillan whom she summoned, and in 1963 it was Lord Home. In each case, her decision was made after consultation, but in both instances there were other candidates with support within the party: R.A. Butler in 1957; and Butler again, along with Reginald Maudling and Lord Hailsham, in 1963.

Although the adoption by the Conservatives of a formal procedure for electing its leader in 1965 meant that the sovereign would no longer have to make such awkward decisions, the remaining prerogatives in respect to the formation of governments and the granting of requests for the dissolution of Parliament could not, nor can they be, easily dispensed with. The general election of 1974 resulted in a situation where the Labour Party won the greater number of seats but had no overall majority. Edward Heath, the Conservative Prime Minister, was within his rights in remaining in office to see if he could strike a deal with the Liberal Party. When this failed, Heath resigned, but the queen could in theory have invited the liberal leader, Jeremy Thorpe, or another politician to attempt to form a government instead of doing as she did and taking the least controversial course by sending for Harold Wilson, whose party had the largest number of seats. There remained the question of whether she had the duty to accede to a request for a dissolution if Wilson should make one. She would have been entitled to refuse if she thought it too soon after the previous dissolution. In the event, she granted Wilson a dissolution after the passage of several months. Labour then gained a small majority at the October election. Had that election again resulted in a hung Parliament, however, the queen might have had to make even more delicate decisions. In short, the queen's powers may be called on every time there is, or seems likely to be, a Parliament without an overall majority for any one party. The case for the continuation of these prerogatives seems uncontestable, for who can make such decisions but the Head of State?

The Silver Jubilee celebrations of 1977 provided an opportunity to review twenty-five years of the queen's reign. All over the country galas and concerts in village halls, far more than processions and formal ceremonies, testified to an enduring loyalty to the Crown. Elizabeth had not only carried out her duties with dignity and grace and won the respect of her governments, but the 'family on the throne', despite the separation of Princess Margaret from her husband, seemed to continue the traditions of domestic harmony of her father's reign. This was not to last.

The troubles of the British monarchy in the final quarter of the twentieth century were in part caused by the deliberate projection of the image of an impeccable family life as a central feature of the monarchy. The long history of the monarchy might have reminded those who so consistently stressed the importance of this that uxoriousness and marital fidelity were not constants of royal behaviour. Over the centuries, the monarchy has regularly had to cope with the problems of errant royal males and straying princesses. When such problems appeared once more, they were exacerbated by changes in the nature of journalism and society. The tame and 'responsible' media with which the royal family had worked for most of the twentieth century was replaced by a press delighting in exposure, gossip and investigation. It was a case of back to the Regency period, but this time with *paparazzi*. The 'permissive' society proved not to be so permissive when it came to its public figures, seemingly expecting standards from them that it had thrown over for itself. Some blame must also be attached to the way that the Crown's public relations team remorselessly exploited the engagements and marriages of the Prince of Wales and his younger brother Prince Andrew, launching the ill-fated 'glamour' monarchy.

The marriage of the Prince of Wales and Lady Diana Spencer in 1981 was treated by the media as a fairy-tale romance. Diana had the charisma and star quality that her husband lacked. Indeed, it was she who resembled that earlier ill-fated Prince of Wales who became Edward VIII: an invitation to every camera; a trendsetter in her dress, her tastes and even her charities; and self-pitying, devious and irresponsible. If the media had found in the royal family a national soap opera, then here was a star whose performance would dangerously upstage the rest of the cast. In Sarah Ferguson, who by her marriage to Prince Andrew became Duchess of York, there was for a while a jollier and heartier supporting role. The enchantment of the glamour or 'celebrity' monarchy was, however, brief. By 1996 the Crown, whose opposition to divorce had been a byword since the unhappy events of 1936, had to confront the fact that four members of the immediate royal family were divorced: Princess Margaret, Princess Anne, the Duke of York, and the Prince of Wales.

The *annus horribilis* for the queen was 1992. Sensational revelations about the royal marriages followed one after the other throughout the year, and in November a fire destroyed important sections of Windsor Castle. Controversy as to who should pay for the repairs to the castle coincided with a revival of a much older debate as to who should pay for the royal family itself. Windsor Castle was clearly not a private royal residence and, like Buckingham Palace and indeed the White House, could be seen as essentially the State's responsibility; but in the atmosphere of the time there was a clamour that the queen should pay for the re-building. Elizabeth II, speaking at a Guildhall banquet a few days later, was frank in her recognition of the monarchy's problems, the marital troubles of her children, the debate over the nature of the institution itself, and her own role. Thistles were grasped almost immediately: it was announced that the Prince and Princess of Wales were to separate; and it was agreed that the queen, as well as paying the expenses of junior members of the family out of the Civil List, would herself pay income tax.

If 1992 was a low point, there were more difficult years to come. A divorced Princess Diana, who was not content to shun the limelight, promised to present the problem that the Duke of Windsor had once done. A nation that had idolized the Princess, was reluctant to accept the Prince of Wales's relationship with his mistress, Camilla Parker-Bowles. The death of Diana in a car crash in Paris, while she was possibly proceeding with a lover, Dodi Fayed, to the house that had once belonged to the Duke and Duchess of Windsor, occasioned an extraordinary period of mourning and hysteria which seemed for a while to threaten the Crown itself. The monarchy had deep roots and would survive, but it was much shaken.

At the end of the century, Queen Elizabeth must have looked back on a reign approaching its half-century with mixed feelings. She had come to a throne grand in style and rich in ceremony to rule over a nation still confident in its greatness. In the course of her reign the nation had become less powerful and, if more prosperous, less contented and less confident in itself and its institutions. The Empire had gone, and not all her ministers shared the queen's regard for the Commonwealth. The monarchy had been important in ensuring that major and often unwelcome changes could take place beneath a reassuring cover of continuity; but it had also been faced with regular and sometimes hostile demands that it should itself change, become more accessible, less dignified and more 'modern'. A monarchy essentially stands for continuity and tradition; as the Japanese put it, it is there 'to tell us what we have been'. To adapt without sacrificing continuity, to curtail grandeur and ceremony without losing dignity, and to evolve without bending to temporary winds of fashion, are difficult tasks. New problems could occur with devolution of constitutional powers to Scotland and Wales, where the mandate of the 'British' royal family is perceived to be less secure: there are hints of the revival of the 'multiple kingdoms' akin to those of an earlier, Stuart, regime. The European Union offers similar difficulties to other surviving monarchies, while the executive government, that 'efficient' part of the constitution, finds its own authority compromised and strained in the same environment.

The monarchy retains enormous loyalty and this owes much to Queen Elizabeth II. She has carried out her duties with care and dignity, combining respect for the constitution with advice to her governments, which most prime ministers have come to value. She is not only the Head of State but the acknowledged leader of civil society. Thousands of links exist between subjects and monarch, whether because of the royal patronage of charities and cultural institutions, those innumerable royal visits, accompanied by her Lord Lieutenants, to towns across the kingdom, or the special relationship with the armed forces. Her knowledge of the culture, the mores and the conventions of British society is unrivalled. Joining in the Millennium celebrations of 2000, which her government chose to open at that ill-fated symbol of 'cool Britannia', the Dome, several newspapers chortled that she was the odd one out in not knowing how to link hands for Auld Lang Syne; it was, as usual, Her Majesty who was correct.

The twenty-first century begins with four generations of the House of Windsor extant: at the two extremes sit the Queen Mother, almost a living national treasure in her personal longevity and the public estimation, and Prince William, exerting the effortless appeal of youth. Prince Charles, with his agonized dedication, has never been a comfortable Prince of Wales; but his virtues have become more apparent in middle age. Queen Elizabeth II will increasingly be the beneficiary of what Joseph Chamberlain called, with respect to Queen Victoria, the veneration accorded to 'ripe old age'. Walter Bagehot's dictum that a family on the throne is 'an interesting idea' expresses a deep truth about monarchy. While presidents and prime ministers stand for the present alone, we find in the institution of monarchy a collective sense of political and cultural continuity.

FURTHER READING

THE KINGS OF THE ENGLISH FROM EARLIEST TIMES TO 1066

F. Barlow, *Edward the Confessor* (Methuen: London, 1985)

N. Higham, *An English Empire: Bede and the Early Anglo-Saxon Kings*
(Manchester University Press: Manchester, 1995)

A.P. Smyth, *King Alfred the Great* (Oxford University Press: Oxford, 1995)

P. Stafford, *Unification and Conquest: A Political and Social History of England in the Tenth
and Eleventh Centuries* (Arnold: London 1989)

THE HOUSE OF NORMANDY

F. Barlow, *William Rufus* (Yale University Press: London and New Haven, 2000)

D. Bates, *William the Conqueror* (Tempus: Stroud, 2001)

C.W. Hollister, *Henry I* (Yale University Press: London and New Haven, 2001)

E.J. King (ed.), *The Anarchy of King Stephen's Reign* (Clarendon Press: Oxford, 1994)

THE HOUSE OF ANJOU

D.A. Carpenter, *The Minority of Henry III* (Methuen: London, 1990)

S.D. Church (ed.), *King John: New Interpretations* (Boydell and Brewer: Woodbridge, 1999)

J. Gillingham, *Richard I*, 2nd edn (Yale University Press: London and New Haven, 2000)

W.L. Warren, *Henry II* (Methuen: London, 1973)

THE HOUSE OF PLANTAGENET

W.M. Ormrod, *The Reign of Edward III* (Tempus: Stroud, 2000)

M. Prestwich, *Edward I* (Yale University Press: London and New Haven, 1997)

M. Prestwich, *The Three Edwards* (Routledge: London, 1990)

N. Saul, *Richard II* (Yale University Press: London and New Haven, 1997)

THE HOUSES OF LANCASTER AND YORK

C. Allmand, *Henry V* (Methuen: London, 1993)

R.A. Griffiths, *The Reign of King Henry VI* (Benn: London, 1981)

C.D. Ross, *Edward IV* (Methuen: London, 1974)

A.J. Pollard, *Richard III and the Princes in the Tower* (Sutton: Stroud, 1993)

THE HOUSE OF TUDOR

S.B. Chrimes, *Henry VII* (Yale University Press: London and New Haven, 1999)

C.A. Haigh, *Elizabeth I*, 2nd edn (Longman: London, 1998)

J. Loach, *Edward VI* (Yale University Press: London and New Haven, 2000)

D.M. Loades, *Mary Tudor: A Life* (Blackwell: Oxford, 1989)

J.J. Scarisbrick, *Henry VIII* (Methuen: London, 1976)

THE HOUSE OF STUART

R. Lockyer, *James VI and I* (Longman: London, 1998)

J. Miller, *Charles II* (Weidenfeld and Nicolson: London, 1991)

J. Miller, *James II* (Yale University Press: London and New Haven, 2000)

J.S. Morrill, *The Oxford Illustrated History of Tudor and Stuart Britain* (Oxford University Press: Oxford, 1996)

THE HOUSE OF HANOVER

J. Black, *An Illustrated History of Eighteenth-Century Britain* (Manchester University Press: Manchester, 1996)

R. Hatton, *George I* (Yale University Press: London and New Haven, 2001)

C. Hibbert, *George III: A Personal History* (Penguin: London, 1999)

E.A. Smith, *George IV* (Yale University Press: London and New Haven, 2001)

FROM THE HOUSE OF HANOVER TO THE HOUSE OF WINDSOR

S. Bradford, *Elizabeth: A Biography of Britain's Queen* (Farrar, Straus and Giroux: London 1996)

S. Bradford, *George VI* (Fontana: London, 1991)

J. Gardiner, *Queen Victoria* (Collins and Brown: London, 1997)

J. Golby and A.W. Purdue, *Kings and Queens of Empire: British Monarchs 1760-2000* (Tempus: Stroud, 2000)

G. Plumptre, *Edward VII* (Pavilion: London, 1995)

LIST OF ILLUSTRATIONS

FRONT COVER:

Edward III in Parliament. BL Cotton Nero D VI, f.72.
Henry VIII by Hans Holbein. TA CD 12, 25.
Portrait of Alfred from a fourteenth-century copy of his laws. BL Cotton MS, Claudius D, ii, f8.
Portrait of Charles I wearing a white, satin coat. Van Dyck. TA CD 12, 1.

BACK COVER

Charles II. TA CD 12, 16.
Jane Seymour. TA CD 12, 28.

1.   Coin of Mercia. TA CD 10, 05/7.
2.   Coin of Cuthred. TA CD 10, 27/49
3.   Coin of Baldred. TA CD 10, 28/52
4.   Coin of Offa. TA CD 10, 14.
5.   Coin of Offa's wife, Cynethryth. TA CD 10, 13/28.
6.   Coin of Peada, son of Penda. TA CD 10, 05/7.
7.   Coin of Ecgfrith. TA CD 10, 47/76.
8.   Coin of King Eadbert. TA CD 10, 49/79.
9.   Coin of Edmund. TA CD 10, 98/163.
10.   Coin of Guthrum (880-90).
11.   An extract from a charter of Æthelbald. BL MS. Cott. Aug. II.
12.   Coin of Ecgbert. TA CD 10, 77/125.
13.   Coin of Æthelwulf. TA CD 10, 78/127.
14.   Coin of Æthelstan. TA CD 10, 97/158.
15.   Coin of Eírik Blood-Axe. TA CD 10, 76/119.
16.   Coin of Æthelred. TA CD 10, 80/132.
17.   Passage from the *Anglo-Saxon Chronicle*. BL Cotton MS. Tiberius B. iv, ff.33v-34.
18.   Coin of Edward the Elder. TA CD 10, 92/148.
19.   Coin of Alfred minted at London. TA CD 10, 88/141.
20.   Manuscript illumination of Christ. BL. MS Cott. Galba A. XVIII.
21.   Coin of Edmund. TA CD 10, 98/163.
22.   Coin of Eadred. TA CD 10, 100/166.
23.   Coin of Eadwig. TA CD 10, 101/167.
24.   Coin of Edward the Martyr. TA CD 10, 154.
25.   Edgar. BL MS Cotton Tiberius A. iii, f2v.
26.   Image of a crowned king. BL MS Cotton Claudius B.iv, f59r.
27.   A charter of Æthelred the Unready. BL MS Stowe Ch. 35.
28.   Part of the Bayeux Tapestry where Harold Godwinsson is seen reporting back to Edward the Confessor. TA CD Bates, William the Conqueror, p80, bottom.

COLOUR SECTION

INDEX

Kings and queens, and princes and princesses without separate titles, are arranged by first name and listed by rank, by country, and in chronological order; nobles, archbishops and bishops are arranged by title and listed in chronological order. Bold type indicates an illustration in the colour section.

ALSO AVAILABLE FROM TEMPUS

The Kings and Queens of Scotland
Richard Oram (Editor)
'the colourful, complex and frequently bloody story of Scottish rulers… an exciting if rarely edifying tale, told in a clear and elegant format.' *BBC History Magazine*
'remarkable' *History Today*
272pp 212 illus (29 col) Paperback £16.99/$22.99 0 7524 1991 9

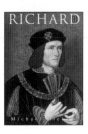

Richard III
Michael Hicks
'This is a most important book by the greatest living expert on Richard… fluently written and force-fully argued, it makes for compulsive reading. A must for anyone even remotely interested in Richard.' *BBC History Magazine*
'important… Where early historians simply accepted the Tudor myth and later ones denied it, Michael Hicks returns to the original sources.' *The Independent on Sunday*
240pp 114 illus (28 col) Paperback £12.99/$19.99 0 7524 2302 9

William the Conqueror
David Bates
'As expertly woven as the Bayeux Tapestry… Stitching together William's life, actions and personality from the scattered threads of information available, particularly French and Norman sources over-looked by previous biographers, Bates reveals an ambitious, implacable man possessed with more than the usual breathless energy typical of a medieval warlord.'
BBC History Magazine
'no one is better qualified than David Bates, with his unrivalled knowledge of the charters of the Conqueror… to interpret King William's character.' *History*
240pp 68 illus. (15 col) Paperback £16.99/$27.99 0 7524 1980 3

The Reign of Edward III
W.M. Ormrod
'Compelling and eloquently written… Nothing of comparable importance has been written on the reign for the past thirty years.' *History Today*
'instantly accessible to the uninformed layman.' *The Observer*
264pp 32 illus. (8 col.) Hardback £19.99/$34.99 0 7524 1773 8

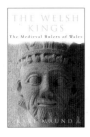

The Welsh Kings: The Medieval Rulers of Wales
Kari Maund
'revealing' *The Western Mail*
'Will be interesting to both medievalists and those interested in their own local history'
The Cambrian News
The untold history of the independent native Kings of Wales from their earliest origins to the destruction of these proud lineages in 1283.
176pp 60 illus. (23 col.) Paperback £14.99/$21.99 0 7524 2321 5

UK ORDERING

Simply write, stating the quantity of books required and enclosing a cheque for the correct amount, to: Sales Department, Tempus Publishing Ltd, The Mill, Brimscombe Port, Stroud, Glos. GL5 2QG, UK.
Alternatively, call the sales department on 01453 883300 to pay by Switch, Visa or Mastercard.

USA ORDERING

Please call Arcadia Publishing, a division of Tempus Publishing, toll free on 1-888-313-2665